THE

JAMESONIAN

UNCONSCIOUS

POST-CONTEMPORARY INTERVENTIONS

Series Editors: Stanley Fish and Fredric Jameson

THE JAMESONIAN UNCONSCIOUS

The Aesthetics

of Marxist Theory

Clint Burnham

Duke University Press

Durham and London

1995

© 1995 Duke University Press

All rights reserved

Printed in the United States of America on acid-free paper ∞

Designed by Cherie H. Westmoreland and typeset in Plantin Light

with Gill Sans display by Keystone Typesetting, Inc.

Library of Congress Cataloging-in-Publication Data appear

on the last printed page of this book.

FOR DANIEL JONES, 1959–1994,

in remembrance

and love

CONTENTS

overdetermination explained, once and for all...shrunken dwarfs, expanded...desire...three interpretive levels...acting out your aggression...lukács: or, marxism and masochism...sex and money...dead soldiers...morganatic marriages...conrad and "easy morality"...a theory of sediment of theory...mass culture, at last...four conrads

critical mass...can the skatepunk speak?...homi don't play that...a sublime quilt...fieldwork in mass culture...platform sneakers remix...the filmic object...miss culture...reification: or, the jaws of life...search for a figure...the heist of class...curious georg...triadic allegories of totality...allegorizing interpretation...ethics and hitchcocK...the existence of jameson...the desire for nostalgia...the end of the chapter...postmodernism is always in taste...vertiginous slime...flannelized jameson...the revenge of the content...postmodernism as liberalism...prolegomena to any fugue of the postmodern...taste and liberalism...the rhetoric of taste...sublime hysteria

ACKNOWLEDGMENTS

This book began as a dissertation I wrote while at York University in Toronto. So my greatest debt is to my Ph.D. supervisory committee: Ian Sowton, Terry Goldie, and Kim Michasiw. Ian is a wonderfully progressive and gentle teacher, and he has taught two or three generations of Canadian intellectuals. I learned a lot working with him, not least to trust my own idiosyncratic methodologies and style. Terry and Kim both kept me working to the edge of my capabilities, and encouraged me to see the relevance of Nine Inch Nails to Hegelian Marxism. My outside examiners, Ioan Davies and Jed Rasula, also provided readings that were both sympathetic and challenging. I don't think I could have written a dissertation and a book on Jameson without the strong support of my committee.

But writing takes place in a larger context than the seminar room or library, and I received support, arguments, and interventions from a lot of people in the Toronto intellectual and writing communities. In particular, the comradeship of the following is gratefully noted: Ken Wilson, Christine Ramsey, Julie Sawatsky, Steve McCaffery, Jinnean Barnard, Peter Fitting, Kevin Connolly, Karen Mac Cormack, Victor Coleman, Libby Scheier, Lola Lemire Tostevin, jwcurry, Stan Fogel, Christopher Dewdney, Stuart Ross, Chris Wodsku, Jim Smith, Graham Barron, Lance La Rocque, and, of course, Paul Mergler. I'd also like to thank the anonymous readers at Duke University Press, and my editor, Reynolds Smith.

Last of all, I'd like to acknowledge the funding I received during the writing of the dissertation in the form of a doctoral fellowship from the Social Sciences and Humanities Research Council of Canada.

C. B.

PREFACE

When Killdozer played in Toronto in early July 1994, they were promoting a new album called *Uncompromising War On Art Under the Dictatorship of the Proletariat* (Touch and Go). Interviewed before the show, band member Dan Hobson commented: "What I miss is bands like Gang of Four and the Mekons because they could deal with politics but have a sense of humour and fun about it. We're not making fun of these ideas even if we do sometimes have a satiric edge. We do believe in what we're saying and I don't think having some fun with it takes anything away from that" (Anderson 30). This is the band, after all, which once put out an album called *Intellectuals are the Shoeshine Boys of the Ruling Elite*. The liner notes for the new album feature plenty of dead capitalists and quotations from Rosa Luxembourg and Fidel Castro; the tour poster rather anachronistically portrays Lenin below the Killdozer hammer and sickle and above Khrushchev's warning, "We will bury you!"

Just to switch into cultural studies mode, then, the new Killdozer says a lot immediately about (a) the politics of indie rock; (b) the death of the Cold War narrative; (c) the way intellectuals look for support in mass culture; and (d) the possibility of engaging in critique while not taking it too seriously. And, coincidence of coincidences, these are some of the themes or lessons of the very book you're now holding in your hand at your local trendy bookstore, deliberating on whether to buy it ("Buy me before good sense insists / You'll strain your purse and sprain your wrists," as Vikram Seth rather cumbersomely rhymes at the beginning of *A Suitable Boy*). Is this what cultural studies is all about: the inability to distinguish between a punk band and an Indian novel? Arguing over the effects of the Mighty Morphin Power Rangers? Ian McEwan is Stephen King for intellectuals: tightly constructed horror stories. We are the richest of the poor.

Cultural studies is apparently in danger of dying from its own success. "You don't have to be Andrew Ross to know [*Cops*'s] rigged for the police's point of view," a *Village Voice* critic commented (Parks 39), a statement with the requisite schizoid subtexts. It probably means you don't have to be as smart as Ross (a rocket scientist) to "deconstruct" *Cops*, but then again, maybe the point is that you don't need Ross's cultural materialism. Good old American know-nothingism. If Ross is in danger of becoming a Leninist Miss Manners, is it really because cultural studies has sold out? Perhaps the multi-culti people are where it's at for a liberal bourgeoisie. Or at least that's John Beverley's conclusion in his provocative essay "By Lacan": "[I]t may be that the 'liberals' have already won the debate, and that multiculturalism and cultural studies are being prepared as the places for a redefinition of educational curricula and disciplinary structures in the period ahead.[1] The conversion of cultural studies from a form of radical opposition to the avant-garde of bourgeois hegemony" (1993, 20) has already started, Beverley suggests. He might have called his essay "bi lacan," suggesting bifurcation as well as the anagram of "Caliban."

So what am I talking about here? MTV Marxism? Yes and no. Yes, if by that term we suggest a catachresis, or a metaphor with no referent (as Spivak would say). There is no such thing as MTV Marxism if I mean a genuinely popular leftist movement in the metropolitan United States. And yet, if cultural studies is about more than just white guys trying not to be white guys, about change in the academy as part of change in the worlds we live in, we have to intervene into our own practice more thoroughly: to objectivate it while knowing about the difference between Killdozer and Stone Temple Pilots. But I also do and don't mean MTV Marxism in a more literal sense: the band I started talking about here, Killdozer, is hardly MTV-friendly. Nor are such bands as Thinking Fellers Union Local 282, Pavement, Super-

1 In *Against Literature* (1993), Beverley says that neoconservatives would hesitate to define themselves as postmodernists; but then, that only demonstrates the view the neo-cons have of postmodernism (which could be a liberal ideology).

chunk, Change of Heart, Nomeansno, Dinner is Ruined, Guh, Sebadoh . . . you get the idea. The specific instances of mass cultural forms I'm interested in here are important not just because a major label is pushing them all over the globe so that Madonna is point woman for the Marines.

So it's MTV Marxism in that deferred (but nevertheless: still *there;* here I part company with Spivak in her notion of the referent not existing) sense of a popular movement, "the insubstantial bottomless realm of the cultural and collective fantasy" Jameson was called upon to defend in the *Diacritics* interview (1982a, 74). Here *The Baffler,* a small journal published in Chicago, is instructive through its vicious attacks on the popular culture industry (the poverty of Madonna theory), and in its conspiratorial nightmare, "Consolidated Deviance." This nefarious allegory is *The Baffler*'s most successful legacy—even more than its *Sassy*-bashing or Steve Albini-led music industry watch. "In the widespread paralysis of the collective or social imaginary, to which 'nothing occurs' (Karl Kraus) when confronted with the ambitious program of fantasizing an economic system on the scale of the globe itself, the older motif of conspiracy knows a fresh lease on life, as a narrative structure capable of reuniting the minimal basic components: a potentially infinite network, along with a plausible explanation of its invisibility; or in other words: the collective and the epistemological. To put it this way is to understand how this imperfect mediatory and allegorical structure—the conspiracy, not yet even the world system itself—offers the gravest representational dilemmas" (*GA,* 9).

"Consolidated Deviance" is a mock corporate report contained in the fifth issue of *The Baffler* (1993: 159–66). "ConDev," as the company calls itself, spikes subcultures, academics, and the corporate media: "The launch of each new SubCult™ must be carefully orchestrated to preserve its patina of grass-roots 'authenticity' " (162–63); "[a] certain variety of scholars, the Company has found, is quite willing to celebrate, help publicize, and lend credibility to certain youth culture ventures *without compensation*" (163); and "ConDev has announced plans to rationalize the process of academic/SubCult™ interface by endowing a number of university chairs and departments of 'subcultural studies,' and by acquiring an interest in one of the country's most influential academic presses. This press has recently published a volume of essays seeking to appreciate the 'libidinal heteroglossia of Grunge' " (163). In ConDev's lubricious conspiracy, even the shape of the

Nike and Puma running-shoe stripes are indications of their economic performance (and thus the Adidas trefoil, so popular in the last year, "fits" with the new importance of pot leaves?). *The Baffler*'s sarcasm and hyperbole render Jameson's epistemological questions difficult, of course, and thus the issue or journal's *Details*- and *Sassy*-bashing, while tiresome and admitting of a certain bad faith (Keith White's article on *Details* sounds like Naomi Wolf on glamour magazines) is a part of the whole package. The style is important, for only by positing such a conspiracy at the level of the university and capital is the discourse able to reason why academics do pimp for free.

For better or for worse, I've taken as my task in the present book an objectivation of theory via the work of Fredric Jameson. And I'm trying to do this in a fairly "Brutalist" manner. The watchwords might be: vulgar, reductive, simplistic, absolutist. I found there to be two representational problems entailed in writing on Jameson's work: while on the one hand the texts seemed to be self-referential in their rhetorical and figural habits, I found it difficult, *from the very start,* to construct in good faith some representational-analytical account, or even "inventory," of these self-referring "folds." This then leads to a rhetorical inflation of the importance of the subject. Sometimes this seems to be dictated by Jameson's "modernist" focus on certain author-subjects or initiators of discourse—Sartre, Lewis, Hitchcock—and sometimes by the return or at least resurgence of author-centered theory— the continuing presence of auteurism, for example, in both high-class film journalism (from J. Hoberman to blurbs written for Cinematheque Ontario), and political criticism (locally: *CineAction*). (In my own practice here, the reader will detect a wild usage of names-as-adjectives: Žižekian, Bourdieuesque, Jamesonian, etc.) The various left and right versions of the end of politics (history, ideology)—Bell, Baudrillard, Fukuyama, Rorty—have led, I think, to a historical demand for the vulgarization of theory itself. Ironically, then, I take the view of some postmodernist critics of Jameson, who see his incorporation of Mandel or Lukács as simplistic; the elegance (there are no doubt less-charitable adjectives) of his sentences belies an insistence on connecting the cultural to the political (an insistence on totalizing) that I also found to be a characteristic of my own discourse (*sans* the elegance, of course).

In the first, introductory chapter, I begin in a high mode of rhetoric, both in terms of semantics and structure. The chapter begins with quotations from Sartre and William Gibson, and then I make claims about Jameson's "career." This habit of collaging/collating my text with short or long quotations, undoubtedly insufficiently commented upon by myself and not even "indented," I practice for a number of reasons: to luxuriate in the prose of another discourse, to negate the separation of "my" writing/analysis from that of others, and to situate both my analysis and Jameson's work in a shifting totality of twentieth-century discourse. My rhetoric at the start of this chapter and elsewhere, then, is usually very hyperbolic—which leads to epistemological problems when the reader cannot determine if "I" am being serious or not. But I now see this technique (which I also loved to find in *The Baffler*) as an example of Jameson's "postmodern sublime," or the vertiginous feeling of being unable to tell the truth from the lie, or the artifact from the natural.

The first chapter's content focuses on two linked issues. I tackle the question of whether the recent political events in Eastern Europe—the 1989 revolutions—are the historical "proofs" of what various poststructuralist theorists—Lyotard, Rorty—have been saying for some time: Marxism as theory and practice is no longer capable of accounting for, or changing, the world in any positive way. The symbolic or semiotic death of Marxism, then, was followed by, if it did not directly cause, the objective death. Between two deaths: the discourse on "the fall of communism" may seem wildly digressive (or even mishandled, since I am evidently not a political scientist), but I think it is important to deal with "popular" conceptions of the relationship between Marxism (in its various academic or theoretical guises) and history (either as current affairs or Lukácsean world-history). I then turn to some more familiar terrain: theoretical objections to or articulations of difficulties with Marxism. First of all, I outline Lyotard's and Rorty's pragmatist critiques, and then I turn to some feminist encounters with Marxism—notably, Showalter and de Lauretis. My point in this section is to demonstrate similarities as well as differences: in a Jameson slogan, "difference relates." I then comment on my methodology in the book (reading in terms of rhetoric and figures); again, the "unrepresentability" of discourse forbids any overly clear statement of purpose there (or here) or anywhere else. I conclude with what will be a practice throughout the book: an autobiographical situating of my own discourse. For me, articulating this in terms of my class background (briefly, a lower middle-class and working-class family with little or no knowledge or competence in so-called high culture, but a bit of pretension via such commodities as *Reader's Digest* and Inuit art) has enabled me to work through my own ambivalence and bad faith in regard to theoretical, political, and aesthetic discourses.

Chapter 2 is primarily concerned with exploring the textual machinery of *Marxism and Form* (*Late Marxism* is used quietly). Considerations of "the example" in Sartre and Jameson, of the footnote in Adorno and Jameson, then, connect in unexpected ways with such theoretical "content" as Sartrean seriality and Adorno's reification. I also initiate here an appropriation of Kojève's method: the quotation mixed with commentary. Here a figurally rich paragraph from Jameson's discussion of Marcuse, Schiller, and Breton is commented on. This technique enables me to combine an apparent facility for close readings with an apparent weakness for wild, unsubstantiated, and unsupportable generalizations and digressions. I also deal with issues like Denis Hollier's important book on Sartre, and the origin of Jameson's concept of utopia in Ernst Bloch.

In Chapter 3, I engage most directly with *The Political Unconscious* (and also, briefly, with *Fables of Aggression*). The chapter weaves around three themes (or, thememes): a molar/molecular dialectic of form, Althusserian overdetermination, and various materialist concepts of power (primarily, Oriental despotism). The molar/molecular distinction comes to us from Deleuze and Guattari courtesy of Jameson's usage of it in *Fables of Aggression* and enables discussions of local figures (in the sentence) versus global rhetoric to be coupled with some consideration of at least one critic of *The Political Unconscious*. Althusser is discussed both in relation to French Marxism (the conceit of "dialogic Marxism," or Jameson's attempts to work with both Hegelian and structuralist modes, is entertained) and in terms of base and superstructure causality.

But this is not, needless to say, an intellectual history of any sort; not only am I probably incapable of such a rigorous project, but, just as Jameson's work seemed less to "represent," say, Continental Marxism (in *Marxism and Form* or *Late Marxism*), or Conrad (in *The Political Unconscious*), I became in the writing of the dissertation (which led to this book) less and less confident of defining just what the "political unconscious" was, or "postmodernism." As Jameson comments on Benjamin and Adorno (in *Late Marxism*): "It is as though, in both these writers, a kind of repressed foundational longing found its way back into their writing by way of these magical terms [aura and mimesis], which are evoked to explain everything without ever themselves being explained, until at length we become persuaded that they could never themselves be explained or grounded" (64). Frankly, I am a little suspicious that intellectual history is what Žižek calls "historicism," and not "historicity" (the demand for a linear and causal narrative), which ignores the (unrepresentable) ahistorical kernel at the heart of history. I make some attempt to account for Jameson's various hermeneutic levels, and then, having briefly explicated what I see as an originary masochism in Lukács, outline Jameson's readings of Balzac and Conrad, providing counterinterpretations or elaborations of my own.

Chapter 4 features a schizoid division of freedom and commitment: while, on the one hand, I felt that one of its objects—mass culture—was an area in which I had a great deal of experience (for all the class reasons rehearsed above), and thus I could engage in an even more strident and absolutist arena of rhetoric (Plato was the first theorist of mass culture, and so on); on the other hand, the other ostensible object—postmodernism—rendered the question of "representing" Jameson even more, or totally, problematic. So here I provide, more than elsewhere in the text, counter-readings and challenges to and expansions on the Jamesonian methodologies; simultaneously, I shy away from actually "engaging" with his argumentative strategies (which I avoid throughout the book anyway), being content with concocting various figures for the *textuality* of *Signatures of the Visible* and *Postmodernism, or, The Cultural Logic of Late Capitalism* (I also discuss the readings of film in the most recent *Geopolitical Aesthetic*). Probably the two most consistent terrains of argument in this chapter are interpretive issues in film criticism (centered around Hitchcock) and the postmodern debate. Here I deal with criticism of Jameson in terms of postcolonialism—Ahmad, Rushdie, Suleri—as well as his stance on postmodernism.

As well as drawing on Jameson's own work for interpretive strategies, the theorists I cite most frequently are Slavoj Žižek and Pierre Bourdieu. Neither is embraced uncritically (although enthusiastically in the manner of the archetypal graduate student not yet sufficiently jaded or cynical about theory), but both theorists or schools seem to offer explanatory models and heuristic methodologies. Žižek's elaborations on Lacan are undoubtedly attractive to me as much because of his rhetoric (hyperbole, most evidently) and his willingness to draw in the mass-cultural, as because of his Hegelian psychoanalysis; and thus my use of him should be judged on all three counts, I think. Bourdieu is mandarin in the way that only Parisian theorists can be (and self-conscious of that problematic more thoroughly than many others), but his concepts of cultural capital and the field are also, I believe, objectively useful.

As I note in the first chapter, I am reluctant to use valorizing political terms like "radical" or "subversive" to characterize, especially, my own stylistic methodology (even if my narrow vocabulary sometimes forces me to resort to them in discussing other theorists). This is not modesty, obviously; I am just uninterested, at some level, in according value based on a differential from what is evidently a corrupt form of discourse (and postmodern style is itself already so reified that "subverts," evidently, is a verb to be found in a headline on an alternative weekly, whether it refers to Mary Stuart Masterson or Vanilla Ice). If there is value in what I attempt here, then perhaps it lies in the fact that this is not philosophy, not aesthetics, and not criticism; rather, it is literary theory trying to develop a form of reading that will replace those older discourses. My attention to Jameson's examples, Lukács's masochism, and *Reservoir Dogs*'s allegory possesses whatever merit it does because the theoretical praxis exemplifies (or tries to) a materialist intervention at the level of the signifier.

If I demonstrate or self-analyze a bad faith at certain local moments in this work, I have tried to shift my own ideological self-view from at least that bad trope. What this means here, at the conclusion of an abstract, is a need to disavow any sort of ownership of this discourse—ownership in the various epistemo-discursive meanings everyone is now familiar with, which is to say that I can neither claim my subjectivity as some "origin" of the meaning nor attribute to my position benefits or punishments associated with this written product. A book, it seems evident, is a prime example (but no less so than a poem or a music video, or a tarred road or swept floor) of "the institution speaking." If there are any positive aspects of the two-hundred-odd pages that follow—range of reference, an aptitude for patches of close reading—these objectively articulate my own social and institutional history. Working in universities on the margins of the North American academic centers, and a class background that forbade any easy acceptance of canons, entailed a certain desperation to my theoretical formation. Similarly, the faults of the following text—these are for the reader to determine—doubtlessly also ensue from instrumental and familial domination. This having been said, my formations and formulations become one story among many, as the author no longer has any particularly privileged authority over this text.

Clint Burnham
Toronto   July 1994

ABBREVIATIONS OF WORKS BY

FREDRIC JAMESON

FA: Fables of Aggression

GA: The Geopolitical Aesthetic: Cinema and Space in the World System

IT: The Ideologies of Theory

LM: Late Marxism: Adorno, or, the Persistence of the Dialectic

M&F: Marxism and Form: Twentieth-Century Dialectical Theories of Literature

PHL: The Prison-House of Language: A Critical Account of Structuralism and Russian Formalism

PM: Postmodernism, or, The Cultural Logic of Late Capitalism

PU: The Political Unconscious: Narrative as a Socially Symbolic Act

S: Sartre: The Origins of a Style

SV: Signatures of the Visible

We have seen Marx *practising* this concept in the use he makes of the '*Darstell-ung*', and trying to pinpoint it in the images of changes in the illumination or in the specific weight of objects by the ether in which they are immersed, and it is sometimes directly exposed in Marx's analyses, in passages where it is expressed in a novel but extremely precise language: a language of metaphors which are nevertheless already *almost perfect concepts,* and which are perhaps only incomplete insofar as they have not yet been *grasped,* i.e., retained and elaborated as concepts.—Louis Althusser, 1968

I blew into the Dôme at 8:30, all agog at the idea of reading *Perry Mason and the Lame Canary,* but then who should show up but Merleau-Ponty, and I can't decently take out a detective story under his very nose.
—Simone de Beauvoir, letter to Jean-Paul Sartre, 13 January 1941

Who is the nonethnic Canadian?
—Gayatri Chakravorty Spivak, 1993

MARXISM

TODAY

virtual marxism

1   In *The Words,* Jean-Paul Sartre describes the origins of his writing (if not of his style): "The first story I completed was entitled *For a Butterfly.* A scientist, his daughter, and an athletic young explorer sailed up the Amazon in search of a precious butterfly. The argument, the characters, the particulars of the adventures, and even the title were borrowed from a story in pictures that had appeared in the preceding quarter. This cold-blooded plagiarism freed me from my remaining misgivings; everything was necessarily true since I invented nothing. I did not aspire to be published, but I had contrived to be printed in advance, and I did not pen a line that was not guaranteed by my model. Did I take myself for an imitator? No, but for an original author" (1969, 88).

2   In *Neuromancer,* William Gibson describes the commercialized version of cyberspace he calls "simstim" (simulation-stimulation), an entertainment version of "virtual reality": "Cowboys didn't get into simstim, he thought, because it was basically a meat toy. He knew that the trodes he used and the little plastic tiara dangling from a simstim deck were basically the same, and that the cyberspace matrix was actually a drastic simplification of the human sensorium, at least in terms of presentation, but simstim itself struck him as a gratuitous multiplication of flesh input" (1984, 55).

3   These two passages can stand, then, as markers for a reified version of Fredric Jameson's career—his work virtually stretches from the totalizing

and unfashionable Sartre to the postmodern, simulated pop culture of sci-fi.
4 Virtual reality as reification: what is truly horrific to watch in the present-
day uses and abuses of cyberspace is how Gibson's ideas (and warnings)
about virtual reality in his novels—simstim as the crack of television, the
cyberspace matrix as site for militaristic Platonism—have been transformed
into that which he himself abhors. Gibson has said that virtual reality is like
freebasing American television: "Just a chance operator in the gasoline crack
of history, officer. . . . Assembled word *cyberspace* from small and readily
available components of language. Neologic spasm: the primal act of pop
poetics. Preceded any concept whatever. Slick and hollow—awaiting received meaning. All I did: folded words as taught. Now other words accrete
in the interstices. 'Gentlemen, that is not now nor will it ever be *my* concern . . .' Not what I do" (1991, 27).
5 A key problem throughout Jameson's work is how to imagine the future—
the maligned Utopia—in a culture that doubly negates such imagination.
First, the culture doubts the possibility of some "better place" than the undoubtedly excellent world of late capitalism (the "reality principle" Jameson
refers to in his discussion of Herbert Marcuse in *Marxism and Form*). This is
the "bad," or negative, or ideological, or neoconservative critique of utopia.
Second, that culture characterizes itself as already nonrepresentational by
doubting the possibility of representationalism (i.e., postmodernism). This
is the "good," or positive, or utopian, or postmodern critique of utopia.
6 The response to all of this—here, as in Jameson's work—will be Hegelian.
For Jameson, the world's postmodern fragmentation demands a totalizing
response and virtually posits that totality in its nexus of fragments. The force
of Jameson's work, then, is not so much that it estranges a certain text
or problem—postmodernism, Alasdair MacIntyre, Chantal Akerman—but
rather that it intervenes into the problematic. This is to read theory itself as
incommensurable, the ultimate differend, a fantasy that possesses its own
symbolic logic—to use terms that will come to be defined in the course of this
introductory chapter.

why marxism (today)?

7 But first, this chapter offers what seems today a doubly redundant task: to
formulate a Marxist theory for reading the works of a Marxist literary theo-

rist. The double redundancy (and redundancies are, in the so-called real world of manufacture and industry, what lead to layoffs, downscaling, restructuring, and so on) seems redundant not only to those critics of intellectual leftism who see in the collapse of Marxist or Communist governments in Eastern Europe a ready subject for university courses or reason for beliefs to be dismissed in the West; for some years various theorists of what Dick Hebdige calls "the posts" have claimed that Marxism is redundant.[1] Thus, or so runs the argument, Marxism constructs a metanarrative of emancipation, one that reflects bourgeois metaphysics even as it attempts to replace them, pursuing a "science" of inquiry that marginalizes the subjectivities of female and Third World subalterns and ends up not being Lacanian or discursive enough in its social theorization.[2]

8   These various high-theoretical dismissals (or reformulations) all offer cogent and unavoidable criticisms of the Marxist tradition, but I would first like to address the more "topical" reasons many find to dismiss socialism and left politics in general, if only because these current events have rarely (thus far) been discussed in a literary-theoretical context. The collapse of state Communism in Eastern Europe does seem to offer a valid historical reason to finally bury Marxism as philosophy or critique. A continuing disregard for human rights, demand-economies that succeeded neither in meeting consumers' needs internally nor in maintaining the nations' economic statures internationally, and the continuing strain of militaristic and near-militaristic activities all led, finally, to a series of initially bloodless revolutions.[3]

1   By "the posts" Hebdige (1988, 181–207) does not mean simply poststructuralism, postmodernism, and post-Marxism as monolithically antimetaphysical theories—he includes Jameson in this category (194), for example.

2   These arguments are made, respectively, by Jean-François Lyotard (metanarratives), Elaine Showalter and Teresa de Lauretis (feminism), Edward Said (the Third World), and Ernesto Laclau and Chantal Mouffe (discourse). I consider the critiques initiated by Lyotard, Showalter, and de Lauretis later in this chapter, and those of Said, Laclau, and Mouffe in chapter 3.

3   Two attempts to account for the slide of Eastern Europe into a very bloody postrevolution are Slavoj Žižek's For They Know Not What They Do: Enjoyment as a Political Factor (1991a), where Hegelian/Lacanian theory is abstracted, and Étienne Balibar and Immanuel Wallerstein's Race, Nation, and Class (1991), where nationalism is seen as the refuge of the working class in a late capitalist system, since "a bourgeoisie can exist only at

9 This hardly can be laid at the doorstep of one figure (be it Boris Yeltsin, Mikhail Gorbachev, or Lech Walesa): as, for example, attempts have been made in the press to connect some monolithic theory (and its present-day irrelevance) to Eastern Europe. In John Patrick Diggins's reductive argument: "[D]econstructionists may have declared the 'death of man' and showed students why the subject must now be seen as the object of history rather than its originator, but the chain of events in Eastern Europe took place because a man named Gorbachev desired to initiate change rather than impede it" (1992, 16). While it is attractive simply to point out the (academic) inadequacies of Diggins's statement (was Michel Foucault properly "deconstructionist" in his famous conclusion to *The Order of Things,* for example, and is not the subject-of-history-versus-the-object-of-history distinction really Louis Althusser's?), this technique would only impose on one field (to use Pierre Bourdieu's terminology)—journalism—the symbolic logic of another—the academy. In this case, the journalistic use of "deconstructionist" is sufficiently open to include both Foucault and Althusser; or, for Diggins, "deconstruction" means a vague and open body of thought. Nevertheless, the speed with which walls and governments fell made the continuing presence of Marxism in Western universities seem to some a little ironic. The taunt to leftists, "Why not go to Russia?" changed to "Marxism is dead—don't you read the newspapers?"

10 There is more than one way to analyze a historical event; relations between contemporary Marxism and state Communism are not direct, and the events in Eastern Europe are hardly cause to abandon a sophisticated theory of economic and historical analysis. First, Marxism has, in the past twenty or thirty years, relied for its moral legitimacy (for better or for worse) more upon progressive and liberation movements in the West (youth, ecology, feminism, antiracism) and the Third World (from Che to postcolonialism) than on Eastern Europe. Second, Marxism itself is more correctly "Marxisms" or "multi-Marxism." The various schools (structuralist, Frankfurt, *Socialisme ou barbarie,* existentialist, British Gramscians) and theorists (Ernst Bloch, Georg Lukács, Rosa Luxembourg, Raymond Williams) have

the world level . . . being a bourgeois means precisely that one cannot be loyal to any community, that one can worship no god but Mammon" (230).

differed in many ways in the past century of thought and activity. Thus, while there are undoubtedly Marxist philosophers who have continued to believe uncritically in the Soviet Union, those whose work contributes most directly to contemporary cultural Marxism (the field in which Jameson's work belongs) have maintained a more independent and skeptical attitude. Third, the revolutions in Europe demonstrate that Marxists are not at all naive or utopian to expect that the masses can opt to take control of their own destinies; and while the revolts are as much about consumer goods as they are about freedom, they also negate latent (or patent) fascist hopes that the masses can be ruled effectively. Finally, Eastern Europe's rejection of state Communism does not mean the abandonment of the Marxist or social-ist programs of many Third World liberation movements, from the ANC to the FMLN; nor does it mean that Marxist analyses of the politics of the Third World (or of elsewhere) are suddenly irrelevant.

11 There are many autobiographical/anecdotal accounts of the resistances to Soviet-style communism from *within* the left since 1917, including Sheila Rowbotham's "Clinging to the Dream" (1990), Lynne Segal's "Whose Left? Socialism, Feminism, and the Future" (1991), and Angela McRob-bie's "Revenge of the 60s" (1991). Alexander Cockburn also provides a simple, if brutal, indication of the importance of "freedom" in Eastern Europe versus the continuing oppressions in (to name only one area of U.S. hegemony) Central America, when he shows that U.S. interventionism led in the past decade to 100,000 deaths in Guatemala, 70,000 in El Salvador, and 40,000 in Nicaragua, whereas, resulting from Soviet imperialism in Europe, 7,000 Hungarians were killed in the 1956 uprising, 92 in the Prague Spring, 21 East Germans in 1953, and 689 in Rumania in 1989 (1990, 66). Indeed, James Rolleston has argued that with "the collapse of state socialism, criticism on the left clearly needs to reposition itself vis-à-vis 'bourgeois society.' Now there really is no outside" (1991, 87).

12 But to return to the central question posed by recent events in Eastern Europe:[4] does the use of violence by Communist governments, and the end

---

4 If these events were "recent" during the initial drafting of this introduction (in the spring of 1992), the neo-ethnic violence now plaguing Eastern Europe certainly over-shadows the 1989 "revolutions'" immediacy.

of various regimes in Eastern Europe, discount the validity of Marxism as
either a political program or a theory? The fall of Communist states in
Eastern Europe, while not without interest as a revamping of various ideologues' imaginaries, can be dismissed as a strong argument against Marxism
because they nevertheless can be explained in Marxist terms. That is, the
late 1980s revolutions are the result of historical changes in the world economic system (the growing globalization of trade that made it all the more
incumbent for the last noncapitalist nations to join the late capitalist system)
and of tendencies in the nations' domestic policies. To give just one example
of domestic changes: Iván Szelényi (1991) argues that the nonresistance of
many Communist parties to change was determined largely by what he calls
the "intellectualization of the bureaucracy," where what Bourdieu calls
"oblates" were replaced in the apparatus by new intellectuals: "As these
'Communist yuppies' replaced the old-line bureaucrats, the ethos of the
Party apparatus changed. These young professional cadres, unlike those
recruited from the working class and peasantry, did not depend exclusively
on political bosses. Their personal fate is not tied to the future of the Party. If
their Party job goes, they believe that with their marketable skills they can
return to their professions and earn better salaries by working for multinational corporations than by working for the Party" (270). Again, the totalizing world system of late capital, it would seem, plays a decisive role. Finally,
state communist violence, across the spectrum from Leninist pragmatism
and Stalinist literary theory to the Moscow trials and various invasions of the
1950s and 1960s, should be addressed, but in the following problematic:
does violence *in the name of* a particular ideology discredit that ideology?

13 The problem is that most world ideologies have benefited from violence
of various kinds. Violence in the name of liberal Western democracies ranges
from the maintenance of class systems and various economic inequalities at
home to the international division of labor which sees various nations maintained in a feudal relationship (a multinational system that is enforced brutally by client states of the West which regularly use torture, assassination,
death squads, and the genocide of aboriginal peoples with impunity). Christianity has an inglorious past (particularly in the cultural genocide and sexual abuse of First Nations peoples in Canada in this century), and in various
present-day incarnations, ranging from the patriarchy of Catholicism to the

extreme right-wing fundamentalisms. The response to these versions of reality falls into one of two categories: either to wish to put oneself "outside" of ideology—the pragmatism of Jean-François Lyotard or Richard Rorty, which will be examined below—or to examine the relationship between the violence and the "authorized/authorizing" ideology.

14 In brief, does violence "in the name of" socialism or democracy or Christianity invalidate that ideology? This is where, to begin, one can mark clearly the difference between fascism and socialism—a difference that has, since World War II, been blurred in the West for the purpose of discrediting socialism (the invention of the term "totalitarianism" is apposite).[5] Fascism is based on violence as its means and end: it is about the exclusion of races and other "deviants," about the superiority of a genetic group, and about the societal and capitalist organization of terror and violence. Violence is not incidental or an unfortunate feature of fascism; it is its reason for existence.[6] Violence is no more essential to socialism than it is to democracy; that is, while Leninist theories of revolution stress the need for a violent overthrow of the existing regime, the violence, like the state itself, is expected to wither away.

15 On the role of violence in socialism, and its relation to democracy, Lenin is quite explicit. Discussing Marx and the Paris Commune, he writes that the Commune "replaced the smashed state machine 'only' for fuller democracy: abolition of the standing army; all officials to be elected and subject to recall. But as a matter of fact this 'only' signifies a gigantic replacement of certain institutions by other institutions of a fundamentally different type . . .

5 As Darko Suvin remarks: "I want to remind people of the strange origins of the connotations of the word 'totalitarianism.' They arose after the [Second World] war, propagated by the Congress of Cultural Freedom, which was associated with such names as Stephen Spender and Irving Kristol and with journals such as *Encounter*, funded by the CIA as it turns out" (Nelson and Grossberg 1988, 359).

6 "Notable . . . is the normalization of the practice of violence as a way of satisfying acquisitive desire and of imposing the will of the powerful on the powerless. . . . In contemporary India communalism is certainly . . . the cutting edge for a fascist project as a whole, but those other violences—of caste, class and gender—are always there to *form* the kind of authoritarian personality upon which the fascist project eventually rests" (Ahmad 1993, 19–20).

democracy, introduced as fully and consistently as is at all conceivable, is transformed from a bourgeois into proletarian democracy; from the state (= a special force for the suppression of a particular class) into something which is no longer the state proper. It is still necessary to suppress the bourgeoisie and crush their resistance. . . . The organ of suppression, however, is here the majority of the population, and not a minority, as was always the case under slavery, serfdom and wage slavery. And since the majority of the people *itself* suppresses its oppressors, a 'special force' for suppression *is no longer necessary!* In this sense, the state *begins to wither away*" (1985, 42–43).

16 According to Lenin's scheme, violence is not necessary to maintain the proletarian state: since there is little of the rationalized division of labor characteristic of capitalism in general, the violence of an organized army or police force is unthinkable. That the Stalinist regime developed a powerful secret police, like democratic and fascist states, only demonstrates both how idealistic Lenin was and how nonsocialist the Soviet Union was already becoming. David McLellan has characterized Lenin's theories as not proto-Stalinist, but utopian: "Lenin's strong insistence on the withering of the state immediately after the revolution has libertarian or even anarchist overtones. His general view seemed to embody the classic socialist formula dating from Saint-Simon that the government of people could give way to the administration of things" (1983, 169).

17 There is also the question of what it means to do violence (or any other action) *in the name of*—and here one may fill in any theory. That is, what does it mean for the theory for an activity to be "authorized"? It is the question of authorization and legitimacy maneuvers in general that Lyotard addresses.

pragmatic objections

18 An elegant and influential argument against Marxism is outlined in *The Postmodern Condition.* Here Lyotard argues that the twin metanarratives of modernity—emancipation and enlightenment—have been discredited in the information explosion since World War II. Thus postmodernism is a period characterized by *petits récits,* or Wittgensteinian language games that only concern themselves with local conditions.

19 Lyotard's concern with the local is comparable to chaos theory and such examples of the latter as the "butterfly effect" (a butterfly flapping its wings in Beijing can cause a thunderstorm in New York), which show that scientific systems like meteorology and demographics are rapidly becoming aware of their own limits. In the case of meteorology, for example, most forecasts after six or seven days are worthless (Lyotard 1984, 58–60; Gleick 1987, 8–23).

20 Chaos theory is a long way from metaphysics and Marxism. Nevertheless, it is interesting that the butterfly effect seems to allegorize Cold War paranoia as the latest in scientific theory.[7] Scientists are loathe to give up their control of forecasting and prediction: Richard Feynman's laconic comment that "physicists like to think that all you have to do is say, these are the conditions, now what happens next?" prefaces the chapter of Gleick's book entitled "The Butterfly Effect" (Gleick 1987, 9). One continuing (and, according to chaos theory, unattainable) goal of meteorology has been, according to Edward Lorenz, the originator of the butterfly effect concept, not prediction, but control (Gleick 1987, 21). Thus capitalism and its economists are loathe to relinquish the reins of social engineering. A recent science fiction novel demonstrates with knowing certitude the links between chaos theory and social control. Michael Crichton's *Jurassic Park* is about a millionaire obsessed with dinosaurs who harnesses scientists and DNA replication to "bring back" the creatures for a theme park.[8] The project collapses, as predicted by a chaos expert, Ian Malcolm, who points out the futility of the project in terms that criticize both science and capitalism: "You create new life-forms, about which you know nothing at all. Your Doctor Wu does not even know the names of the things he is creating. He cannot be bothered

7 That the lepidopterist Nabokov and the plagiarist Sartre would stand on different sides of anti-communism notwithstanding. Perhaps this dialectic realizes its fullest contemporary text in the "Ayesha" sequence of *The Satanic Verses*, particularly in how Rushdie introduces these magical butterflies: "On the fateful morning of his fortieth birthday, in a room full of butterflies, the zamindar Mirza Saeed Akhtar watched over his sleeping wife" (Rushdie 1992, 216).

8 One predictable reaction to Spielberg's 1993 film of the novel centered on its marketing of the dinosaurs, indeed, of the idea of a "Jurassic Park," but in the sequence near the end of the film when the gift shop is destroyed, we see the commodities themselves (identical to those you could purchase that summer) burned or crushed.

with such details as *what the thing is called*, let alone what it *is*. You create many of them in a very short time, you never learn anything about them, yet you expect them to do your bidding, because you made them and you therefore think you own them. . . . You know what's wrong with scientific power? It's a form of inherited wealth. And you know what assholes congenitally rich people are" (Crichton 1991, 305–6).

21 Crichton's Marxist critique of science shows the critical aspects of chaos theory and is also not without a certain Foucauldean moment in seeing a fundamental problem with modern science as the absence of apprenticeship (some period of waiting and endurance, as in the pre-rationalized cultures of martial arts or spiritualism).[9]

22 Economics and other forms of social engineering are also not immune from the allure of forecasting. The most notorious and influential example of this is probably Daniel Bell's theory of "post-industrialism." Bell begins *The Coming of Post-Industrial Society* with the comment that, while the book "is an essay in social forecasting," one cannot predict the future, "if only for the logical reason that there is no such thing as 'the future'" (1976, 3). Forecasting, for Bell, is restricted to determining limits in policy decisions and, as if to confirm William Gibson's worst fears, he argues that "[m]ost technological forecasting is still based on what an imaginative engineer or writer can dream up as possible. . . . [E]xpectation is 'poetry,' because little attention is paid to constraints, especially economic ones. Fantasy may be indispensable, but only if it is disciplined by technique" (1976, 199). Forecasting is the precise opposite of a utopian commitment.

23 Lyotard sees the origins of Marxism in the resistance to encroaching modernity—the proletarianization of the rural working class (1984, 12). He argues that the Marxist critique has since become the basis for either liberal reform, in the West, or a totalizing society in the Eastern bloc. " 'Traditional' theory is always in danger of being incorporated into the programming of the social whole as a simple tool for the optimization of its performance; this is because its desire for a unitary and totalizing truth lends itself to the

---

9 After a comment like Žižek's "*Richard II* proves beyond any doubt that Shakespeare had read Lacan" (1991b, 9), I feel justified in my own, more modest imputing of Marxist motives to Crichton.

unitary and totalizing practice of the system's managers" (Lyotard 1984, 12). Totalities, Lyotard argues, lead to totalitarianism.

24 Lyotard locates the metaphysical problematic of Marxism specifically in the realm of two "grand narratives," a term he uses to mean the legitimacy maneuvers with which education has been formulated. The two narratives are education in an emancipatory role in the service of the nation (the Napoleonic ethos) and education for its own, university-defined speculative sake (the Schleiermacher option). The grand narrative, per se, Lyotard argues, "has lost its credibility, regardless of what mode of unification it uses, regardless of whether it is a speculative narrative or a narrative of emancipation" (37). The cause of this decline in metanarratives is the proliferation of "techniques and technologies" over the last fifty years.

25 So grand narratives suffer like the father in Marcuse's nightmare of 1950s alienation, *Leave It to Beaver*-style: "within the system of unified and intensified controls, decisive changes are taking place. . . . The superego is loosened from its origin, and the traumatic experience of the father is superseded by more exogenous images. . . . The repressive organization of the instincts seem to be *collective,* and the ego seems to be prematurely socialized by a whole system of extra-familial agents and agencies. As early as the preschool level, gangs, radio and television set the pattern for conformity and rebellion. . . . With this education, the family can no longer compete. In the struggle between the generations, the sides seem to be shifted: the son knows better [i.e., *Beaver Knows Best*]; he represents the mature reality principle against its obsolescent paternal forms. [The father's] authority as transmitter of wealth, skills, experiences is greatly reduced; he has less to offer, and therefore less to prohibit" (Marcuse 1974, 95–97; see also Jameson's comment [*M&F* 108–9]).

26 For Marcuse here the break with the older Freudian schema is precipitated by the growth of technology beyond the patriarch's knowledge: the male epiphany comes not, as Sartre commented, when you are older than your father, or even when you are stronger, but when you know more than your father.

27 But Lyotard does not contend, à la George Grant or Bell or Heidegger, that the technological is therefore the basis of the social. In the end, "science plays its own game; it is incapable of legitimating the other language games"

(1984, 40).[10] As John McGowan comments in *Postmodernism and Its Critics* (1991), "Lyotard makes it clear that the category of grand narratives includes not only nationalist stories of manifest destiny and humanism's celebration of autonomous selves but also Marxist schemas of emancipation—in other words, any generalizable explanation or purpose (*telos*) to which local action must be answerable" (183).

28 If Marxism is simply another grand narrative that has fallen by the wayside in the postmodern rush to performativity and language games, then intellectuals must create local rules in a "pragmatic" fashion, for the Rorty-like "conversation" to take place (Lyotard 1984, 17). Lyotard's vigilance offers an incisive critique of Leninist politics, replacing the vanguardism of Marxism with a local politics of the "micro." A Marxist reply to this critique would note that a host of socialist and Marxist philosophical and activist strategies have long given up on the vanguardist theory (see Segal or Rowbotham). And, as Eagleton remarks, "the micropolitical . . . sometimes seems to mean a politics so tiny as to be invisible" (1990b, 92). Lyotard's politics mirror in a left fashion Daniel Bell's "post-industrialism," and both point to the need for Marxism to shift from a fetish of the (masculine) model of the factory worker (a shift already underway in the imaginary of trade unions, for example, which recognize that organizing office and high-tech workers must be their future). Margaret Thatcher's praxis may derive from Lyotard's theory.[11]

29 This dubious distinction between the forecast and the real is no doubt structurally parallel to that between fantasy and the real, a distinction commented upon by Slavoj Žižek in *Looking Awry*. There Žižek shows that the Lacanian notion of surplus enjoyment is based on Marxist surplus value and that surplus enjoyment means the reversal of symbolic codes leading to "a nostalgic yearning for the 'natural' state in which things were only what they were" (1991b, 12–13). For Žižek, the fantasy as promulgated in popular

10   The "incommensurable" is important to Lyotard and to his notion of the postmodern. See *The Differend: Phrases in Dispute* (1988), where he writes the following: "Is this the sense in which we are not modern? Incommensurability, heterogeneity, the differend, the persistence of proper names, the absence of a supreme tribunal" (135).

11   A valuable account of the 1984–85 British coal strike is *Digging Deeper: Issues in the Miners' Strike* (Beynon 1985).

culture (Robert Heinlein, Fritz Lang, Patricia Highsmith) typically horrifies us because it is true: we are really the murderous professor; our world is really a Sartrean nothingness. The forecast world of economists, meteorologists, and postmodernists is more real than reality *precisely because it is the fantasy of theory that creates their subjectivities.*

30 As has been pointed out elsewhere,[12] Lyotard's critique, based as it is on a certain causal relationship between grand narratives and local actions, is more suited to a culture of powerful communist parties and unexamined Stalinism than the less rigorous Marxism to be found in the Anglo-American tradition. Whether we are to characterize the interpenetrating spheres as pragmatic language games, as Lyotard does, or as Habermassian spheres (or as Negt and Kluge's proletarian counter-spheres [see Jameson 1988]) matters little. An important flaw in Lyotard's analysis is that he overestimates the aforementioned causality.

31 Rorty's notion of the "conversation" and his anti-foundationalist pragmatics is the opposite of Marx, particularly if we take seriously the famous thesis that the point of philosophy is not to interpret the world, but to change it. That is, Rorty's concept of philosophy as a conversation means that there is no "truth" out there in "reality" since truth is an aspect of language, a linguistic category embedded in sentences. Therefore, as Rorty remarks of Wittgenstein and Heidegger, edifying philosophers "do not think that when we say something we must necessarily be expressing a view about a subject.

12 Most recently, for example, the long interview with Derrida in *The Althusserian Legacy* demonstrates the institutional strictures of 1950s and 1960s Parisian intellectual praxis: "But, quite naturally, I was paralyzed because at the same time I didn't want my questions to be taken for crude and self-serving criticisms connected with the Right or the Left—in particular with the Communist party. Even though I was not a Party member, I understood the situation. I knew that the accusation of theoreticism or of scientism could be formulated from the Party's point of view, for example, and, moreover, it was formulated by them in quite summary fashion—or in terms, at least, to which I would have been the last to subscribe" (Derrida 1993a, 188). Derrida saw, then, that to criticize Althusser and his colleagues from his deconstructive stance (of theoreticism or "newfangled scientism") could be appropriated by the monolithic Party structure to maintain pressure on Althusser's otherwise anti-Stalinist philosophies and praxis. Is this an example of the "positive" effects of "p.c.-ism?" See also *Remarks on Marx* (Foucault 1991).

We might just be *saying something*—participating in a conversation rather than contributing to an inquiry" (1980, 371). Rorty's critique of representation attempts to foreground in philosophy a system of linguistic difference all the while recognizing that his own discourse can be no more representational, that is, is not itself *about* its own content. In a sense, however, and without trying to flatten the differences between Rorty and Marx, the two systems can be reconciled in some way: Marx's desire to move beyond "interpretation" should be read as a critique of that word in its weak form (not the now-famous Nietzschean sense, that is, where explanation is seen as the other binary term). Interpretation in Marx's phrase is akin to representation (*Darstellung*),[13] or merely the continuing attempt in classical and bourgeois philosophy to create some theory of the world *instead* of intervening into it.

32   Frank Lentricchia is less positive about the place of Rorty in progressive theory, however. He writes in *Criticism and Social Change:* "No single anchoring goal for the conversation is possible because our various vocabularies will never project or describe the same thing. The voices will tend to merge in a cacophony, a Babel-like chorus of unconstrained and incommensurate interpretations" (1985, 16). Lentricchia allows that "[e]difying philosophy, down deep, has a goal—it must be both critical and utopian" (17), but Rorty's choice, between either a totalizing realism or a multitude of individualisms, is too extreme (Lentricchia identifies the missing term as "the social"). Eagleton, too, argues that some degree of commensurability is necessary to conflict: "[W]e are not politically *conflicting* if you hold that patriarchy is an objectionable social system and I hold that it is a small town in upper New York state" (1991, 13). He also dismisses Rorty for not providing a political way out of the conversation: Rorty "will have to come out from behind the cover of general theories of belief or anti-foundationalism or anti-logocentrism or the ontological ineluctability of micropolitics and let

13   Althusser discusses this most famously in *Reading Capital* (Althusser and Balibar 1979), in the passage on pages 192–93 (from which one of this book's epigraphs is derived). Hobsbawm comments on this in his essay "The Structure of *Capital*," (Hobsbawm 1994, 8), reprinted in the Althusser critical reader (ed. Elliott, 1994). See also Benjamin's "Epistemo-Critical Prologue" (1985, 27–56), which I discuss at the end of chapter 2.

us know a little more clearly why [he] would like us to remain in NATO" (1990b, 93). For both Lentricchia and Eagleton, Rorty's genteel vision of philosophy smacks too much of the polite conversations that have dominated literary criticism from Addison and Steele to deconstruction (as Lentricchia would put it) or from the *Spectator* to poststructuralism (in Eagleton's terms).

33 Nonetheless, Eagleton has theorized from Marx's writings a critique of representation analogous to Rorty's. In reference to the famous "poetry of the future" passage of the *Eighteenth Brumaire*, Eagleton writes that "[w]hat is at question here is the whole concept of a representational aesthetics. Previous revolutions have been formalistic, engrafting a factitious 'phrase' or form onto their content; but the consequence of this is a dwarfing of the signified by the signifier. The content of socialist revolution, by contrast, is excessive of all form, out in advance of its own rhetoric. It is unrepresentable by anything but itself, signified only in its 'absolute movement of becoming,' and thus a kind of sublimity. The representational devices of bourgeois society are those of exchange-value; but it is precisely this signifying frame that the productive forces must break beyond, releasing a heterogeneity of use-values whose unique particularity would seem to refuse all standardized representation" (1990a, 214–15).

34 In the next chapter, I analyze Jameson's concept of the "figure" and how he has theorized this question of the "politically unrepresentable"; similarly, there the relationship between exchange-value and philosophy in Adorno is analyzed in relation to *Late Marxism*. The point for now is to assert that there is no great chasm separating a bad and realist Marxism from a good and post-referential anti-foundationalism.[14]

35 Finally, and on a lighter note, these two theoretical and historical moments (the fall of Communism, the follies of Marxism) may be countered at once. As Eagleton acerbically states, "No doubt President Ceausescu spent his last moments on earth reminding his executioners that revolution was an

14 As Greig Henderson put it in a review of Eagleton's *Ideology,* "Marxism survives as a rhetoric of social change, its ideas being part of the active struggle to establish proletarian class consciousness, but its materialist analysis of sociohistorical formations loses its scientific status" (1991, 286).

outmoded concept, that there were only ever micro-strategies and local deconstructions, and that the idea of a 'collective revolutionary subject' was
hopelessly passé" (1991, xiii).

technologies of marxism

36 In articulating the differences between feminism and Marxism, this is not
the place for a final argument for the supremacy of Marxism as method or
practice: the ability of Marxist theory to work through other methodologies
and "come out the other side" has been demonstrated by Jameson. And it is
interesting to note that most other theoretical approaches remain in the
mode of dialectical opposition to competing methods; no doubt it is something to do with the postmodern affection for "particularism" that little
thought is given by Elaine Showalter, say, to engage with Marxist theory and
use it itself to show its patriarchal inadequacies.

37 This is not to say that Showalter's engagement with Marxism, as in her
essay on Terry Eagleton in *Men in Feminism* (Showalter 1987, 127–30), lacks
substance. Showalter's essay is a critique that unites the structure of demystification with a content of feminism: "By possessing feminist criticism,
so to speak, Eagleton effectively recuperates for himself its 'phallic' signifying power. In his synthesis of feminism, Marxism and poststructuralism,
Eagleton also intermingles (or ignores) critics, so that there is no sense of a
background of feminist readings of Clarissa" (1987, 128).[15] And Showalter's engagement with Eagleton, as the context of her entire article on "critical cross-dressing" demonstrates, is as much concerned with the ability of
poststructuralism to erase feminine specificities as with Marxism as a patriarchal discourse: that last formulation might be too global or even *theoretical* for Showalter.

15 Showalter, it should be noted, is not overly hostile to Eagleton. Later in this article
she adds that in *Literary Theory*, Eagleton gives feminist criticism "a full measure of
autonomy and respect" (1987, 130). But am I being "fair" in a neat and bourgeois manner
by noting this, by saying that "it should be noted"? Probably just a betrayal of male anxiety
at not wanting to seem antifeminist.

38 A feminist theorist who in her work appropriates Marxism for her own practice is Teresa de Lauretis, in *Technologies of Gender* (1987). De Lauretis intervenes first into the problematic of ideology and interpellation; she engages with Althusser's statement that "*All ideology has the function (which defines it) of 'constituting' concrete individuals as subjects*" (Althusser, 1971, 171, emphasis his; qtd. de Lauretis 1987, 6). "If I substitute *gender* for *ideology*," de Lauretis then adds, "the statement still works, but with a slight shift of the terms: Gender has the function (which defines it) of constituting concrete individuals as men and women" (6). Gender interpellates a split *in*, or *between*, subjects (and not simply the Lacanian split-subject), unlike classic Althusserian ideology, which simply interpellates all individuals as subjects.

39 The terrain of the "all" here varies with class, but remember that Althusser is concerned with getting away from a class-oriented Marxist humanism (associated with Lukács and his notion that the consciousness of the proletariat has a priority due to reification). Althusser does not argue that ideology will disappear in a new socialist society: "[T]he problem of ideology's function in a classless society must also be posed. This can be resolved by showing that the deformation of ideology [Lacan's "misrecognition"] is socially necessary as a result of the very nature of the social whole. . . . Owing to the opacity of the social structure, the representation of the world indispensable to social cohesion is necessarily *mythical*" (Althusser 1965, 30–31; qtd. Elliott 1987, 174). Althusser's insistence on cohesion and social structure, then, means that a postrevolutionary society would not be anarchistic (which would be grounded in the Lacanian Imaginary), and that history would still be some unrepresentable (the Lacanian Real): in other words, social structure will still be characterizable as the Lacanian Symbolic, a structure of representation bound by rules.

40 For de Lauretis, Althusser's analysis is "blind to its own complicity in the ideology of gender, [and] can itself function as a techno-logy of gender" (1987, 6). But she is not engaged in the sort of *Ideologiekritik* that we saw above with Showalter. De Lauretis aims less to demonstrate some problem or failing in Marxism than to use Marxism to arrive at a feminist problematic. Taking Althusser's insistence that ideology depends on individuals in order that it may "create" or interpellate a subject, she argues that this is

"central to the feminist project of theorizing gender as a personal-political force both negative and positive" (9). So, unlike the Marxist formulation which dictates that we are always in ideology, female subjects are both inside gender—as Woman, some eternal and fixed essence, represented in tropes like the Angel of the Hearth, or the Dark Continent—and outside it—as women, or shifting and deterritorializing subject positions (114).

41 What is relevant to my purposes here is that de Lauretis is neither "deconstructing" Marxism nor simply arguing that its premises, since they exclude gender, are invariably masculinist. Here is less a critique of Marxism than an appropriation of its theory for a feminist purpose. Do I "prefer" this to Showalter's technique? Probably. Because it is more theoretical, more sophisticated? Sure. (But, as will become evident in the discussions in the next two chapters, I also prefer it to deconstructions of Marxism by critics like Denis Hollier and Geoff Bennington.) Because I think that de Lauretis's method is akin to what Jameson sets out to do, that is, work through a competing methodology?

42 De Lauretis also uses Jameson's *The Political Unconscious,* and especially his hermeneutic engagement with history as a "prior textualization" (*PU,* 21; qtd. de Lauretis 1987, 111). This notion informs her reading of how feminist film (Yvonne Rainier) rewrites a prior historical or ideological subtext, where that subtext is now an en-gendered one, framed specifically in terms of de Lauretis's dialectic of Woman and women. This use of Jameson's theory is not at all critical and is merely one of many such instances in the theory of the past decade.[16]

43 My point in this consideration of a third critique of Marxism (after the first, and unduly historicist one of "current events," and the second, disingenuous one of poststructuralism) is that there is more at stake in a dispute between two practices that both claim a political urgency. That is (to utilize proleptically two terms which I elaborate upon in the third chapter of this work), there are antagonisms at work here and there are alliances. So

16 A bibliography prepared for Jameson's 1991 Wellek Library lectures at UC-Irvine lists some 150 texts that deal at length with Jameson's work, and approximately 1,500 that do so briefly (Yeghiayan 1991). Jameson is also apparently one of the three most-cited authorities, according to an MLA survey (Sprinker 1993, 22).

the Lyotardian "differend" or Rortyesque "incommensurability" does not mean, to my mind, that difference is everything.

reading marxism reading

44 Summarizing a philosophical and political movement requires the well-known Freudian rhetorical strategies of condensation and displacement—saying exactly what Marxism is would be no different. The tradition of Marxist inquiry into which Jameson's work can be most accurately slotted is Western Marxism—one that originates with Lukács's attempts to think in a formal and anti-Kantian way about modern subjectivity. Concepts like "the commodity" and "reification" were imbued with a philosophical dignity, and along with Althusser's "overdetermination" and "ideological state appara-ratuses," Sartre's "seriality," Bloch's "anticipatory illumination," Benjamin's "aura," Theodor Adorno and Max Horkheimer's "culture industry," and Antonio Gramsci's "hegemony," led to the modern and rich semantic field of Marxist theory.

45 The word "field" was chosen carefully—in many ways, Western Marxism constitutes what Bourdieu calls a field or *champ*. (A field is "any system of social relations which functions according to a logic of its own that must be taken into account in explaining its development" [Boschetti 1988, 3].) While Bourdieu has attempted to evade what he sees as the more simplistic or deterministic class and economic analyses of Marxist sociology, his the-ory of the field depends on economic metaphors. The "symbolic logic" of a field is that certain activities carry a symbolic profit, while others realize none.

46 The interpretative activity offered in this book constitutes itself as inter-stitial and counter-hegemonic. It is interstitial because what is normally forgotten or stepped over in reading, and especially in the reading of politi-cally driven literary theory—the infamous "cracks" that will "break your mother's back"—is here foregrounded in order that a "rhetoric of Jameson" may be arrived at. And the theory is counter-hegemonic in three senses. First, readings of this sort, and surely Paul de Man's is the most influential still, are usually attempts to "undo" the text and somehow find what was repressed by the author, attempts that end up affirming some subversion of (authorial) intent by the text.[17] I see my project as, instead, in solidarity with Jameson's. Second, what is "interstitial" in the work of Marxists like Jameson is usually glossed over by progressive or left readers: tropes and figures are secondary, it is still felt, to the hard work of the class struggle (even if reading theorists like Jameson is a struggle that frequently takes place in a classroom). Third, unlike most readings of rhetoric, I also locate in the *content* of the work a certain political importance—and content is, again, marginal to poststructuralism.

47 In "Writing and Method," Charles Bernstein argues that "[i]f philosophy is to be characterized as a form consisting of clearly exposited arguments whose appeal is to the logic of validity, then it would systematically be limited by the limits of expository practice. I don't think it makes sense to restrict philosophy to this particular mode of discourse both because it would rule out some of the best work in philosophy and because it suggests that reason's most 'clear' expression is exposition. Rather it seems to me that, as a mode, contemporary expository writing edges close to being merely a *style* of decorous thinking, rigidified and formalized. . . . It is no longer an enactment of thinking or reason but a representation (and simplification) of an eighteenth-century ideal of reasoning" (1986, 221).

48 Bernstein's target is clearly the linear passage of an idea through a sentence, developed carefully with due thought for clarity and readability. Similarly, my stylistic aim is simply to appropriate the rhetoric of poststructuralism without importing (all of) the ideology.

49 My interest in the interstitial in Jameson's work leads in some fairly eclectic directions, not least because I am interested both in an analysis of the function of structuring and politicizing narratives in the texts (the notorious "intrinsic" in Jameson's and de Man's dichotomies [Jameson, *LM* 4; de Man 1979, 4–5]) and in a situating (in the proper Sartrean sense) of these inter-

---

17 Thus Geoff Bennington writes: "I shall . . . return to some of those privileged operators of Jameson's method, to re-turn them (for I take this to be a necessary, if far from sufficient, operator of any deconstructive reading) against the text which puts them to work" (1982, 26). So Bennington sees deconstruction as working "against" a text that "puts" certain operators "to work."

stices within a larger or social field—the figure in the ground, then (here, the "extrinsic"). This methodological twinning of analyses (and Jameson is the great theoretician of outlining important twin or dialectical concepts) is founded neither upon some Ur-opposition nor in an economy of origin. The desire on my part for such a bifocal approach entails falling smack into the center of the liberal eclecticism of contemporary theory.

returning to normal

50 I would like to reverse Thomas Kuhn's influential hierarchy of "normal science" and "paradigm shifts" and argue that it is in the work of scholars in the "normal" teaching and writing about literary theory today that the so-called research of the field takes place. Kuhn argues that scientific research is characterized by certain paradigms, ways of theorizing a given field (of astronomy, organic chemistry, etc.). "Normal science," or the work carried on by most scientists, supports paradigms through "empirical work undertaken to articulate the paradigm theory, resolving some of its residual ambiguities and permitting the solution of problems to which it had previously only drawn attention" (1968, 27), refining the theory of the paradigm through theoretical discussions, "not because the predictions in which they result are intrinsically valuable, but because they can be confronted directly with experiment. Their purpose is to display a new application and to increase the precision of an application that has already been made" (30). Normal science, Kuhn argues, is simply the "determining of significant fact, matching of fact with theory, and articulation of theory" (33)—is simply, Kuhn sarcastically and quietly shows, "puzzle-solving" (35–42). When a scientific community is forced to confront "anomalies" that will not fit into its paradigm, a crisis results, and a revolution occurs in which a new paradigm is formulated.

51 The central problem with Kuhn's theory lies in its similarity to avant-gardism in the arts and vulgar Leninism in politics. In all three cases, the masses are assumed to be blind to real problems (trapped in the normal, in the mainstream, in ideology). If the Kuhnian analysis is applied to literary theory—to cultural studies in general—an obvious heuristic benefit results in

seeing a "paradigm-shift" from humanistic studies to structuralism and poststructuralism. In such a narrative, figures like Barthes, Derrida, and de Man are valorized for their recognition of "anomalies" (gaps in texts, phonocentrism).

52 In the contemporary context, an elitist and synchronic hierarchy (Kuhn's model is mostly diachronic) could be constructed by relegating the majority of garden-variety scholars to the halls of the normal school and the hundred or so theorists to the pantheon. I would rather invert Kuhn's pyramid, locating in the work of the "normal" both a site for the actual *production* of the paradigm as well as its shift. That is, while the elite produces a fairly narrow and monologic discourse, the normal critic engages in a radically dialogic practice. I am still willing, however, to see Kuhn's theory of "progress through revolutions" as useful. While his discourse is flawed—as elsewhere he consistently refers to scientists as men and considers science to be insulated from the social world—the most important of his conclusions is that while science progresses *from* some primitive/inarticulate morass, it does not do so *toward* a goal—truth or pure and total knowledge (169–72).

liberalism and marxism

53 High-profile literary theorists tend to produce a monologic discourse; while the work of other theorists is acknowledged *this is primarily to correct/supplement* that work. Thus de Man or Spivak or Lentricchia in their work produce a "de Manian discourse" or "Spivak effect" or "Lentricchia textuality," composed of the advancement of a certain heuristic/explanatory argument (which can certainly be analyzed in terms of narrative semiotics: the "rhetorical" exploration of alternatives that are then discarded, the vanquishing/incorporation of other theories, the quasi-heroic arrival at a satisfactory solution). This "plot" or story is also "illustrated" via the acceptable plagiarism of quotation and "colored" (in the novelistic sense of "local color": and certainly Spivak's rhetorical technique of consistently deferring her "theorizing" with reflections on the local conditions in which she began to write or deliver the article in question is the most sophisticated example of this) with the critic's "voice" or "style." Even the critic's awareness of

his/her strategy does not negate its importance, as when Lentricchia admits to pitting de Man against Burke in his *Criticism and Social Change* (1985, 19–20).

54 Like the famous Chekovian revolver (on the wall in Act One, used to murder later on), theoretical or critical discourse also leaves embedded or proleptic land mines as it were: what appear to be minor arguments that will later in the text be expanded or exploded to provide another explanatory function. Synthesizing for the moment the work of Jameson and J. Hillis Miller, narratologically this is a repeated shifting of gears—a dialectical repetition.[18] And in the present work, for example, this mini-theory of the narratology of literary theory is later used to comment both on Jameson's reflections on narrative in philosophy and on the narratives at/as work in his texts.

55 In contradistinction to the monologism of theorists, the discourse of the technician is unrelentingly dialogic. The question of whether a critic's place in the hierarchy determines her monologism or dialogism or is determined *by* it is the topic for a work other than this one. My own feeling is that while "monologic" technicians will prove to be quite boring—think of the pedant in your own faculty department for verification of this—"dialogic" theorists are quite rare, for their allegiance to the methodology of the technicians-proletariat, as it were, almost ensures a marginalization of their work. This dialogism—radical dialogism is the "good" or utopian side of the figure; liberal eclecticism is the ideological version of it—by the way, is a key aspect of Jameson's work.

56 I am interested in a Marxist interpretation of discourse, which, as I see it, would not only determine how ideology is "*intrinsic* to the business of formal analysis" (*LM*, 4) but also how the analysis of form as a structural cause of social and ideological factors is part of the class struggle and *in*formed by the class struggle. This metatheory, then, necessarily involves reference to and incorporation of a number of contemporary and historical theorists.

57 Jameson argues somewhere that the "theorist" is a postmodern phenom-

18 The archetypal moment in the novel for this figure is undoubtedly Jim's various leaps in *Lord Jim*—like the two leaps that Joe Gold (played by Joe Mantegna) takes in David Mamet's *Homicide,* both resulting in his dropping his gun (the second time unnoticed, when he almost dies) (Mamet 1992, 66, 118).

enon, corresponding both to the triumph of "structural guilt" in the various disciplines and subdisciplines of the humanities, and to the postmodern need to integrate what was formerly fragmented. Thus the formation of the "critic" in the nineteenth century was a reaction to the separation of the aesthetic from the industrial;[19] while the integration of philosopher, critic, theoretician (in the past, "theoretician" had the more limited meaning of a specialist dealing in the "theory" of a given profession/discipline) and perhaps even poet/novelist into the theorist is a reaction to the totalizing hegemony of late capitalism (it is no accident that we live in the age of inter/multidisciplinarity *and* multinational "synergy"—what is more Bataillean in terms of excess and limits and transgressions, the various border-blur genre-hopping experiments of po-mo poets and video artists, or such new media forms as infotainment and Macjournalism, or the dismantling of national boundaries and tariffs of late capitalism?).

58   But to return to the question of the technician's dialogism or liberal eclecticism as source for my own method: the garden-variety academic teaching and writing about literary theory (the "real" theorist writes literary theory, not merely *about* it) embodies, ironically, what Rorty sees as essential in the literary critic for a moral philosopher: "Ironists read literary critics, and take them as moral advisers, simply because such critics have an exceptionally

19   As is usual, Raymond Williams is perceptive and illustrative on this point (I suppose I am rather old-fashioned to still be reading Williams [and Said, for that matter; his recent *Culture and Imperialism* (1993) seems to be a monumental summing-up of his career] to be both relevant and theoretico-critically sophisticated): he writes, in *Culture and Society* (1990), of the *fin-de-siècle* new aesthetics, that "[w]hat we sometimes suppose to be a change in ideas is perhaps properly identified as a change—a change for the worse—in prose. . . . The elements of continuity in this statement [Pater, who remarks that "the end of life is . . . to withdraw the thoughts for a little while from the mere machinery of life, to fix them, with appropriate emotions, on the spectacle of those great facts in man's existence which no machinery affects"] are clear: the distinction between 'being' and 'doing,' the criticism of 'mere machinery,' the description of this 'true moral significance of art and poetry' as 'culture'—this *to the very words* is no more than a summing-up of the long preceding tradition" (166–67). I take Williams's "prose" to be his private code word for what I am calling "rhetoric" or "figures," as Pater's "very words" of "mere machinery" thus transcodes between the industrial penetration of Britain and the precapitalist figure of the machine.

large range of acquaintance. They are moral advisers not because they have special access to moral truth but because they have been around. They have read more books and are thus in a better position not to get trapped in the vocabulary of a single book. In particular, ironists hope that critics will help them perform the sort of dialectical feat which Hegel was so good at. That is, they hope critics will help them continue to admire books 'which are prima facie antithetical by performing some sort of synthesis" (1990, 80–81).

59 Bracketing for a moment the idea of literary critics as moral advisers, it is easy to see how well this description of the literary critic as type fits Jameson. This is true both because of the breadth of his reference and because of how he manipulates those references. In the first case, for example, and keeping in mind Rorty's remark that literary theory essentially means the addition of new proper names to the canon, one can see *Marxism and Form* as the addition of Adorno, Lukács, and Benjamin to the then-nascent theory canon (the proper names of Sartre and Bloch have fared less well). In terms of Jameson's dialectical feats, the manipulation of Northrop Frye, Althusser, and A. J. Greimas in *The Political Unconscious* similarly acts to make the book remarkable in an objective (nonevaluative) sense. In Bourdieu's jargon, the symbolic logic of the field of literary criticism is such that the breadth and manipulation (the common code word for this "accomplishment" will typically be "rigor," which has replaced "genius," which smacks too much of Romantic cultism) are valued apparently "for [their] own sake."

60 I see the value of Jameson's work as political, however, and not ethical:[20]

---

20 Here is my (Rorty-influenced) distinction between what I see as a no-longer tenable sense of the ethics and still-important politics. I was recently postering in my neighborhood when I saw an altercation between three men and a woman. I turned off my Walkman and drew closer. The three men were drunk outside the local beer store, where they usually are, sitting on a car. I asked the young woman if the car was hers; she told me it was not, but that her friend would be angry "if she saw these guys sitting on the hood." My decision to intercede at this point overrode what would otherwise be a political solidarity with the three lumpens: it is their space, and the car had invaded it. But their verbal violence directed at the woman seemed more important, more of an immediate issue. But this was not an ethic: my solidarity with women as a class or group in terms of street violence seemed to be paramount in this case, and my so-called "decision" was neither individual in terms of my own consciousness (to use a Sartrean vocabulary, my "free

and here a certain contradiction will be admitted. If Jameson's work is so counter-hegemonic in terms of its radical dialogism (in my description), why has it achieved an undeniable level of success and visibility (major publishers, wide availability, a Wellek Library lecture, etc.)?[21] This question is a subset of the larger question of the role of Marxist criticism in a capitalist state: in both scenarios, the success of Jameson indicates the very real (if terribly contingent) liberalism of the field and state. That is, first of all, while the paradigm is shifting in cultural studies toward liberal eclecticism, Jameson's work meets with approval even as it is criticized for precisely this liberalism (see Weber 1987). And second, the democratic state and its various ISA's work hard at maintaining an appearance of liberalism and free expression—and thus the attacks on "political correctness" must necessarily follow the line that leftism in the U.S. is itself censoring (and thus can be again curtailed).

the two clints

61   "Psychoanalysis is less merciful than Christianity," reads the blurb on the back of Žižek's *For They Know Not What They Do: Enjoyment as a Political Factor* (1991a): "God the Father forgives our ignorance; psychoanalysis holds out no such hope." Žižek's condemnation of the vulgar notion of "bad

---

choice" was determined by my situation) nor in terms of identifying with or feeling "protective" of the woman; finally, my actions were not ethical because they were not based on some grand narrative of "humanity" (in which case, of course, I would have been stymied, I think).

21   Christopher Norris argues that "any theory that *claimed* to be 'radical' but in fact enjoyed widespread acceptance—or even a modest degree of comprehension among like-minded colleagues—would for this very reason have to be seen as part of an existing consensus, no matter how small or how marginal its membership" (1991, 116). But see Eagleton on "conflicting" (1991, 13). And Bruce Norton sees precisely Jameson's popularity as a hopeful sign. Noting that the *Postmodernism* book won the 1990 James Lowell Prize of the MLA, he writes: "To my knowledge, no work positing capitalism as the product of a logic of capital has ever achieved similar recognition in general academic circles in the United States" (Norton 1994, 67n4).

faith" is also pertinent to another dyad that I analyze more than once in the following pages: the theorist versus the artist. Clint Eastwood, in a recent interview, pointed to the popular disavowal of analysis so prevalent as to be a trope: "Hitchcock once told me, when I was analyzing a lot of things about his pictures, 'Clint, you must remember, it's only a movie'" (Eastwood 1993, 38).[22] The theorist, confronted with a similar "Clint" who is "analyzing a lot of things," can make no such objection: "Clint, you must remember, it's only a theory." Theory demands its own interpretation and quite frequently encodes such demands and first steps into its own text; similarly, a common trope for readers of theory is to immediately turn the theoretical text's modest heuristic or critical discovery back onto that text: out-Foucault Foucault, perhaps, or deconstruct deconstruction. Rest assured that this is not my project here, to show the "political unconscious" of Jameson's various texts. The image of the critic (or graduate student) as some belligerent "deconstructor" of texts (Nabokov's *Pale Fire*, of course) has its mirror in mass culture: the obsessed fan or "stalker," also mentioned by Eastwood: "There was one [stalker] recently where the FBI had gone to see the guy because he had made some threats over the phone and left it on tape. And they said the guy seemed quite normal until they mentioned my name and he went crazy" (76). The stalking critic also obsesses at this level of the signifier (in both cases some economy of the Name-of-the-Father would seem to be at work)—picking up journals for articles by the Object, or flipping through book indexes for mention of the Object.

62 This minor technique, that of linking academic theory to mass culture, is evidently determined in part by my class background. Two processes are at work here: one, by eliding, methodologically, the "difference" between high theory and low entertainment, I can receive the greatest possible returns on my investment of cultural capital (Bourdieu 1984, 87).[23] Since my child-

---

22 But Eastwood also later differentiates his desire for a cinema of characters and story values from the formulaic, based on the future fate of the latter: "A lot of dumb pictures have made a lot of money but that doesn't mean they're going to be anything cinema students will revel over in the future" (1992, 40).

23 Would Žižek have achieved quite his notoriety or popularity if he didn't talk so much about Hitchcock and other mass-cultural texts widely available in the Anglo-American world?

hood was bereft of high culture but steeped in mass culture, I valorize the latter utilizing a technique, "theory," that seems to be, in its anti-canonicity, oppositional to the former. I come from a lower middle-class background (my mother was a bank teller, my father is in the air force), which means that while my family's financial security was never absolute, we had some pretensions to culture that linked us more to working-class families than to more solidly middle-class ones. But the "culture" I grew up with contained the most degraded specimens of the North American commodification processes: *Reader's Digest* vied with encyclopaedias for space on the bookshelves. In the living room there was a painting of mountains and rock that would make work by the Group of Seven look cubist, and hung in my parents' bedroom was a shellacked jigsaw puzzle, also of a forgettable and puerile "scene." A devotion to reading meant some Pierre Berton, the Hardy Boys, and Nancy Drew; and the music was almost unclassifiable in its obduracy—not high, middle, or lowbrow, but rather no-brow, or mono-brow—101 Strings, Mantovani, Hagood Hardy. This served as "supper music" for special occasions.[24]

63 There was no serious literature, classical music, or nondecorative visual art in our home, for my parents knew that such stuff was not for people like us. These various levels of artistic culture function to maintain a class system; if later my parents tried to signal a rise in class (a rise so monologic and economically microscopic as to be insignificant) by suddenly listening to *Hooked on Classics* or serving shrimp cocktail with tartar sauce, these cultural markers can only, in the implacable gaze of the Other, incite ridicule. From the point of view of the underclass, the Other is the educated, cultured snob, the white guy in a silk dressing robe listening to jazz or classical music. And thus when I left home and started drifting in and out of universities—and since I had for whatever reason started writing poetry in high school (do I have to say how well that was received at home?)—culture seemed to offer

24 When a version of this account appeared in a magazine, the editor wrote beside the preceding paragraph: "[T]his is a 'pretension to culture'?" My point is that the emphasis should be on the pretension (and this is what links my culture more to the working class than to the middle class). But what is more pathetic, believing that surrounding yourself with Book of the Month Club reprints of Sherlock Holmes is "culture," or yearning after first editions of Thomas Mann?

me a refuge from my class background. More bluntly: I was a class traitor; to use the African American vernacular, I was trying to "pass." Eliot, Beethoven, Atwood, Joyce, Camus—here were things my parents had no competence in (even if the eclecticism of the list might for some readers signal a lack of discipline or knowledge). What sealed off my past, but also made me self-conscious about my class heritage, was an event as fatal as taking a suicide pill: I started to do well in the academic field.

64 The success meant a virtual erasure of my past, which is the point of this account. A commonplace of progressive critiques of the various institutions of late capitalist society is that these institutions erase one's specificity: women have to be "masculinized" even down to their dress in order to succeed in business; Natives are Christianized in residence schools. This symbolic loss is just as real for working-class and lower middle-class men and women when they begin careers in intellectual fields—the arts, the academy, the media. When a working-class student (who has to try harder than upper middle-class students, who have the "benefits" of private schools, role models in one's own parents, and connections) graduates from university, he or she suddenly loses his or her class: you are now a member of the upper middle-class elite. University-educated, you regard the cultural pastimes of your youth and heritage with suspicion—watching football is simultaneously mind-deadening and sexist, soap operas are either tools of patriarchal oppression or pathetic melodramas compared to Shakespeare or Beckett.

65 More recently, and only during the editing of my dissertation, my economic and class configuration took another fatal turn. Most of the class trajectory that I found myself on in the past eleven or twelve years, even as I drifted in and out of university and various semiskilled jobs (notably, bartending and legal editing), was based on an invisible infrastructure: a long-term relationship. When this ended during the writing of my dissertation, my economic situation changed dramatically and my praxis joined my theory. Interestingly, I began to articulate myself in a more class- and sexuality-conscious manner; notably, dressing in that complex of parodic and working-class youth codes sometimes designated as skinhead or grunge (shades of Dick Hebdige!), made all the more complicated by my coming out and moving to Toronto's gay ghetto (where skinheads are as likely to be Queer Nation activists or leather dykes as street kids or neo-Nazis). Other

changes in my body I have initiated include an interest in body-piercing, recreational drugs, and bodybuilding; what is of interest (and possibly only to me) is that I initially articulated these desires for change in terms of masculinity; it was only more recently that I was able to articulate this to myself and others as becoming queer or bisexual.

66 My point is that a change in sexual-economic circumstances led to a change in how I viewed my body and how I immersed myself in mass culture . . . all the while maintaining a Rortyan ironist's scepticism about my own location. Theory previously, it seems, acted as my mass culture (I had a voracious appetite for buying books, was almost a groupie in the classical sense of that term, and so on), and mass culture was the exotic other, whereas now the terms seem to be reversed and intractably contaminating each other; if I am listening to Suicidal Tendencies as I enter this on the computer, with three Adorno books and *Late Marxism* piled on my desk, I might as easily be listening to John Coltrane or CBC-FM as I read *Vibe*, or *Details*. But this is only really a case of the theorist playing catch-up to the masses, who possess a wonderfully heterogeneous sense (ideology) of the lack of barriers even as their practices affirm those barriers (i.e., disparaging supermarket tabloids while disavowing their competence to read a "difficult" novel; attacking television and Stephen King while "devouring" science-fiction fantasy novels).

2

POSTMODERN

MARXISM

apostrophe 's'

67 The beginning of Jameson's *Marxism and Form* seems to fall into the rhetorical category of the apostrophe: "To whom can one present a writer whose principal subject is the disappearance of the public?" (*M&F,* 3). But the apostrophe here is about the difficulty of apostrophizing; or about the difficulty of addressing Adorno's work (to an audience that, according to Adorno's own analysis, is disappearing). Here the apostrophe, which swings between the address of a dead or absent entity and the address of one (person) and *not* the "general" public, already encodes the dilemma of Jameson's reading of Adorno: the difficulty of reconciling *form*—an address or presentation—with content—Adorno's thesis of the disappearance of a certain public.

68 So what Jameson's apostrophe or meta-apostrophe alerts me to is the formal effect his work desires/needs (for this dichotomy, see Jameson on Sartre's move from existential lack to Marxist need: *M&F,* 232)—as well as the necessity to avoid merely cataloging his tropes in a late capitalist version of Quintilian. For in this age of the secularization of rhetoric—and the various catalogs of the ancient art represented on the one hand by McLuhan and on the other by college handbooks—Jameson's demand is not to list, for easy consumption, the various tropes of the trade that a Marxist should keep her eyes peeled for. What such rhetoric should do is to demonstrate the incommensurability, already, of the writers Jameson discusses (Adorno, Sartre): the necessity to allegorize, or apostrophize, or use symbols or metaphors because of how reified these philosophies, how removed, they already are. Thus the apostrophe is utopian in its desire to reach (the reader) and to convey (the politics).

69 By calling the philosophies that Jameson treats in *Marxism and Form* "already reified," I am not arguing for the inadequacy of Marxist theory. Rather, I am following Jameson's contention in *Late Marxism* that reification theory itself frequently is "a kind of spiritualizing moralism" (21) and that "Adorno's objection would frequently seem to be the (pertinent) one that most often the concept of reification is itself reified." Really, Jameson continues, "Adorno criticizes 'reification' in the name of the moment of truth of reification theory" (22).

70 But this is to proceed as though there were nothing problematic or obscure about Jameson's discussion of Adorno and reification in *Late Marxism,* or as if this very problem of address were not being addressed in the later text. Jameson typically works, of course, the other way entirely (for better or for worse), which is evident in a commentary on another Marxist problematic: "The dilemma of the cultural has in fact very significant consequences—as Adorno demonstrates in one of the most brilliant 'fragments' of *Minima Moralia,* entitled 'Baby with the Bath Water'—for what has often been thought of as one of the essential working principles of the Marxist tradition: the distinction between base and superstructure: it being understood that very serious qualms and reservations about this, ranging all the way from the most drastic proposals for its total removal, are also a recurrent part of the Marxist tradition, virtually from Engels himself onward" (*LM,* 45). But this is only the beginning, of course, an introduction to the fervent discussion of the problem of *figuring* base and superstructure; since there is evidently no need at this juncture to give the reader a "flavor" of Jameson's prose (and especially since that dubious "sample" is soon to follow this section of my text), I will rapidly gloss the issues Jameson raises: (1) figuration and causality; (2) *Überbau* and *Basis* refer to rolling stock and railroad; (3) Engels's "reciprocal action" as positivism versus Gramsci's hegemony as non-landscape metaphor; (4) Benjamin's suggestion of superstructure expressing base; (5) Sartre's "situation" as infrastructure to free choice;

(6) which is akin to the Marx of *The Eighteenth Brumaire* (and thence Lukács); (7) Adorno's stereoscopic universal/particular; (8) nothing here suggests a fatalistic determinism; (9) what is so relevant is the centrality of the relationship to Marxism, which (i.e., the question of base and super-structure) must always be addressed locally; (10) and hence the Rortyan conclusion that there is to be no "decid[ing] in advance," (*LM, 47*) or you end up throwing out the baby with the bathwater.

71 Without going into the horrific implications of the baby and bathwater figure (even just in terms of its anachronism: or is it only I who somehow sees a tub of water thrown out of a second- or third-story turn-of-the-century European window, the baby landing in the street next to a disinterested horse or *flâneur?*), I should like to return to Jameson's and Adorno's reflections on reification. Adorno is quite clear on this in the baby section of *Minima Moralia* (as opposed to the "Tough Baby" section: 45–47): "[T]he notion of culture as ideology . . . appears at first sight common to both the bourgeois doctrine of violence and its adversary, both to Nietzsche and to Marx. But precisely this notion, like all expostulation about lies, has a suspicious tendency to become itself ideology" (Adorno 1989, 43). This ideology is reification: what Adorno focuses on elsewhere in the section is the dominance of the economic ("the thought of money and all its attendant conflicts extends into the most tender erotic"; "If material reality is called the world of exchange value"; "free and honest exchange is itself a lie . . . in face of the lie of the commodity world").[1] As Jameson stresses in his readings in *Late Marxism,* Adorno's philosophy utilizes as master-code or narrative the Marxian trope of the economic, a dialect which places him closer to the unreconstructed Benjamin or Brecht than is usually thought; but this is all, for Adorno, in order that he might better work through the "lie" of ideology or reification—since culture is that document of barbarism, that great allegorical lie or gang-bang of history, a dialectical response must neither reject the culture wholeheartedly nor embrace the material in some Nietzschean or Spenglerian violence of ressentiment, for "[p]eople who belong together

---

1 As I will explicate more fully in my fourth chapter (on "triadic allegories"), I am not under the illusion that signifiers of the economic are therefore unmediated signs, or, to speak more locally, that Adorno's use of economic figures here is not, um, figural.

ought neither to keep silent about their material interests, nor to sink to their level, but to assimilate them by reflection into their relationships and so surpass them" (Adorno 1989, 45).

reading marxism (ii)

72   "*[I]t pleases me for another moment* [here we see momentarily the introduction of the personal shifter, a rare event in Jameson's work] *still to contemplate* [note: not "to still contemplate"—unlike Chandler, on whom he has written (1983 and 1993), Jameson has no love for the split infinitive, even where it might be more sensible] *the stubborn rebirth* [stubborn: a Jamesonian Keyword] *of the idea of freedom, in three such profoundly different shapes* ["shape" is very important to Jameson, as a sensual trope or constellation] *at three such profoundly different moments in history:* [the repetition here is important not only because it stresses the parallelism of the repetend, but also because it dares to be ponderous, "Germanic"] *its reinvention* [the idea of freedom is always being reinvented because it never possessed a Golden Age—see *M&F,* 39–43, the discussion of Adorno on Beethoven] *by the historian-playwright* [Schiller: un-named, because here the ludicrousness of occupation as signifier is to re-mind us of the individual in the very absence of the proper name; or, as Sartre remarks, "[N]or do [poets] dream of *naming* the world, and, this being the case, they name nothing at all, for naming implies a perpetual sacrifice of the name to the object named" (Sartre 1965, 6; but see Benjamin on naming in *The Origin of German Tragic Drama,* discussed below)], *dreaming the heroic gestures of political eloquence in his tiny* [the gestures' heroism needs a full-scale Brechtian analysis of the gesture; the eloquence signals Jameson's hope for a political dimension to his own formidable eloquence; the word "tiny" is smaller than the commas that punctuate Jameson's twenty-one-line sentence-paragraph] *feudal city-state* [un-named, like Schiller: but why? To allow Jameson the full play of adjective and noun: to name would seal off the *jouissance*] *open to the fields,* [the vulnerability of the fields, city-state (in all its anachronistic feudalness), and historian-playwright are all constructed here] *stimulated* [Jameson's "simstim" Marxism—"simulate-stimulate," that is] *by the news* [Benjamin sees news as the

degradation of knowledge and experience—see his essay "The Storyteller," Benjamin 1969, 83–110] *of revolutionary victories there where in a few years the shock* [Jameson's interest in shock is important, polysemic, politically direct, and revolutionary: from Breton, for example] *of Napoleonic armies* [which created, Lukács argued in *The Historical Novel,* the national peoples (1976, 21–22)] *will cause the earth to tremble;* [the verb tense here (one I also am fond of) cuts through the layers of history] *by the poet,* [an almost Central American appellation: I am thinking of Tomás Borge's (1984)] *stalking* [a hunter or a word-hunter—see his essay on "The Great American Hunter" (Jameson 1972b)] *his magical fun-park* [here I am uncertain—I was the first couple of times reading this—are we with Breton, or, "poet" meant in a mystical way? Marcuse? What fun-park? The irony, also, of magical—the Surrealists' stress on the magic of the everyday—as cathexis, I suppose] *for the neon omens* [the anagramlike pairing of neon and omen belies the anti-*Dialectic of Enlightenment* project being carried out here—omens that are neon (and today we certainly have invested a lot of nostalgic energy in neon) certainly contain none of the degradation of the noumena attacked by Horkheimer and Adorno] *of objective chance,* [the aleatory tyranny, or Steve McCaffery's "fetishization of chance" (McCaffery 1986, 117)] *behind the hallucinatory* [here the connection with the 1960s is suggested] *rebus* [Freud certainly] *of the street scene* [the primal scene for Jameson, you might say] *never ceasing to hear the pop gun volleys* [the juxtaposition of childish simulation play with the polysemic "volleys" renders the phrase intensely arcane] *of the vicious, never-ending* [here, as in the repetition of "three such" earlier, anaphora (with "never ceasing") almost becomes orgasmic] *military pacification of colonial empire;* [the combination of rococo adjective-driven description and shifting reference (*which* military? what empire? where? when?) allows both rhetorical play and political decisiveness] *by the philosopher, in the exile* [paradigm from Adorno or Marx to Bhabha, Spivak, Ahmad, Brennan, and Said] *of that enormous housing development which is the state of California* [California is so mythic its name is less specific than, say, Pennsylvania or Saskatchewan (Newfoundland is similarly mythic in Canada, for instance), and can thus be named, whereas Schiller and his city-state were not; it is also a metonymic inflation that sees the Steinbeckian wish become a rhetorical cul-de-sac] *remembering, reawakening, reinventing* [more repetition]—*from the rows of products in the supermarkets,* [Eagleton's "supermarket of theory"?] *from the roar* [rows] *of the freeways and the ominous shape* [shape, again] *of the helmets of traffic policemen,* [here the acronym-prosopopoeia of popular culture— CHIPS, S.W.A.T.—are renegotiated as primal fascism] *from the incessant overhead traffic of the fleets* [the mixed metaphor here—traffic and fleets— recalls the very politically unrepresentable nature of the military] *of military transport planes, and as it were from beyond them,* [but also, importantly, *from* them—from the very horrific excess of power and money embodied in the U.S. military] *in the future—the almost extinct form* [the style, then, or utopia as a form] *of the Utopian idea.* [*M&F,* 116: and if utopia is linguistically and grammatically the telos of this paragraph-sentence, it is nonetheless a concern all the way through the writing, as the very form of the phrases, rhetoric, and lexicon.]

dissing for tenure

73 Is there a class struggle in this text? I was reading Jonathan Arac on whether Jameson presents adequately the "political unconscious" in the book of the same name (Arac 1987, 263). I wanted to step back from this argument and deskill myself a little: when I read *The Political Unconscious* for the first or second time, I did not "catch" such a problem. If this argument is examined from the "outside," perhaps it is all just intellectual finery. Following Pierre Bourdieu's analysis in *Homo Academicus,* I would argue that this sort of critical interaction is simultaneously economic (the generation and stockpiling of cultural capital) and concerned with power (patriarchal display, the safeguarding of rights to administer "correction," "punishment").

74 Jameson admits to a species of bad faith in this regard at the start of his essay on Claude Simon when he asks if "the seeming gratuitousness of talking about Simon or even reading him confirm[s] Bourdieu's blanket condemnation of the aesthetic as a mere class signal and as conspicuous consumption?" (*PM,* 132). Bourdieu comments on precisely this interpretation: "[T]his is to mistake the iconologist for the iconoclast," he remarks, adding, however, that "a certain iconoclasm of the disenchanted believer could have facilitated the break with primary belief necessary to produce an objectifying analysis of cultural practices. . . . The artistic field is the site of

an objectively oriented and cumulative process engendering works which, from purification to purification, from refinement to refinement, reach levels of accomplishment that decisively set them apart from forms of artistic expression that are not the product of history. (I have an unpublished post-face to *Distinction* where I tackle the problem of cultural relativism. I took it out of the book because I thought: I have affected a critical questioning of aesthetic belief, of the fetishism of art shared; and now, at the very end, I give them an escape? The God of Art is dead and I am going to resuscitate him?) Durkheim raises this question in *The Elementary Structures of Religious Life* when he asks: is there not something universal about culture? Yes, ascesis" (Bourdieu and Wacquant 1992, 85, 87). Bourdieu does go on to make some relevant, if at times questionable, claims, particularly that art in a shopping mall is without history; but his tortured position as cultural relativist (the Vancouver poet Jeff Derksen comments, "Something deep inside liberal cultural relativism says, 'Yes I can'" [1993, n.p.]) does not really negate Jameson's comments here or his remarks that link Bourdieu to Spengler, Huxley, and Veblen's "anti-cultural, anti-aesthetic impulse" (*LM,* 44): "Bourdieu renews this position in our own time, with the powerful anti-cultural and anti-intellectual demystifications of books like *Distinctions*" (*LM,* 255n. 29).

75 The proper reply to make to Jameson's bad faith at this point (as this text enacts the figure of aposiopesis) is not to agree too slavishly with *another* Jameson (the "author" of *The Political Unconscious*) who remarks that "everything is 'in the last analysis' political" (*PU,* 20). Not to agree without pondering for some time the significance of both " 'in the last analysis' "— that is, the Althusserian "in the last instance" which frees up the text, literary or otherwise, from a bald-faced determinism—and the act of "analysis," which stresses the hermeneutic, interpretive activity necessary.

76 It is an error to resort to this facile politicization, the "conscience [salve] of the American academic on the left," as Arac puts it (265), because, as John Frow argues convincingly in the conclusion to his *Marxism and Literary History* (1986), "These questions do not allow of simple answers in the case of literary study, precisely because of the highly mediated relations between social class, power, and literary discourse. Certainly, within current institutional structures, literary study cannot relate directly to the political needs of the working class, nor can it contribute directly to the formation of organic working-class intellectuals" (234). While this is probably correct, it is only

so if "organic working-class intellectuals" does not as a category include working-class writers or artists, who are directly affected by and, it is to be hoped, participating in, such problems of literary study.

77 But the question of "current institutional structures" also leads to Samuel Weber's *Institution and Interpretation* (1987), where he contends that "the professional" is a middle-class category dependent on the twin marks of scarcity (the body of knowledge) and specialization (the reified, late capitalist hyper-division of labor) (18–32). Weber notes that the professional "seeks to define his services as exclusively determined by public need, and hence, as predominately a *use-value,* not an exchange-value. It is precisely to distinguish himself from the businessman . . . and from the worker . . . that the professional finds it necessary to cultivate the professional ethos and 'culture' " (27). A group "seeking to define and to maintain a certain identity in the face of an extremely dynamic, unsettling, and powerful reorganization and transformation of society" (27) may refer to any emerging (to use Raymond Williams's useful word) group; but the projection evident here is problematized more fruitfully in terms of what Barbara and John Ehrenreich call the "Professional-Managerial Class" (Ehrenreich and Ehrenreich 1979), and which is raised in Jameson's essay on *Dog Day Afternoon* (*SV,* 35–54: see my chapter 4).

78 But what I am after here, as announced at the start of this discussion ("Is there a class struggle in this text?"), is the formal and political struggle that goes on in my reading of and around Jameson and in my writing about that reading. For I have to "scheme," to put it all down on paper: I must try to make it readable, to show both what I have done (establish professional credentials as a researcher) and what I can interpret from that research (produce some cultural capital as a Marxist). My anxiety here in this writing is also unprofessional: for the general economy of the profession of the academy is that the "vicissitudes of a generalized and unpredictable *competition* are replaced by the calculability of *competence*" (Weber, 31).

/for example/, for example

79 Terry Eagleton remarks in *The Ideology of the Aesthetic* that "[t]he esoteric and the everyday, the aesthetic as both solitary splendour and mundane

conduct, commingle in the very structure of *Dasein*, as they do in a different sense in Heidegger's writing, with its bathetic mixture of the oracular and the ordinary. His style is well practised in the device of investing humble particulars with ontological status, elevating something as empirical as bad temper into a fundamental structure of Being . . . this device impresses with its demonic flavour: how liberated of philosophy to stoop for its staple themes to hammers and forest paths—to allow you, as the excited young Sartre was to realize, to do philosophy by talking about the ash tray" (1990a, 303). This is the generally correct assumption regarding Sartre's indebtedness to Heidegger: A. J. Ayer's notorious comment that *Being and Nothingness* was just a translation of *Being and Time* into French is pertinent. Or at least Eagleton's sarcasm is an attractive inroad, here permitting me to construct a theory of philosophical examples and pretexts, a theory of how they change from Heidegger's Black Forest and peasant to Sartre's Left Bank and cafés. A similar shift is visible from Sartre to Jameson, and there are certain problematics involved in "commentary" (of one writer on another's work): *not* as a representational aporia, but instead as something quite different.

80   For example, in *Critique of Dialectical Reason*, when Sartre first begins his discussion of seriality, he uses as an example "the grouping of people in the Place Saint-Germain . . . waiting for a bus at a bus stop in front of the church" (Sartre 1991, 1: 256). This example is a typically Sartrean "situation": dependent on the collectivity still prevalent in French society. Jameson, meanwhile, in his summary/exposition of Sartre's theory, offers the following example: "Thus, when performing most of the acts characteristic of industrial civilization—waiting for a bus, reading a newspaper, pausing at a traffic light—I seem alone" (*M&F,* 248). The *inflation* of Sartre's signifiers to three acts is important for a number of reasons: first, it shifts the Sartrean specificities of situation to a list (form par excellence, one might say, of both epic and postmodern literature). Second, by shifting from the bus, via the newspaper, to "pausing at a traffic light," the exemplary signification moves from the European collective to the degraded, individualistic world of North American consumerism. A bus might be seen as metonym for the European (and Canadian, I might add) social-democratic contract, whereby the state still provides public means for the people, whereas in the U.S.A., mass transit is notoriously abandoned to the underclass and the automobile reigns supreme.

81   The newspaper is a middle term in the royal road from mass transit to individual consumerism (one does not *consume* a bus—one is consumed in a Bachelardian fashion by it?—as one consumes a car). For the newspaper, while common to both cultures, is in the U.S. usually a conservative vehicle for the upper class, as Noam Chomsky, or Michael Parenti (1986), have shown us, while the presence of such left-liberal dailies as *Libération* and *The Guardian* in Europe ensures that a slightly wider range of opinion and "facts" are reported. The third reason that the *inflation* of Sartre's signifiers into Jameson's discourse is important is that my figure of "inflation" links the formal device of Jameson's text to another example Sartre uses to show seriality: the inflation wreaked on Europe by the Spanish importation of gold in the seventeenth century (Sartre 1991, 1: 166–78). Thus Jameson's technique reveals an incipient seriality of his own discourse: in positing an Elsewhere (Western Marxism), it awaits the third party (a social democratic movement in America) that itself awaits the creation of a Marxist intelligence in America.

82   In a *Diacritics* interview, Jameson remarked, "I happen to think that no real systemic change in this country will be possible without the minimal first step of the achievement of a social democratic movement, and in my opinion even that first step will not be possible without two other preconditions (which are essentially the same thing): namely the creation of a Marxist intelligentsia, and that of a Marxist culture, a Marxist intellectual presence, which is to say, the legitimation of Marxist discourse as that of a 'realistic' social and political alternative in a country which (unlike most of the other countries in the world) has never recognised it as such. This is the perspective in which I would want my own efforts to be understood, and I suppose my own particular contribution to such a development would mainly lie in showing the capacity of Marxism to engage the most advanced currents of 'bourgeois' thinking and theory, but that is only one task among others" (1982a, 73). Charges of voluntarism or idealism are probably best countered with the reminder that Jameson is not declaring that "the creation of a Marxist intelligentsia" is the only precondition for that social democratic movement; the growing importance of intellectuals has not a little to do, I would think, with the importance of culture in general: "[I]t does seem to me that unless the question of the changing status and function of culture today

is taken into account, an effective cultural politics can scarcely be devised" (77).

examples, ii

83 Derrida treats the problem of "examples" and "mentions" by foregrounding what was previously marginal.[2] In his essay on J. L. Austin and speech-act theory, he deconstructs Austin's relegation to the sidelines of the "infelicities" of parasitic or nonserious speech (Austin 1975, 21). For Derrida, "[i]t is also as a 'parasite' that writing has always been treated by the philosophical tradition, and the rapprochement, here, is by no means fortuitous" (1982, 325). Derrida's suspicion—in Ricoeur's use of the word—is disallowed by Richard Rorty's Sartrean contingency. Rorty's pragmatic philosophy teaches us that it is only a coincidence that Western philosophy has been until Nietzsche (Heidegger? Derrida?) metaphysical: only a series of historical random events. Derrida asks, "[I]s not what Austin excludes as anomalous, exceptional, 'non-serious,' that is, *citation* (on the stage, in a poem, or in a soliloquy), the determined modification of a general citationality—or rather, a general iterability—without which there would not even be a 'successful' performative?" (325).

84 For Derrida, speech-act theory slips up when problems such as the fuzzy distinction between citation and parasitism are expanded so that all of language is citation, not only in nonserious or special cases. So an example is not merely the decoration to a text. As Eagleton argued above, Heidegger's *Dasein* originates in his examples in all their mundaneness. An example is the entry point of lived experience as *content* into the text (Bourdieu argues that Heidegger's admixture of the academic and the peasant stems from his class trajectory). John Searle, in his reply, remarks that "Derrida in this argument confuses no less than three separate and distinct phenomena:

---

2 Here you might want to make a distinction between the epistemological, or structural-marginal, and the ontological, or social-marginal. That is, the contribution of Derridean theory to feminist and postcolonial theory seems to be based on the "false friend" of the term "marginality."

iterability, citationality, and parasitism" (1977, 206). Searle desires to maintain the formal hierarchies, because traditional philosophy must maintain a Kantianism after the death of Kant (Kantianism understood here as a formal separation of the mind, where the various faculties and their sharply limited powers are the outcome of a bourgeois detachment).

85 One commentator, surveying the Searle-Derrida debate, writes that it is precisely the hierarchy between "use" and "mention" that Derrida contests (Culler 1984, 119n), and that, furthermore, "Derrida is quite right to claim that use/mention is ultimately a hierarchy of the same sort as serious/non-serious and speech/writing" (120n). Culler's domestication of Derrida is evident here in his desire to effect an equal status for the various sorts of hierarchies.

86 Any model of clear and inductive writing would suggest that now is not the point to regress further from whatever point I am supposed to be making here. Be that as it may, the mention I am making of Derrida and others, which will only be elevated to the superior position of use if I comment rigorously upon the mention and show its relevance to my text—this mention suggests my desire to use the techniques and rhetoric of poststructuralism (self-consciousness, the foregrounding of style, deconstructing textual oppositions) without importing the underlying philosophy of the theories (I will discuss below, via Rorty, whether there is such an "underlying" [foundational?] philosophy). That is, I seek to use the rhetoric without suggesting some ultimate lack of referent or indeterminability for writing. It might be argued that this utopian desire retains, then, a certain pre-Derridean nostalgia for the difference between use/mention: I want to mention all of these theorists but not use them, since I would be afeard of being used in my own rhetoric.

87 There is domestication, and there is domestication: the link between Rorty's rhetoric of the "privatization" of ironism and the 1980s' Thatcher-inspired orgy of the privatization of public services is surely less contingent than the ironist would have us believe. But Rorty is also at pains to distinguish himself from the college handbook approach to deconstruction: "Culler and others believe that Derrida has discovered [a method]" (1990, 135n), he writes, dismissing what Derrida has called, in memory of de Man, "deconstruction in America." To accept Rorty's privatization of the enjoyment of

philosophy "means," he suggests, "giving up the attempt to say, with Gashé and Culler, that Derrida has demonstrated anything or refuted anybody (e.g., Austin)" (134). Again, for me it is a question of using Rorty's rhetoric without his philosophy; you do not need a second-rate Barthesian attitude to agree on the (essential) incommensurability of various discourses, to agree, that is, that "[r]econtextualization in general, and inverting hierarchies in particular, has been going on for a long time" (Rorty 1990, 134). The point is not to engage in a modernist fetish of the "new," to argue that Sartre or Derrida or Jameson or Rorty was there first (said it first): philosophical examples are not virgins. Rather, the question to ask is: What happens when such a new example (a "recontextualization") is introduced? What happens when Heidegger takes as an example Van Gogh's paintings of a peasant's shoes, when Sartre talks about a waiter in a café, when Eagleton talks about the execution of Ceausescu? If we agree that for my purposes, "the use-mention distinction is just a distraction" (Rorty 1990, 135), how is my new discourse affected by the insertion of an example?

88 In terms of a narratology *of* narratology, the sub-concern of much of this book, it is evident that the introduction of an example into a text begs for a contextualization for that example, like a new character introduced into a work of fiction, who must be described in some fashion (whether realistically or absurdly). If the discourse does not sufficiently contextualize, the example is considered to be ill-placed, or inappropriate (the high school teacher's imperative—"Explain your quotations"—is exemplary). An example of how this works in a work of theory could be the following. I buttressed the mention of "using" and "mentioning" with the example from Derrida with Rorty's brief comments on Culler's use of Derrida, prefacing those comments with the observation that Rorty's determination to argue for a privatized ironism (and a public liberalism) in *Contingency, Irony, and Solidarity* is politically conservative. That observation, if left on its own, might be as unimportant to the narratives of the present volume as some insignificant detail to a character's clothing in a novel. But it is also possible to tie this character-example to a main thread of my argument: one of the examples Rorty offers of a strong recontextualizer is Proust, and what Proust does, Rorty argues, is to describe and redescribe the people he met. "[P]arents, servants, family friends, fellow students, duchesses, editors, lovers [are] *just*

a collection, just the people Proust happened to bump into" (100). And for Jameson "the hidden significance of such passions as snobbery and social climbing is at once revealed . . . [as] the mystified figures of that longing for perfection, of an as yet unconscious Utopian impulse" (*M&F,* 153). What Rorty sees as radically contingent and the mark of a heroic shape-shifter, Jameson sees as the anticipatory mark of a determinate utopianism. Thus Rorty's own private ironism, in a Jamesonian reading, is revealed to be, like Proust's novel, a "mystified figure" for the utopia of plenitude and, further, Rorty's division of philosophy into public and private would be the formal reaction in his text to the late capitalist integration of public and private. (These thematics of postmodern space, discussed also in my chapter 4, are discernible in the current attempts to reintegrate work and home in public planning—"workburbs"; daycare, gyms, and cafeterias in the business; and downtown highrises with malls in their basements and apartments above.)[3]

stretching language

89 The above drawing-together of Rorty's private utopia and Jameson's public one demonstrates, or is an *example* of, the discursive pressure in a theoretical work to provide a cogent argument. Perhaps another way of coming at the problematic of how writers use each other as examples lies in the relations between style and ideology. Jameson reformulates these relations in terms of style and utopia, on the one hand, and *content* and utopia, on the other (I say this remembering Jameson's key deconstruction of the putative opposition between ideology and utopia). Another theorization of this relationship has been offered by the North American school of poets and theorists known as the L=A=N=G=U=A=G=E writers. In such collec-

---

3 Hakim Bey, for example, in "The Temporary Autonomous Zone" (1991, 97–141), discusses "as an image of anarchist society, the *dinner party,* in which all structure of authority dissolves in conviviality and celebration" (105). Bey, rather disingenuously of course (but that is all part of his hyperbolic rhetoric), like the anarchist Stephen Pearl Andrews, from whom he draws this theory (Bey 1991, 140–41), ignores the infrastructure that will make itself felt in that so-called autonomous zone (see Said [1993] for his discussion of *Mansfield Park* [80–97]).

tions as *The L=A=N=G=U=A=G=E Book* (Andrews and Bernstein, eds., 1984), *Codes of Signals* (Palmer 1983), *Content's Dream* (Bernstein 1986), *North of Intention* (McCaffery 1986), *The New Sentence* (Silliman 1987), and *A Poetics* (Bernstein 1991), a series of manifestos, reviews, and critical engagements have articulated a fairly unambiguous commitment to the politics *of* form, as opposed to a politics *in* language. As George Hartley comments in *Textual Politics and the Language Poets* (1989), if "language determines the consciousness of the members of . . . society, then poetry, as a language practice, plays a role in ideological production and is an indicator of the social assumptions about language" (63).

90 Hartley is working with Ron Silliman's contention that "words are never our own. Rather, they are our own usages of a determinate coding passed down to us like all other products of civilization, organized into a single, capitalist, world economy" (1984, 167). The various L=A=N=G=U=A=G=E writers assert that the best way to attack capitalism is through the style of the literary work; that is, as bourgeois culture demands clarity, simplicity, a transparency of meaning, and lack of ambiguity (in order to better interpellate and indoctrinate, as well as to facilitate the steady stream of economic order), politically progressive writing must resist not through a realist depiction of the horrors of capitalism (which *style* would only affirm the bourgeois subject in its self-knowing status), but in a writing that defamiliarizes, dereifies, and foregrounds the production of signification. There is something anachronistic in the L=A=N=G=U=A=G=E school's position—the "plain style" so important to the bourgeoisie was born in the Puritan era, flowered in the nineteenth century, and now has segued painlessly to a postmodern emphasis on style, confusion, and the foregrounding of the signifier (music videos are only the most obvious example).

91 This familiar critical position, practiced by the L=A=N=G=U=A=G=E group as a poetics, also necessitates a hostility toward some of the older political agendas, a hostility with an Oedipal dynamic.[4] An example of this

---

4 In a more Nietzschean and therefore anxious tone, the dynamic is simply the "distant hint of ressentiment in this assessment of an older generation by a younger one," as Jameson remarked on Derrida's scorn for Sartre (Jameson 1985b, iv: see also Norris 1987, 12, for an anecdotal account of Derrida in this regard).

resentment can be seen in Charles Bernstein's essay "Writing and Method" (1986, 217–33). There Bernstein contends that Sartre, in his "Self-Portrait at 70" (an interview in *Life/Situations* [Sartre 1977, 3–92]), "argues that while literature *should* be ambiguous, 'in philosophy, every sentence should have only one meaning' " (219). Bernstein goes on to say that he thinks that "*Being and Nothingness* is a more poetic work than *The Age of Reason*." There exists a clear and significant parallel, Bernstein argues, between the "history of our contemporary plain styles, with their emphasis on connective, a tight rein on digression, and a continual self-glossing" (223) and what Jameson and Sartre call the Taylorization of capitalist society, or what in other idiolects is called rationalization (Weber), reification (Lukács), integration (Adorno), Fordism (Gramsci), or normalization (Foucault).

92 Why attack Sartre? Surely, for one thing, rhetorical strategies like self-glossing (which Sartre, Bernstein, and Jameson are experts at) are not simply the textual instrument of Foucauldian "exclusion" (as Bernstein argues: 223). What might be a better example of exclusion lies precisely in the "use" Bernstein makes of Sartre to validate his argument (a strategy—"validation"—that Bernstein criticizes Sartre's novels for). This rhetoric of "using" another (philosopher's) text brings me back to the overall narrative of this work (since the quotation from Eagleton on Heidegger); that is, how are we to theorize this movement between texts?

93 Bernstein's "use" of Sartre is significant for what it excludes in order to construct Sartre as the out-of-date philosopher, the antiquated writer who could not know what his own texts are doing, and who used that ignorance as the basis for formulating a crass opposition between philosophical texts and literary ones. Bernstein, however, ignores other comments by Sartre from the same interview which would not support his argument, such as "I do not mean to say that philosophy, like scientific communication, is unambiguous" (8), or that in literature, "[N]othing that I say is totally expressed by what I say. The same reality can be expressed in a practically infinite number of ways" (8). Bernstein also ignores the exigencies of the interview itself; the interviewer *asked* Sartre to compare his philosophical writing to his literary writing; later, when asked if "a truth [can] be expressed independently of the person who expresses it," Sartre replies that "[i]t is no longer interesting then" (14). Elsewhere, Sartre makes a distinction between poetry

and prose along roughly the same lines as that between philosophy and literature. For Sartre, the poet *"is in a situation* in language; he is invested with words" (Sartre 1965, 7), whereas "[p]rose is, in essence, utilitarian. I would readily define the prose-writer as a man who *makes use* of words" (13). Bernstein, like myself, has to stop somewhere.

digressing as example

94 The relationship between texts, formally constituted when one uses another for an *example,* is similar to the rhetoric of examples in general, and always necessitates a violence of decontextualization and appropriation. Thus Heidegger's everyday and rural philosophical examples are changed by Sartre to Parisian ones, which are then changed by Jameson to American examples. When Jameson appropriates Sartre, a certain inflation takes place, whereby the new text distorts the original specificity (and perhaps intent, to reintroduce the author). Like Baudrillardean simulation or Leiris's *mise-en-abŷme,* the inflation of exemplification spirals outward. Bernstein's criticism of Sartre relies on the same technique for which he attacks bourgeois writing: exclusion. In a similar way, another technique deplored by Bernstein, self-glossing, is an attempt to limit or construct a textual linearity (or at least comprehension).

95 My digression-as-method is also permitted by Jameson's style, which he calls the semantic richness of Marxism. "Jameson's cumulative, integrative sentences allusively build up totalities out of multifarious discursive material" (Frow, 32); "the infamous Jamesonian sentences appear full-blown" (Kellner 1989b, 7); "it is . . . unimaginable that anyone could read Jameson's . . . magisterial, busily metaphorical sentences without profound pleasure" (Eagleton 1986, 66); "Jameson's analyses . . . are undoubtedly rich and dense" (Bennington 1982, 26); and (finally): "[T]here is the private matter of my own pleasure in writing these texts: it is a pleasure tied up in the peculiarities of my 'difficult' style (if that's what it is). I wouldn't write them unless there were some minimal gratification in it for myself, and I hope we are not yet too alienated or instrumentalized to reserve some small place for what used to be handicraft satisfaction" (Jameson 1982a, 88).

seriality and inflation

96 But I would like to return to Jameson's serial appropriation of Sartre's example. Jameson's "list" inflates Sartre's situation into an excess, an over-determined structural causality (i.e., not the totality of the Sartrean text). Formally, Jameson's "use" of Sartre exemplifies the utopia of inflation. Jameson has commented that the "6o's are . . . an immense and inflationary issuing of superstructural credit" (qtd. Sprinker 1982, 70); this metaphor of inflation is to be understood dialectically both as the excessive demands for freedom and inequality issuing forth from the Third World as well as the youth and ethnic groups of the metropolis, *and* as the pre-1970s (economic) inflation of consumerism and production demand that was shortly to burn out in a Mandel cycle of crisis.

97 This is my position on the use to which Jameson puts Sartre: inflation, in Sartre's analysis, demonstrates the positive-negative contradictions of totality: as everyone gets richer (earns more), they become disastrously poorer (their money buys less). Similarly, *Marxism and Form* arrives at the beginning of a theoretical inflation in the U.S. academy: the pluralization of theories, paradigms, and agendas designated sarcastically by Eagleton as the "supermarket of theory." In the midst of such an abundance of theoretical positions, any one position is thus worth (relatively) less.

98 The "example" of waiting for a bus, in Sartre's text the first site for seriality, now is, in Jameson's version, but one of three. Here the nominal condensation and displacement of Sartre is replaced by inflation and utopian anticipation. That is, one way to posit the relation of commentary to text is "manifest content" to "latent content": Freud's model of the unconscious. So my job would be to interpret what has been repressed in/through the "translation" from Sartre to Jameson. But the issue is not interpretation; Jameson's commentary renders the relationship between Sartre's book and his chapter not the hierarchical master/slave one (whether the master is the original text or the [Freudian] interpretation).

99 "In literary terms, this means that society is conceived of at any given historical moment as that preexistent and indeed preformed raw material which ultimately determines the abstractness or the concreteness of the works of art within it" (*M&F,* 164).

footnote as commodity

100 How to theorize the footnote, here, without digressing into that accoutrement? This last word, defined in the *OED* as "equipment," betrays a certain technologism[5] in my discourse, akin to what Jameson criticizes Benjamin and McLuhan for (*M&F,* 74), but close also to Jameson's characterization of Western music as "a tiny history of inventions and machines" (*M&F,* 14). Indeed, this tiny form, the footnote, is significant in the case of Jameson because of how frequently his poststructuralist critics resort to accusations of "totalizing" (how very 1980s) as if totality is automatically a guarantee of totalitarianism. Geoff Bennington, for example, argues that in *The Political Unconscious* Jameson uses footnotes (particularly the note on page 23) for the "containment of what he calls the contemporary 'Nietzschean and antiinterpretive current' in France" (Bennington 1982, 28). I have to confess that one of the aspects of *The Political Unconscious* that I enjoyed most, particularly the first few times reading it, was precisely the footnotes, where Jameson (and the reader) would be freed from the criticonarrative demands of Conrad, or George Gissing, or Althusser, and then make comments on immanent criticism (*PU,* 282–83n) or U.S. versus French social organizations (*PU,* 54n), or provide a quick lesson on the origins of Sartre's distinction between freedom and necessity (*PU,* 17n).[6]

101 And certainly nothing is more surprising than seeing a translator of Derrida (Bennington co-translated *The Truth in Painting*), whose important and early deconstruction of Heidegger's *Being and Time* (Derrida 1982) is based on a *footnote* (Heidegger's meditation on Hegel's concepts of spirit and time), attack the form of the footnote as "containment."

102 My weak-kneed "defense" of Jameson's footnoting is based on his own commentary on the form, relating specifically to Adorno, early in the discus-

---

5 Or, as one of my commentators noted, a "fashion-sense." And then the predictable forays into Barthes and queer theory would no doubt ensue.

6 Steve McCaffery has said that the footnote "draws off digressionary matter from a main text" (1992, 1). He also credits Jameson's discussion of footnotes in *Marxism and Form* with suggesting some avenues of inquiry for the Toronto Research Group: "[W]e had been made aware of [the footnote's] dialectical potential by Fredric Jameson, who promotes it to the status of a minor genre" (McCaffery and Nichol 1992, 14).

sion in *Marxism and Form* (9n). Jameson sees "the footnote as a lyrical form," whose "very limits" allow or determine the "release of intellectual energies," and, finally, in a parody of his own immanent Sartreanism, the footnote is seen pursuing "its fitful existence in the small print at the bottom of the page." This text lies in small print at the bottom of page nine of *Marxism and Form*. And following the repeated urges on Jameson's part to read philosophy like a novel (*M&F,* 283, for example), this meta-footnote now assumes a spiral relation with the uses of footnotes in such canonical late modernist or postmodernist novels as Beckett's trilogy, Nabokov's *Pale Fire,* or Gilbert Sorrentino's *Mulligan Stew.* Those meta-fictions (as well as *Finnegans Wake,* Alasdair Gray's *1982 Janine,* Nicholson Baker's *The Mezzanine*) all parody the scholarly apparatus of footnoting, as well as the fictive puritanism that rejects such accoutrements. Jameson appropriates the novelist's appropriation of the footnote as form, it would seem: for his intensely self-conscious moment here, "in small print," allows as much an escape from the intellectual rigor of theorizing itself, as it does from the linear narrative of his text.

103 When Jameson remarks that "we will not be able to understand Bloch's ultimate response [to death] without a long detour through the present itself" (*M&F,* 135), he is remarking as well on his own practice, on the necessity in dialectical thinking to see connections with the totality. Thus, there is almost never a "linear narrative" in Jameson's discourse—it is more properly rhizomatic. For as Jameson divides Marxism into two codes, the subjective (class struggle) and the objective (materialism), his own text is composed of a number of codes and idiolects: the "representation" of a particular thinker's thought; the "self-glossing" of itself into a fairly coherent narrative; the recourse to metaphor and device; the invocation of dialectics as a master-code; and the list goes on.

ontinkel: the figure as illusion

104 "seriality is a vast optical illusion" (*M&F,* 248); "the experience of living in a numbered and historical decade is something that no one feels at the time: it is an optical illusion of the historian" (*M&F,* 258); "such issues as those which seemed to oppose Marxism and the Weberians turn out to be optical illusions" (*M&F,* 6); "[t]his optical illusion of our own centrality"

(*M&F,* 368); "an optical illusion of totality projected by what is in reality only an artificial isolation" (*M&F,* 315); "are here by Sartre subjected to a phenomenological analysis which reveals them to be a kind of optical illusion: they are, indeed, the optical illusion of the outsider" (*M&F,* 269); "[s]o the world-oriented novel (which Lukács calls the novel of *abstract idealism*) proves to be based on a kind of optical illusion" (*M&F,* 174); "from the standpoint of *Hope the Principal* existentialism itself is a kind of optical illusion" (*M&F,* 139); "the transitional indeterminacy of the period in which Hegel lived granted him a fortunate mirage, the optical illusion of Absolute Spirit" (*M&F,* 48); "[Stravinsky's] modernness is therefore the result of a kind of optical illusion" (*M&F,* 33); "a Fascist system is a contradiction in terms, not thought but the optical illusion of thought only" (*M&F,* 118–19); "[t]he most successful audition of a work by Schoenberg yields, not a plenitude, but rather a kind of shadow work, an optical illusion" (*M&F,* 37–38); "it is this optical illusion of the substantiality of thought itself which negative dialectics is designed to dispel" (*M&F,* 57); " 'the negative dialectic' represents an attempt to save philosophy itself, and the very idea of philosophizing, from a fetishization in time, from the optical illusion of stasis and permanency" (*M&F,* 58).

105 Jameson in other places also uses visual metaphors, and in his discussion of impressionism in Conrad in *The Political Unconscious* argues that the visual in impressionist painting and in Conrad's descriptions are utopian compensations for the reification of the senses caused by capitalism. Marx and Engels, in the well-known passage of *The German Ideology,* remark that ideology is like a camera obscura (see *M&F,* 369–70). It is evident that Jameson's, like Marx's, fondness for the images owes a great deal to the ease with which they can be harnessed to a dialectics: reversal, inversion, setting things on their feet or head. But the point is less to dive into a genealogy of Marxian imagery than to understand what function the figures have in Jameson's text. In general, the use of visual imagery is rhetorical: it posits indirectly a relation, the ontinkel, between perception and ideology.

casual relations

106 The problem is how to relate one text (this one) to another (Jameson's). A paragraph here and there may demonstrate a fragmented technique, and

yet this technique must be justified theoretically. The relationship between my text and Jameson's is similar to how Marxism formulates that between art and society; that is, (how) does my text "represent" Jameson's? This problem is one of mediation. Marxist criticism has been traditionally focused on this problematic: the relationship between society and its artworks, which developed from the mimetic theories of reflection through structural causality and into the various postmodern Marxisms and post-Marxisms of today's Spivak, Baudrillard, Laclau and Mouffe, Eagleton, and Jameson.

107 Arac points succinctly to the problematic as Jameson encounters it: "The issue [is] how a social totality is to be conceptualized. Is the whole implicit in each of its parts (a model like the rhetorical figure of synecdoche), or are the parts related to each other only by adjacency (a model like the rhetorical figure of metonymy)? Despite his use of Althusser's 'structural causality,' which followed the metonymic model, we have seen that Jameson also defended 'expressive causality,' which holds to synecdoche. If the whole is fully reflected in every part, then aspects of the whole not immediately visible in a part must be latent within it, repressed or unconscious within it" (264).

108 This sums up admirably the model Jameson is working with, in part, in *The Political Unconscious*, the text Arac deals with most closely. Arac suggests that Jameson's mediation between text and society, based on a Freudian schema of repression, might better be apprehended with Foucault's notion of "production" (as in the Victorian discourses on sexuality produced, rather than repressed, sexuality; as in prisons "produce" prisoners). And we can look at Arac's own textuality to see a good example of this production/repression dialectic:[7] "At decisive moments in his remarkable chapter

---

7 The rhetoric in Foucault's *History of Sexuality* is so heady that sometimes it seems as if some malignant "repressive hypothesis" objectively existed; but apart from a brief mention of Steve Marcus (who inadvertently provides the title for the first chapter, "We 'Other Victorians'"), no theorist of repression is mentioned (although of course Freud and Marx are implicitly suggested). But a careful reading of Foucault's useful little book leads neither to the notion that power relations always produce their dissent nor to the idea that repression does not exist. Rather, it seems he is out to show that power and repression are not monolithic. Andrew Parker, in a paper delivered at the 1994 Institute on Culture

on romance (a masterpiece of condensed comparative reflection) and in his chapter on Conrad (the richest consideration of *Lord Jim* that I know), as well as in his conclusion (which radically revises our understanding of 'ideological' criticism), Jameson drew on Nietzsche's attacks against ethics to strengthen his own position" (265). Arac's sentence, *pace* Geoff Bennington's hierarchy of textual privilege in prose (made implicit when Bennington links the footnote with containment), *represses* his admiration for Jameson, and the possibility of seeing Jameson's work in a positive light, by literally bracketing all of Arac's praise—in the three successive parentheses. But following the Foucault/Arac paradigm, the parenthetical remarks *produce* that space for admiration: using parentheses, Arac qualifies and undermines his account of Jameson's use of Nietzsche (which for the most part he is critical of).

109 This foray into Arac's text illustrates the possibilities of re-thinking how literary texts relate to society; that is, it is necessary to theorize "on the run," without sinking into the (liberal) optical illusion of eclecticism. Althusser's theory of structural causality holds that the superstructure (the various state apparatuses and ideological state apparatuses) is economic only in the final instance, but it is economic nonetheless. And if that economic determination is repressed in the literary text, it is the task of the dialectical critic to interpret the text for the latent content amid the manifest forms.

110 Arac seems to have forgotten the subtitle of *The Political Unconscious:* "Narrative as a Socially Symbolic Act"—that is, "Kenneth Burke's play of emphases, in which the symbolic act is on the one hand affirmed as a genuine *act,* albeit on the symbolic level" (*PU,* 81). But the symbolism of Jameson's and Burke's theories leads back to problems of the figure in *Marxism and Form.* This perhaps is the clue to how Jameson not only figures the relationship between literature and society, but also how he can theorize it— that is, how he is forced to theorize it, based on the "raw material" presented him in the form of Western Marxism. Expressed in a vulgar way, literature is both ideological, implicated through and through with the traces and stains

---

and Society, suggested that his students' continual (mis)readings of Foucault (as being in *favor* of the repressive hypothesis) stem in large part from the rhetoric of unattributed quotation and rewriting (which Parker calls Foucault's "ventriloquism").

of its repressive raw material, and utopian, symbolizing a future world, by implication, that has not yet arrived and hence is not yet represented.

barbarically long quotations

111   These contradictions are rooted in two favorite passages from Benjamin. The first is from the seventh thesis on history: "Whoever has emerged victorious participates to this day in the triumphal procession in which the present rulers step over those who are lying prostrate. According to traditional practice, the spoils are carried along in the procession. They are called cultural treasures, and a historical materialist views them with cautious detachment. For without exception the cultural treasures he surveys have an origin which he cannot contemplate without horror. They owe their existence not only to the efforts of the great minds and talents who have created them, but also to the anonymous toil of their contemporaries. There is no document of civilization which is not at the same time a document of barbarism. And just as such a document is not free of barbarism, barbarism taints also the manner in which it was transmitted from one owner to another. A historical materialist therefore dissociates himself from it as far as possible. He regards it as his task to brush history against the grain" (1969, 256–57).
112   The other Benjamin passage is from the ninth thesis, on the Klee painting of the Angelus Novus: "This is how one pictures the angel of history. His face is turned toward the past. Where we perceive a chain of events, he sees one single catastrophe which keeps piling wreckage upon wreckage and hurls it in front of his feet. The angel would like to say, awaken the dead, and make whole what has been smashed. But a storm is blowing from Paradise; it has got caught in his wings with such violence that the angel can no longer close them. This storm irresistibly propels him into the future to which his back is turned, while the pile of debris before him grows skyward. This storm is what we call progress" (1969, 257–58).
113   These two passages illustrate the dialectical play in Jameson's work between reification and utopia, or between *figure:* the way in which cultural products—"documents of civilization"—"represent" the history and barbarism of the past in a repressed way, demanding the interpretative activity, the

negative hermeneutic, of the political critic; and *narrative:* progress, which hurls the cultural product toward the future, demands of the political critic a positive hermeneutic that, driven by a belief in that "as yet unimaginable collective future" (as Jameson will say again and again), elicits from the documents the hope for something still unrepresentable. It is the dialectic of metaphor and narrative that, keystone to Jameson's dialectics of interpretation, also forms the allegorical container for his work itself—his work is a utopia.

114 In some ways I am an old Eagletonian, by which I mean I treasure above almost anything else the Marxist traditions. This falls, and I suppose you could have predicted this periodization, into the realist-modernist-postmodernist narrative. Thus from Marx and Engels on up to the Second International, Rosa Luxembourg, Bernstein and the revisionists, the October Revolution, and possibly Lukács are the realists. Lukács is on the cusp, like a child born on the twentieth of the month, and the modern Marxist tradition starts with or after him, with Gramsci, the Frankfurt School, Mao, Castro, and Che, Sartre, Brecht, and Benjamin, and including British Marxists like Williams and Eagleton. Postmodern Marxism means essentially the work of Eagleton (again, on the cusp: in a talk he expresses ambivalence about theory, referring to it as "crack" [1992, 30]),[8] Jameson, Spivak, Althusser (hangover from a previous epoch),[9] the heterodox Sandinistas in Nicaragua, and even Chiapas.

115 Think of those of us who began reading theory in the mid-1980s. There appeared in libraries and bookstores to be three distinct forms of textual semiotics. One group was made up of largely hardcover texts, it seemed, or

8 But then there is his collaboration-cum-debate with late gay filmmaker Derek Jarman over the film about Wittgenstein (Eagleton et al. 1993). Is this Lukács-Brecht all over again, or is the homosocial too evident at this juncture?

9 If Althusser seemed through much of the 1980s to be an embarrassing relic from another age, consider the extraordinary renaissance in French Marxism in the past couple of years, including the publication of his memoir, a new work by Balibar collected in English, two collections on Althusser (ed. Kaplan and Sprinker 1993; ed. Elliott 1994), and even Derrida's recent "conversion" (*Spectres de Marx,* 1993). What still remains, in even these preliminary gestures at making available this rich tradition, is some translation or collection of Macherey's work, including his *A quoi pense la littérature?* (1990).

in dully colored covers in the political science section of the bookstore. This was the old German and French stuff: Marx and his immediate followers. The second group was almost exclusively from New Left Books and Verso (with some Monthly Review Press co-printings): the series of covers with Robert Natkin paintings that looked like pastel burlap. This was modernist Marxism and included the Frankfurt School, French Structuralists, Raymond Williams, and Eagleton. Most of these books were published in the mid to late 1970s, it seemed. I have sitting next to my keyboard right now Althusser and Balibar's *Reading Capital;* I bought it for $6.95 at a used bookstore in Victoria, B.C., probably in 1987. It was published in paperback in 1979. The third group began in the early 1980s and can be described most succinctly as the decade of Minnesota and then Routledge. This is the great era of, on the one hand, translations of every interesting or even uninteresting Continental theorist with concomitant, indigenous (Anglo-American) theorists and their younger colleagues' dissertations (the last forming the bulk of the Routledge catalog, it seems). Theory suddenly exploded from the confines of structuralist rigor and escaped the "restrictions" of its European roots to provide *the* lingua franca for the world scholarly community. In this postmodernist Marxist world, Baudrillard, Laclau and Mouffe, and Menchú are all published by a Verso which is suddenly oriented toward the demographics of "progressive" graduate students.

116 In the context of this shifting tradition, I have to admit that I really admire the use to which Anne McClintock puts Benjamin in her 1992 essay "The Angel of Progress: Pitfalls of the Term 'Post-Colonialism'."[10] The essay takes Benjamin's "storm called progress" notion to bear on the "career" or figure of the term "post-colonialism." And so she declares: "Metaphorically poised on the border between old and new, end and beginning, the term heralds the end of a world era, but within the same trope of linear

10 Another recent use of Benjamin in the context of postcolonial criticism can be seen in Edward Said's essay on Commonwealth literature (1990): Said argues that Benjamin's "document of civilization and barbarism" dialectic is instructive in his argument that the underbelly of new "world" literatures is the totalizing control of the transnational media institutions. In this sense, the Third World—or the dominated nations—produces mass culture even while Rushdie or Naipaul are held up as postcolonial literature. This argument of mine is developed a little further at the start of the fourth chapter, in the context of Jameson's Third World literature essay.

progress" (85). McClintock also argues that the term "post-colonialism" has caught on because it reduces the varying experiences of nations under and after (or between) colonialism(s): "[T]he singular category 'post-colonial' may license too readily a panoptic tendency to view the globe within generic abstractions voided of political nuance" (86).[11] This of course is also an argument made against Jameson for his use of "Third World" theory, although it does seem as though the chief fault with "Third Worldism" is that it is too vulgar. Announcements of diversity and multiplicity seem often to be liberal humanism in some guise or the other. Policing of the term "post-colonial" is undoubtedly occasioned by the problematics of the U.S. academy, as Shohat makes clear in her comments (1992: esp. 99–100).

non-place

117 Complex to the point of being an unbreakable code, Jameson's theory of utopia has three sources/implications: the positive and negative resonances in Marxist discourse; its secular label of artistic "content"; and its theologico-formal metaphysics. The first ensemble is explored in *Marxism and Form* most thoroughly in relation to Marcuse, Schiller, and Bloch, but also has important connections with the futurity of the Sartrean-existential "project"; the second connotation is for the most part developed outside of *Marxism and Form*, in such essays as "Reification and Utopia in Mass Culture" (*SV,* 9–34), "Progress Versus Utopia, or Can We Imagine the Future?" (Jameson 1982b), and many others; the third ensemble is the nar-

11 It should be noted that one pitfall or limit of McClintock's article is its tendency to engage in the "poco-Oedipal" game common to postcolonial theory, whereby a previous theorist or (especially) anthologist is held up for scathing critique: in this case, McClintock accuses the authors of *The Empire Writes Back* (Ashcroft et al. 1989) of running the risk "of a fetishistic disavowal of crucial international distinctions that are barely understood and inadequately theorized" (McClintock 1992, 87). In the same issue of *Social Text,* Ella Shohat's notes also rehearse this gesture: the term "postcolonial" is used by the authors of *EWB* (as we all refer to the beast nowadays) in a way that "masks the [Canadian or Australian] white settlers' colonialist-racist policies toward indigenous peoples" (Shohat 1992, 102)!

rative container of Jameson's work: of his career as a whole (from book to book: from an individual writer—Sartre; to whole traditions—Western Marxism, formalism, and structuralism; to the entire space of contemporary cultural and political (re)productions—postmodernism); of his various essays, chapters, and books with their structural and narrativistic and rhetorical exigencies and apodicticies; and of actual sentences—as Sartre said of his own work, "[E]ach sentence is as long as it is . . . only because each sentence represents the unity of dialectical movement" (Sartre 1966, 329; qtd. *M&F*, 209).

118 The three ensembles of utopianism in and of Jameson's work can be summarized in Schiller's *Naïve and Sentimental Poetry* (1966); speaking of the naive, Schiller writes: "*They are what we were; they are what we should once again become*" (85). But Benjamin is less relaxed about the role of the future:[12] speaking of German Social Democrats' reformism, he writes that their "training made the working class forget both its hatred and its spirit of sacrifice, for both are nourished by the image of enslaved ancestors rather than that of liberated grandchildren" (1969, 260). Benjamin's dichotomy does not oppose the past against the future, but asks whether the future can possess an *image* to drive the revolution—that is, inquires into the political unrepresentability of that utopia.

119 Jameson's work refers to or depends upon a golden age before the onslaught of capitalism; he characterizes (or, to be narratological, adjectivizes) that period; in a symmetrical fashion, his theory depends equally on the hope that there can be a future space which will see the triumph of collective and creative forces against the fragmenting and dehumanizing armies of the various world orders. This ethical and political position is a narrative: it implies a sort of prolepsis of the moment. Every sentence contains within it the potential for a dialectical glimpse of that future.

form and content

120 "society is conceived of at any given historical moment as that preexistent and indeed preformed raw material which ultimately determines the

---

12 While Benjamin has not been reified in the manner of the Young Marx or various Freuds, it nevertheless is necessary to point out that his pronouncements—like Althusser's, for example—on this and other topics varied throughout his writings.

abstractness or the concreteness of the works of art created within it" (*M&F*, 164); "what is more important is the influence of a given social raw material, not only on the content, but on the very form of the works themselves" (165); "In the art works of a preindustrialized . . . society, the artist's raw material is on a human scale" (165); "in the language of Hegel, this raw material needs no *mediation*" (165); "the most important aspect of this feeling of totality for us is not at the moment the ideological explanation given it but rather its immediate presence or absence in that particular social life from which the writer draws his raw material" (169); "the names of Scott and Balzac may be associated with this initial stockpiling of social and anecdotal raw material for processing and ultimate transformation into marketable, that is to say *narratable,* shapes and forms" (10).

121 Formed, or preformed—this is the condition of raw material (for Adorno, "society") when its organization predetermines the styles of the aesthetic.

122 Subjectivity and personality: Jameson narrates a change from the naive poetry of preindustrial times to the realist novel, where the resulting texts must, confronted with a situation (the growth of the commodity society, where the human labor in products is fast vanishing under fetishization) of "a dissolution of the human" (*M&F*, 166), resort to characters as "personalities."

123 Utopia is an optical illusion. The angelus novus is only new. Utopian activity is fundamentally, for Jameson (*M&F*, 173), realizable in "concrete narration"—this differs from Bloch, who sees all works of art, in their becoming, as utopian. Jameson's idea parallels his later theory in *The Political Unconscious* that the narrative is the primary way to theorize society (not just to be utopian, but also critical). His theoretical works are themselves concrete narratives. Ontological utopianism versus secular utopianism. Jameson is quite suspicious in *Marxism and Form* of secular utopias, or the narrative with a story of a utopia: "[W]hen the literary work attempts to use this utopian material directly, as content, in secular fashion, as in the various literary utopias themselves, there results an impoverishment which is due to the reduction of the multiple levels of the utopian idea to the single, relatively abstract field of social planning" (*M&F*, 145–46). However true this may be, this rather stern dictum is slightly too Adornoesque (meaning: like Adorno's disparagement of political art, Jameson here is too hasty) in its dismissal of

popular and political uses of utopia, as is borne out later in Jameson's and others' work.[13]

124 Sartre in *Critique of Dialectical Reason* writes that the "raw material" of the group is the gathering (he opposes the group to seriality: 633): here is the raw material of Jameson's metaphor. For Jameson, the raw material is always preformed (like the sculptor's idea that the statue is already inside the stone). So the logic of the content dictates what form the literary work will take—this is his exposition/appropriation of Lukács.

125 The politically unrepresentable is that which discourse cannot admit: Jameson argues that for the bourgeois novel, this was increasingly "work." This is Jameson's "loss of immediate comprehensibility" (*M&F*, 167).

126 So it is evident that Jameson's "raw material," which determines the shape and form of his text, is the relationship and structure theorized by Marxist criticism and implicit in its praxis. An examination of one local instance of such raw material—Bloch—will show how this comes to be.

utopia and emotion

127 Bloch's aesthetics coordinates the twin functions of ideological surplus and utopianism. The first principle he argues is what lifts a cultural work, in orthodox Marxist terms, "part of the superstructure," out of the limitations of the "base" (the economic and historical situation). The utopian role of art is its essence, in that the art contains, and promises, a future world beyond the present. Art in its very Being is a wish for that place. "[I]n other words, there is a relative return of the cultural superstructure even when the base disappears" (Bloch 1989, 34).

128 For Bloch, and Jameson, art is utopian because it contains the Benjaminian barbarism—the work is ideological and utopian simultaneously. "The fruits of art, science, and philosophy always reveal more than the false con-

13 See "Reification and Utopia in Mass Culture" (*SV* 9–34); "Progress Versus Utopia, or Can We Imagine the Future?" (Jameson 1982b); Tom Moylan's *Demand the Impossible* (1986); Fred Pfeil's essay on science fiction (1990, 83–94); and Michael Denning's "The End of Mass Culture" (1990).

sciousness that a society has about itself and that it uses for its local em-
bellishment. In particular, the fruits can be lifted from their initial local-
historical ground since they are essentially not bound to it. The Acropolis
admittedly belongs to the slave-holding society and the Strasbourg cathedral
belongs to the feudal society. Nevertheless, they did not vanish with their
base" (Bloch, 1989, 116). Here Bloch contends that the art "survives" not
because of its literal concreteness—the relative permanence of books as
physical objects (as they tell young painters in art school: "Don't worry
about your materials. If your work is great, it'll be restored."). Because the
works themselves reveal the inner contradictions of their time, and, in that
revelation, contain the hope that those contradictions will be overcome at
some future time, they remain relevant to future generations.

129 You might say that Bloch is being idealist, if not for at least two aspects of
his philosophy: his theory of emotions, and his practical literary criticism.
The anticipatory illumination, as Bloch labels art's utopianism, also pre-
cludes the stasis induced by positivism or idealism, for the work of art (even
in these large, abstract schemes) nevertheless always beckons to the future.
Thus Bloch sees "The Stage Regarded as a Paradigmatic Institution," as one
of his essays is titled, as the place where "the spectator does not only remain
in expectation, for the exciting, lively actors arouse him for more" (1989,
225). So even at the present moment, the work is arousing desire, and that
arousal is accomplished with *illusion*, or what Adorno calls the "false copy."

130 In Bloch's theory, emotions are divided into "filled effects or emotions"
and "expectation-effects"; the former "project their wish into a psychic
space which is properly unreal [and] ask for fulfillment in a world at all
points identical to that of the present" (*M&F,* 126)—so no change is desired,
only plenitude. Bloch's "expectation-effects," whether positive and hopeful
or negative and anxious, are fetish-free, desiring instead "the very configuration of the world in general or at the future disposition or constitution of the
self" (127). Thus Bloch's distinction fuels Jameson's preference and necessity of the formal: for its formal change is properly utopian.

131 Bloch's literary criticism also contains a dialectical dynamic of narrative
and metaphor. In his essays on the detective novel and the artist-novel, Bloch
sees the first form as an Oedipal meditation-riddle on Being that can be
answered only "when the world passes over into Utopia" (*M&F,* 131). Bloch

is also incisively political in his analysis, however: "Agatha Christie's character Hercule Poirot . . . no longer stakes his 'grey little cells' on the inductive
card [of Holmes], but instead intuits the totality of the case in accordance
with the increasingly irrational modes of thinking characteristic of late bourgeois society" (Bloch 1989, 251). Holmes's villains are rationalists; Poirot's
are hysterical.

132 The metaphor at the heart of the artist-novel stands dialectically to that
barbarism of the detective novel's fallen world. The utopianism of the artist-
novel lies, like the detective novel's unknown past crime, in an absent center:
"[T]he empty space of that imaginary work of art which alone confers upon
the novel's hero his right to be called an artist," and it is for Bloch the novel's
"ontological value as a form and figure of the movement of the future still
incomplete before us" (*M&F,* 131–32).

style and the man

133 If we understand Bloch's mystical theorems as the raw material of
Jameson's "theologico-formal metaphysics of Utopia," it becomes easier to
see a bifurcation in Jameson's praxis: his use of metaphor, and his use of
narrative. Thus it is evident that this utopia of his form is identical to his
doubled hermeneutics (positive and negative). Utopianism acts as a container of meaning and dialogism—"container" meant dialectically, both negative restriction and positive enabling device.

134 Jamesonian utopianisms: his frequent, gleeful, and sensual resort to examples, metaphors, symbols, rhetorical devices. All of these "formal orna-
ments" I tried to show, in the discussion of Sartre and Jameson above (bus
versus car), have political and philosophical importance. So what is typically
seen, in bourgeois criticism, as an expression of the author's "individuality,"
his or her style, is in my analysis rather a formal manifestation of the social
and the real—style here ranges from "stream of consciousness" and the
unreliable narrator down to the very minutest detail of the sentence.

135 Jameson must use metaphor for the same reason he argues (summarizing Lukács) the novelist uses symbolism: as a sign of the loss of the human in
the world of the text. That is, as the everyday objects of the novel's world—
furniture, the city, work—lose their connection with human labor because of

reification, the novelist tries through "subjectivity to evolve a human world completely out of itself" (*M&F,* 198). So the symbols, allegories, and rhetorical devices of Jameson's text instantiate the reification of Marxism itself— into either the meaningless "vulgarities" (noting the problematics of class entailed in this world) of older non-Hegelian and typically prescriptive criticism, a criticism which we could say was all-too-totalizing; or the furious fragmentation of academic Marxism, especially in the U.S.A., and as practiced in the social sciences (a target also confronted by Adorno in *Negative Dialectics*).

the fetish of the category

136 Jameson notes in *Late Marxism* that Adorno's "struggles within a postwar . . . German sociology . . . according to the structure of social contradiction itself . . . aimed as much at promoting a certain kind of empirical research within an otherwise relatively metaphysical and speculative tradition as at criticizing the unreflexive and merely operational use of contradictory categories as though they were classificatory concepts" (*LM,* 41). This is analogous to Jameson's own castigation of academic sociology, which, beguiled by its Kantian idealism even while it projects its disciplinary categories and divisions of labor onto its object of study (viewed dialectically, the differences between psychology, sociology, and anthropology are inconsequential and mystifying justifications for the Nietzschean self-perpetuations of the academic);[14] for Marxism "differs from the purely sociological kind in

14 See, for certain roots or origins or parallels to Jameson's praxis, "Sociology and Psychology" (Adorno 1967). Thus, as Jameson summarizes Adorno's argument, "The rift between public and private, social and psychological, is a dramatic externalization (although not the only one or even the only type) of the epistemological contradictions of 'a society whose unity resides in its not being unified' " (*LM,* 39). Thus the disciplinary differentials are both objective (anthropology takes as its mission the colonization of the hinterland, sociology the pacification of the working classes, and psychology the marginalization of the dissident) and subjective (like the aesthete grappling with the unresolvable dilemma of whether a certain *word* is form or content, the social scientist must eventually decide that his or her praxis is rooted in liminal institutions—class, behavior, the tribe—or risk confronting the unsaid of the discipline).

that it describes not simply the affiliation between a doctrine and a class but also the functional role of that doctrine in *class struggle*. . . . Whatever its philosophical presuppositions, the sociological view is *formally* [it is a matter of form!] wrong to the degree that it allows us to think of the individual classes in a kind of isolation from each other . . . just as surely a hypostasis as the notion of the solitary individual in eighteenth-century philosophy" (*M&F,* 380–81).

137 This is to say that for Jameson the class categories are not figures on the ground of society, but battlements or ramparts, shifting as the various classes do combat (Gramsci). This was signaled recently in the early-1990s concept of "Generation X," where the lack or lacunae in the "X" (which usually did not mean Malcolm) signified the "lack" of representability as well as the subjects' "refusal" to participate (a.k.a. "slackers").

138 In his turn, Adorno's most profound enunciation of the dialectic of the subject and the object, which forces the sociologist to consider his or her situation and thereby negates the illusions of freestanding objectivity even while it demands the methodology of such a "false empiricism of the false copy," comes at a certain point in *Negative Dialectics:* "To give the object its due instead of being content with the false copy, the subject would have to resist the average value of such objectivity and to free itself as a subject. It is on this emancipation, not on the subject's insatiable repression, that objectivity depends today" (Adorno 1987, 170–71).

139 Of course for all his rigor (or indeed because of it!), here Adorno is being intolerably idealist: if "idealism" can be positive in the same way that Jameson sees utopia as positive.

140 That is, Adorno's idealism here (or the positive-capability of his positivism?) argues that while we should not be content with the "false copy," that is frequently all we have, and all we shall have, to work through, until that as-yet-unrealizable future moment. This is the meaning of Jameson's metaphoricity; and the spiral of logic becomes more sickeningly twisted (inducing a roller-coaster nausea not only Sartrean, but also dialectical in Jameson's sense—"something of the sickening shudder we feel in an elevator's fall" [*M&F,* 308]) when I say that it is the "false copy" itself that leads to the subject being able to free herself from Adorno's "average value" of objectivity into true emancipation. What we go to art for (or to Adorno, Sartre, or Jameson) is precisely that *jouissance* of the false copy.

elevated language

141 Jameson's comment about the elevator can perhaps allow a site for a brief exploration of his figures and narratives as utopian formalism and container of meaning. The passage is Sartrean because of the objective role it accords physical sensations in a kind of dialectical synesthesia of nausea and dialectics. It is simultaneously Blochian for the utopianism which it elicits—or which is generated—out of these philosophico-somatic sensations. And it is the shock or juxtaposition of these heterogeneous or enclitic philosophies that marks Jameson's overall utopianism of his career and lifework. Therefore the passage can stand as a synecdoche, like a shrunken dwarf, to the larger totality of his project.

142 "This is indeed the most sensitive moment in the dialectical process: that in which an entire complex of thought is hoisted through a kind of inner leverage one floor higher, in which the mind, in a kind of shifting of gears, now finds itself willing to take what had been a question for an answer. . . . There is a breathlessness about this shift from the normal object-oriented activity of the mind to such dialectical self-consciousness—something of the sickening shudder we feel in an elevator's fall or in the sudden dip in an airliner. That recalls us to our bodies much as this recalls us to our mental positions as thinkers and observers. The shock indeed is basic, and constitutive, of the dialectic as such" (*M&F*, 307–8).

143 The somatic-spatial metaphors are obvious: elevators rising but as if propelled from within; a car shifting gears to travel all the faster; the almost Sartrean (a Sartre of *Nausea* and *Being and Nothingness*) attitude toward the body as example; the Breton-like emphasis on shock. And this, my list, recalls also the impossibility of thereby leveling out Jameson's rhetoric and metaphors to some catalog of effects, for the rhizomatic quality of his writing here is quite stunning. That is, the play of metaphors, in an attempt to *exemplify* the dialectic, leads to a dialectical "shifting of gears" itself, for the reader is confronted here with the text itself as a formal encoding of dialectical movement.

144 Indeed, the shock of Jameson's writing is designed again and again to reintroduce the frustration of his project;[15] for the very lushness of his prose

---

15 There is a danger in fetishizing the notion of "shock." Poet/critic Alan Davies has written of the L=A=N=G=U=A=G=E poets' analogous desire to "startle": "It has been

signals the not-yet-arrived quality of the dialectic: he needs these examples and metaphors not as some individual pleasure or filigree, but instead as utopian compensation for the loss of the object (like the symbolist's analogous loss)—the object being a visible and readily apparent class struggle.

145 For Jameson, not only is the future utopia not discernible, but so too is the necessity of moving in that direction, in a post-Freudian world dominated by the reality principle; as Marcuse shows in *Eros and Civilization* (1974), "[P]hantasy (imagination) retains the structure and the tendencies of the psyche prior to its organization by the reality, prior to its becoming an 'individual' set off against other individuals . . . imagination preserves the 'memory' of the subhistorical past when the life of the individual was the life of the genus, the image of the immediate unity between the universal and the particular under the rule of the pleasure principle" (142). Jameson's metaphors, traces in the Blochian sense of the imagination as much as of dialectical thinking itself, thereby harken to that subhistorical or transhistorical unity. Organized into narratives, the language of Jameson's text thereby refutes both the fragmentation of thought made imperative by the division of labor and alienation of capitalism: manifested in both the academy as the "multiversity" and in the marketplace as the "job."

146 But Jameson's metaphors also recall his borrowing from Sartre announced earlier in this chapter: specifically, Jameson's "shifting of gears" seems to continue the Americanization of dialectics begun when Jameson translated Sartre's example for seriality.

in defense of sartre as hero

147 This problematic can best be approached by way of Denis Hollier's *The Politics of Prose* (1986). Hollier's book is for the most part a Lyotardian or Derridean essay, which seeks to deconstruct Sartre's claims to commitment, realism, and phenomenological truth by way of his metaphors and rhetoric. Thus if Sartre in *What Is Literature?* claimed that writing is like using a

---

posited (meaning or no meaning) that the reader has to be startled. Presumably out of complacency or something of the sort. But startled people don't think. They don't understand anything they didn't understand before" (1991, 4).

gun (1965, 18), Hollier shows how this lack of self-consciousness sabotages Sartre's claims. Hollier's work, in my view, is more interesting for how he can write in a highly libidinal manner (spinning off puns as the structure for his work) than for its critique of Sartre (which can be reduced to a plea for a pun-driven [the word "driven" will come to be significant] *écriture;* and which derives its ethical strength from the privilege accorded to language).

148 But Hollier's work is also interesting for one of its central ensembles of meaning, which is based on Sartre's linkage of writing to the automobile.

149 Hollier's critique generates his own writing—and thus considerations of the automobile allow puns on *conduire,* which can refer to driving, behavior, and conduct; "auto-" can lead to considerations of the self, or automobilisation.

150 Hollier shows how Sartre's metaphors drive his theories and critiques of language and literature; thus writing waits for the proletariat to take the front seat, the wheel; Sartre is against Baudelaire, "who does not see that 'the arrow indicates the direction of the road'" (Hollier 1986, 17); he castigates Faulkner: "'[I]t appears that Faulkner's vision of the world can be compared to that of a man seated in a convertible car and looking out the back'" (17). But, Hollier asks, what does this metaphor entail? This is the first of many Sartrean aporia, whose "automobile's front seat remains empty" (20). Sartre's vaunted "determination of the present by the future" turns out to be centered not on an automobile but on an airplane, at the controls of which is Antoine de St-Exupéry: "[T]he bourgeoisie is not surpassed by the proletarian future it feared but by a return of the aristocratic past—the ex- in place of the neo-" (21).

151 Hollier exemplifies the poststructuralist unease with a novel or a theory of writing that refers to anything outside of the text. Jameson points out elsewhere that theories of the signifier that seek to erase the referent are like political theories that call for the end of ideology (or of history): "[W]hat we do with the [realist] works that show the functioning of all those realities of capitalism that have not changed substantially since the time of the great naturalists—wage slavery, money, exploitation, the profit motive—is to decree that since they cannot be said to be untrue, they are boring and old-fashioned. . . . So the death of the referent has been greatly exaggerated; at best, it has only gone underground" (*IT,* 2:68).

152 This also explains Hollier's displeasure with Sartre's rhetoric of machines like guns and cars: "When one uses a rifle, one thinks of the target. When one uses a car, one thinks of the road" (Hollier 1990, 54). But this is surely phenomenologically false: when I use a rifle, I also feel intensely the rifle on my shoulder, its weight—like language, it is unfamiliar and I have to trust it, I have to be *capable*. Similarly, when I drive a car, I have to do more than just look out the window (Robert Pirsig notwithstanding)—it is also important to be aware of the progress of the machine. Hollier would have us believe Sartre's theories are a monologic discourse of monologism—Sartre is always saying the same thing, and it is bad.

153 Hollier is unhappy with Sartre's utopianism, that is, with his politics, which do not align with a poststructuralist politics mired in language. For it is in Hollier's text that we see the usual claim that "utopia" is merely negative (and here the translator's choice of a lower-case "u" is surely intentional): "Sartre decided the ideal of committed literature was utopian" (28); "[a]nd yet, at the heart of this egalitarian utopia, not just anyone can serve as an example" (54); "[t]he utopian banana republic proposed by *Qu'est-ce que la littérature?* as an ideal to the committed writer in reality produces only dream-bananas" (93). Hollier's negative concept of the utopia ("Sartrean shifters, Barthes would have said, are intensely atopian" [86]) is ironic in part because it reveals that his discourse is similar to an older, even pre-Sartrean Marxism, where "Utopian thought represented a diversion of revolutionary energy into ideal wish-fulfillments and imaginary satisfactions," whereas now, in a post-Freudian era, "in our own time the very nature of the Utopian concept has undergone a dialectical reversal. Now it is practical thinking which everywhere represents a capitulation to the system itself. . . . The Utopian idea, on the contrary, keeps alive the possibility of a world qualitatively distinct from this one" (*M&F,* 110–11).

154 Jameson's formulations of a utopian and libidinal Marxism contradicts violently Hollier's project, which rejects any concept of the future as a metaphysics, a teleology that suppresses the differend via a totalizing grip on the present. This is the theory behind Hollier's further critique of Sartre's rhetoric of temporality—Sartre writing, for example, "I am looking at a blank sheet of paper," which is obviously a fiction about writing, while simultaneously militating against self-consciousness in art.

155 This fiction or utopia is also why Hollier is troubled by Sartre's fragmentary manuscripts: a "book is unfinished, save for a few fragments" (Hollier, 18); and "[a]lthough they were sufficiently strong not to prolong themselves, the *Chemins* were cut short in the matter in which existent things perish. . . . A swoon cuts short the future of a narrative which has not even broached its finale. And which it leaves in suspension, truncated, as though mutilated, on an unresolved chord" (28).

156 Hollier's aversion to Sartre's utopianism and to the unfinished nature of Sartre's work can be linked also to a more fundamental problematic, that of Sartre's seriality: "Sartre came to elaborate the concept *series*, a polemical concept based on which one can envision a first approach to the singularly abrupt breakdown cutting short *Les chemins de la liberté*" (28).

157 This is where I again propose the notion of circularity; for the logic of the content of this essay, of the examples and their play, dictates a return to my earlier meditation on Sartre and Jameson. Hollier, that is, proposes that Sartre's Paris is *already* Americanized: "Sartre finds by looking out his own window the example allowing him to analyze the serial group: the line forming at a Parisian taxi station. Each individual has taken his number and waits for his turn to come. Paris has become Americanized" (32).

158 Hollier's focus on the automobile corresponds as well to Jameson's notion of the dialectic as a shifting of gears. And Hollier's critique of the immanent contradictions in Sartre's notion of the airplane suggests Jameson's idea of the dialectic "in another sense the ever-widening nets of the exposition, in which each topic seems to recapitulate the previous one in a different context and on a higher plane" (*M&F*, 309)—as if to demonstrate the metonymy at work here, shortly after this remark Jameson illustrates the dialectic at work in the air-superiority race between the Soviet Union and the U.S. immediately after World War II.

159 What does Hollier's comment on the series mean in terms of the conclusions that I drew earlier? First, it is important to note that Hollier is nowhere able to deal with either the dialectic as Sartre's form of argument (he is firmly on the trail of the wayward metaphor), and second, Hollier similarly ignores the importance in the *Critique* of the dynamics of the group.

160 For the group is, for Sartre, precisely that utopian moment or possibility—always a potential for any serial collective. For the seriality of modern

life is "the Elsewhere of all Elsewheres (or the series of all series of series)" (Sartre 1991, 1:324).

161 Hollier realizes that deconstructive criticism, in its dismissal of dialectics as totalizing and relying on binary oppositions, in its refusal to imagine a future, is resigned to the seriality of what we might call a lettrist-idealism. That is, the superstructure of language is fetishized as the origin of meaning, the privileged site of its manufacture, which thereby mystifies the human labor involved in the production of meaning.

162 Language, or the structure of rhetoric and metaphor, takes its place as the latest form of what Sartre calls the "practico-inert," or those machines and structures that demand, in a commodity version of the vampire, our energy to maintain their working order.

against clarity

163 The apodictic: this word, which recurs again and again in Sartre's *Critique*, destroys itself—meaning "a clear demonstration," it is so obscure and beguiling that I am tempted, à la Hollier, to remonstrate against its catachresis. But Sartre's works are apodictic because they pretend to be clear, reasonable, and straightforward *even while they are not*. So if Jameson tries to "demonstrate" Sartre's ideas, he must also formalize and stylize his writing, in the utopian demand that there will be a time and place for such naïveté— "I hope we are not yet too alienated or instrumentalized to reserve some small place for what used to be handicraft satisfaction" (1982a, 88).

164 De Man declares that Sartre's "self-assertion took the form of a frantic attempt to maintain a firm inner commitment in open and polemical contact with the changing trends" (1988, 61). What are "changing trends," or, rather, what is (the phrase) "changing trends" but the attempt to trivialize a theory or methodology by linking its worth or value to its (inflated?) popularity? The ascetic critic also fears blindly the idea of "commitment" since this implies that literature has some use or role outside of intrinsic self-scrutiny.

165 Jameson writes in *Late Marxism* that "Adorno's sociological propositions tend towards a lapidary concision that transforms brief essays . . . into

verbal objects of great density, like shrunken dwarfs: this is to be explained by the fundamental asymmetry between subject and object, and by the consequent fact that 'society,' the universal, the system itself, is as 'fictive' and non-empirical as it is real. The social totality 'cannot be grasped in any immediate fashion, nor is it susceptible of drastic verification.' In practice, this means that Adorno's sociological theorization will always be metacritical" (*LM*, 38).

166 The spiral or *mise-en-abŷme* (seriality?) of simulation and origins allows me to turn this statement back onto Jameson's own work: the ideal of a satisfactory mediating term between society and art (the ideal, that is, of a satisfactory dialectical criticism). This is why it is useless, I think, to engage in a handbook of Jameson-isms—for it is as impossible to "represent" Jameson's technique as it is for his own work to represent Marxism, and thus Jameson resorts to metaphor and the engine of the dialectical sentence in a utopian gesture of weary energy.[16]

no subject

167 But this hesitation before the body of work, like the paver's hesitation before pouring the tar onto the scraped and vulnerable roadbed, is illusory. I cannot tell a story "properly," hence, I do not believe in narrative. Adorno, in the *Negative Dialectics,* provides the necessary example of avoiding the subjective and re-claiming the formal. First, he remarks that the subjective impulse in philosophy is figuratively (and thus literally) a feature of the dinosaur: "[P]hilosophy's stress on the constitutive power of the subjective moment always blocks the road to truth as well. This is how animal species like the dinosaur Triceratops or the rhinoceros drag their protective armour with them, an ingrown prison which they seem—anthropomorphically, at least—to be trying vainly to shed. The imprisonment in their survival mechanism may explain the special ferocity of rhinoceroses as well as the un-

16 Or of energetic sleepiness: Sartre's remark that he took speed while writing the *Critique* [Sartre 1977, 18] stands as Marxist philosophy's emblematic version of Hemingwayesque drinking or Charlie Parker's heroin.

acknowledged and therefore more dreadful ferocity of *homo sapiens*. The subjective moment is framed, as it were, in the objective one. As a limitation imposed on the subject, it is objective itself" (1987, 180). "Style" is one of the various contemporary pseudo-subjectivities by which domination makes its insidious effects on the subject known through the object; therefore fetishizing, in turn, the unrepresentability of discourse itself, as though this would free the politics or the text, turns the very possibility of the text existing in system (the mythic marketplace of ideas) into some subjective quality of freedom ("the very subject Kant calls free and exalted is part of that natural context above which freedom would lift it"—Adorno 1987, 180).

168 So I can see little point in claiming some individualist subjectivity on behalf of the Jameson-text—style makes the man. The problem, the central tension in Adorno's work, is that there remains "some last remnant of absolutely subjective categories which the desubjectifying impulse cannot wish to dissolve" (*LM,* 123). This articulates Adorno's work to postmodernism in general: both links and severs that link, like a trailer-hitch. While, like the poststructuralists, Adorno wishes to demolish the subject as some transcendental illusion, unlike theorists of the post, and especially in his aesthetics, Adorno still values experience (Raymond Williams).

169 Adorno argues that the trailer-hitch of the subject, somehow articulating between the object and history, stunts all philosophy to the role of after-the-event rationalizer of brutality.[17] This is the full-dress Marxist critique of ethics and morality: "[W]e criticize morality by criticizing the extension of the logic of consistency to the conduct of men; this is where the stringent logic of consistency becomes an organ of unfreedom. The impulse . . . is immanent in moral conduct and would be denied in attempts at ruthless rationalization" (Adorno 1987, 286). Adorno critiques knowledge or mimesis (and philosophy itself) as midwife to ethics: the latter must instead be

---

17 And not only of "brutality." Christian Metz, in a passage cited by Jameson (*SV,* 99): "Another case, and just as frequent a one, is that of conceptions of the cinema which aim to be theoretical and general but in fact consist of justifying a given type of film that one has first liked, and rationalising this liking after the event" (Metz 1982, 10). (I discuss varieties of the "epistemophilic" versus the "libidinal" forms of criticism in chapter 4.)

instantaneous and untheorized (in this way he is close to Foucault's critique of the traditional intellectual, or to Rorty's theory of pragmatic philosophy, but see, also, the critique of "spontaneous" love, which "in this supreme independence [is] precisely the tool of society" [Adorno 1989, 172]). Thus the persecution of Nazi war criminals decades after the war is less a matter of some transcendental "justice" (in the archaic notion that the guilty must be punished: which depends on a stable notion of guilt and the subject) than a "falsified" process, "compromised by the same principle on which the killers were acting" (Adorno 1987, 287).

170 The critique of ethics applies to aesthetics in a way that makes me uneasy. That is, it raises the problem of valorizing in theory a certain practice (in this chapter, Jameson's style). For, in the end, there can be no philosophical or political need to conduct such an appraisal. That is, Jameson's absurdly rich style is there, and that is neither to the good or the bad; rather, the important question is, does his work lead into an encounter with Marxist and bourgeois thought?

171 This can be answered in part by turning to questions of rhetoric, writing, and philosophy. But first, I would like to qualify my use of "archaic" above, as in "the archaic notion" of justice. The adjective "archaic" should not be taken as negative. This false historicism (as opposed to what Žižek calls "historicity") is critiqued in a particularly bristling passage of *Late Marxism* (but are there any passages which are not?): "These new 'ideas' [capital, bureaucracy, dictatorship, Nature, History] are not to be seen as some 'fall' of the Platonic problematic into the secular dynamics of modern times. Rather, these new abstractions—like Adorno's system or totality, they are at one and the same time utterly non-empirical (not given as knowledge or immediately) and the realest matters to us in the world, the matters which constrain us the most absolutely—pose new 'epistemological' problems to which Benjamin's deliberately *archaic* solution provides a fresh answer that is retained in *Negative Dialectics*" (*LM*, 56: my emphasis). Jameson argues that the "archaic" sense of Benjamin's adamic stress on naming in the 'Epistemo-Critical Prologue' to *The Origin of German Tragic Drama* (1985, 27–56) "influences" Adorno in the *Negative Dialectics*. This question of influence (and specifically of Benjamin's influence on Adorno) might best be described (instead of "the transfer of some new thought from one person's

head to another") as "the awakening of new interests (not to say a whole new problematic) in the mind of the individual on the receiving end of the 'influence' in question. . . . 'Influence' in this new sense would then describe the ways in which the pedagogical figure, by his own praxis, shows the disciple what else you can think and how much further you can go with the thoughts you already have; or—to put it another way, which for us is the same—what else you can *write* and the possibility of forms of writing and *Darstellung* that unexpectedly free you from the taboos and constraints of forms learnt by rote and assumed to be inscribed in the nature of things" (*LM*, 52; emphasis in the original). So Benjamin in the "Epistemo-Critical Prologue" writes that "[t]he idea is something linguistic. . . . Ultimately, however, this is not the attitude of Plato, but the attitude of Adam, the father of the human race and the father of philosophy. Adam's action of naming things is so far removed from play or caprice that it actually confirms the state of paradise as a state in which there is as yet no need to struggle with the communicative significance of words. Ideas are displayed, without intention, in the act of naming, and they have to be renewed in philosophical contemplation. In this renewal the primordial mode of apprehending words is restored" (1985, 36–37).[18] Without ascribing some influence or even intertextuality, consider this deconstructive passage from *Negative Dialectics:* "In its dependence—patent or latent—on texts, philosophy admits its linguistic nature which the ideal of the method leads it to deny in vain. . . . [T]he persecutors of the rhetorical

18 Note on Benjamin's use of "primordial": Surely Jameson is right to warn against simply ascribing some linear narrative to intellectual biographemes of Benjamin (the "Epistemo-Critical Prologue," like the *Origins* itself, is idealistic and mystical, whereas the *Passagenwerk* is more thoroughly materialist [*LM*, 51–52]—a similar, if inverted narrative, is usually laid over Lukács's career, of course); similarly, then, I would warn the hearty deconstructionist from blanching at the "primordial" or the eponymous "origin" of Benjamin's thought; as the following passage should make clear, his vision of the terms is (in)finitely complex (and also punning, obviously, on the polysemic *Ursprung*): "Origin, although an entirely historical category, has, nevertheless, nothing to do with genesis. The term origin is not intended to describe the process by which the existent came into being, but rather to describe that which emerges from the process of becoming and disappearance. Origin is an eddy in the stream of becoming, and in its current it swallows the material involved in the process of genesis" (1985, 45).

element that saved expression for thought did just as much for the technification of thought, for its potential abolition, as did those who cultivated rhetoric and ignored the object. In philosophy, rhetoric represents that which cannot be thought except in language" (Adorno 1987, 55). This last sentence, as well as Benjamin's emphasis on the act of naming as a restoration of the primordial, allegorically substantiates my chapter's findings regarding the importance of Jameson's style—objectively (and here the invectives against post-hoc valorization as theory are answered), the difficulty and ornateness of Jameson's prose demands a political attention to the dialectic (in the act of reading) both as form and content. To give only two examples from this chapter, the use of "examples" instantiates a trans-Atlantic political economy of the figure and the tropes of the dialectic and the hermeneutic quest for those tropes demonstrate the Anglo-American or North American poverty of radical philosophy that must begin anew, with each generation, to construct an epistemology and ontology based on concrete needs and desires.

3

THE JAMESONIAN

UNCONSCIOUS

always red

172 *The Political Unconscious* is the book for which Jameson is best known: it resides in the realm of the "always already read," that kingdom of works known before they are encountered. I first came across Jameson's work as an undergraduate when our instructor warned us of its difficulty. She noted that in teaching theory to graduate students even an essay on Joyce's *Ulysses* (Jameson 1982c) caused numerous difficulties. In one class, during a discussion of an essay on *Lord Jim* (Miller 1982, 22–41), the instructor held up a copy of *The Political Unconscious* at the head of the seminar table and proceeded to summarize its argument, warning us of the immense difficulty entailed in reading the initial chapter and the hard work of understanding Jameson on Conrad. Thus the instructor divided the course into books or articles that were "easy" or accessible enough for undergraduate students actually to read (Eagleton, Derrida, Gilbert, and Gubar) and those that would only be summarized for us (Jameson, Lacan). The following summer, two salutary events occurred. First, while making my way through a library copy of *The Prison-House of Language,* I excitedly photocopied the following passage: "The rich analogical content of the various local studies of value—Marx's analysis of money and the commodity, Freud's of the libido, Nietzsche's of ethics, Derrida's of the word—is itself a sign of the hidden interrelationships of the categories which govern these various di-

mensions: gold, the phallus, the father or the monarch or God, and the myth of the *parole plein* or spoken word" (180–81). This analysis seemed to me, sitting in a student pub, to be the apex of the Marxist and deconstructive project.

173 Or is this quite how it all took place? One's first reading of a book is remembered as if it were a dream, particularly if that book is already famous or deemed important; later retellings of the putatively primal event are liable to be distorted and managed (both consciously and unconsciously) to re-direct attention and to valorize the teller.

174 Reading, interpretation, position, the unconscious . . . these form, then, the crux or prothesis of this chapter's examination of *The Political Uncon-scious* and *Fables of Aggression.* The former book set the agenda for political-literary criticism in the 1980s. Here I will discuss three interlocking problem-atics: the textual machinery that contains the various antagonistic theories Jameson examines and applies; Althusserian theory as master-code for the interpretive activity outlined in the first chapter; and the politics of readings that are carried out in the following chapters.

175 But these interpretive aims must negotiate with two discrete textual apparatuses: *The Political Unconscious,* and the writing of this chapter. I describe *The Political Unconscious* as a system of alliances and antagonisms, a libidinal apparatus that manages the reader's narrative and ideological de-sire, and which disposes that reader never to stray far from the garden path of form. Or, rather, I wander that space like Marlow in Stein's garden in *Lord Jim* (Conrad 1989, 300–302), searching for a political narrative distinguish-able from the bamboo brakes which halt meaning. In terms of this writing, here a certain slipperiness or spin of reference is inevitable (the bamboo grove is a "spinney"): which chapter is under inspection—Conrad's, Bal-zac's, Jameson's, mine?

molar/molecular antagonisms

176 An instructor of mine once remarked that the difficulty of the initial hundred pages or so in Umberto Eco's *The Name of the Rose* is intended to ensure that only the smartest of readers continued on. This professor

doubted if many of the novel's millions of purchasers made it through this baptism by fire. The first chapter of *The Political Unconscious* poses a similar challenge for the unwary reader. Unlike the strict attention, author-by-author, evinced in *Marxism and Form,* here is a wild corralling of Althusserian causality, patristic hermeneutics, Lévi-Strauss, Propp, and Frye. This method possesses a positive symbolic value in the terms established by Bourdieu and Rorty: utilizing a variety of (previously deemed) incommensurable "proper names," the text accumulates value in the pluralistic North American academy.

177 And it is precisely this formal "fit" of *The Political Unconscious* into the academy that attracted me to this work. I studied theory in my first year back in university after I had dropped out and bartended. The first and only member of my family to graduate from university, I lacked the cultural capital to properly situate the course-content I began accumulating as an undergraduate. That is, unlike a middle-class or upper middle-class student, whose education in "the humanities" reaffirms certain familial verities, the working-class or lower middle-class student necessarily comes to culture differently (remember the importance Sartre and Jameson place on the family). Culture for me was an Oedipal weapon: a way of distancing myself from the family romance of art as middlebrow pictorialism (anonymous, vulgar and hopelessly out-of-date), books as degraded decoration (the smooth vinyl of Reader's Digest Condensed Books where you could read the abbreviated *Jaws* or *Mrs. 'Arris Goes to Moscow*) and music and television as audiovisual white noise (TVs on in every room, the radio tuned to a local AM station "for the weather" and left on for the dog when the house was empty). This Oedipal figuration is dialectical: I sought out culture for something my family had no competence in, and it, in turn, taught me that the culture of my family was of no value—through the fetish of the author, the reification of the autonomous, iconic art-object, and the valorization of complexity and difficulty. As if to affirm this Bourdieuizing-on-the-run, my family rejected my newfound enthusiasms as soon as they emerged. When I was sixteen, my parents, on learning that I had started writing poetry, told me they thought I was mentally ill. Two incidents should further demonstrate how the complexities of my dialectical turn to culture worked in the family drama. Both events have to do with James Joyce, for some reason, whose work I studied in a summer course, during which I visited my parents'

home. I was wearing a T-shirt with Joyce's face and name on it, and my maternal grandmother, a Newfoundlander, asked with genuine curiosity, "Oh and who's he when he's at home?" And at some point I was sitting in the basement reading *Ulysses* when my father, walking by, said, "That's supposed to be a really difficult book." To which I replied, "Oh no, it's racy and it's been banned and stuff!" My point is that the turn toward culture for someone of my class background is oppositional, a rebellion. "Theory," in the mid-1980s, at least, had precisely this allure, thus explaining my eagerness to study it and "claim" it for my own.

178 So in *Homo Academicus,* Bourdieu writes that structuralism succeeded because its practitioners "seemed to bring a miraculous solution to the contradiction which confronted a whole generation of professors and students . . . by enabling them to remain on the level of 'science' " (1990, 122). Bourdieu argues diagrammatically that the power of the "new disciplines" lay in a spatial or interstitial situation: sociology, ethnology, linguistics, and the other sciences of man were between the sciences and the arts and thus were able to use the techniques of both (rigor and mathematics from the one, stylish writing and grandiose statements from the other) to accrue capital. Rorty, then, in *Contingency, Irony, and Solidarity,* argues that literary theory, in its impact on the American academy, has added new proper names (the stuff-in-trade of Continental philosophy, he says) "to the range of those among which equilibrium was sought" (1990, 81n).

179 But Jameson's comments on pluralism complicate this use-value I have just postulated: "[I]n the ideological climate of a contemporary American 'pluralism,' with its unexamined valorization of the open ('freedom') versus its inevitable binary opposition, the closed ('totalitarianism') . . . [p]luralism means one thing when it stands for the coexistence of methods and interpretations in the intellectual and academic marketplace, but quite another when it is taken as a proposition about the infinity of possible meanings and methods and their ultimate equivalence with and substitutability for one another" (*PU,* 31). This comment functions in the Jameson-text in a curious way: just as the reader is becoming accustomed to the incongruity of seeing a Marxist critic updating, or at least "postmodernizing,"[1] the "medieval

---

1   This last gerund is not a major concern of *The Political Unconscious,* but surely the reception of the book is both part of the (*fin-de-la*) *condition postmoderne* and, in ways,

system of the four levels of scripture" (*PU,* 29), having already dismissed Barthes (18), moved through Deleuze and Guattari (21–23), commented briefly on Benjamin and McLuhan (25), and summarized Althusser (23–28). Dominick LaCapra calls Jameson's appropriation of the medieval levels a "limited attempt to rehabilitate theological hermeneutics" (1983, 256), while Cornel West concludes that Jameson's "fundamental aim is to preserve *the old Christian notion*—and Marxist affirmation—that history is meaningful" (1986, 130; emphasis mine).

180 Embedded in Jameson's daunting interpretive chapter, his comment about American liberalism can be read, to use his own analysis of Wyndham Lewis, as "sentence-production [or] a symbolic act in its own right, an explosive and window-breaking *praxis* on the level of the words themselves" (*FA,* 8). So the few sentences on pluralism are on the molecular level in comparison to the molar level of *The Political Unconscious* as a whole. The molecular level designates the here-and-now of immediate politics or of local action, the production-time of the individual sentence, the electrifying shock that the text I am reading takes place in a social and institutional *place* and not just as some transcendental analysis (the place being the locale of the American academy, itself within the confines—or containment, if you will—of the U.S. state itself), and that it cannot be removed from that context without some very real pain.

181 The politics of the "local" posited here is quite different from that of, say, Geoff Bennington's article "Not Yet," which he begins with a Lyotardian play on Jameson's dialectical demand for the subject to be part of analysis: "A constant injunction in Jameson: reckon the place of the analyst into the analysis. When I analyze Jameson, is my place defined geographically, politically, or in the topology of some schema of intellectual or institutional sites? Am I writing in (or from?) Oxford, Paris, 'poststructuralism'?" (Bennington 1982, 23).

---

creator of that finale. Jameson is also categorically fascinated with the possibility of interpreting various earlier writers as postmodern—Wyndham Lewis is an obvious example throughout *Fables of Aggression* (see especially 19–20), as is Adorno in *Late Marxism* (227–52), and Joyce, Flaubert, Rimbaud, and Baudelaire in various essays (1982c, 1984a, 1984b, and 1985c); Jameson comments on the "thoroughgoing rewriting into the postmodern text" done by himself and others in *Postmodernism* (302–3).

182 The Jameson-text consists of these two forces: a microscopic fragmentation at the level of the molecular or immediate (recourse to footnotes, the deferral of the sentence, the sudden intrusion of the political); and the molar, which designates all those large, abstract, mediated, and perhaps even empty and imaginary forms by which the social seek to recontain the molecular: the narrative of *The Political Unconscious*, the anti-idea of a political unconscious (and its concomitant notions of interpretation, levels, the transcendence of Marxist criticism). The ultimate manifestation of the molar is "the notion of the organic unity of the work of [criticism]. This distinction allows us to respect the specificity of the narrative level, while grasping its function to recontain the molecular proliferation of sentences on the stylistic level" (*FA*, 8). But lest a misconception arise that Jameson's use of the term implies some decentered heterogeneity of textuality, his warning that the "value of the molecular in Deleuze, for instance, depends structurally on the preexisting molar or unifying impulse against which its truth is read" (*PU*, 53) is a reminder the molecular is not purely a formal code.

183 The function of the molar/molecular antagonism is dialectical: it disengages the reader from his or her serene thought-patterns and dereifies the text's objective status by emphasizing the subjective forces at work. These forces include reading and writing operations and the Marxist subjective code: the class struggle. In *Marx Beyond Marx*, Antonio Negri uses the term "antagonism" to describe Marx's *Grundrisse*, where the heterogeneity of the economic system analyzed in Marx's notebooks is matched by a polyphonic style: "[T]here is no linear continuity, but only a plurality of points of view which are endlessly solicited at each determinate moment of the antagonism, at each leap in the presentation, in the rhythm of the investigation . . . the *Grundrisse* constitutes a 'plural' universe" (1991a, 13). Negri detects in Marx's method, as I do in Jameson's, "the passion for totality . . . in the form of a multiplicity of sequences and leaps" (13). The antagonisms are an example of how the Jameson-text has methodologically assimilated the lessons of poststructuralist textuality—the breathtaking meandering of Derrida, the bloody imagery of Foucault,[2] the frustrating obscurantism of Lacan—to create a discourse that is both totalizing *and* polyvocal.

---

2 I am thinking of the beginning of *Discipline and Punish* (1979), where Foucault quotes at length from accounts of the public torture of Robert-François Damiens.

and yet,

184 Geoff Bennington argues that the textual apparatus of *The Political Un-conscious*—metaphors, rhetoric, footnotes, digressions—deconstructs and delays his political agenda (delaying, to give a minor example, any useful encounter with key elements like the notion of the political unconscious[3]). Bennington's critique is based on a misrecognition of the antagonisms in Jameson's text. The molecular rejects a univocal text, and this disconcerts Bennington because it does not provide him with a straw man, or a mono-lithic narrative, to attack. The heterogeneity of the Jamesonian text—or whatever code word for postmodernism one chooses—does not abandon meaning or truth. Rather, Jameson claims that Marxism is an " 'untranscen-dable horizon' that subsumes such apparently antagonistic or incommen-surable critical operations, assigning them an undoubted sectoral validity within itself, and thus at once canceling and preserving them" (*PU*, 10). The operation is Hegelian in the sense of the *Aufhebung* or "sublation" of dia-lectics. But the debate surrounding Jameson's horizon often overlooks the necessity of demonstrating Marxism's claim to "priority," to "semantic rich-ness," in opposition to an ultraleftist desire simply to dismiss all other meth-odologies. Jameson's universalism is also reminiscent of Spinoza, for whom the move in a text between social, ethical, and philosophical topics is an assertion of reason's "implied universalist promise" (Norris 1991, 100).

185 Like Macherey, Althusser sees Spinoza, and not Hegel, as the true pre-cursor to Marx. In his essay "On the Young Marx" (1986, 49–86), Althusser argues that Marx does not move in a dialectical manner from Hegel, he does not "sublate" Hegel or stand him on his head or negate him, for the dialectic implies some essentialist continuity from thesis to antithesis. Althusser's theory of an epistemic rupture in Marx means his finds an ancestor in Spinoza, for whom the "relation between the first and second kind[s] of knowledge . . . in its immediacy (abstracting from the totality in God) pre-supposed precisely a radical *discontinuity*" (Althusser 1986, 78n40). This

---

3 LaCapra, on the other hand, notes that the "guiding principle of a 'political uncon-scious' is in Jameson's usage as richly connotative and associative as in any 'master' term or title that is defined—insofar as it is at all—only by its multiple uses" (1983, 236).

is the discontinuity between ideology and science, conceived of as two separate or incommensurable spheres of knowledge. If Jameson's Marxism is as much Spinozist as it is Hegelian, then the simultaneous embrace of totality and discontinuity (or openness, which Negri found in Marx) awakens the deconstructive critic's fear of totalities. This is what happens when Bennington tries to argue against Jameson's contention that alliance politics is the most important form of organizing for the U.S. left.

186 Jameson comments on this point in a footnote (*PU,* 54n), where he adds "a final comment about the coded political resonance" of the debate on totalization. He argues that an alliance of "[e]thnic groups, neighborhood movements, feminism . . . rank-and-file labor dissidence, student movements" is the most effective way for the American left to succeed. In practice, of course, real obstacles frustrate such hegemonic blocks—as the vicissitudes of the NDP in this country and the Rainbow Coalition in the U.S.A. confirm—but alliances for Jameson are "the strict practical equivalent of the concept of totalization on the theoretical level." Totality, like history, is an "absent cause" (a Spinozist-Althusserian term elaborated on below) to the structure of the political organization. Here, again, form meets content: the "alliance" politics discussed in the footnote (or, content) bespeak the antagonistic "alliance" of the molecular and molar (or, form) to be found throughout Jameson's text, particularly at this juncture. The footnote itself is molecular, digressing as it does into contemporary politics (albeit briefly). And the insight that the molecular and molar are both allied with and antagonistic to each other can subdue the otherwise masculinist rhetoric (the aggressiveness of "antagonisms" for example) in so much of my analysis.

187 Bennington cannot tolerate Jameson's discussion; the concept of the alliance, as either political content or formal totality, is unacceptable to Bennington's version of Lyotardian deconstruction. There is an alliance between the footnote and the main text, and the antagonism of the molecular and the molar is not divisive but productive. Bennington sees the footnote as "a not very nice way of silencing or neutralizing Americans" (30). He proceeds to "show" that Jameson's text is as infected with the ideologeme of ressentiment as are those of Gissing or Nietzsche, and that history, as both absent cause and *telos* of *The Political Unconscious* narrative, is therefore nowhere and doomed to the deferral of the "not yet."

188 Contrary to Bennington, I believe that the molecular molar dialectic indicates that *The Political Unconscious* is "always already red" in two important senses. First, Jameson's use of various "proper names" not only postmodernizes them but "Jamesonizes" their theory. Second, the molecular *bouleversement* accomplished on pages 31 (pluralism) and 54 (alliance politics) means that the molar argument and narrative is already located in a maelstrom of specific and social contingencies: the academy and the state. Molar-molecular antagonisms materialize *formally* both the totality of the social real and the contradictions that bedevil that totality: "The Marxist method is a constituting one in so far as the class struggle constitutes explosive antagonisms" (Negri 1991a, 13).

189 The molar/molecular dialectic in Jameson is an important element of the final chapter of *The Political Unconscious*. There, as part of a discussion of Marxism and the subject, and after the predictable (and no less pertinent) gesture toward a "whole new logic of collective dynamics" suggested by Sartre's *Critique,* Jameson rounds up yet another bourgeois theorist into his interpretive corral—Emile Durkheim. This leads to a comment on Marx's notion of the "Asiatic mode of production," where the Asian peasant community transfers its identity onto the unity of a higher proprietor.

a materialist theory of power

190 The various forms of Asiatic or Oriental theories proposed by Marx and Engels—in their articles for the *New York Daily Tribune,* and in Marx's *Grundrisse* and *Capital*—have been criticized by Marxists (see Turner 1983). But as a species of psychological analysis, the analysis possesses a rich tropology. A passage in *Grundrisse* runs as follows: "[P]roperty . . . the objective, nature-given inorganic body of [the individual's] subjectivity—appears mediated for him through a cession by the total unity—a unity realized in the form of the despot, the father of many communities. . . . Amidst oriental despotism and the propertylessness which seems legally to exist there . . . part of their surplus labour belongs to the higher community, which exists ultimately as a *person*, and this surplus labour takes the form of tribute etc., as well as of common labour for the exaltation of the unity, partly of the real despot, partly of the imagined clan-being, the god" (Marx 1973, 473).

191   Here only the leader or Father can be an individual, but he himself is recipient of such dubious honors (the ermine cloak of subjectivity, as well as the rotten fruit of tithes) only because he embodies some deferred being or god. Marx alludes to the economic and psychological formation of Authority. The leader gets the goods, which might as well be destroyed by the clan-members: the potlatch, for all its Lévi-Straussian or Bataillean glamour, is a "danger" only for Eurocentric value.[4] Žižek makes this point about the *"mystique of the Institution"* (1991a, 249), where an unfair leader fronting for a real institution is more powerful than a fair leader with no institution behind him.[5] Thus the warning from a mother: "Just you wait till your father gets home!" is more literally transmitted in another idiom, uttered by the returning breadwinner: "I'd like to have a word with you, young man!" Authority is imminent and immanent: always deferred, but contained in the word, or, as Žižek puts it: "[U]ltimately founded in the power of the signifier, not in the immediate force of coercion—[authority] implies a certain surplus of trust" (1991a, 250). So authority is immanent in the structure of intersubjectivity: in the deferral to and from the female partner. The death of a mother or wife will frequently leave the father not helpless (or hapless in the manner of a television sitcom) but powerless, for authority and emperors are never naked.

a brief foray into novels

192   The so-called Oriental despot is better seen as a figure of power removed

4   Just as the Canadian government once outlawed the exchange/destruction, French theory rendered the potlatch an event "outside" the law of European capitalism. The potlatch, as a First Nations' cultural or social phenomenon, possesses its own positive value (and value based on difference) within the context of aboriginal traditions, not merely in contradistinction or contribution to Western theory. Indeed, history shows that Canadian attempts to outlaw the potlatch and other indigenous rituals for the most part failed (Miller 1989, 192).

5   See also Jameson's remarks in "Imaginary and Symbolic in Lacan" on the "discourse of the master" in relation to Marx, Mao, and Castro (*IT,* 1:114). A useful example that Žižek gives is of Socrates agreeing to the judgment condemning him because although the individual judge may be acting vindictively, the Law behind him cannot be questioned.

from that which is merely historicist or contingent.[6] This is evident in the power structures in three of the novels analyzed in *The Political Unconscious: Lord Jim, Nostromo,* and *The Black Sheep.* Reading these novels with the benefit of Jameson's analysis, one could see despotism as a Lacanian gloss on the actant-actor structuralism of Greimas. This is not immediately apparent, or at least it was not so to me. In *Lord Jim,* a hasty reader (myself) may deduce that the Rajah, or even Doramin (the two leaders Jim fights with in the second half of the novel), are transparent figures of this detested despotism; that reading would be correct to the extent that, figured as Doramin is in the novel as an almost-European humanist (in the way that his son the Rajah is an almost-European warrior),[7] this characterization demonstrates that the analysis of despotism is not an ethical one. The despot is a structural position created by narrative and psychology (action and description). So, describing Doramin, Marlow says: "[T]here was nothing of a cripple about him: on the contrary, all his ponderous movements were like manifestations of a mighty deliberate force" (Conrad 1989, 234). This illustrates the psychoanalysis contained in description—in summarizing and choosing physical and metaphysical details (physical details function like Barthes's sign-

---

6   I am using "historicist" in Althusser's sense to designate the over-hasty adherence to some linear chronology (or regional background or socio-ethnic heritage) as a determination of effects: see Jameson's brief discussion of this in *The Political Unconscious* (26–28 and note), and also the essay "Marxism and Historicism" (*IT,* 1:148–77). Of course, in his comments on historicism in Marx (Althusser and Balibar 1979, 119–44), Althusser focuses for the most part on Gramsci's Crocean uses of concepts like organicism, hegemony, and traditional intellectuals; but this is construed to separate Gramsci's attacks on "the bookish phariseeism of the Second International" (129: Gramsci's title "The Revolution against *Capital*" is evoked by Althusser here) from just that linear, causal narrative.

7   The "Europeanization" of the native or indigene in colonial fiction no doubt is the mirror image of the figure of a European "going native." As Terry Goldie has argued in another context, that "indigenization" itself functioned as an anxiety point for European desires (1989, 13–14, 46–47); similarly, the native or Oriental other who can be "like" the European signifies both anxiety over just what European identity means and a desire to control the other by coding him or her as quasi-European. See Said on Kipling (1993, 132–62) for a discussion of this anxiety and desire (which Said calls "the pleasures of imperialism") in *Kim.*

system in *Mythologies*): the power of the father is "contained" in a strategy that manages the libidinal forces of fascist authority-worship.

193 To see the Rajah or this kind, gentle giant (Doramin), as the despots of *Lord Jim* only because of their strength is too limited: even if it serves the liberal function of showing how Conrad maintained the thread of Orientalism in European letters. This simply repeats the Orientalist semiotic field (only Orientals can be despots), lazily castigating a Modernist (Conrad) in the bargain. A more psychological-materialist view of Doramin stresses his actant function: he does kill Lord Jim, after all.

194 On this point the gesture of postmodernizing Jung might help: a "dark side" racialist ideology updated to a Lacanian signification. A better task might be to inquire into how Jungian readings of Conrad will erase class (for "The Secret Sharer"), race (*Heart of Darkness*), and imperialist designs (*Lord Jim, Nostromo*), rendering the rich content of the texts instead into some eternal play of anima and animus.

195 Similar to Jung's split-subject is the play in *Nostromo* between the anti-hero Nostromo, man of the people,[8] and Charles Gould, the son seeking to right his father's injuries with a silver mine (shades of Clark Coolidge!). Here, the splitting of the despot into two (Greimassian) actors mystifies the imperialist ethic of the text's political unconscious even as it generates it. Jameson points out the novel bifurcates revolutionary activities into a "good" or European or populist Garibaldism and a "bad" or Latin American or "indigenous Monterista variety" (*PU,* 274). A similar bad mirror image exists between the taciturn Gould who digs (through the proxies of workers) the silver *out* of Costaguana and the verbose Nostromo who plants the silver on an island—again, through a proxy: the European-trained Decoud, who is only a *pétit* Gould (the Decoud/Gould rhyme is significant).

196 Whereas historically the absent father was Napoléon, in *The Black Sheep* the despot is evidently Phillipe, the older of the two brothers. Phillipe leads a

---

8 Speaking of Nostromo (and *Nostromo*), am I the only fan of *Alien* to suspect that the screenwriter thought *Nostromo* (the name of the giant spaceship in the movie) was the name of some great ship in Conrad? Sigourney Weaver as "woman of the people"? I think not. Although apparently the "treatment . . . was unique in writing each role to be played by either a man or a woman" (Penley 1989, 133).

dissipated life before, toward the end of the novel, suddenly being structurally transformed into a hero. The translation of the novel's title from *La
Rabouilleuse* (rendered in the text as "the Fisherwoman" [Balzac 1970, 161])
was probably a marketing decision that *also* served to Conradize the narrative. By this I mean that the English title emphasized or constructed the
ethical dilemma. The translator asks rhetorically: "But which of [the broth-
ers] *is* the black sheep?" (Balzac 1970, 8). It is as if we are, once again, in the
throes of ethical debate—the dominant mode of literary interpretation in the
Anglo-American world, both within theory (which is mostly engaged in a
liberal-humanist mode) and outside of it. The despot is *evidently* Phillipe,
but this is problematized by the narrative, where Phillipe (as Greimassian
actor) switches from the actant of a libertine or prodigal son (as Madame
Descoigns calls him [65]), to an almost Stendahlian hero (when he van-
quishes Max), to "vanishing mediator" of the monetary transition from
aristocracy to bourgeoisie (*PU,* 172). And the despot of the text may turn
out to be Balzac—or even Balzac's father!—following the Lacanian psycho-
biography proposed in *The Political Unconscious* (176–77, 179ff.).

the power of materialism

197 If Marx's theory of the Oriental despot works better as formalized psychoanalysis than as historical analysis, the ensuing "deconstruction" of Oriental despotism (this is an important deconstructive moment for Bennington [1982, 31]) fulfill Žižek's belated prophecy: "Father's authority is to
be fully trusted, yet one should not put it to the test too often since, sooner or
later, one is bound to discover that Father is an imposter and his authority a
pure semblance. . . . And it is the same with the King: his wisdom, justice and
power are to be trusted, yet not too severely tested" (1991a, 250). When this
wisdom is tested, it is as applicable to the exotic locale of Conrad's Asian
villages as it is to the rarefied atmosphere of Jameson's Marxist theory. More
correctly: thus far a materialist theory of power. As Sartre remarks in the
first *Critique,* "[D]isturbances, which are quickly repressed, *never* serve as a
lesson, or as an indication of the depth of popular discontent, precisely
because it is always the Other who rebels or makes a demand: the Other, the
alien, the suspect, the trouble-maker" (1991, 1:656). When authority is
viewed as a structure, rebellion suddenly appears overdetermined, or purely

an epiphenomenon of the rebel suddenly reified as Other. Troublemaking, like gift-giving, always refers back to the leader. And that master is then maintained in the structure.

198 The adventures of the concept of Asiatic despotism (within the larger scheme of Asiatic modes of production) are now evidently circular, as what was wrenched out of mere historicism returns to the materialist theory of collectivity promulgated in Sartre's *Critique* (alluded to by Jameson [*PU*, 294]). That is, to follow Sartre and typify bureaucratic structure as an instance of the "practico-inert," where relations between individuals are reified, is not to indulge in an ethical judgment: the critique is directed toward an objective structure. This is true particularly if we can adjust "reification" to a post-Althusserian vocabulary, where reification is seen not as "soul-destroying" but as an effect of late capitalism. The relation of the collective to the master, Sartre writes in the second *Critique*, is unambiguous: "As a common individual, Stalin was not a mere *person*. He was a human pyramid, deriving his practical sovereignty from all the inert structures . . . his totalizing praxis was transcendence and preservation of all structures . . . since his praxis was the synthetic temporalization of that entire inert structuration" (1991, 2:199). Read in conjunction with Marx's theory, Sartre divulges a conception of power that is located in specific structures *and their abuses*. This last is what is unthinkable for the Foucauldean notion of power, where there can be no "abuses," since that would imply some normal practice of power. Cornelius Castoriadis notes sardonically (referring apparently to post-1968 French philosophy), "[P]ower as such does not exist because its 'networks' are everywhere (*except*, please note, in the *Collège de France*), and . . . if, moreover, fascism does exist, that is because those who are tortured, exploited and so forth libidinally enjoy their condition" (1984, 101). As noted in the previous chapter, the Foucauldean notion of power implicitly under attack here is nonetheless exemplary, but as a structure not unlike Jameson's notion of totality (an idea that is probably as repugnant to a card-carrying Foucauldean as Castoriadis's attack).

marxism and orientalism

199 For Bennington, Marx's concept of the investment of unity in the body of the despot calls to mind—and is deconstructed by—Lyotard's warning:

"[T]here is no whole body" (Lyotard 1974, 37; qtd. Bennington 1982, 29).[9] Edward Said has critiqued Marx in terms of the latter's Orientalism. Said argues that Marx's concept of Asiatic society is erroneous: in this way the Father's authority can be both present (as object of critique) and absent.[10] Since Marx's concepts *resemble* the Orientalism of his contemporaries, Said argues, the fault of the concept does not lie in the individual (Said 1979, 155).

200 It should be noted that Said's critique of Marx is not so much directed at Marx's anthropology of Asiatic society than at his conviction that British imperialism in India was necessary to break the Indians out of the spell of Asiatic despotism and to prepare the way for a Western (and then socialist) society:[11] "England has to fulfil a double mission in India: one destructive, the other regenerating—the annihilation of old Asiatic society, and the laying of the material foundations of Western society in Asia" (Marx 1984, 332). Said argues that Marx's "Romantic-Orientalist vision" authorizes the "idea of regenerating a fundamentally lifeless Asia." This all comes from Goethe, which meant that a "censor" embedded in Orientalist lore (Goethe's *West-östlicher Diwan*) overwrote Marx's sympathy for Asians (Said 1979, 153–55).

201 The most powerful rejoinder to Said on this point has been Aijaz Ahmad, in his recent *In Theory: Classes, Nations, Literatures* (1992).[12] There Ahmad argues that Said's reading of Marx is based on a scanty knowledge of Marx's work, that Said fails to see Marx's characterization of colonialism is

9 Interestingly, while Bennington calls Lyotard's line a "non-dialectical negative" (29), suggesting Adorno's *Negative Dialectics,* he does not see its precursor in Adorno's great anti-Hegelian moment in *Minima Moralia:* "The whole is the false" (1989, 50).

10 My own method reflects a desire not to reify Jameson's work into an object, a method which is not dissimilar from Spivak's "catachrestic" method: see her definition in *The Post-Colonial Critic* (1990): "[A] metaphor without an adequate referent" (154). Two good examples in Spivak's more recent work of this catachrestic deferral are the beginning of the essay "Limits and Openings of Marx in Derrida" (1993, 97ff.), or her use of MLA program notes in an interview (1990, 153).

11 Turner argues that the "Marxist categories [may] become a justification for colonialism" (1983, 33).

12 A useful analysis of the Ahmad-Said-Jameson debate is offered by Michael Sprinker in his essay "The National Question: Said, Ahmad, Jameson" (1993). See also my chapter 4.

parallel to his view of capitalism in Europe, and that Said too quickly adduces a racist intent based on a nonmaterialist or even nonrigorous scholarship (221–42). Ahmad is quite severe in his own characterization of Said's motivations for the attack on Marx in *Orientalism,* as he sarcastically remarks, "One of Said's notable contributions to the American Left, in fact, is that he, perhaps more than anyone else, has taught this Left how to build bridges between the liberal mainstream and avant-garde literary theory," adding that "the notable feature, underlying all the ambivalences [of Said's work], is the anti-Marxism and the construction of a whole critical apparatus for defining a postmodern kind of anti-colonialism" (222). (Ahmad also is forthright, at the start of a longer chapter criticizing *Orientalism,* about his own motivations: "I disagree with [Said] so fundamentally on issues both of theory and of history that our respective understandings of the world . . . are simply irreconcilable" [159].)

202 Ahmad is also critical of Said for ignoring similarities between progressive Indian historians both contemporary to and after Marx; thus the essays collected in *Selected Subaltern Studies* (Guha and Spivak 1988) are particularly useful because of how they, in Spivak's phrase, "deconstruct historiography." Previous left and right histories are shown to be "cognitive failures" (Spivak 1988, 6–7), based both on epistemological error and narratological fallacies.[13] Ranajit Guha's essay on "The Prose of Counter-Insurgency" reads colonial descriptions of revolt in terms of semiotics: "To rebel was indeed to destroy many of those familiar signs which [the peasant] had learned to read and manipulate in order to extract a meaning out of the harsh world" (1988, 45). Marx's theory of Oriental despotism, however, was based primarily on the erroneous notion of absence of property.[14]

truth, error, contradictions

203 In his essay "Heidegger's Exegeses of Hölderlin" Paul de Man makes a distinction between benign "mistakes" and destructive "errors." Here, in de

13 For the cognitive versus narrative distinction, and the way that "each is used to undermine the primacy or priority of the other" in contemporary semiotics, see Jameson 1987b, xi–xiv.

14 See also Blaut (1987). Marx himself was later reluctant to elevate the Asiatic stage of modes of production to a general historical principle (Kiernan 1983, 73).

Man's classic dialectic of blindness and insight, Heidegger's empirical mis-understandings (misquotation, bad drafts of the poetry for his study, mis-readings: "Heidegger's heresies against the most elementary rules of text analysis" [de Man 1988, 250]) give rise to Heidegger's ontology. Christopher Norris believes that de Man's comment recalls Spinoza's movement, which is not *between* philosophical texts and political tracts, but instead between philosophy and politics in the same text (Norris 1991, 93–97). Thus Negri terms *A Theologico-Political Treatise* as a "savage anomaly" of radical disunities (Negri 1991b, 120: the treatise is so both because of its refoundational interruption of the *Ethics* and because of its internal conclusions); for example, in Spinoza's methodological chapter on interpretation, he remarks that "[t]he nature of God . . . Scripture nowhere teaches professedly, and as eternal doctrine. . . . Now as such teaching was only set forth by the prophets in times of oppression, and was even then never laid down as a law; and as, on the other hand, Moses (who did not write in times of oppression but—mark this—strove to found a well-ordered commonwealth) . . . ordained that an eye should be given for an eye . . . submission to injuries was only valid in places where justice was neglected, and in a time of oppression, but does not hold good in a well-ordered state" (Spinoza 1951, 104–5). Deleuze argues that there really is, for Spinoza, little difference between such apparently discrete spheres as statecraft and theology, since the immanence of God means that both are *expressions* of univocity (1990, 180–86).

204 The connection between Spinoza and de Man lies in the latter's errors (in the strong, if not moral, sense) in his wartime writings, which demonstrate again how discourse will be grounded in history.[15] As Macherey put

15 As with the de Man controversy, the Rushdie affair (affairs?) was also irritating for the disingenuousness of his defenders. Aamir Mufti (1991), for example, argues that it is bad faith for Rushdie and his supporters to be astonished that the masses demonstrating against his book have not read the novel: "A reconceptualization of reception appropriate to the realities of the postcolonial 'global ecumene' . . . must account for forms of mass 'consumption' other than 'reading' in the narrower sense of that word. Extracts published in the print media, in English and in translation, commentary in print, on the airwaves, and from the pulpit, fantasticated representation in the popular cinema, rumours and hearsay, such are the means by which the novel has achieved circulation in the Islamic world" (97). Mufti also points to the post-McLuhan (my term, not his) fascination with

it, error is overdetermined by history (1979, 79). Spinoza, anticipating de Man's errors, disavowed any real difference between metaphysics and politics. Throughout the *Ethics,* then, Spinoza frequently turns "aside from the business of argument *more geometrico* and [strikes] a more combative, polemical tone" (Norris 1991, 97). The implications are relevant to my present readings of Jameson: the molecular antagonism in his text is a Spinozist[16] injection of the transitory, the "only contemporary," into the more rigorous or theoretical.

205 These various texts' molar recourse to the political could be seen as an example of Althusserian "overdetermination." Freud maintained that a manifest symptom or dream element is determined by a variety of latent causes (both important and unimportant ones); Althusser adjusted overdetermination to mean that a specific realm (culture, or the state) reflects the material conditions of the structure in dominance (1986, 209). Bourgeois philosophy is immediately important to Althusserian Marxism—without overdetermination as a guiding concept, "[W]e will be unable to explain the following simple reality: the prodigious 'labour' of a theoretician, be it Galileo, Spinoza, or Marx . . . the elaboration of an 'obvious' theory . . . the realization in their own personal 'contingency' of the Necessity of History" (Althusser 1986, 210). These philosophies are bourgeois only "in the last instance," for to deem them merely the unmediated expression of a certain class would mean to throw out the bathwater with the baby (or vice versa).

206 The relationship between overdetermination and the molar/molecular dialectic can be seen more clearly in another of Althusser's discussions of

---

media in *The Satanic Verses* (and elsewhere in Rushdie, of course) as indications of how the novel was in some ways *about* its reception. And certainly if I and my partner, as "progressives" elect not to go see the musical *Miss Saigon* and instead scalp the tickets we were given, "believing" it is a racist play, we are acting in a similar way. That said, it is also necessary, because of the institutions in which Rushdie's discourse receives a wide degree of so-called support (*The New York Times, The London Review of Books*) that such a rhetoric of disbelief be adopted; the question then is, how does such a liberal-democratic rhetoric and politics depend on a demonization of the Islamic masses?

16 Norris uses the term "Spinozist" to refer not merely to thinkers who engage with Spinoza (Deleuze, Macherey), but to methodological tendencies in Spinoza and to modern controversies that seem to be anticipated by problems Spinoza dealt with.

overdetermination, where he refers to Mao Ze-dong on antagonistic and nonantagonistic contradictions (1986, 101n).[17] Mao's dichotomy guides the Negri formulation I base my own figural reading of Jameson on in this chapter in that, for Mao, antagonistic contradictions (which require a violent or revolutionary resolution) and nonantagonistic contradictions are not essences but shifting positions. Similarly, Mao was to write twenty years later that "contradictions between ourselves and our enemies are antagonistic ones. Within the ranks of the people, contradictions among the working peoples are nonantagonistic" (1970, 231). The value of Mao's analysis lies in its combination of a subtle formalism and a grounded or situated politics.

207 Mao's pragmatism entailed a flexible politics, and he was concerned to show that the identity of a class was not fixed: "The term 'the people' has different meanings in different countries, and in different historical periods in each country" (1970, 229). These *formal* antagonisms present in a concept ("different meanings") were buried when critical attention was directed toward "deconstructing" Marxism. Ernesto Laclau and Chantal Mouffe, in their groundbreaking work of "post-Marxism," *Hegemony and Socialist Strategy*, are primarily concerned with resurrecting a Tocquevillean (or Lefortian[18]) notion of "democracy" with the aid of a poststructuralist Gramsci. "Only in the enumerative practices of the popular fronts period does the 'people,'" they write, "re-emerge, timidly at first, in the field of Marxist discursivity," but "the concept of 'class alliance' is . . . inadequate to characterize a hegemonic relation" (1987, 64). Like Bennington's discourse, Laclau and Mouffe's situates itself in opposition to "alliances" per se, which function as a red flag of totality in the (Laclau-Mouffe) discursive-field.

17 John Beverley applies the same Maoist distinction to the testimonial documents of Latin American people; nonantagonistic contradictions "best captures . . . the nature of the relations between narrator, interlocutor-compiler, and reader in the testimonio" (1993, 81).

18 Claude Lefort, theorist of democracy as "empty chair of power," as Žižek put it (1991a, 267–70), holds the radical conception that "democracy is instituted and sustained by the *dissolution of the markers of certainty*. It inaugurates a history in which people experience a fundamental indeterminacy as to the basis of power, law and knowledge, and as to the basis of relations between *self* and *other*, at every level of social life" (Lefort 1988, 19).

They do make the following curious statement, however: "Mao's analyses of contradiction—despite their near-to-zero philosophical value—do have the great merit of presenting the terrain of social struggles as a proliferation of contradiction" (64); evidently what we have here is a non- or pre-Spinozist conception of the philosophical or political as mutually exclusive monoliths. 208 Nevertheless, Mao's theory offers a subtle formulation for considering the molar/molecular play at work in *The Political Unconscious:* the dialectic or contradiction between molecular and molar is an antagonistic contradiction at one level of discourse—a unitary or homogeneous model of text. But viewed in another historical light, the dialectic is a nonantagonistic alliance, within the totality of Jameson's book and its function as Marxist theory. 209 Bringing an antiquated theorist like Mao into this discussion—was he a tyrant? a philosopher? a writer? it is a mark of how Mao has not yet been "postmodernized" that we do not possess a category for this "faulty"[19] thinker—may seem both vulgar and naive. As Jameson remarks of Maoism in "Periodizing the 60s," theories "are often liberated on their own terms when they are thus radically disjoined from the practical interests of state power" (*IT,* 2:189). Referring to the so-called excesses of Western Maoism, Jameson warns that campaigns to discredit Maoism, either on a worldwide scale or as a Western political agenda, were mostly part of the Reagan-era attack on the 1960s and their concomitant heady hopes (Utopianism) and mass demonstrations (see also Fields 1985; Elliott 1987, 260–74). The taint or "Stalinization" of Maoism as state ideology in China proper, then, is susceptible to the same "defenses" offered up in the name of Marxism at the beginning of this work. Commenting on the place of Jameson's work, and poststructuralism, in an analysis of theory and power, McCaffery com-

---

19 I use the term in Macherey's sense; he sees Verne's novels as *en défaut* by dint of their ideological nature (1989, 159–239). Mao and other "proper names" of Marxism are still ideological: "To say, then, that the Marxism of Lenin, or of Che, or of Althusser, or of Brecht (or indeed of Perry Anderson, or of Eagleton, not to speak of myself) is *ideological* now simply means, in the critical sense of the term, that each one is situation-specific to the point of encompassing class determinations and cultural and national horizons in its proponents" (*LM,* 6). Althusser is equally adamant that there is not a clarity obtainable outside of ideology, even in a postrevolutionary society (1965, 30–31). (But see, also, my discussion of the logical impossibility of labeling Marxism as ideological, in chapter 4.)

ments: "The effectiveness of theory's application is totally dependent on the hierarchical placement of the theoreticians in the dominant ideological apparatus. Where theory radiates from a position of power then its application is simple and efficient" (1992, 18). Mao's contradictory politics and Jameson's antagonistic text, viewed together, disallow such an efficient practice.

dialogic marxism

210 To return to Jameson's molar excursion on despotism: that is itself accomplished in yet another molecular moment, when Jameson, typically, both in "local" footnotes and in the main text, comments briefly on the (then nascent) "post-Marxist"[20] critiques of Asiatic modes of production (*PU,* 295–96). After this digression, Jameson proposes one of his major heuristic points: "[A] Marxist negative hermeneutic, a Marxist practice of ideological analysis proper, must in the practical work of reading and interpretation be exercised *simultaneously* with a Marxist positive hermeneutic, or a decipherment of the Utopian impulses of these same still ideological cultural texts" (*PU,* 296). Jameson's great metacommentary here twins a hermeneutics of suspicion with a positive project—and thus the garden-variety deconstruction contemporary to the moment of *The Political Unconscious* (shown most strongly by Bennington)[21] fails precisely because it remains satisfied with a

20 The early sense of the word "post-Marxist" is perhaps stronger than its present-day one. That is, Hindess and Hirst (and such French critics as Jacques Rancière) have made a definite break with all concepts of Marxist thought, whereas arguably what is now known as post-Marxism—the theories of Laclau and Mouffe—bears the same relation to Marxism that postmodernism or poststructuralism do to their antecedents. I mean to suggest less a total break than a (Serres-esque) parasitic or (Wittgensteinian) familial—generational—relationship.

21 If the shrunken dwarf or toad in that garden is for most readers (including this one!) Paul de Man, then Susan Wells's (1985, 1–19) excursus on de Man and Jameson remains exemplary; notably the following faux conclusions: "What is needed, I think, is an understanding of these relations that is dialectical in two senses: in seeing the deep relationship of interdependence between reading and reference, and in opening its own presuppositions to critical reflection" (17). That Jameson's reading of de Man in *Postmod-*

negative hermeneutic. In this sense Jameson's metacommentary functions as a proleptic critique of the strong deconstructions of his own text. But this also means that it is a mistake to think that Jameson's molecular discourse mentioned above—the sidebar on post-Marxism—is simply an attack on post-Marxism.

211 Jameson is as much dialogic in his harnessing of varying Marxist traditions—proper names—as in his uses of bourgeois theorists like Northrop Frye or Norman Holland. The danger in eclecticism, as any Hegelian knows, is that one is simultaneously too eclectic and not eclectic enough. Samuel Weber lays the former charge, while the latter, in respect to post-Marxism, is made by Bennington. Jameson deals briefly with the Marxist and post-Marxist debate, but this very tendency to summarize quickly theories and debates has left him open to attack by those who would rather their theological turf were left alone: "An even more disturbing 'blindness' or short-circuit undermines Jameson's claim of having assimilated the lessons of deconstruction into his totalized historical methodology. One has a choice, it seems to me, of either accepting the rules of the deconstructionist's game—the premise or ground rule that no totalized solution may offer an access to Truth—or of rejecting that premise, and refusing to engage in that particular game. But to claim to have selected out elements of the deconstructionist position—which is, in the final analysis, a refutation of the validity of totalization—to be recuperated back into a total system, is, it seems to me, to be guilty of a kind of misdiagnosis or critical malpractice which must prejudice one's analysis" (Flieger 1982, 54).

212 Jameson reins in his own discourse[22] and remarks that "we have perhaps

---

ernism (217–59) should reveal the proto-Althusserian mixed with the historicist in the Belgian waffler (after a—for Jameson—uncharacteristically hilarious set piece on primitive hominid Adorno trying to theorize instrumentality amid cave-persons straight out of *One Million Years B.C.*, which then leads to Rousseau's "they might be giants" philosophizing) only foregrounds, I think, the deep or ultimate triumph of theory itself as class alliance above and beyond the so-called "merely" political.

22 The notion that such molecular moments have to be curbed or reined-in is a suspiciously metaphysical one: Julian Symons, commenting in his introduction to *The Revenge for Love* on Wyndham Lewis's writings after *The Apes of God*, says: "[H]e provided a plot, and modified the texture of his prose to make it more easily readable" (Lewis 1983,

said enough to show that the *problem* of the symbolic enactment of collective unity is inscribed in that problematic by Marx himself at this point, whatever solution may ultimately be devised for it" (*PU,* 296). This is Foucault's notion that figures like Marx and Freud are "initiators of discourse";[23] Jameson also notes in a footnote that, if Barry Hindess and Paul Hirst declare a problematic of "forms of ritual and social cohesion . . . has nothing whatever to do with Marxism" (Hindess and Hirst 1975, 55; qtd. *PU,* 296n), then he "is tempted to add: in that case, too bad for Marxism!"

213   Bennington argues that the Jameson-text here deconstructs itself by admitting the failure of Marxism when faced with its post-Marxist critiques: "I shall not attempt to analyze the gestures of inclusion and exclusion going on in [Jameson's] text, although such a rhetorical analysis would of course be necessary if we were here concerned to reinscribe the problems of the body, the corpus and so on. But it may well be that the implications of the work of Hindess and Hirst are indeed 'too bad for Marxism,' or at least for the type of

---

xi). Jameson has compared Lewis's writing to a "sentence-producing mechanism" (*FA,* 35): to be sure, Symons's characterization sounds as though he were describing a new model of car with luxury options like plot and a more readable texture!

23   Foucault's essay "What Is an Author?" (1984) is the canonical forum for this notion, but note that Foucault is careful to say that these "founders of discursivity . . . have established an endless possibility of discourse" (114). Jameson's deathless repetition of "*problem* . . . problematic" in his passage just cited poses another, well, "problem" (sorry; among the innumerable Jamesonian stylistic patches [in this case, that I have been censured for enough to remove] of my own writing has been precisely this repetition—the one that I most recently edited out was "proposes . . . proposition"); that is, first, what is the relation between a "problem" and a "problematic," and what is the Jameson-text doing here (regardless, say, of whether the "tic" is conscious or not)? Quickly, then, a "problem" would seem to be a local or tactical issue—in the idiolect of my book, it is "molecular," whereas a "problematic" is more likely a global or strategic issue—again, the "molar." And as my jocular "deathless" hinted at, Jameson's text in its repetition of the Marxemes/ signifiers instantiates the death drive of classic Freudian or Lacanian symptom-formation (a blot or stain, then, to update to Slovenia). As becomes evident in the ensuing debate, Bennington, in his take on the passage and its repetition, focuses on (fetishizes) Jameson as an authoritarian (totality = totalitarianism) critic out to purify some "Marxist problematic" (a.k.a. Lyotardian "whole body": see below) and thus ignores the prevalent dialogism of Jameson's simultaneity of Marxism. 'Nuff said, needless to say!

Hegelian Marxism here defended by Jameson" (1982, 31).[24] Jameson, Bennington has just noted, "sidesteps [post-Marxism's] attempt to expunge the concept from Marxism by insisting that 'the *problem* of the symbolic enactment of collective unity is inscribed in that problematic by Marx himself at this point, whatever solution may ultimately be devised for it.' " This means that the location of an origin of the problematic with Marx is suspect: " 'Marx himself': another [Lyotardian] 'whole body'? Does Marx's own inscription of the Asiatic mode necessarily situate it as a problem in the problematic? What would be the status of a Marxist's expulsion of Marx's 'own' problem from that problematic?" (Bennington 1982, 31).

214 Bennington interprets Jameson's argument with post-Marxism only in a negative manner. But deconstruction's fatalism is instructive: it would seem that Marxism is doomed to create the problem-children that will disown it. Here Bennington, a non-Marxist, dictates the concerns of Marxist theory. Bennington wants to see Marxism itself fail: as he writes, if, according to Hindess and Hirst, "the mode of production is no longer a coherent concept, then all the other mainstays of Jameson's 'untranscendable horizon,' which he calls Marxism, are equally undermined" (32). Bennington's bad faith here manifests itself in his necessary blindness to Jameson's utopianism: while Jameson allows that the problem "of the symbolic enactment of collective unity" originates with Marx, he does not dictate a solution. (I suspect that, given his aversion for any sort of collective unity or alliance, Bennington can see "utopia" only as a delusion.)

215 Furthermore, Bennington gets it exactly wrong in his comments on the "too bad for Marxism" footnote. In part, this is because he wants to show how really "bad for Marxism" is the post-Marxism of Hindess and Hirst; but Jameson is saying that it is too bad for Marxism *if it cannot accommodate a Durkheimian problematic.* Jameson criticizes Hindess and Hirst because, in *Pre-Capitalist Modes of Production,* they exclude forms of ritual and social cohesion. Here, Jameson's comment, "too bad for Marxism," means that Marxism should be more open to alien bodies of thought (i.e., less of a Lyotardian "whole body"—perhaps more of a Deleuze and Guattarian "Body

24 But see the discussion of Žižek on authority, above, and his chapter "Much Ado about a Thing" (1991a, 229–71).

Without Organs"—see the discussion of Frye, below). The molecular antagonisms in Jameson's text turn back onto the molar arguments and contexts,
and prove to be too difficult even for Bennington's recondite analysis.

216 My point is less to "defend" Jameson's text, or Marxism, against either
post-Marxism or deconstruction, than to argue that, in some important
ways, the machinery of *The Political Unconscious* anticipates the arguments
posed by deconstructive critics, who see in Marxism a straw figure of ironclad totality.[25] That is, *The Political Unconscious* posits an open, eclectic, or
dialogic Marxism. Bennington is too busy looking for some gap or fissure in
the text where he can insert his deconstructive crowbar.[26]

a return to althusser

217 As noted above, the ease with which Jameson enlists various traditions of
Marxism—notably the Hegelian and structuralist ones—can be disconcert-

25 In a recent and fascinating article on the Frankfurt School and Disney, Miriam
Hansen (1993) uses the wonderful phrase "the iron bath of fun" (34), which I think she
gets from *Dialectic of Enlightenment* (viz., "Amusement under late capitalism is the pro-
longation of work"—Horkheimer and Adorno 1972, 137). Marxism, then, for the post-
Marxist or libidinal philosopher is the ice bath(water) of rule, a theory implicated in a
society of psychiatrization.

26 In a review of *Late Marxism,* Michael Rothberg makes a number of points similar to
my claims. Most importantly, he argues that Jameson's use of Adorno's "baby and bathwater" aphorism from *Minima Moralia* teaches us that to overestimate sheer difference
(and discount totality or base-superstructure causality) is a poststructuralist mistake that
would discard the important insights and strategies of Marxism, a "totalizing critique,
which [post-Marxists] equate, through a kind of poetic license, with a totalitarian politics"
(1992, 116). Pertinent to this question of "strategies" is Wells's assertion in *The Dialectics
of Representation* (1985) that "[f]or Jameson, however, totality is a *strategic* rather than a
transcendent concept. It is a mark of a systemic attempt to objectify the world, and to
establish the boundaries of a system's coherence, simultaneously marking them as boundaries and warning the reader to test the truth of the relations that hold within them" (11).
But here I would like to mark the exhaustion of the "tactics" versus "strategy" binary (I
used to play an American wargame called "Strategy and Tactics" in the 1970s). Whether it
is Clausewitz or Gramsci, Marxist gun-envy (in Lisa Frank's phrase) and military metaphors have led to a reified usage of the "Is this a tactical meaning? In which case, what is
your strategy?" variety.

ing, or at least once the reader realizes that they are different traditions. To
see how wide the gap has become between different forms of Marxism, see
how Gregory Elliott, in *Althusser: The Detour of Theory*, recounts the attacks
on French humanist Marxism initiated by Althusser in the early 1960s: "In
order to escape Hegel and rescue Marxism from the discredit into which it
was apparently falling by its association with him, Althusser carried out an
adroit philosophical reversal of alliances. Perceiving a convergence between
the astringent anti-humanism of structuralism and his own Marxist positions, Althusser informed the Italian Communist newspaper *Rinascita* in
1964 that Lévi-Strauss was more of an immediate ally of historical materialism than Sartre" (1987, 62).

218 Althusser's broadside, coming shortly after Lévi-Strauss and Sartre's
battles over dialectics and materialism, is unequivocal.[27] It demonstrates
antagonisms inherent to Marxism itself and supports my contention that
Jameson's enlisting of the various discourses and problematics into one project (or even into a series of projects) is dialogic in an important sense. The
Adornoesque estrangement of the classical music concert at the beginning
of *Marxism and Form* is an object-lesson here, and my more modest ambi-
tion is to show how Jameson uses various Marxist traditions. One possible
objection to my present estrangement could point out that the genealogy of
Althusserian Marxism is hardly relevant to the North American academy, or
even to understanding Jameson's argument.[28] But the role of Hegel in Althusser's thought articulates the displacement of theory into a social discourse that is the specialty of the Jamesonian molecular text. The first chapter of *The Political Unconscious* analyzes the relationship between cultural
products and their social history; there Jameson attempts to move beyond
"the vulgar Marxist theory of levels" (*PU*, 32) or base and superstructure.
For the necessary first step in this "polemic program" (21), the "enterprise
of constructing a properly Marxist hermeneutic" (23) deals with the con-

27 See Sartre's *Critique*, and Lévi-Strauss's response to Sartre in *The Savage Mind*
(1966, 245–61).

28 Jameson makes precisely this point in his discussion of the "subject" in his essay on
Lacan (*IT* 1:109). As I pointed out in a previous chapter, it is now possible to speak of a
return "of" Althusser and French Marxism in a way that was scarcely thinkable during the
early 1980s.

temporary poststructuralist critique of hermeneutics and interpretation, encapsulated in Althusser's notion of structural causality.

219 In *Reading Capital,* Althusser posits structural causality as a break with both mechanistic causality (Cartesian billiard balls) and Hegel's expressive causality (expressive of some inner essence). Jameson argues, however, that both earlier forms of causality, often thought to be dead in the postmodern universe of surface and quotation, possess a "purely local validity in cultural analysis" (*PU,* 25). Referring specifically to expressivity, he adds that "to switch it off at the source entails the virtual repression of the text of history and the political unconscious in our own cultural and practical experience, just at the moment when increasing privatization has made that dimension so faint as to be virtually inaudible" (34).

220 Jameson then explains the difference in Althusser's theory between economic determinism (the strong form in which Hegelian expressive causality finds itself in orthodox Marxism) and the relative autonomy, or "semi-autonomy," of various levels in the Althusserian structure:[29] "The insistence on the 'semi-autonomy' of these various levels—which can so easily strike the unwary as a scholastic quibble, but which we have now been able to grasp as the correlative of the attack on Hegelian expressive causality in which all these levels are somehow 'the same' and so many expressions and modulations of one another—may now be understood as a coded battle waged within the framework of the French Communist party [PCF] against Stalinism. As paradoxical as it may seem, therefore, 'Hegel' here is a secret code word for Stalin (just as in Lukács's work, 'naturalism' is a code word for 'socialist realism')" (*PU,* 37). Here, then, Jameson typically insists on reading the text of the internecine battles of French Marxism as allegories for historical struggles, even if his analysis uses the same police or espionage vocabulary of "codes" that bedevils so much contemporary literary theory.[30]

---

29 Althusser wrote of "the poor man's Hegelianism, the evolutionism which has . . . taken the form of economism" (1976, 186; qtd. Elliott 1987, 142). The levels being modes of production, culture, ideology, the judicial, the political, the economic, relations of production (classes), and forces of production (technology, population, the environment) (*PU,* 32–37).

30 Jameson hints at the problematic of "code-shifting" in semiotics, or the embrace of information theory (*IT,* 1:26–27) but, as his example in those pages from Barthes's semi-

221 Elliott concurs with Jameson's allegory: "[T]he Marxist-Leninist version of historical materialism secreted a Hegelianism—[in Althusser's phrase] 'the rich man's evolutionism'—that dared not speak its name: economism. Behind Stalin, paradoxically, stood Hegel. So any critique of Hegelianism and Second International orthodoxy was simultaneously—albeit cautiously—directed against theoretical Stalinism and its spectres" (1987, 143–44). Elliott earlier notes that Althusser's great productions of 1965–66 were dominated by the Twentieth Congress of the Communist Party of the Soviet Union and the Sino-Soviet split (16).[31]

222 Jameson's comments on decoding Althusser (*PU*, 37) are another molecular antagonism, a leap into willfully dry, it seems, debates having to do with Stalin and superstructure; the passage may appear reminiscent or repetitive. And his warning that the debates may "strike the unwary as a scholastic quibble" recalls the earlier footnote, which admitted that the discussion of Althusser and causality "will inevitably strike certain readers as scholastic exercises within the philosophically alien tradition of Marxism" (*PU*, 23n8). The entire and heuristic device of determining that "Hegel" is a code word recalls yet another footnote, where Althusser's "polemic against 'historicism' is part of the more general Althusserian offensive within the PCF against Stalinism, and involves very real practical, political, and strategic consequences" (*PU*, 27n). His molecular nexus (or rhizome), then, both antagonizes the linear hegemony of Jameson's text and brings into an alliance (totalizes) the disparate commentaries being constructed.[32] It also recalls formally the place that Althusser's theorizing had in a historical situation: if Spinoza had to encode his deliberations within the language of

---

nal essay on James Bond suggests, surely the detective analogon is much more pertinent to the literary theorist's self-conception (see also Rée 1985, 337)?

31   This can be adjudged more directly in Althusser's memoir, *The Future Lasts Forever* (1993); see also Elliott's excellent summary, "Analysis Terminated, Analysis Interminable: The Case of Louis Althusser" (Elliott 1994c).

32   As Jameson notes, the "negative and methodological status of the concept of 'totality' may also be shown at work in those very post-structural philosophies which explicitly repudiate such 'totalizations' in the name of difference, flux, dissemination, and heterogeneity" (*PU*, 53).

theology (Norris 1991, 45–49), Althusser no less had to encode his within the language of idealist philosophy.[33]

223 Examining Althusser's theory "out of this encoding," free of the mundane or boring matters of PCF internal politics, is sternly forbidden. "More plausible," as Norris remarks on Spinoza, "is the reading that interprets such language *on both levels simultaneously*" (1991, 47). Jameson therefore argues that Althusser's work "addresses two distinct publics at once" (*PU*, 32). So the "problem" of a code is misleading, or at least this "false problem" has only become a problem with the passage of history (and because Althusser's work, like most "French theory," is subject to wild redescriptions in its translation outside metropolitan France). Certainly Althusserianism can be characterized as an attempt to break Marxism out of its Hegelian mold: this is the important lesson to be learned by Jameson's citation of a long passage from *Reading Marx* (*PU*, 23–25).

224 In part, the counter-hegemonic interpretation of Marx begun by Althusser realigns Marx with Spinoza. Althusser's concept of how structure overdetermines depends on Spinoza's absent cause. "The only theoretician who had the unprecedented daring to pose" the problem of structural causality, Althusser writes, "and outline a first solution to it was Spinoza" (Althusser and Balibar 1979, 187). The absent cause in the structure, Jameson makes clear, is history itself—and thus it is easier to see how attention to one level of interpretation (of Althusser in this case, i.e., reading him solely as a philosopher) will wander to another level. Or: the antagonism between the molecular and molar is also an alliance. With history as absent cause (and

---

33 In terms of my phrase "historical situation," recall Jameson's comment in *Late Marxism* that Sartre's version or vocabulary-shift of base and superstructure was "situation" and "choice" (46)—as, brutally Sartre reminds us in the conclusion to *Saint Genet* (1963): "What is noteworthy . . . is the vacillation of the self that occurs in us when certain minds open before our eyes like yawning chasms: what we considered to be our innermost being suddenly seems to us to be a fabricated appearance; it seems to us that we have escaped only by an incredible stroke of luck from the vices that repel us most in others; we recognize, with horror, a *subject*" (633). If, as is argued in Marc Huestis's documentary *Sex Is . . .* (1993), the queer eroticization of safer sex in the late 1980s was effectively an instance of queers becoming the subjects of their (out) history, then surely the "horror" with which this is greeted in the straight community is a similar, Sartrean reaction.

Hegel in a temporary trashcan),[34] the historical contingencies of Althusser's theory, the ways in which it is overdetermined at every point, are once again evident.

overdetermination explained, once and for all

225 Althusser's concept of overdetermination functions as a master-code for *The Political Unconscious:* it both explains the variety of methodologies Jameson brings together and functions as the "last instance" of how the absent cause of history will affect cultural products. Jameson proposes an alliance of two fairly antagonistic interpretive schemes in his first chapter: patristic hermeneutics re-conceived as a Lukácsean "expression" of history, and the structuralist project seen as the "imaginary resolution of real contradictions" on a formal level.

226 Althusser provides the clearest demonstrations or definitions of over-determination in two essays: "Contradiction and Overdetermination" and "On the Materialist Dialectic," both in *For Marx.* In the first essay he presents as a starting point Lenin's theory of the "weakest link": Russia was the first state to fall to communism because it was the weakest link in the chain of imperialist nations, being both primitive and advanced at the same time (vestigial serfdom and Petersburg Symbolism). What this means is that a ruptural event can be caused not by some primary contradiction, but by the structure of relations. The figure is structuralist in the sense that Saussurean linguistics will say that a signifier "means" not because of the signified but because of its place in a structure of difference. The " 'contradiction' is inseparable from its formal *conditions* of existence," Althusser writes, "and even from the *instances* it governs; it is radically *affected by them,* determining, but also determined in one and the same movement, and determined by the various *levels* and *instances* of the social formations it animates; it might be called *overdetermined in its principle*" (1986, 101). So the structure itself determines, through its networks of phenomena, the catalog of effects.

34 The model I am thinking of is the "trash can" icon to be found in Macintosh computer GUI's (graphic user interfaces), where a "file" can be dumped into the trash but is not "lost" (its address on the hard disk erased, that is) until the trash is "emptied."

227 The term "overdetermination," as noted earlier, Althusser took from Freud (Althusser 1986, 206n) in an attempt to create a new, non-Hegelian dialectic: "[W]ithin the reality of the conditions of existence of each contradiction, it is the manifestation of the structure in dominance that unifies the whole" (206).[35] In this dialectic of antagonism and alliance the various levels are semiautonomous, but the structure in dominance unifies the whole. Elliott comments, "Althusser's preservation of the base/superstructure topography (determination in the last instance by the *economic*) is thus conjoined with a reconceptualization of the conformation of social formations: the political and ideological levels enjoy relative autonomy, but not independence (determination in the *last instance*)" (1987, 154). What this "last instance" means is much debated, but Althusser is quite unambiguous at one point: "From the first moment to the last, the lonely hour of the 'last instance' never comes" (1986, 113).

228 The totality promulgated by overdetermination is exceedingly heterogenous, but it is still a unity: "This complexity implies domination as one of its essentials: it is inscribed in its structure" (Althusser 1986, 201). Still, Jameson insists not only on the "local sectoral validity" of a Marxist allegorical hermeneutic, but also on its fairly equal status with a more postmodern structuralist methodology based on Propp and Lévi-Strauss.

229 The role or value of these two approaches—totality and structure—lies precisely in their relationship: that is, neither is able to deal sufficiently with cultural productions in a way that is both up-to-date and Marxist. An allegorical interpretation is finally neo-Romantic, postmodernized Lukács; structural interpretation is overly anti-subjective, beholden to the prisonhouse of signification. A more recent attempt to align or bring into alliance Hegelian dialectics and structuralism provides some help in this regard. Žižek, in *For They Know Not What They Do*, a set of lectures on Hegel and Lacan, is engaged in a project analogous to Jameson's. Žižek is determined to show that Hegel, postmodernized, is a structuralist *avant la lettre*. Identity already means difference; a common label applied to the Canadian city of

---

35 Freudian and Lacanian usages of the word "overdetermination" are to be found in the authoritative J. Laplanche and J. B. Pontalis work, *The Language of Psychoanalysis* (1973, 292–93).

Victoria, for instance, is that it is "more British than the British." This means not so much that the category or notion of the "British" may already be lacking, but that Victoria itself is lacking (it is too prettified, artificial, or tourist-oriented): "The lack of identity which impels movement in judgement of the Notion is thus not the lack of identity between the Notion and its realization, but extends to the fact that the Notion can never correspond to itself, be adequate to itself" (Žižek 1991a, 133).[36]

230 Žižek also locates a Hegelian structuralism around the issue of over-determination. The category is not anti-Hegelian, he notes, because it "designates precisely this inherently Hegelian paradox of a *totality which always comprises a particular element embodying its universal structuring principle*" (45). Totality (in Žižek's vernacular, "the Universal") is implied in the particulars but not now in an expressive sense, nor even in a metonymic way that reduces the individual pieces of the pie to mere representatives of the whole. In this sense, allegorical and structuralist interpretations are valid not because they express the anomie of modern critical folkways, but because in their relation with each other, in the verbal structure of *The Political Unconscious* as a whole, they are cogent and heuristic.

231 Jameson does not hesitate to show why the allegorical hermeneutic is still valid: "[T]he system of four levels or senses is particularly suggestive in the solution it provides for an interpretive dilemma which in a privatized world we must live far more intensely than did its Alexandrian and medieval recipients: namely that incommensurability referred to above between the private and the public, the psychological and the social, the poetic and the political" (*PU*, 31). Jameson retrofits the Christian hermeneutic for political criticism. Jameson's attitude toward Christianity is best summed up in *Marxism and Form,* where he counters the argument that Marxism is a kind of religion with the assertion that, on the contrary, religions are forms of Marxism (*M&F,* 117). Jameson appropriates for materialism the patristic hermeneutic, a way of reading the Bible as a four-level text—the literal, allegorical,

---

36 Henry Abelove makes a similar point in a Marxist Literary Group talk. There he located the origin of the "identity" in "identity politics" in Eriksonian psychology, noting the always already differential status of "identity." Of course, today "identity politics" is often the Stalinism of our time, in the sense of a bogeyman for both the left and the right.

moral, and anagogical. For example, the "literal" bondage of the Israelites in Egypt is allegorized first as proleptic figure for the sufferings of Christ, then as a moral lesson for the Christian reading, and finally as an anagogical text for the history of the Christian world and the coming Last Judgement.

shrunken dwarfs, expanded

232   The problem that Jameson then tackles is how these levels of interpretation are to be connected, since, having assimilated the lessons of Althusser, pure expressivity is no longer an option. His answer for this mediation lies in the neologism "transcoding," which is the operation whereby "the same terminology can be used to analyze and articulate two quite distinct types of objects or 'texts,' or two very different structural levels of reality" (*PU*, 40). This heuristic method is the cornerstone to the architecture of Jameson's technique (or perhaps, to postmodernize the metaphor, the gift shop of his Frank Gehry-designed hotel of techniques).

233   Transcoding offers a similarity between two or more different levels (which have been separated in an Althusserian method only because they *are* related) that is figural; but that allegorization is then negated by the realization that the world is one totality or whole. (Slightly later in *The Political Unconscious*, Jameson quotes from Sartre's *The Reprieve*, "in which totality is affirmed in the very movement whereby it is denied, and represented in the same language that denies it all possible representation" [*PU*, 55]; this stands for this particular dialectic of the part and the whole.)

234   Transcoding, for Jameson, is as much an affirmation of difference as it is an interpretive tool, and here Althusser's prior highlighting of the concept is pertinent (he "regarded multiplicity, difference, as primordial" [Callinicos 1985, 90]).[37] In *Reading Capital,* the French Marxist stressed that a "*plurality* of instances must be an essential property of every social structure . . . the problem of the science of society must be precisely the problem of *the*

37   Elliott comments on this and also remarks that "in an unpublished text dating from c. 1970, Althusser suggested that the two (commendable) concepts dominating Mao's writings are '*difference*' and '*unevenness*'" (Elliott 1987, 153n. 144).

forms of variation of their articulation" (1979, 207). This problem of "artic-ulation," no less important to the post-Marxist work of Laclau and Mouffe (1987, 105–14), where it is also grafted onto or supplemented by the more Lacanian notion of "suture" (47–48, 88n. 1),[38] is fundamental to Jameson's transcoding. The various levels of a text and its history, interpreted in such a way that permits them to articulate and to be articulated, means that the critic "can restore, at least methodologically, the lost unity of social life . . . [while doing] justice to the autonomy or semi-autonomy of aesthetic lan-guage" (*PU,* 226).

235 "Articulation" is evidently a pun: it means both linkage (in the sense of articulated joints or lorries) and speech. That first meaning then can break down into both connection and separation: two limbs are both joined and separated by cartilage; two truck-trailers are joined. Transcoding searches out that point of mediation or joining—the gristle that connects even while it separates—and the transcoding operation is performative.

236 The difficulties inherent in transcoding come to the fore in the extended discussion of the most important mediatory code in *The Political Uncon-scious,* "reification." Jameson writes: "To read Conrad's 'will to style' as a socially symbolic act involves the practice of *mediation,* an operation that we have already characterized (in Chapter 1) as the invention of an analytic terminology or code which can be applied to two or more structurally dis-tinct objects or sectors of being. As we there argued, it is not necessary that these analyses be homogeneous, that is, that each of the objects in question be seen as doing the same thing, having the same structure or emitting the same message. . . . In the present case, this means the invention of a descrip-tion of Conrad's stylistic practice (and of that of impressionist painting) which is adequate in its own terms . . . but which at the same time, by articulating the description of a quite different type of reality—in the event, the organization and experience of daily life during the imperialist heyday of industrial capitalism—allows us to think these two distinct realities together in a meaningful way. . . . It has no doubt already become clear to the reader

38 See also, for a commentary on both articulation and suture, Barrett 1991, 65–68. The idea of "suture," and its more modernist precursor in Adorno's idea of the "scar," is discussed in the following chapter.

that the mediatory code I have found most useful here is that variously termed rationalization by Weber and reification by Lukács. Yet the reader should also be reminded that Marxism knows a number of other such mediatory codes, the most obvious ones being social class, mode of production, the alienation of labor, commodification, the various ideologies of Otherness (sex or race), and political domination. The strategic selection of reification as a code for the reading and interpretation of Conrad's style does not constitute the choice of one kind of Marxism (let us say, a Lukácsean one) over others. . . . This said, it remains to show how the language of reification and rationalization, whose applicability to the increasing standardization of capitalist daily life has already been argued, can be useful for an account of style, either literary or pictorial" (225–26).

237 A number of problematics are signaled in the passage above. Jameson historicizes impressionism, arguing that the aesthetic style is simultaneously ideological and utopian. Vision, then, is a sense now seen as a grossly over-developed one[39] (like the Fatboys of *Lord Jim:* the German captain and Doramin). If the narrator of *The Black Sheep* anticipated "a fine array of names" to be a characteristic of science in the twentieth century (Balzac 1970, 29), then this proto-Rortyan comment is borne out in the metalinguistic tendencies of the passage—Jameson's strategy of inventing "an analytic terminology or code." Reading *Lord Jim* as a "socially symbolic act," in the Lévi-Straussian sense of an "imaginary resolution of real contradiction" itself is a socially symbolic act. For, in his discussion of Lévi-Strauss, in the first chapter of *The Political Unconscious,* Jameson argues that "to specify this

---

39 As Arthur Kroker notes, "McLuhan always accorded [Georges] Seurat a privileged position as the 'art fulcrum between Renaissance visual and modern tactile. The coalescing of inner and outer, subject and object.' McLuhan was drawn to Seurat in making painting a 'light source' (a 'light through situation'). Seurat did that which was most difficult and decisive: he switched the viewer into the 'vanishing point' of the painting. Or as McLuhan said, and in prophetic terms, Seurat (this 'precursor of TV') presented us with a searing visual image of the age of the 'anxious object'" (1985, 58). McLuhan was the great technologist, perceiving in that mode a liberal engine of modern society, and thus he focuses on the technique of the painting as technique, and not as expression of history in the way Jameson does (see also Jameson's discussion of the brush stroke, 1979b).

individual text as a symbolic act is already fundamentally to transform the categories with which traditional *explication de texte* (whether narrative or poetic) operated and largely still operates" (77).

238 Deconstruction, as practiced by such avatars as Paul de Man or J. Hillis Miller, has not deviated significantly from the earlier New Criticism in this *historicized* respect (as Frank Lentricchia [1980] and Terry Eagleton [1987] have argued). That is, the semiotics of rhetoric proposed by de Man in *Allegories of Reading* reaffirms the text as a site of an authorized undoing (instead of New Critical iconicity). Lentricchia charges that "de Man's rhetoric projects the image of the philosophical realist, in full possession of the knowledge of being" (1980, 294), and Eagleton adds that de Man does not acknowledge the "ideological character of an irony which gazes contemplatively at the whole authentic scene" (1987, 100). In the semiotics of ethics practiced more recently by Miller, "[i]t is impossible to get outside the limits of language by means of language. Everything we reach that seems outside language, for example sensation and perception, turns out to be more language. . . . Such is the rigour of Paul de Man's affirmation of an ethics of reading. It imposes on the reader the 'impossible' task of reading unreadability, but that does not by any means mean that reading, even 'good' reading, cannot take place and does not have a necessary ethical dimension" (Miller 1987, 59). This may seem to constitute a deconstruction of politics, as has been claimed (Readings 1989), but Miller's slip from *reference* (i.e., getting "outside language") to *ethics* merely returns reading to the individual (if ironized) subject.

239 Jameson renders Lévi-Strauss's analysis of Caduveo body art (from "The Structural Study of Myth," [Lévi-Strauss 1967]) into a dialectical movement. For Lévi-Strauss, the art resolves societal contradictions *formally:* he is not interested in the designs themselves, but in their structural role, which is to compensate for a lack in the Caduveo's social organization. Jameson argues that these findings, applied to cultural productions in general, mean ideology is not then merely the "content" of the form, but rather that the "production of aesthetic or narrative form is to be seen as an ideological act in its own right, with the function of inventing imaginary or formal 'solutions' to unresolvable social contradictions" (79).

240 The transcoding operation, which determines a mediatory code in the

hopes of articulating how Conrad's text is a socially symbolic act, is self-referential; or, rather, Jameson's description of his method, his "elaborate hermeneutic geiger counters" (*PU,* 215), turns in on its own codification; this fold pushes to the limit the relationship between the molecular and the molar. This reflexivity is a frequent theme and textual machination in *The Political Unconscious.* Chapter 2, with its rehearsal of the three interpretive levels described in chapter 1 (and worked out at more leisure in chapters 3, 4, and 5), is a chapter of "containment" that also releases the libidinal-interpretive energies of the text. In chapter 5, much of the political unconscious of *Lord Jim* is seen to originate in the bifurcation of the novel into an artistic first half (which owes to Henry James and Ford Madox Ford) and a male-romance second half (which owes to Robert Louis Stevenson and leads to W. Somerset Maugham). But that division of the Conrad novel proper is problematized by the actantial role played in the first half by "light holiday literature" (Conrad 1989, 47), which sets Jim onto his course of seafaring *and* incapacitates him.

241   In chapter 4, the Lacanian dialectic of Imaginary and Symbolic in Balzac's *The Black Sheep* results in a division of the novel similar to that of *Lord Jim.* Here, the novel splits between Joseph's prelinguistic desire to be an artist and Phillipe's Machiavellian machinations to get the gold. As Jameson argues, the energy of the novel comes both from the simultaneity of psychological and historical overdetermination for Phillipe's malice (*PU,* 171–74) and from the discomfort with which we read the prophesy and (wish) fulfillment of Joseph's artistic career. Thus the novel begins with an aside: "[T]he conjunction of facts and circumstances which is the prelude to this story may contain the generative causes to which we are indebted for Joseph Bridau, one of the great artists of the contemporary school of French painting" (Balzac 1970, 43); and it closes with this: "Joseph . . . already has a private income of 60,000 francs a year. Though he paints magnificent pictures and gives much help to artists, he is still not a member of the Institut. By virtue of a clause in the deed of entailment he is now known as the Count de Brambourg, which often makes him howl with laughter when he is in his studio with his friends" (339).

242   The sheer willfulness, the childishness, of Joseph's success and its un-alloyed innocence embarrasses the reader in the same way that we are em-

barrassed by a dream recited to us by a friend, as Freud noted in "Creative Writers and Day-Dreaming" (cited by Jameson [*PU,* 174–75]). From a writer we get pleasure or compensation because the "writer softens the character of his egoistic day-dreams by altering and disguising it" (Freud 1988, 141), whereas the dream is too evidently still in the realm of desire.[40] In terms of a reified psychoanalytic interpretation of Balzac, where Joseph is his projected self in the novel, it is discomforting to see how much the author desires that success. That desire is still in the realm of the Imaginary because it pretends to be untainted by power (Joseph is not in the Institut, and he laughs at his title, *even* while he retains it), and because the phallus has not yet been affixed, as it were, to the penis (hence Joseph's apparent bachelor-hood—the novel is in a series called *Les Célibataires*—and he is still the virgin hanging out with the guys).

243 The thematic and textual figures which I suggest reside in *The Political Unconscious* may be summed up in Stein's particular collection in *Lord Jim*—but not his insect collection, which is merely the materialization of the lugubrious ethical "theme" of Conrad's novels (how do you know you are courageous, or a butterfly and not a beetle?). Rather, the collections I'm thinking of are "the famous gardens of Stein, in which you can find every plant and tree of tropical lowlands" (Conrad 1989, 300–301). A species of the Adornoesque "shrunken dwarf" (itself a privileged mode of argument), the garden is interesting because it is a space of imperial domination and quantitative grasping *within* the empire, that is, in the hinterland or margin of the empire and not at the center as a zoo or botanical garden would properly be (which has been submitted to John Berger's analysis in "Why Look at Animals" [1980]). The garden is also not the site for a neat bifurcation of personality and morality (as Stein's beetle and butterfly collection smugly serves to be), but rather as the place for, simultaneous to the (necessary) final unraveling of a narrative thread, a muddying of textual-ethical

40 This dialectic might be at the base of the split reception between two art-house successes of 1993: Jane Campion's *The Piano* and Mike Leigh's *Naked.* In both films, an artist-type is "held back" or in check by the social—piano-playing or chaos-theory philosophizing—so that when the desire spills over into sexuality (or is expressed as such), the result in both cases is a curious admixture of feminist and postfeminist violence.

possibilities: "They [Stein and Jewel] disappeared beyond that spinney (you may remember) where sixteen different kinds of bamboo grow together, all distinguishable to the learned eye" (Conrad 1989, 302).

desire

244 If a parlor game of word association were to be conducted at a gathering of intellectuals, there is perhaps no critic less likely to suggest "desire" than Northrop Frye. And yet Frye's status in *The Political Unconscious* is most firmly announced or valorized in a discussion of precisely this theoretico-sexual term.[41] Jameson notes that desire is contingent on the very forces of modernization and reification that constitute a master-code for his hermeneutic; if we now read Freud in a mode where it "is not sexual experience but rather wish-fulfillment, or its more metaphysical variant, 'desire,' posited as the very dynamic of our being as individual subjects" (*PU*, 65), then that desire itself is only capable of being described or theorized because our experience of subjectivity has been thoroughly fragmented and disintegrated. But Jameson's discussion of desire then turns from the expected, the au courant book-machines of Deleuze and Guattari, to that stodgy Canadian minister Frye. Jameson is interested in archetypal criticism primarily, it would seem, because Frye maintains a (tenuous) link with ideas of community and the social, "the most vital exchange of energies inevitably takes place between the two poles of the psychoanalytic and the theological" (*PU*, 69), which two poles, of course, might stand as the markers for a Marxist pathway laid by Benjamin, Bloch, and Marcuse.

245 Frye's argument is almost Althusserian in its concept of autonomy: "The close resemblance between the conceptions of anagogic criticism and those of religion has led many to assume that they can only be related by

41 But see Castoriadis's astringent remark, presumably addressed to Lyotard, and Deleuze and Guattari: "[H]ardy and improbable philosophy professors transformed suddenly into prophets of schizophrenia, erstwhile orthodox Marxists longing to besprinkle the universe with their libidinal flux, a whole tribe of pen-pushers who have found a remedy against advancing age in the elixir of modern 'sexual liberation' and to whom, at long last, 'desire' was revealed" (1984, 101).

making one supreme and the other subordinate. . . . But for the purity of each the autonomy of each must be guaranteed. Culture interposes, between the ordinary and the religious life, a total vision of possibilities, and insists on its totality—for whatever is excluded from culture by religion or the state will get its revenge somehow" (1973, 127). My mischievous labeling of Frye as proto-Althusserian, and the Freudian tone of his revenge of culture (the return of the repressed) notwithstanding, the primary flaw in Frye's argument lies in his Conradian view that culture has a "total vision of possibilities." It is Jameson's contention that the figures of sight which figure so prominently in the past few sentences are themselves concomitant with the reification of the senses that also led to the privileging of the visual in impressionist painting and Conrad ("above all else, to make you see").

246 But Frye is not afraid to link religion to Marxism (a brave-enough theorem in 1950s North America), if mostly in a negative manner, making the Popperian charge that the Marxist or religious state, like the Platonic one, has no room for the unanswerable poet. Nevertheless, he does also say that "Christian theology is no less of a revolutionary dialectic, or indissoluble union of theory and social practice" (127), a view originating in some way with the Canadian tradition of the Christian left.

247 Frye is a fellow traveller because of "his willingness to raise the issue of community and to draw basic, essentially social, interpretive consequences from the nature of religion as a collective representation" (*PU,* 69). Discussing Frye's use of the medieval hermeneutic, Jameson contends that the ultimate level of Frye's system, the monadic-anagogical one (Frye 1973, 115–16), depoliticizes the medieval code, a "significant strategic and ideological move, in which political and collective imagery is transformed into a mere relay in some ultimately privatizing celebration of the category of individual experience" (*PU,* 74). In *Anatomy of Criticism,* the passage in which Frye arrives at the anagogical level of the libidinal body is a point of the text's deconstruction that marks its own limit: "This is the only type of image I can think of" (1973, 124), Frye admits.

248 The movement to the body is, in *Anatomy of Criticism,* rich both in its meditation on identity and difference, and as a species of textual aporia: "In the anagogic aspect of meaning, the radical form of metaphor, 'A is B,' comes into its own. Here we are dealing with poetry in its totality, in which

the formula 'A is B' may be hypothetically applied to anything, for there is no metaphor, not even 'black is white,' which a reader has any right to quarrel with in advance. The literary universe, therefore, is a universe in which everything is potentially identical with everything else. This does not mean that any two things in it are separate and very similar, like peas in a pod, or in the slangy and erroneous sense of the word in which we speak of identical twins. If twins were really identical they would be the same person. On the other hand, a grown man feels identical with himself at the age of seven, although the two manifestations of this identity, the man and the boy, have very little in common as regards similarity or likeness. In form, matter, personality, time, and space, man and boy are quite unlike. This is the only type of image I can think of that illustrates the process of identifying two independent forms. All poetry, then, proceeds as though all poetic images were contained within a single universal body. Identity is the opposite of similarity or likeness, and total identity is not uniformity, still less monotony, but a unity of various things" (Frye 1973, 124–25).

249 Here, the sentence that begins "This is the only type of image" betrays a certain gap in Frye's text. That is, this self-consciousness signifies the coming to realization of the apparatus or machinery that a figure (or metaphor or image) generates analysis (and not the other way around).[42] Frye's de Manesque blindness manifests itself when he writes that he believes that the image "illustrates the process" and not that the image generates a conceptual tool for thinking of that process. The anagogic metaphor is akin to Jameson's use of transcoding: a term that asserts a unity without obliterating difference.

250 What kind of body is being proposed here, that Jameson can call it a "libidinal" one? (We can bracket, while noting, the Platonic-homoerotic tone of Frye's text at this point, which places him as a theorist of desire a bit more acceptably, perhaps.) Evidently an Althusserian totality, the figure varies between idealism and materialism: the first is evident in the notion that "man" at seven feels himself to be the same as an adult; the second in the self-conscious turn to the body as a metaphor.

---

42 I am basing this point on de Man's essay on metaphor in *Allegories of Reading* (1979, 135–59), especially the discussion of the "blindness of metaphor" and language confronting itself (153).

251 The body cannot be contained: it is a "Body without Organs." This figure seems to be even more of a mystification: "Why such a dreary parade of sucked-dry, catatonicized, vitrified, sewn-up bodies, when the BwO is also full of gaiety, ecstasy, and dance?" (Deleuze and Guattari 1987, 150). One way to explicate Deleuze and Guattari's figure, and to reassert the importance of Frye's turn to the body, is to see it in terms of Jameson's transcoding. The BwO is another mediatory term between the text, the individual, and the social. The Body without Organs is also the State without Organs, without the organs to defend itself or to purge itself (Chomsky's joke that a language is a dialect with an army and a navy is pertinent here). The figure is both utopian and ideological, however: nothing is more liberal or bourgeois than the fantasy that the state is such a benign entity; or, to turn around the figure, what can be more middle class than the desire to escape from the material senses, the "organs" of sight, hearing, and (especially) smell? So the BwO, or the libidinal body, is the body of the text conceived in a Lacanian way as a site for readerly desire, but a desire (for interpretation) itself located in the social realm. Jameson's use of Frye is not secondary to the former's political hermeneutic; for once Frye's radicalness is in turn recognized (reorganized or postmodernized), his place in Jameson's scheme is evident.

252 Jameson's *Fables of Aggression* appropriates the vocabulary of Lyotard and the concept of a "libidinal apparatus" (*FA*, 10–11). Here, "the objective preconditions of the narrative structures that inform Lewis's imagination, far from being familial or archaic, are rather to be sought in . . . political history" (11). The "quasi-material inertness" of the apparatus is an advantage since it functions as a mediation between the historical and the textual. For the political critic, the job is to determine just how that apparatus will manage desire, and to what end: "[A] social hermeneutic will . . . wish to keep faith with its medieval precursor [and] must necessarily restore a perspective in which the imagery of libidinal revolution and of bodily transfiguration once again becomes a figure for the perfected community" (*PU*, 74). This passage is similar to the one from Frye quoted at length above: but the move from a disinterested critic to a desiring theorist shows that the Jameson-text is not merely a postmodernized Frye-text. The difference is that, where Frye will gently admit that the body is the only kind of image he

can think of (as if embarrassed to bring it up) and stoutly hold that the metaphor illustrates the concept, Jameson is interested in the figure *as material*, as self-conscious source for a dialectical criticism. The difference between method and figure is never easy to decipher in the Jameson-text: but suffice to say that metaphor will release the political desire (for libidinal revolution and bodily transfiguration) in *The Political Unconscious*, and not restrict or contain it. The textual strategies that *form* Jameson's book are then realized in the critical readings of Balzac, Gissing, and Conrad.

three interpretive levels

253 As the squares that illustrate the cover of *The Political Unconscious* show,[43] Jameson's architecture of interpretation posits three levels or horizons: political history, or "punctual event and a chroniclelike sequence of happenings in time"; society, as the less temporal "constitutive tension and struggle between classes"; and history as "the sequence of modes of production and the succession and destiny of the various human social formations" (*PU*, 75). Significantly, Jameson's three levels allow a contingent or local form of criticism that is otherwise unfashionable in a postmodern hermeneutic; as discussed above, the first level, where the text is seen to play a socially symbolic role, is fairly functionalist. But the use of Lévi-Strauss here wonderfully problematizes the French anthropologist's functionalist tendencies, and New Critical aestheticism is similarly avoided: "[S]ymbolic functions are . . . rarely found by an aimless enumeration of random formal and stylistic features; our discovery of a text's symbolic efficiency must be oriented by a formal description which seeks to grasp it as a determinate structure of still properly formal *contradictions*" (77). So Jameson uses a structuralist anthropology to argue that a text, in its formal construction, provides an imaginary resolution of a real contradiction. Jameson shifts from Lévi-Strauss with the notion that politics at this basic level (elections, wars, and so on) is the *pensée sauvage* or mass consciousness of nontribal societies (80). The text articulates these *contradictions* of savage thought in terms of

43   The American edition, that is.

Greimas's semiotic rectangle, the site where the oppositions of dialectics meet the binaries of structuralism (83).

254 The second level is where again the notion of contradiction (this time between classes) differentiates Jameson's method from garden-variety sociology, which will see classes as merely the strata of society (even the welcome strata: for the social scientist, methodological formalism is a respite from the messy Real): "The constitutive form of class relationships is always that between a dominant and a laboring class" (83). The perspective on the text is then dialectically raised to a higher plane, from which the text is seen as an utterance of that class relationship, and characterized in terms of the Saussuresque neologism—the "ideologeme." Jameson's theory of the ideologeme, like Raymond Williams's phrase "structure of feeling," allows Jameson to organize class discourse into a linguistic structure, with the ideologeme as its minimal unit. The ideologeme is "an amphibious formation, whose essential structural characteristic may be described as its possibility to manifest itself either as a pseudoidea . . . or as a protonarrative" (87). A key ideologeme is ressentiment, which is important for its role in class discourse centered around the subject. It is the adventures of that last concept, from a pre-centered subjectivity in Balzac to a stale one in Gissing and a disintegrating one in Conrad, that forms the narrative of the remainder of *The Political Unconscious,* with an appendix on the postmodernization of Wyndham Lewis in *Fables of Aggression.* Jameson also utilizes ressentiment to demonstrate the poverty of ethical criticism. This latter project can be said to be an important subtextual "class struggle in criticism" being carried out throughout *The Political Unconscious.*

255 Jameson's third level is even more rudely Marxist; if the discussion of political history can be politely accommodated by the academy (lately under New Historicism) and if even class is admissible to literary criticism as a form of local color, then the assertion that texts are ultimately about "modes of production" is not scandalous (since everything is scandalous nowadays) but vulgar or crude. Jameson stresses here both his alliance with and his antagonism toward the orthodox Marxist theories of modes of production, noting "the notion of a cultural dominant or form of ideological coding specific to each mode" (89). He quickly sketches the two main theoretical arguments with Marxism over this master-narrative: the Orwell-Foucault-

Weber vision of a totalitarian future contained in our present, and the Huxley-Baudrillard-Bell version of consumption and post-ideology. The first argument holds that Marxism leads to and participates in totalitarianism both theoretically and practically, and the second that Marxism is no longer sufficient to explain "postcapitalism." Modes of production are, appropriate to a Hegelian argument, both too explanatory and not explanatory enough. Modes of production here contradict each other.[44] The contradiction is realized in and outside the text as the ideology of form. That is, form is seen as a Frygian "body," reformulated as a space for the signs of these contradictory modes of production, the dynamics of which make up "the determinate contradiction of the specific messages emitted by the varied signs systems [and where] 'form' is apprehended as content" (98–99). The absent cause of this text is then History itself: here seen, finally, as "the experience of Necessity," a horizon untranscendable because of the basic human-biological status of necessity, realized socially in the modes of production in which that necessity is both satisfied and denied.

acting out your aggression

256 How is desire managed in the text? This is where Jameson's use of Greimas's theory becomes important, and where an explanation of that system will conveniently move us from the previous explication of Jameson's interpretive levels to a following application of those levels in Balzac and Conrad. Greimas's structure of actants and actors and the accompanying semiotic rectangle are initially treated in the first chapter of *The Political*

---

44 Jameson derives this from Nicos Poulantzas and "his suggestion that every social formation or historically existing society has in fact consisted in the overlay and structural coexistence of *several* modes of production all at once, including vestiges and survivals of older modes of production, now relegated to structurally dependent positions within the new, as well as anticipatory tendencies which are potentially inconsistent with the existing system but have not yet generated an autonomous space of their own" (*PU,* 95). The similarity to Raymond Williams's residual and emergent discourses is noted later (218); but Williams does not stress enough the conflict between the discourses (this might also be said of Deleuze and Guattari in their idea of the rhizome, especially since their figure is evidently a dialectical response to the "arborescent" model of tree-ness [1987, 3–25]).

Unconscious (46–48, 82–83), as well as in the Balzac and Conrad chapters. Greimas's working contention is that a narrative will articulate a contradiction by posing not merely opposites but antinomies, or opposites with their own binaries. As spelled out in his essays "The Interaction of Semiotic Constraints" and in "Elements of a Narrative Grammar," the system works by combining *semiotics* with *semantics*. Here meaning returns to imbue form in a dialectical sublation: "The project of a fundamental semantics, a semantics that differs from the semantics of linguistic manifestation, is absolutely dependent on a theory of meaning. . . . This elementary structure . . . must be conceived of as being the logical development of a binary semic category, of the type *white* vs *black,* whose terms are in a relation of contrariety and that can also, each one, project a new term that would be its contradictory" (Greimas 1987, 65–66). So white and black each generate an opposite, nonwhite and nonblack. This is how narrative, Greimas argues, generates meaning. That is, if a narrative is disposed to work with the problem of sexuality, terms like "potency" and "impotency" (or "fertility" and "sterility") are *given meaning* through the narrative by being juxtaposed not merely with each other but with their semantic contraries: the narrative "fills in the slots," and it does so through characterization. The semiotic rectangle is the graphic representation that permits the otherwise obscure relationships to be interpreted.

257   The second tool of Greimas—the actor/actant binary—is significant in that the semiotic rectangle projects four positions, which are the actants in the narrative. The various characters are then actors who will fill in these actantial roles. The desire at work here is both figural and literal: Greimas frequently uses Balzac and his narratives of sexuality and economics as illustration. And it is evident that from a larger theoretical perspective, the narrative desires to "fill in" the slots, or to arrive at a meaning (narrative here including the interpretation of that narrative).

lukács: or, marxism and masochism

258   Jameson's great precursor in reading Balzac is Lukács. In *Studies in European Realism,* Lukács contends that it is the "discrepancy between intention and performance, between Balzac the political thinker and Balzac

the author of *La Comédie Humaine* that constitutes Balzac's historical greatness" (1978a, 21). Here are, it seems, all the sins of humanist Marxism: a fetish for "intention," an evaluative stance that seeks some "greatness," and the prescriptive desire to valorize realism as the *telos* of literary and aesthetic activity. Lukács's role is not simply as methodological precursor, although some of the topics or approaches founded by him are central to Jameson's project. Lukács heralds a *conservative* writer as the most effective critic of his historical period, focuses on characterization as a site for political interpretation, and privileges the situation of a writer in history. But the very centrality of these methods announces a place for Lukács in Jameson's crucial maneuver in *The Political Unconscious:* the theory of the political unconscious itself. That split in the social text, the forcing underground in modernist culture, as in everyday bourgeois life, of the political "by accumulated reification" (*PU,* 280) that is the *telos* of Jameson's chapter on Conrad, finds its origin in Lukács, first, in a masochism that demands to read bourgeois literature, and, second, in a determination that writers themselves are split-subjects.

259 Balzac's work had an important place in Marxist criticism before Lukács: in Marx and Engels's brief remarks on Balzac's "typical" characters and critical relation with capitalism.[45] Lukács's enthusiasm for Balzac's realism and "historical luck" (as Jameson puts it elsewhere [*M&F,* 203]) was damaging to Lukács's stature and to his conception of the relationship of literature to society, as the so-called Brecht-Lukács debate shows.[46] But nonetheless, if realism today is discredited as a style, being irredeemably tied in with reification (Hartley 1989, 53–75) or naïveté (the Althusserian position), the *practice,* or the actual novels that now suffer under that label,

---

45 See Raymond Williams's comments in *Marxism and Literature* (1988, 201).

46 Documents in that debate are collected in *Aesthetics and Politics* (Bloch 1986). Terry Eagleton, in *Criticism and Ideology,* takes Lukács to task for believing that Balzac was able to write free from his ideology, and instead sees Balzac in a more properly Althusserian way as inserted into ideology. The Brecht-Lukács debate is commented upon by Jameson in his afterword to the Verso collection (*IT* 2:133–47); Werner Mittenzwei makes the point that Lukács was interested in Balzac in part because he saw the latter's attitude of being critical of the ruling class without definitively breaking with it as a good model for socialist writers in a socialist state (hence "critical realism": Mittenzwei 1973, 210).

perhaps has to be interpreted in a new light. There are other ways in which Lukács, writing on Balzac, has influenced Marxist critics: first, the privileging of the situation of a writer in history introduced or foregrounded the problem of mediation, or how artistic works are affected by the social. This is the logical explanation for the lengthy first chapter in *The Political Unconscious* and is also a key moment in Sartre's *Search for a Method*. Second, the view that realism is about a unity or totality of the individual and the world should not sidetrack an inquiry into precisely why *realism* is accorded this position.

260 Terry Eagleton begins an essay on Conrad with a sarcastic apology that *The Secret Agent* "is altogether too convenient a text to select for discussion . . . it is, self-evidently, a 'political' novel, and a materialist criticism should not give itself an easy ride by choosing as its object texts which 'spontaneously' conform to its method. Better, surely, to select an 'innocent' work—a Bides verse-tragedy or medieval love-lyric—than to risk the perils of methodological circularity, a mirror-image reciprocity between 'approach' and object" (1986, 23). In typical form, Eagleton parodies here that Lukácsean imperative to demonstrate one's Marxist rigor by not simply reading socialist literature or explicitly political texts (and finding in them one's preformed themes)—a parody that reaffirms the importance of that selfsame Homeric (or "homeric," as Wyndham Lewis writes) task. And if Eagleton's form here is typical—that is, he uses sarcasm to encapsulate in a lively form the terms of the debate—his images are also uncanny in the suggestion of just what is at stake. The "methodological circularity" of a criticism that seeks to take the easy way out (a political reading that looks for political texts) is satisfied with the "mirror-image," or, in Lacan's terms, remains trapped in the harness of the mirror-stage of criticism, where the text functions to reassure the baby-critic that his position is secured in the jolly-jumper of rigor. A Marxist criticism that is not satisfied with this criticism of the Imaginary will then run the risk of being labeled masochistic, or at least perverse. Where Lukács is mandarin in his treatment of this issue, Jameson is more revealing. Lukács remarks that it might appear "we are involving ourselves in a serious contradiction, demanding on the one hand the politicization of literature and on the other hand attacking insidiously the most vigorous and militant section of left-wing literature" (1978a, 10). Jameson, arguing with

an imaginary interlocutor, writes that it "will also be observed that it is on the face of it rather perverse to seek to deny the commodification of desire in a work such as Balzac's" (*PU,* 170).

261 In *Criticism and Ideology,* Eagleton writes that seeing "the fissuring of organic form [as] a progressive act has not been a received position within a Marxist aesthetic tradition heavily dominated by the work of Georg Lukács" (1990b, 161); and yet the very act of finding various exemplary modes of resistance to capitalism in Lawrence, Joyce, and Eliot is a very Lukácsean move.[47] Lukács's founding methodology is also important because of its implications for psychoanalytic approaches to the author, as Jameson points out in *Marxism and Form:* "[T]he newer kinds of psychological analyses, such as Sartre's of Flaubert, are merely refinements, using psychoanalytic techniques, on [Lukács's] basic model. Thus the formal practice of Flaubert is seen as reflecting his detachment from the possibilities of lived action in his situation as a second son to whom the practical fulfillments of middle-class life seemed denied" (203). That is, Lukács's greatness lies in splitting the author's subjectivity into a manifest-content of "intent"/"wish" and a latent-content of (historically determined) "genius" that then are synthesized in the literary text.

262 "The central category and criterion of realist literature is the type," Lukács wrote in 1948, "a peculiar synthesis which organically binds together the general and the particular both in characters and situations" (1978a, 6). If this formulation again seems problematic, because of its valorization of the organic and its didactic tone, its dialectical relation to what Lukács saw as false literatures and its focus on the character are still relevant. Lukács opposes his formula to the "lifeless average" of naturalists like Upton Sinclair and the dissolved self of modernists like Joyce, so the "type" must be seen in that dialectical relationship if its importance is not to be disintegrated into a static and mandarin pronouncement from the bad old days. More relevant to Jameson's chapter on Balzac, and to his focus on the bourgeois subject throughout *The Political Unconscious,* is the place here of the character, conceived as the center of the fiction, the site for the most explicit politics of the

47 Jameson's like move would be the way he encounters a vigorous anticapitalism in Wyndham Lewis in *Fables of Aggression.*

novel to come to the fore. Here, then, Jameson's use of both Lukács and Greimas is more explicable.

263 As the "organic" tone of the previous pronouncement should remind us, Lukács's theories of realism rely on how "great realism . . . depicts man and society as complete entities" (1978a, 6). But if Lukács's master-code is organicism and totality, then it may now be argued that this is not too different from the various master-codes of structuralism, poststructuralism, feminism, postcolonialism, or post-Marxism.[48] Lukács emphasizes organicism, but, *pace* Eagleton, that can now be interpreted as a Gramscian dichotomy (Gramsci 1975, 14–23): Balzac is not a "traditional" writer, who would float freely above the debates of early nineteenth-century France, but is instead an "organic" one, whose interest for a Marxist lies in the dialectic of a critical stance *and* a conservative desire. For Lukács, the all-important question is the following: "[D]oes a writer live within the community or is [he] a mere observer of [it, which] is determined . . . by the evolution of society" (11). In my interpretation, organicism may seem as little "Gramscian" as it is Lukácsean, then, for what I am bringing to the fore is a split-subjectivity common to both Marxists. But Gramsci, as his influence on post-Marxism makes evident, saw intellectuals not *intrinsically,* but as a position "in an ensemble of the system of relations in which their activities . . . have their place within the general complex of social relations" (1975, 8).[49]

264 Lukács's situating of Balzac in history has also been tremendously important for its dialectical anticipation of the "death of the author," where the Barthesian Oedipal drama is shown to have been negated before it was even begun. The focus on the author is both negative and positive: he is valorized by Lukács as a great man, but his greatness is historically contingent, which makes the usual label of Lukács as a late Romantic dubious. The subject, in Lukács's discourse, is therefore *both* humanist and Althusserian, both an agent of history (or at least an agent of creativity) and an object slotted into a

---

48 Eagleton makes the point that Jameson's *The Prison-House of Language* shows a "totalizing Lukácsean for whom structural thought is inherently congenial" (1987, 58).

49 It should also be noted that Eagleton stresses the difference between the "organicism" he treats in *Criticism and Ideology* (1990b) and Gramsci's concept of the organic (102n).

specific formation—the "realist." This second actantial role which Balzac plays in Lukács's text anticipates "interpellation" of a specific sort: "Balzac painted this tragedy of the aristocratic large estate with all the richness of his literary genius . . . yet, as the great realist that he is, he gives a monumental and perfectly balanced picture of the forces locked in struggle on both sides" (Lukács 1978a, 28). The focus on the author is self-evidently a problem only if some ethical dilemma transforms the complexities of Lukács's discourse into the bogeyman of "humanism."

265 Perhaps the solution to this false problem lies in pursuing that humanism, in embracing it, then. For Lukács, Balzac as author—the category of the author—is the mediating term between history and the literary text. Lukács's use of Romantic codes for creativity—greatness, genius—should not obscure this; unlike the Romantics, Lukács does not see the literary text originating in the author's consciousness; rather, that consciousness is "great" because of the objective qualities of the work (i.e., not the other way around). And that literary object is great not because of its fidelity to an ahistorical touchstone or principle, but because of its political and critical realism. Lukács is commonly misread as "merely" Romantic, or his philosophy as merely Romantic anti-capitalism. But his standing of Romantic codes on their head and appropriation of "Romantic ideology," in Jerome McGann's suggestive phrase, show that Lukács's Romanticism is quite different from the reified aestheticism prevalent now. If Romantic art was essentially "a symbolic abstraction" (Williams 1990, 47), an assertion of "the integrity of the biosphere and the inner, spiritual self" (McGann 1983, 67–68), then the organic totality trumpeted by Lukács was of a distinct order and is probably closer to de Man's theory of Romanticism.

266 De Man, in "The Rhetoric of Temporality," holds that the Romantic text resorts to allegory "in the repetition . . . of a previous sign with which it can never coincide, since it is of an essence of the previous sign to be pure anteriority" (1988, 207). Lukács's is a "secularized allegory" of realism, a figural master-code of totality and organicism, and his Hellenic epic comes close to de Man's sign of "anteriority." The "dialectical relationship between subject and object is no longer the central statement of romantic thought, but this dialectic is now located entirely in the temporal relationships that exist within a system of allegorical signs" (de Man 1988, 208). The appropriateness of de Man's comments to Lukács's brand of Romanticism is

evident when Lukács addresses head-on what I earlier called his "originary masochism." Lukács acknowledges his debt to Engels, writes that privileging Balzac over Zola might lead the reader to think that "the *Weltanschauung* and political attitude of serious great realists are a matter of no great consequence" (Lukács 1978a, 10) and then admits that this is for the most part true. Weltanschauung and political intent—the baggage of the subject-writer—are now deferred in favor of the writer releasing the characters of his fiction.

267 Here, in a great Oedipal drama, Lukács is explicit: "[T]he characters created by the great realists, once conceived in the vision of their creator, live an independent life of their own: their comings and going, their development, their destiny is dictated by the inner dialectic of their social and individual existence. No writer is a true realist—or even a truly good writer, if he can direct the evolution of his own characters at will" (11). Lukács sees in the dialectic of literary characters' social existences, almost free-floating signifiers, the test of the realist's greatness. What is important to my purposes here is a formal similarity between Lukács's theory of character and de Man's notion that the "dialectic is now located entirely in the temporal relationships that exist within a system of allegorical signs." Characters are allegorical and signs for Lukács as well: he censures the "second-rate" writers who try to force their own worldview through the literary work. The solution, for Lukács, does not lie in a willful "truth," but in the libidinal release by the author of his or her character-signs.[50]

268 This said, Lukács's solution is not the only "humanist" Marxist theory of artistic mediation: the other great one is Sartre's theory of the family in *Search for a Method* (1968). Sartre asks how Marxism should proceed in its "situating" of the artistic object (36). So, while Marxists may argue that Flaubert is dealing in his realism with the development of the petit bourgeoisie in the Second Empire, that methodology "*never* shows the genesis of this reciprocity of perspective. We do not know why Flaubert preferred literature to everything else, nor why he lived like an anchorite, nor why he wrote *these* books rather than those of Duranty or the Goncourt brothers.

---

50 My scattered comments linking Jameson's practice to de Man are in part to show similarities to de Man are of a radical nature, not a conservative one. Terry Collits connects de Man to Jameson to suggest that neither is out to "disturb the canon" (1989, 308).

Marxism situates but no longer discovers anything. . . . It is neither his rental income nor the strictly intellectual nature of his work which first makes Flaubert a bourgeois. He *belongs* to the bourgeoisie because he was born in it; that is, because he appeared in the midst of a family *already bourgeois*" (57–58). A psychoanalysis of Flaubert's family, of the artist in situation in the family (a *Sartrean* psychoanalysis, for better or for worse) will reveal the sedimentation of class conflict and historical progress that, in turn, form the individual. The insertion of the individual into the family constitutes the Sartrean mediation between history and the artistic object (62).

269 The attraction of realism for a Marxist critic lies primarily in the aesthetic mode's claims to a cognitive superiority: "Realism . . . is not some sort of middle way between false objectivity and false subjectivity, but on the contrary the true, solution-bringing third way" (Lukács 1978, 6). What must be recognized, however, is that this epistemological claim is based on a certain moment of early capitalism, and on the nascent and "progressive" forces of modernization—the secularization of the world, as Marx and Engels described it in *The Communist Manifesto:* "All fixed, fast-frozen relations, with their train of ancient and venerable prejudices and opinions, are swept away. . . . All that is solid melts into air, all that is holy is profaned, and man is at last compelled to face with sober senses, his real conditions of life, and his relations with his kind" (Marx 1977, 224). And certainly these celebrated and poetic words would seem to privilege literary realism: if capitalism stripped the feudal relations and religious veils from nineteenth-century Europe in its drive to reduce all relations to money, then a style that eschewed symbolism and prolix filigree would seem to be appropriate. But there is a crucial passage omitted just now in the quotation from the *Manifesto:* "[A]ll new-formed ones become antiquated before they can ossify"; the new relations, replacing the old, are themselves replaced in short order. A criticism with dialectical claims cannot hold onto a static model of realism, demanding that realism maintain its hegemony in an unchanged manner.

sex and money

270 Jameson's project is to provide a newer and more satisfying version of what goes on in Balzac, as well as to account for the role of realism in the

creation of the bourgeois subject. He first of all asserts that this form plays the role assigned to capitalism in *The Communist Manifesto:* "[T]hat processing operation variously called narrative mimesis or realist representation has as its historic function the systematic undermining and demystification, the secular 'decoding,' of those preexisting inherited traditional or sacred narrative paradigms which are its initial givens . . . [and the] 'objective' function of the novel is . . . producing as though for the first time that very life world, that very 'referent'—the newly quantifiable space of extension and market equivalence, the new rhythms of measurable time, the new secular and 'disenchanted' object world of the commodity system" (*PU,* 152). This analysis is focused, in Jameson's Lukácsean problematic, then, on the subject—as both reader and character, in order that the emergence of that "centered subject" can be determined. The poststructuralist objection to the subject, or *one* objection, is that the subject as such restricts libidinal flow; Jameson then begins with a novel that offers desire *before* the subject as such has been constituted: Balzac's *La Vieille Fille.* Description is posited as arriving here with a libidinal investment *sans* subject, as in the scene Jameson quotes, where the text breathlessly offers: "What peace! what calm! nothing pretentious, but nothing transitory" (Balzac, qtd. *PU,* 155).

271 Jameson here is taking desire (the fragmentation of the totalized subject) and historicizing it. The realist project, then, manages a precapitalist wish (the Blochian paradigm of the fairy tale), rendering it into a bourgeois materialism. This is what Bloch calls "Balzac's incomparable art of painting the attitude of *Enrichissez-vous*" (1989, 211). The question of how this aesthetico-political management functions narratologically in *The Black Sheep* and *Nostromo* is addressed below; what is more immediately relevant is Jameson's conclusion that this libidinal investment is utopian: "To juxtapose the depersonalized and retextualized provincial houses of Flaubert with this one is to become perhaps uncomfortably aware of the degree to which the Balzacian dwelling invites the awakening of a longing for possession, of the mild and warming fantasy of landed property as the tangible figure of a Utopian wish-fulfillment" (*PU,* 157).

272 The critic to take up this challenge, to see just how description is depersonalized and retextualized in Flaubert (and at the same time to take issue with Barthes's attack on realism in "The Reality Effect" [1986]) is Jameson

himself, in the essay "The Realist Floor-Plan" (Jameson 1986a).[51] Jameson
analyzes a paragraph from Flaubert's *Simple Heart,* which is seen to betray
the "bourgeois cultural revolution" that Jameson, as we have just seen, describes as the political agenda of nineteenth-century realist fiction. What
Barthes considers to be insignificant notation, only locatable in the twin
narratives of analysis or realism (thus the "reality effect": Barthes 1986,
142–43), is instead open to a historicist analysis. In Flaubert's story, the
house's floor is described as lower than the garden; Jameson then juxtaposes
the new space of bourgeois decoding with the older, sacred space of the
(Frygian) garden. The musty smell of the house denotes a nostalgia for the
past with a Body without Organ's distaste for that residual olfactory aura.
Finally, "the symbolic readings I have alluded to end up as a dramatic recon-
figuration of an ideological and formal production process which works the
raw materials of the older mode of production over in the very moment in
which the forms, practices, and daily life of the new mode of production are
being for the first time produced" (Jameson 1986a, 382).

273 But the utopian register in terms of which Jameson reads Balzac's description in *La Vieille Fille* signifies a collective, not yet unified, subject of the
narrative: the "wish-fulfilling or fantasy investment . . . dissolved the biographical into the Utopian" (*PU,* 169). The passage where Jameson shifts
his analysis to another Balzac novel, *The Black Sheep,* contains a peculiarly
Frygian-Lukácsean moment: many novels by Balzac use desire to the ends
of a "monadic bourgeois subjectivity," and Jameson admits the perversity of
denying "the commodification of desire in a work such as Balzac's, which is
so saturated with object-hunger of all kinds" (170). Lukács's masochism
here is genuinely figured as a desire that is thwarted by some imaginary
Father (against the "perverse")—no doubt the same reader urged to skip
ahead past the Althusser in chapter 1. Or, rather, here are two fathers: one,
the critic put off by the theology of Marxism (Raymond Williams's nose-
sniffing at Goldmann is remembered),[52] the other, is the Marxist off-put by

51 But see also "The Ideology of the Text" (*IT,* 1:17–71). There Jameson contrasts
Barthes's conclusion (to "The Reality-Effect") that "realist narrative is defined less as a
structure of discourse in its own right than as an optical illusion" to the more insistently
visual-spatial discourse of *Mythologies.*

52 See Eagleton's comments on Raymond Williams disavowing interest in Marxist
"heresies" (Eagleton 1990b, 32–33).

the disingenuous Lukács who will not admit that Balzac is a capitalist ideologue. Both the "No!" of the Father and the "Name" of the Father (*Non/Nom*) are at work here, denying the simple mirror-reading and the other functioning as a source of authority.[53]

274 The split-subject of this Father-despot helps to explain why it is, then, that in *The Black Sheep* the critic detects first and foremost an etiology of desire, a genealogy that leapfrogs the subject and splits it in two: first, in the form of the two feuding brothers, and then in the twin explanatory codes (historical and psychoanalytic) used to suggest why Phillipe is so "bad." Jameson's distance from Lukács's theory of the author as split-subject is not so great, then; Lukács's humanist mediating point is refigured as Jameson's notion of the Sartrean psychology in Balzac's family. Here Lukács's theory of a political unconscious is revealed to be too unquestioningly historicist: he is right to pinpoint Balzac's schizoid politics (or perhaps, to use a more current term, Balzac's "Multiple Personality Disorder"), but Lukács's theory of "types" will not admit that Phillipe's ethical position in the novel is pre-individualistic. This point underlies the two incommensurable narratives of *The Black Sheep*. The first is a rivalry between two brothers: Joseph, the artist, and Phillipe, the dissolute soldier. The second is the battle between the two lines of the Rouget family, pitting first Joseph (who fails) and then Phillipe (who succeeds) against Max, another dissolute soldier. As Jameson remarks, the power of the novel lies in how "each of these axes or *agons* will stage its principle exhibit—Phillipe—in a different register and for quite different narrative ends" (*PU*, 171).

dead soldiers

275 Phillipe's military career is made up of only two brief moments, virtual shrunken dwarfs in the novel, a couple of longish paragraphs separated by 283 pages. The first quickly outlines Phillipe's service to Napoleon (Balzac

---

53 Rorty's recent discussion of proper names is relevant, as is Barthes's assertion in *S/Z* that action in a narrative (the proairetic code) is fundamentally about "the unfolding of a name" and that reading "is to proceed from name to name. . . . This is proairetism: an artifice (or art) of reading that seeks out names, that tends toward them" (1985, 82–83).

1970, 54–55), the second his campaign in Algeria (338–39), ending with his decapitation, "overwhelmed by the earliest Third World guerrillas represented in modern literature" (*PU*, 172). In between these moments of glory, Phillipe functions most thoroughly in the actant-role of the dangerous and debauched soldier. This function is the first of three significant roles soldiers play in modern Western culture; it stresses the dangerousness of the soldier on half-pay who, accustomed to the glory and recklessness of war, must now make do with building a capitalist order (this is represented in *The Black Sheep*). The second, in properly modernist culture, stresses the problematic of the dead soldier, the carnage of the Great War represented conveniently by Brecht's sarcastic poem, "Legend of the Dead Sodier," or by the title of the Canadian antiwar novel *Generals Die in Bed*. The third function of soldiers, associated with the break between modernism and postmodernism, stresses the problem of atrocities in World War II.

276 Where the first problematic, like that of realism, was a break with a ritualistic past (the uniform as precapitalist encumbrance), and the second problematic struggles with how to represent adequately the destruction and horror of war (referentiality, the Heisenberg principle), the third one foundered on what atrocities like Auschwitz meant for conceptions of the "human." But more recently a fourth function has emerged: here we see the Vietnam veteran as marauding killer, either in a negative sense (the villain of TV shows) or as a hero (Rambo).[54] This last function of the soldier in culture is, of course, a return to the first, which leads to two important conclusions to this lengthy digression. First, the repetition of actantial roles suggests that a similar *social* function is being demanded of the returning soldiery: discard the frippery of Asiatic false gods (drugs, sympathy with the Vietnamese peasantry, miscegenation) and get to work building a new capitalist world order. Second, what is telling about the function of the marauding vet in popular culture (like, say, the crack dealer of more recent fare) is the *formal* role that vet plays as container for transferred anxieties. You have,

54   The soldier functions as actant-villain for the most part in late 1970s and early 1980s popular U.S. culture, which function was then assumed by the Latin American or black drug dealer, a switch overdetermined by, on the one hand, getting over the "Vietnam syndrome," and, on the other, getting over post-1960s liberalism.

on the one hand, a repetition of the "Victorian fantasy-image of the lumpen-proletariat at his most threatening," (*PU*, 171), and on the other hand, as with the crack dealer, the vet reassures the "reader" that the Third World is to blame for metropolitan ills.

morganatic marriages

277 Although the last appearance of the soldier-actant in this brief survey is in popular culture, I do not want to argue that *The Black Sheep* prefigures or contains the popular/high culture divide: that honor, Jameson asserts, belongs to Conrad's *Lord Jim*. The translator of the Balzac novel, in his introduction (1970), tries to claim, no doubt for marketing purposes, that "no story in the world is more exciting than *The Black Sheep,* combining as it does the compelling readability of the blood-and-thunder with the deeper insights of literary art" (7). The translator ignores the incommensurability of this project, of "combining" the excitement of a James Fenimore Cooper or Sir Walter Scott with proto-Flaubertianisms. What we now call popular culture is at this point in time simply a matter of hierarchy: lowbrow versus highbrow.[55] This is demonstrated in *The Black Sheep* when Max and Flore (the other soldier and the fisherwoman) congratulate themselves for having duped the artist Joseph (they gave him some paintings—the value of which they are ignorant—to fob him off): " 'Tomorrow morning [Max is speaking] Kouski and I between us will take out all these canvases and send them over to the artist so that he has them when he wakes up. We'll put the frames in the attic and redecorate the dining room wall with those glossy wallpapers which have scenes from *Télémaque* painted on them, like I've seen at Monsieur Mouilleron's.' 'Yes, that'll be much prettier,' said Flore" (Balzac 1970, 227). 278 Balzac's irony demonstrates that any marriage between popular and high culture is doomed to remain a "morganatic" one; this term denotes the aristocratic version of a "common-law" marriage (Balzac 1970, 71–72), but one also where the lower partner (usually a woman, sometimes not royal or

---

55 These are anachronistic terms as well. *The Making of Middlebrow Culture* (Rubin 1992) is a good start.

noble) would give up any fiscal or lineal claims (*OED*). Here, with the comments on the paintings, low culture, the so-called culturelessness of the low (Flore comes from the peasant class, Max was the bastard son of an army officer and a clogmaker's wife) assumes a narrativistic function. This was signaled earlier in the novel, when the lack of culture in the town of Issoudun was credited with leading to the young men's lawlessness in the "Knights of Idleness" (138). When Flore and Max realize the paintings have value (of course our pure hero Joseph only treasured them for their artistic worth), their anger precipitates a crisis, playing a small part in the "framing" of Joseph for the attempted murder of Max. But this narrative function of low culture is a minor one, and that unevenness between the two spheres of culture is symptomatic of the morganatic nature of the marriage. Low culture is still, in Balzac, a purely negative term, both ethically and nar-rativistically.

conrad and "easy morality"

279 Perhaps the most original literary-critical finding of Jameson's chapter on Conrad is that the division of *Lord Jim* into two stories is "not merely a shift between two narrative paradigms, nor even a disparity between two types of narration or narrative organization, but a shift between two distinct cultural spaces, that of 'high' culture and that of mass culture" (*PU*, 207). Jameson makes other noteworthy conclusions: that the descriptive passages are instances of (almost) postmodern *écriture* (219),[56] and that repressed in the underbelly of the text are the unconscious machinations "of a world of work and history and of protopolitical conflict" (207). Jameson remarks on the following noises that float above the sleep of the Muslim pilgrims: "[S]hort metallic clangs bursting out suddenly in the depths of the ship, the

56 Eagleton makes a similar point in *Criticism and Ideology:* "Dickens is perhaps the last historical point at which sheer verbal exuberance has not come to signify "writing-as-object—*écriture* . . . Conrad's calculated linguistic colourfulness offers a significant con-trast" (1990b, 136). It is important to recognize that neither Eagleton nor Jameson asserts that Conrad is a postmodernist—as Terry Collits does (1989, 304): so Jameson warns himself at the start of *The Political Unconscious* (17–18).

harsh scrape of a shovel, the violent slam of a furnace-door, exploded brutally, as if the men handling the mysterious things below had their breasts
full of anger" (Conrad 1989, 57). For Jameson, this description figures repressed labor, and his interpretation of that passage sublates both ethical
criticism, "the moral problem of the 'sleepers,'" and the problem of style,
"the finally consumable verbal commodity—the vision of the ship" (*PU*,
214).

280 Conrad provides a neat figural operator in this phrase: "[A]s if the men
handling the mysterious things below had their breasts full of anger." An
interpretation of these words lead in two metacritical directions: there is no
"as if"—the men are angry and have a right to be so; and it is these very men
who not only provide the labor power for the ship but will get it into port
when the Europeans have jumped ship. My first comment, which may seem
to lead to a vulgar Marxism that searches out the worker in any text, instead
argues that Conrad's fear that harsh noises *express* an angry proletariat is
essentially true—the *as if* must be inserted as a prophylactic against that
phallic truth. The second comment leads further into the vagaries or inadequacies of ethical criticism: better the anger of the workers dealing with
mysterious machines than the exquisite self-doubt of absconding Europeans. For the limits of ethical criticism (was Jim a coward to jump?) are
both individualistic and colonialist. This first limit is demonstrated in Jameson's reading in section 4 of this chapter (*PU*, 242–57). Jim's ethics are
evidently on trial as the novel begins, but more than one individual is on trial;
the embarrassing dilemma is that a European sailor failed, and failed in the
face of Oriental Others who stay with the ship.

281 When the French lieutenant tells Marlow about towing the *Patna* into
port and standing ready to cut the rope if the lame ship started to sink, there
is no ethical dilemma in his mind: "'Because, mind you (*notez bien*), all the
time of towing we had two quartermasters stationed with axes by the haw-
sers, to cut us clear of our tow in case she . . .'" (146). The apparent
cowardice of this deed is then mitigated when we learn that the naval officer
was stationed on the *Patna* for those thirty hours.

282 Jameson utilizes Greimas's semiotic rectangle to propose that *Lord Jim*
deals with two antinomies: "activity" and "value." Jameson elaborates on the
terms in the following manner: value with nonactivity is represented by the

pilgrims, who are traveling to Mecca but are not working now; activity without value is represented by Gentleman Brown, the ceaselessly agitated *Übermensch* responsible for Lord Jim's downfall; nonactivity with no value is represented by the various deck-chair sailors or worthless Europeans of *Lord Jim*'s first part, who are so lackadaisical that they would even work for Asians. This last category is evidently what the Europeans associated with the *Patna* case wish to extricate Jim from. The French lieutenant says that Jim ran away with the others (150), Judge Brierly drowns himself after the trial, and Marlow narrates a novel.

283 But the category reserved in Jameson's rectangle for Jim is the utopian one of both activity and value: only the Jim who fills in this slot is not the hero of the aesthetic novel that takes place in the first section of *Lord Jim*, but rather the Tuan Jim or Lord Jim of the second, light half. So, "the ideal synthesis of the two major terms of the contradiction and thus the latter's unimaginable and impossible resolution and *Aufhebung;* the union of activity and value, of the energies of Western capitalism and the organic immanence of the religion of precapitalist societies, can only block out the place of Jim himself. But not the existential Jim, the antihero of the first part of the novel: rather, the ideal Jim, the 'Lord Jim' of the second half, the wish-fulfilling romance, which is marked as a degraded narrative precisely by its claim to have 'resolved' the contradiction and generated the impossible hero, who, remaining problematic in the *Patna* section of the book as the Lukács of *The Theory of the Novel* told us the hero of a genuine novel must do, now solicits that lowering of our reality principle necessary to accredit this final burst of legend" (*PU,* 255–56).

284 *Lord Jim*'s shift to a vulgar nautical tale, so unbecoming to a Flaubertian, is necessary for the imaginary resolution of the real contradiction—the historical contradiction of how to valorize in residual (if not feudal) codes the vicious activities of nineteenth-century capitalism. And here Jameson's analysis of *The Black Sheep,* finding two explanations for Phillipe's behavior (one historical, one psychoanalytic), suggests an alternate strategy of containment of the ethical in *Lord Jim.* That is, the theory of despotism situates Jim's activities in a more psychoanalytic way. Jameson suggests that Jim's career offers Jim an Oedipal *Aufhebung* over his father's calling—Jim tries "to re-enact in reality what his father achieves symbolically, in speech and idea"

(*PU*, 211). Where his father was content to act as mediatory ideologue between the landowners and the villagers in the Sussex countryside, Jim, training "in the fore-top" and looking down on the fields, roofs, and factory chimneys (Conrad 1989, 47) literally "raised himself above" his father's merely spiritual vocation.[57] Jim tries to do this, and the novel shows how he fails in this regard. So he must lose his father, kill him by not replying to his last letter, full of what Marlow calls "easy morality," but which Jim carries with him to his death (Conrad, 294–95). Jim has no patronymic.

285 The limits of ethical criticism are the following: Lord Jim is redeemed, the novel suggests, by offering himself to Doramin to kill. Redemption lies in submission to the Oriental despot. Since the novel is all about repetition, Jim again and again offers himself up to an authority figure: the maritime court, Marlow as affable advice-monger, Gentleman Brown (Jim does not attack him), and, finally, Doramin. These Fathers (the letter that we read at page 294 is already a dead one by the time Jim is on trial) are variously tedious, prolix, and vicious, until there is one who is moral *and* authoritative—Doramin. What Doramin represents is the unthinkable synthesis of Žižek's two terms of authority: fairness and power (Žižek 1991a, 249). This interpretation is forbidden by the ethico-imperialist stance of the novel itself, however, where Jewel's remonstrations to Stein and Marlow center around Jim's failure—as if the center of non-European destinies lie in European ethics. What is never questioned is the ethical dimension of Doramin's activities; he is, after all, just another Oriental despot.

a theory of sediment of theory

286 Treating canonical novels is difficult for the Marxist critic: bourgeois critics have to be accounted for, but their readings occlude a politics of the

---

57 Jim is "in the fore-top" early in his training period, still in England. The childishness of this period recalls the reader's embarrassment I earlier posited in relation to Joseph's ambitions in *The Black Sheep*. Jameson's notion that the mass-cultural "degraded narrative" succeeds only because it "solicits [a] lowering of our reality principle" (*PU*, 256) means, then, that both Balzac and Conrad discomfort us because, like someone relating a dream, their text's perfection seems too much like naked desire.

text. This can be summed up in the idea of the "sedimentation of readings," or the notion that previous readings, institutional strictures, and pedagogical practices influence our "reading" of a text even "before" we read it. Jameson's solution to this problem is to make the sediment of previous readings part of the text, or at least to take, say, Leavis's comments on the bifurcation of *Lord Jim*, or existential analyses of the novel, as starting points for his own interpretation.

287 "Each sentence shows the displacement one-eighth of a cycle later than the sentence above it. After sixteen cycles of residue, I think i am hearing the moon. A more violent form of sedimentary transport is the treated text. Freeze frees the writer as poacher. A plagiarist in twilight who moves the coral amplex to adjacent beds."

288 The foregoing passage, from Steve McCaffery's *Theory of Sediment* (1991, 111) articulates and provides figures for the dilemma I just announced. Jameson takes the problem at hand in his analysis of senses and synesthesia in *Nostromo;* Conrad, creating the scene for Charles Gould's proposal to his future wife, describes "in mid-air the sound of a bell, thin and alert . . . like the throbbing pulse of the sunset glow" (Conrad 1985, 83). The aesthetic intensity of the prose at this point is a due compensation, both for the deprivation of sensory input because of the encroaching forces of capitalism (the Romantic project), and for the gaps in Conrad that decenter the Act itself (the Modernist anti-referentiality). Jameson argues that the event, in Conrad, is always deferred.[58] Jim's jump is never narrated in the present, the dictator never arrives in Sulaco on his donkey, and when Gould proposes to his future wife, she faints: "[T]he marriage proposal—the prospect of a new and very different life in Costaguana—opens up a hole in time and a void at the center of reality" (*PU,* 240). But what occasioned this proposition, and how does Gould finally get compensation for his father's mine, turning it into a success?

289 The death of the father. When Gould finds out his father has finally been

---

58 Eagleton argues: "The bomb-explosion in *The Secret Agent,* like Jim's leap from the ship, cannot be directly presented: it suggests a kind of cataclysmic transformation, an unpredictable 'leap' in an organically evolving Nature, which the novel's conservative ideology can accommodate only as impenetrable mystery" (1990b, 138).

killed by the politics of his country, his wife-to-be is "the first person to whom he opened his lips. . . . He had walked straight out of town with the news, straight out before him in the noonday sun on the white road, and his feet had brought him face to face with her in the hall of the ruined *palazzo*, a room magnificent and naked. . . . Charles Gould was dusty with the white dust of the road lying on his boots, on his shoulders, on his cap with two peaks. Water dripped from under it all over his face, and he grasped a thick oaken cudgel in his bare right hand" (82). A reading of this text informed by "sedimentary transport," the sentences' displacement and residue, a reading that plagiarizes Jameson's method, is startled by the subtext of sexuality. Who or what is "magnificent and naked"? Whose lips are opened, for the first time, to whom? Is it a palazzo that is ruined, or a body? The white, sedimentary dust seems suspiciously seminal, forming into two (twin!) peaks, as "water" drips onto Charles's face while he grasps his cudgel, opening his lips for the first time after his father has been killed—as he will soon open a mine that his father could not (but always with the threat of closing it for good).

290 If Lukács the father has been killed, the royal road to interpretation will still be dusty, due to seminal readings like Said's of *Nostromo*, like Eagleton's in *Criticism and Ideology*. This is the strategy of containment of ressentiment, which in *Lord Jim*, Jameson argues, "transformed a modernist text into the precursor of a mass cultural one (a best-selling subgenre)" (*PU*, 271). In *Nostromo*, ressentiment limits Conrad's historical reflections (the splitting of politics into the good Blancos and bad Monteristas), but, at the same time, the ideologeme itself is contained by the narrative of Conrad's novel. As the central gap or hole—the flight of the dictator Ribiera—is deferred textually by the novel's *récit*, ressentiment is limited by *Nostromo*. The sediment of theory that covers the Jameson-text at this moment (when he shifts to a consideration of Nostromo and Decoud as metonyms for nineteenth-century populism and industrialism) is a strict Althusserianism of the first order: an Althusserianism, that is, outlined by Eagleton in *Criticism and Ideology*. Eagleton argues that the "absent centre of *Nostromo* is in part Nostromo himself, but also the silver of which he is the agent—the inert, opaque matter around which the human action frenetically swirls. As the determining structure of which the novel's characters are the bearers (the true protagonist of the book, as Conrad commented), the silver has for Conrad no

coherent historical intelligibility, it is a principle which must of necessity be dramatically absent. It is precisely in these absent centers, which 'hollow' rather than scatter and fragment the organic forms of Conrad's fiction, that the relations of that fiction to its ideological context is laid bare" (1990b, 138–39).

291 Eagleton's absent center is raised dialectically to become, as interpretation, the sedimentary absent cause of the *Nostromo* interpretation in *The Political Unconscious*. The meditation on silver as a sedimentation of value—Sartre's practico-inert is alluded to here, with all of its rich suggestion that this inertness signifies an absence[59]—and determining structure "remains locked," as Terry Collits argues, "into an Althusserian grid" (1989, 303). The interpretation that the absent silver disfigures Conrad's organicism is itself a central event in Marxist criticism which can only be "present/absent in the most classic Derridean fashion, present only in its initial absence, absent when it is supposed to be most intensely present" (*PU*, 272). Eagleton's is an absent sedimentation—not the present sediment of Raymond Williams, Stephen Zelnick, or Georg Lukács. Williams's reading of *Nostromo* as the disappearance of social value is unacceptable (*PU*, 228n), and, as Jameson comments on Zelnick, "[A]ny effort of Marxist criticism to articulate the 'progressive' content of a classical work . . . needs to be accompanied by a reminder of what is essentially 'reactionary' about it, as so much in Conrad unquestioningly is" (*PU*, 235n). Lukács's attacks on existentialism and modernism vitiate Jameson's project, for, while Lukács's anti-modernism was in error only for the ethical load placed on "reification" (and otherwise was essentially correct: *PU*, 226–27), the Hungarian philosopher's attempt to historicize existentialism is "an object lesson in how not to do this particular job" (*PU*, 259).

292 Where you might expect Eagleton's interpretation to be most intensely present, as founding act in an Althusserian approach to Conrad, there is instead "this hole at the center of the narrative" as Jameson re-places the events and silver in *Nostromo*, replacing them as allegorical emblems for the utopian figuration of collective action. "Jameson's (undeclared) argument

---

59 " 'The silver is gone [Charles Gould "declared, firmly"], and I am glad of it' " (Conrad 1985, 346). The silver is actually more effective in its own absence, as the doctor tells Mrs. Gould: " '[T]he shadow of the treasure may do just as well as the substance.' "

with Eagleton over *Nostromo* turns on a question about form," Collits declares (306). But what sort of argument is going on, an "(undeclared)" one,
that can only be declared so in parentheses, an argument in which, Collits
says, Jameson's text "can be seen as a move beyond the Althusserian closure
of Eagleton's Conrad" (306), but a "move beyond" that Collits then quickly
adds is an " 'advance' " only if we frame it in quotation marks?

mass culture, at last

293   *"[I]t does not take much reflection* [to which one might reply: it takes a lot
of reflection, especially to determine the function of this sudden and molecular jump to the thematics of the "Reification and Utopia in Mass Culture" essay (*SV,* 9–34), a moment again antagonistic to the putatively ironclad narrative of *The Political Unconscious,* and which is then treated in this,
my chapter, as a capitulation of tropes that also segues to the following chapter on postmodernism and mass culture in a way that attempts to vitiate the
normative "chapter" division] *to see that a process of compensatory exchange*
[here the two poles of mass culture as drug and mass culture as freedom are
negated at once, with the proposition that there exists an *exchange* between
audience and medium] *must be involved here* [the "must" is one of Jameson's
most problematic operators], *in which the henceforth manipulated viewer* [the-
ories of manipulation mistake Althusser's ISA's or Gramsci's civil society for
the more naked manipulation of the police and the soldiery: the great finding
of Chomsky is that a liberal state (usually) *does not need* to use violence on its
own people] *is offered specific gratifications* [first: they are specific: this is not
totality as a system of one, but of difference, and thus mass culture accom-
modates the heterogeneity of viewers; second, the gratification ranges from
sexual titillation to vicarious violence—but these *are* pleasurable, as is the
transferred dream and envy of the ethnic family in *The Godfather* (*SV,* 32–
33)] *in return for his or her consent to passivity* [this last reminds us that
Jameson is not saying mass culture audiences are "activists" or de Cer-
teauesque "poachers"—*Star Trek* fans are not the new (generation) proletariat,[60] but the question of a consent that must be nonetheless elicited

---

60 Henry Jenkins's essay on fandom (1991) is the most extreme example of this, but
see also Constance Penley's essay on "slash" or homoerotic fan writing by women (1991).

reminds us of the Sartrean imperative that the subject is free]. *In other words* [a convenient duplication of intent or layering of signification], *if the ideo-logical function of mass culture is understood as a process whereby otherwise dangerous and protopolitical* [the protopolitical because political impulses or desires are only possible in the collective or Sartrean group] *impulses are 'managed'* [the scare-quotes around Norman Holland's term belies the im-portant figure—the way in which culture uses and directs libidinal energies is thus a business trope] *and defused* [thus stressing the anti-masses nature of mass culture], *rechanneled* [into object-fetishes of consumer goods, of essen-tially *wrong* political action] *and offered spurious objects, then some preliminary* [the "then" here serves to remind the reader that the foregoing way of under-standing mass culture, "as a process whereby otherwise," is the originary moment for a theoretical project] *step must also be theorized in which these same impulses* [the repetition of these "same" impulses from the subordinate clause immediately preceding this clause is akin to the Conradian (and Bloomsburyan) recuperation of a minor character to play a pivotal actantial role, as in the "background" Indians in *Lord Jim* whose dog is the occasion for Marlow and Jim meeting—that meeting, terribly overdetermined, almost ended in violence, because Jim thought Marlow was calling him a "cur" and, while Marlow was not even the addressee of the yellow beast, his comment that he was "getting a little angry, too, at the absurdity of this encounter" (Conrad 1989, 95) shows that the impressionistic epistemology and indeter-minacy of *Lord Jim* has some very violent effects—but anyway, the bringing of a semic element in the "ground" to the central "figure," in Jameson's text if not in Conrad's, bespeaks a collective dialectics, "in which the ideological would be grasped as somehow at one with the Utopian, and the Utopian at one with the ideological" (*PU,* 286)]—*the raw material* [current events as our "savage mind"] *upon which the process works—are initially awakened* [mass culture must, nevertheless, dance with the political in the audience] *within the very text that seeks to still them. If the function of the mass cultural text is meanwhile seen rather as the production of false consciousness* [false conscious-ness is still a useful category for Marxist thought, then] *and the symbolic reaffirmation of this or that legitimizing strategy* [while that "production" is the text's "symbolic action" in the Burke/Lévi-Strauss sense, the "symbolic re-affirmation" here is the allegory at work in the text (the second and first of

Jameson's three interpretive horizons, respectively)], *even this process cannot be grasped as one of sheer violence (the* [Gramscian] *theory of hegemony is explicitly distinguished from control by brute force* [repeating the warning against seeing manipulation everywhere, or left-conspiracy-theoryism]) *nor as one inscribing the appropriate attitudes upon a blank slate, but must necessarily involve a complex strategy of rhetorical persuasion* [where rhetoric is not seen just as a cataloging of media] *in which substantial incentives are offered for ideological adherence. We will say that such incentives, as well as the impulses to be managed by the mass cultural text, are necessarily Utopian in nature"* [*PU,* 287: this will be the subject of the next chapter of my work; for now, it is not difficult to find a moment in *The Political Unconscious* where Jameson or the text gestures beyond the immediate, or the macro-narrative, where the immediate (the molecular) gestures to other concerns, in a move encompassing the dialectic of antagonisms and alliances as (mass) culture encompasses utopia and ideology].

four conrads

294 There are at least, finally, four or five Conrads, or versions of Conrad that are graspable in postmodern theory: there is the Conrad of Flaubertian or Jamesian irony, the Conrad of mass-culture boys' lit, the Conrad of diaspora and multiculturalism, the Conrad of miscegenation, and the Conrad of Wyndham Lewis excess. The first two of these positions are amply demonstrated in Jameson's readings, where the aesthete meets postmodernism; the dialectic of pulp literature enables the recourse elsewhere in *Lord Jim,* for example, to Sollers-esque textuality. The Conrad of diaspora and multiculturalism[61]—*Almayer's Folly*—is largely determined by the "base" of the international imperial projects that considered Latin America, Africa, and

---

61 Conrad's documented racism will make this claim seem grotesque to some: my point is not to apologize or explain away that racism but instead to locate his texts, in spite of the author's biographical politics, in an objective context of an imperialism whose effects—including emigration and "deterritorialization"—he seemed to be especially sensitive to, no doubt because of his own Polish background.

Asia to be storehouses for European capital. But Conrad's technique also played a small part, as Ian Watt shows: "Many of the details given in *Lord Jim* about the *Patna* are based on the actual incident, but Conrad made a number of changes. For instance, he internationalized the cast: the actual captain of the *Jeddah* was English, not German; and the rescuer was in fact not a French but a British officer" (1981, 266). The characters' constant limbo, homeless or in diaspora, is not just a function of their service for the empire. When the Assistant Commissioner in *The Secret Agent* decides to go look for the anarchist Verloc himself (as in his former days as a *colonial* policeman), Conrad describes his minor disguise thus: "And he himself had become unplaced" (1990, 152). This is in the context of the narrator ruminating upon the "atmosphere of fraudulent cookery" (Conrad 1990, 151) in an Italian restaurant; what more fitting symbol of postmodern nomadism is there than the ethnic restaurant, with all the ensuing arguments as to whether the cuisine is authentic or not?[62] *The Secret Agent,* then, fits in as a precursor to Lewis's own excesses, not only stylistic, but also political. Formally, as Eagleton has noted, the novel is hysterically anti-naturalist (Eagleton 1986, 24). It also foreshadows Lewis's greatest political novel, *The Revenge for Love:* in both cases, descriptive *jouissance* is allied to a limiting misanthropic critique that, by focusing on supposed radicals (anarchists in the one, Communists in the other), "shows" that progressive politics are a sham. It will be with a later political novelist, E. L. Doctorow, that formal and political concerns find a greater harmony or alliance: ironically, that novelist and his work will then be contemplated as a typical postmodern artifact.

62 Žižek mentions somewhere that nothing more authentically bespeaks the lack of ethnicity than a restaurant. Jameson's image of Marxism in postmodernity being like a faded Russian restaurant in a gleaming postmodern hotel (*PM,* 297) recalls, like a ghostly afterimage, the figure at the beginning of Conrad's *Victory:* "[T]here is a fascination in coal, the supreme commodity of the age in which we are camped like bewildered travellers in a garish, unrestful hotel" (Conrad 1979, 19). Of course, that casual trope of Conrad's is then revealed to be a shrunken dwarf all its own, as, during the course of *Victory,* a succession of actors come to audition for the actant of the "bewildered travellers" in the German Schomberg's hotel: the women's orchestra, perhaps, or Heyst himself, or maybe even Davidson. The Bloomsburyan play of minor/major characters in the novel—Heyst is absent for so much of it—leads me to suspect that perhaps the hotel really prefigures the island getaway Heyst is holed up in with his English girl.

4

THE HYSTERIA OF

MASS CULTURE

critical mass

295 As Eric Havelock argues in *Preface to Plato*, there is now little doubt that Plato was the first theorist of mass culture. *The Republic* is not a work of political theory. Havelock got it partly correct when he argued that *The Republic* was about how to forge an education system to ensure a smoothly operating state. He too is wrong: as the famed passages on Homer and poetry show, Plato narrowed down his concern even more, beyond even "writing" (McLuhan 1968, 25), to the role of mass culture in his contemporary Greece. That mass culture was what we can call (following Havelock's notion of the Homeric encyclopedia) Homeric TV or movies: "performance of poetry was fundamental in adult recreation" (Havelock 1963, 37).

296 Critics have traditionally fallen into one of three psychological-ethical stances: the hysterical, the obsessional, and the pervert. "The *hysterical* ethical imperative is to keep desire alive at any price" (Žižek 1991a, 271): this is the Arnoldian fetish for art, where the critic sees his role as a promoter of aesthetic bliss: Nabokov or John Metcalf would be obvious examples. The "*obsessional* desire is the Other's demand," which sublimates art to some ideal or metaphysical project of "accessibility" or "commitment." This ethic ranges from the ridiculous Zhdanov to the sublime Sartre. The pervert, who seeks "to work for the Other's enjoyment, to become an object-instrument of it," now sees the Other as precisely the opposite of the obsessed critic (or as theory), and seeks only to make the reader "work" for it; here a paradigm might be the L=A=N=G=U=A=G=E poet-critics.

297 Plato falls into the second category: faced with a populace that is learning the wrong lessons from art, he does not try to understand why he thinks those lessons are wrong (he thinks this because of his metaphysic) or how to reeducate the people; his response, that is, is to obsess on the inadequacies of the art form itself. What is it in Homer that is so bad? And do not reach for the easy answer of "representation."

298 There are two guiding principles behind Plato's critique of poetry—the latter being the MTV of Athens. First of all, the masses were and are a *hysterical* mass, a group whose desire was only to desire, as Lacan would put it. This desire to desire means first of all a desire to enjoy art for all the right reasons—but the masses cannot: they have been deracinated and expelled and thus they can only desire to desire (Horkheimer and Adorno's parable of the oarsmen is not so anachronistic after all). It means secondly that the masses, if they cannot enjoy Homer as art, will *use* it as mass culture. This last means that if godlike virtues are not learnt from the *Iliad,* then how to attack your government will be. This is the true mass-culture meaning of the "Homeric encyclopedia" of methods and arsenals, where an encyclopedia is not seen as some eighteenth-century document of enlightenment but as a twentieth-century middle brow compendium designed for the edification of the masses—a university for the working class. Havelock remarks that he will "deliberately adopt the hypothesis that the tale itself [of the *Iliad*] is designed as a kind of literary portmanteau which is to contain a collection of assorted usages, conventions, prescriptions, and procedures"—shades of Will Durant![1]

299 Why are the masses hysterical? The answer to this lies in the second "reason" for Plato's take on Homer, which can be found in Luce Irigaray's critique of Plato. That is, Plato's horror of the cave, his horror of his own allegory, is predicated on a misogyny directed at the womb or *hysteron.* As far as Plato is concerned, the masses are chained into the womb—chained, and watching TV. Irigaray describes the implications of Plato's phallocentric

---

1 Joan Shelley Rubin describes Durant's role as creator of philosophical outlines and guides in *The Making of Middlebrow Culture* (1992, 209–65).

critique as follows: "So men have lived in this cave since their childhood. . . . The cave cannot be explored in the round, walked around, measured in the round. Which means that the men all stay there in the same spot—same place, same time—in the same *circle,* or circus ring, the *theatrical arena* of that representation" (1987, 244–55; original emphasis). The man-child of Irigaray's rewriting of *The Republic* has been forced since birth (mass culture is always most pernicious in its effect upon the young) to sit in a row, in a space that cannot be explored (the cool, non-space of the television or movie screen), in a *theatrical* space at the same time (Saturday afternoon movies, after-school cartoons). Without Plato's twelve-step program, "they are condemned to look . . . toward the metaphorical project of the back of the cave, which will serve as a *backcloth* for all the representations to come" (Irigaray 1987, 245). The speculum with which Plato would drag the prole, squalling, out of the cave, is of course ideal speculation itself, which replaces the Homeric TV with the bright lights of the great lens man.

300 The role of the critic discussed above, a prophylactic of the phallic proletariat,[2] is evidently different from that proposed in Terry Eagleton's *The Function of Criticism.* There Eagleton puts forward the utopian project that critics can participate in the construction of a public sphere, an undertaking in the past that meant the coffeehouse culture of the nascent English bourgeoisie.[3] But whereas that public sphere was dissociated from the "intimate sphere" of the family (Eagleton 1987, 115–18), the family is now, under the blinkless gaze of late capitalism, "no longer the privileged site of subjectivity." When right-wing ideologues pin their hopes on the family, a fantasy island pitted against television in which the latter is somehow both a product of an elite and a moral vacuum, the desperation of the gesture is

2 I use "phallic" here not as a synonym for "phallocentric" as that latter word usually denotes, but instead in Žižek's sense of that which "sticks out" and thus *betrays* patriarchy. This distinction is discussed below in the sections on Hitchcock.

3 Aamir Mufti (1991) argues that the pan-Islamic reaction to *The Satanic Verses* demonstrated the presence, and strength, of an Islamic public sphere, "in which resistance to neototalitarian movements and discourses is marginalized or brutally suppressed" (107). Mufti argues that the novel is not so much irreligious as participating in a critique from *within* that sphere. (See also Suleri, who argues that *The Satanic Verses* suggests "blasphemy can be articulated only within the compass of belief" [1992, 191].)

probably overemphasized by both sides of the debate—media mavens, like their academic counterparts during the p.c. debate, are not a little flattered at the attention. But if mass culture, as Eagleton argues, has taken on a political function in late capitalism (in common with the canon and political correctness debates, the "function" is simply as a site for struggle—Poulantz—as the state and other spheres are in classic Althusserian theory as outlined in my previous chapter) that is both progressive and reactionary. Mass culture, Eagleton writes "displaces the family as the arena in which needs and desires are negotiated, and indeed progressively penetrates the family itself" (1987, 121); the television in particular is both *in* the family spatially and *about* the family discursively.

301 One of my strategies in this chapter will be to overemphasize Jameson's work on mass culture and film, just as in the previous chapter I dwelt for so long on questions of Althusserian interpretation, and in the one previous to that, the role of Sartre. I favour the rhetoric of hyperbole here because exaggeration opens up a space for deliberation otherwise closed to the discreet or subtle reading. An uncharitable reader might oppose to hyperbole not subtlety but accuracy; but here a parallel argument might be made with respect to the earlier critique of "shock" mentioned in chapter 2 (based on Alan Davies [1991]). Deleuze has suggested that in Hitchcock, shock is replaced by suspense (1989, 164); suspense is more drawn-out, providing the space for reflections and anticipations both false and real (here the true-false dichotomy is irrelevant, for suspense is designed to mislead and thus can only work if wrong events are anticipated as well as right ones). But while this may work for the proper modernist canon of Hitchcock, what of horror in its postmodernist guise: Tobe Hooper, John Carpenter, Clive Barker? In *Candyman* (Bernard Rose, 1992), adapted from a Barker short story, the suspense is so overwhelming that fright replaces cognition.[4] In a like man-

---

4 Like *The People Under the Stairs* (Craven, 1991), *Candyman* articulates a post-Reagan shift in horror and suspense from the Freudian problematic of the *family* (Robin Wood's [1986] thesis) to the public space of racial and class violence. So in *Candyman*, the two heroines, an African American woman and a white woman, are both as frightened by the prospect of entering Chicago's Cabrini Green housing project as they are at investigating the "truth" of the Candyman, a myth with connotations of both urban legend and

ner, hyperbole in its present-day, postmodern usage (Baudrillard, Žižek, Foucault) can also be a tool to shut down critical distance and analysis. So it may not be accurate then, to argue that unlike accuracy or subtlety, which fetishizes a bourgeois truth-content and a slavedom of the Right, hyperbole and exaggeration, in their suggestion of the possible, provide a space for investigations undeterred by their eventual falsity. To pursue this filmic endeavor: shock and suspense can be completed dialectically with the proper third term "tension." Some recent films demonstrate the function of tension in cinema as both a space for introspection and distancing. In Quentin Tarantino's *Reservoir Dogs,* a torture scene is, the first time viewed, horrific not only because of the blood (there has been blood all the way through the movie) nor the actions of Michael Madsen's character (as he cuts off a policeman's ear). Rather, it is the *tension* that is pure cinema at this moment: the feeling of open-endedness and indeterminacy. *We do not know what will happen.* Similarly, in Nick Gomez's *Laws of Gravity,* three characters walk into a five-and-dime and shoplift. The erratic camera, the swiftness with which the men, in particular, take folded bags out of their waistbands and begin filling them with cosmetic and household goods, all of this is *negated* by the feeling that *they must be caught.*

302   But it is space, not time, which is the central concern of postmodernism, whether it is formulated in terms of a vulgar-Marxist emphasis on the "geographical transfer of value" in Soja's *Postmodern Geographies* (1990, 112–17), or Jameson's more rarefied recent meditations on Heideggerian space in Hitchcock, Chandler, and world cinema (1992; 1993a; *GA*). As Soja explains Greek architect/planner Costis Hadjimichalis's notion of the geographical transfer of value, it is "the mechanism or process through which a part of the value produced at one location, area, or region is realized in another, adding to the receiving region's localized accumulation base" (113).[5]

---

suppressed African American historiography. See, for a less epistemological view, an essay on suspense by Bonitzer (1992).

5   Soja notes (114n) that the parent notion for this concept is Marx's idea of antagonism between town and countryside; another offspring of Marx's notion would also be Harold Innis's long-standing ruminations on Canada's essentially inferior position in terms of staple economies (cod fisheries, the fur trade) and the concomitant "conquest of

303 Jameson, then, sees as a key recurrent theme in postmodern culture the will-to-roam, or the nomadism of the film: "*The Parallax View* enfolds a variety of landscapes within itself by way of documenting its model of the social totality as conspiracy. As with *Videodrome* (and also, in a different way, *North by Northwest*), the multiplicity of landscapes becomes something like an *analogon* for aesthetic as well as epistemological closure" (*GA*, 63). This "closure" reiterates the essential mass-cultural nature of Jameson's object: hence the clichéd idea that mass cultural texts are more conservative aesthetically is turned back onto itself and shown to be a necessary precondition of their encapsulating the reactionary nature of late capitalism itself; just as the "conspiracy" motif of the films Jameson discusses in the first half of *The Geopolitical Aesthetic* (*Videodrome, The Parallax View, All the President's Men*) embodies the politically unrepresentable nature of totality itself (rather like the hardly visual images we will be offered on the nightly news of a stack of dollar bills or coins—Loonies?—reaching up to the moon to "represent" the federal deficit), so the films' narrative closure, their abnegation of Godardian open-ness, more accurately reflects the anti-Foucauldean conclusion that the world is not carceral, but is instead "the more intense nightmare of . . . a world conspiratorially organized and controlled as far as the eye can see" (*GA*, 60). The hysterical or invaginatory nature of Jameson's trope "enfolds," then, repeats earlier notions of the footnote as a container, totality-as-negative methodology that can somehow reflect back onto the totality of the late capitalist system. In the more esoteric senses of space, Jameson extends the totality notion literally to its own edge. Discussing the filmic movement across the United States in *North by Northwest*, Jameson remarks that "this sequence of spaces generates a sense of completeness (or a 'totality-effect') which can scarcely be explained by content alone. Comparable formal problems (and 'solutions') can be found in Raymond Chandler's equally episodic (and spatial) detective stories, where the successful mapping of the Los Angeles region—in other words, our sense that, in spite of necessary selectivity, 'totalization' has been achieved—is structurally dependent on the inclusion of some ultimate boundary or verge of

---

'geographic barriers'" (Kroker 1985, 94). A more recent Canadian theory of space is Rob Shields's *Places on the Margin: Alternative Geographies of Modernity* (1991).

Being itself (in *Farewell, My Lovely*, the sea) [see Jameson 1993]. In the Hitchcock film, the stereotypical or imaginary frame is clearly some phantasmic United States. . . . Yet here too, as in Chandler, the completeness of the enumerated elements (of such a map-phantasm) is not enough: we must also come to the ultimate edge of all this, in order for it to recohere retroactively as a satisfyingly exhaustive itinerary" (Jameson 1992, 56). The reterritorialization of the movie, as it literally "moves" across the world, is an attempt on the part of mass culture to decolonize the geographic space that has been imperiously claimed by late capital as it reorganizes, in a symptom-like repetition of nineteenth-century imperialism, the global terrain into unequal zones of *maquiladoras*, silicone valleys, and "reforested" watersheds.

304 Mike Davis, in his pre-rebellion article "The L.A. Inferno" (1992a), provides a chilling image of the geopolitical movement of peoples and capital when interviewing a Honduran immigrant smashing computer equipment for salvage: "Miguel is about to deliver a massive blow to the VDT of a Macintosh when I ask him why he came to Los Angeles. His hammer hesitates for a second, then he smiles and answers: 'Because I wanted to work for your high technology economy.' I wince as the hammer falls. The Macintosh implodes" (60). Davis's *City of Quartz* also documents exhaustively how Los Angeles's place in the "Pacific Rim" geo-economy affects the most disenfranchised (1992b, 105–45). Davis's work seems to demonstrate a revenge of Althusserianism (see also his two Open Magazine pamphlets)—that is, Los Angeles, in Davis's "excavations," enfolds the geopolitical structure-in-dominance, so that the city's progressive loss of economic self-determination is reflected in its various carceral and virtual "scanscape" reterritorializations. Jameson, in his chapter on Godard in *The Geopolitical Aesthetic,* argues that a certain event in the film "serves to block out the great spatial opposition in *Passion* between the film studio and the factory, between superstructure and base, the image of the thing and the thing itself, reproduction and production, aesthetics and political economy, the technology of the postmodern period and the older assembly-line technology of the previous (or monopoly) stage" (*GA,* 173–74).

305 But mass culture possesses a spatial component that has rarely been analyzed: the place of the television in the living room or bedroom or kitchen, the full-frontal "nudity" of magazine displays versus the more discreet

spines of books, the collective space of the movie theater—and, finally, the space of the text itself (see de Certeau 1988, 134–35), here conceived of through the figure of the quilt, a figure that is about the search for a figure which occupies so much of Jameson's work. Two recent instances of quilt- ing are the re-valorization of women's work under the proper name of Judy Chicago (see her *Embroidering Our Heritage: The Dinner Party* [1980]), and, the NAMES project or AIDS quilt. Like other linguistic memorials—the Vietnam memorial in Washington, D.C., or the Toronto AIDS memorial, the NAMES project works in large because of the accumulation of identities as proper names—because of their being quilted together, that is. As my own development of "cognitive mapping," mass culture emerges as an under- class to the more elite forms of culture and entertainment. And my emphasis on the place of mass culture seems to me to be as satisfying in terms of understanding the "objects" of Jameson's inquiry as is the recent tendency of postcolonial critics to use concepts of the Third World to critique Jame- son's work on postmodernism. So Santiago Colás argues that the Third World "is at the heart of Jameson's pathbreaking assertion that postmodern- ism is 'the cultural logic of late capitalism'" (1992, 258). The parallel is not disingenuous: mass culture, like the cultures of the Third World, has lately been ossified into cultural studies, like postcolonial studies, in no small part because of the attraction both hold for middle-class and First World intellec- tuals. Mass culture is not a "dark continent," in Freud's dubious metaphor, but a bright incontinence, a mindlessness attractive to intellectuals who have "forgotten" or never had a heritage of trash, bright and without shadow (see Hebdige 1988) in the way of so many Kubrick or Pakula films.

can the skatepunk speak?

306 When Gayatri Chakravorty Spivak asked the original version of this question, she cast radical doubt into the minds of many professional theo- rists around the globe who wanted to "let the people speak." Many readers here are no doubt outraged at the travesty of this section's title, as if that serious project cannot be compared with my love of trash culture, but surely to divide one's political and cultural projects is the same disingenuous sort of

classification that various movements of "the post" are seeking to move beyond. This title "refers" to a specific text (the song "Silent Kid" by the California group Pavement), and to my uncanny feeling recently, reading Sara Suleri's *Meatless Days* (1989) that *this* was like listening to Pavement, in the flux of discourses similar to both, that is. Pavement most effectively captures the radical mass-cultural stream the band's constituency finds itself in: a combination of boomer-dominated FM (that's why they're so much like The Beatles, why they sample Led Zeppelin), Mexican and Central American pop and salsa, light jazz (Dave Brubeck), 1980s British Alternative (The Fall), hip-hop, and discordant punk (indeed, who can listen to Beck's album *Mellow Gold* [1994] without hearing Cypress Hill, as well as bluegrass, hardcore, and folk?).[6] A Pavement song mentions skateboarding as the epitome of nostalgic moments in order to "authorize" its critique of the Stone Temple Pilots. For Suleri, this flux is determined both by history (Pakistan in the 1970s) and by the framing of that history via the family and the media (the function of gossip, then, as a "record" of the war), all rendered in the language of language: "For Ifat's gold was in her speech, in language that reflected like a radiance from her: they would find nothing at her interior. My father did not deserve to be so questioned, making him look up with anger, when he had to spell out such obviousness—'*I* India, *F* Frank, *A* Apple, *T* Thomas'" (1989, 174).

6 In a like manner, music popular with the Toronto-area skate scene (with crossovers and alliances with scooter clubs, snowboarding, and downtown hardcore) will include local bands like PolitiKill InCorect [*sic*], YAP (Yet Another Posse), Armed and Hammered, and Hev's Duties, as well as better-known groups like De La Soul, Fugazi, A Tribe Called Quest, Dr. Dre, Snoop Doggy Dogg, and House of Pain. Commenting on fan reception, Jeremy Dove, rapper with YAP (they're all suburban white kids), said: "One night there was a couple of neo-Nazi skinheads at a gig in Oshawa. They didn't actually say anything to us, just walked around the bar going 'Get this fuckin' shit outta here.' And somebody wrote on the bathroom wall: 'Fuck all this grunge hip-hop shit/Keep '80s British Alternative alive!'" (O'Connor 1994, 26). These alliances of taste cultures are always unstable, then: see, on the one hand, Chris Wodsku's (1994) argument that indie "pop" (Velocity Girl, cub, jale) constitutes a new synthesis of aggro-punk and pop melodies, and Terry Bloomfield's (1991) exploration of precisely the vexed question of "British Alternative."

307 But I am more interested in how it now seems texts from the "under-developed" worlds or zones are so immediately allegorical that Jameson and Rushdie (to take two names out of a hat) must, in turn, be enfolded into their very texts. It seems to me that critiques of Jameson's project or essay ("Third-World Literature in the Era of Multinational Capitalism" [1986b]) falter precisely at this connection of mass culture and the "literature of the Third World" (both terms are equally problematic), and this is why, in the comments I have seen on Jameson's essay (including Colás, Ahmad 1992, but also Prasad 1992, Suleri 1992 [13–14], Sprinker 1993, and Beverley 1993), there has been little or no mention of the founding importance Jameson accords to mass culture in his essay. (But see the transition from "Latin American Postmodernism" to "Postmodern Music" in John Beverley's *Against Literature*.) On the first page, Jameson compares "admitting" Third World texts to the canon to the attempts to read Dashiell Hammett as great literature, and comments that "[t]his is to attempt dutifully to wish away all traces of that 'pulp' format which is constitutive of sub-genres" (1986b, 65). Hence Tarantino. More relevantly, Jameson argues that the "conclusive nail" in his argument that First World intellectuals *must* enlarge their (our) reading practices is that "we all do 'read' many different kinds of texts in this life of ours, since, whether we are willing to admit it or not, we spend much of our existence in the force field of a mass culture that is radically different from our 'great books' and live at least a double life in the various compartments of our unavoidably fragmented society" (1986b, 66–67).

308 Now this is what really interests me about Jameson's essay, and it recalls both Cornel West's comment in an interview that such European theorists as Habermas and Lyotard typically have little to say about mass culture (West 1988, 272–75)—that is, their discourse excludes or marginalizes that "private" realm of pleasure—and Said's comment (again, in an interview [Wicke and Sprinker 1992], the interview being the place for admitting to private pleasures, after all) about his own *lack* of knowledge of contemporary popular music (Wicke and Sprinker, 247). For what constitutes the intellectual in contemporary society may be said to be, that she or he forbears "what are essentially private pleasures" for the autotelic or at least autonomous (but finally *rigorous*) pursuits of the object; that is, that which constitutes a lack

precisely because pleasure has been deferred or sworn off. "Cultural studies" does little to address this in its eagerness to embrace every icon produced by a corporate monstrosity; semiotics is for ad agencies, however, and a Canadian beer debuted in 1994 with the slogan "alt beer," suggesting the "alt.sex.bondage" newsgroups on the Internet. Cult.studs transforms low culture into an object. But Jameson's work challenges this division of the subject (which, since the private is always historical, reproduces the class division of the social) through his repeated admissions or references to "private pleasure." Geeky stuff like science fiction? Yeah, I like it. Shoot-'em-up cop movies like *Dog Day Afternoon*? Right on, dude! Frequently in his recent work, that is, Jameson figures himself as a projection of American progressive/imperialism (in the sense of a progressive middle class which realizes it is complicit).

309 Jameson's essay on Third World literature, then, is rife with these sort of moments which are a lot like the comment on "looking over" a colleague's shoulder in *Signatures of the Visible*. The essay begins with a meditation on First World unease toward Third World texts, culminating in a properly sarcastic acknowledgment of the importance of a Reaganite philologist: "We may therefore—as 'humanists'—acknowledge the pertinence of the critique of present-day humanities by our titular leader, William Bennett, without finding any great satisfaction in his embarrassing solution" (1986b, 67). "[W]e ourselves are (perhaps without fully knowing it) constitutive forces powerfully at work" (68), and it "is a matter of some shame for an American to witness the cultural curriculum in a socialist setting" (74), and yet "it seems to me that one of our basic political tasks lies precisely in the ceaseless effort to remind the American public of the radical difference of other national situations" (77). Finally, however, Jameson concludes on a less than optimistic note: "It strikes me that [for] we Americans, we masters of the world . . . [t]he view from the top is epistemologically crippling" (85). So in some ways Jameson's essay should be read "in the institution" (that is, the American academy) or viewed in a Robbins-Fish-Foucault paradigm as being *produced* by that institution; he seeks to use the changing composition of comparative literature to carry out the political task of educating the American public.

310 Jameson's discourse is also produced by the institutional struggles which

have resulted in "postcolonialism" (with or without the hyphen) as an attempt to normalize the threats to liberal humanism by Third World struggles, an attempt critiqued by Anne McClintock: "[A]dmittedly another p-c word, 'post-colonialism' is arguably more palatable and less foreign-sounding to sceptical deans than 'Third World Studies.' It also has a less accusatory ring than 'Studies in Neo-colonialism,' say, or 'Fighting Two Colonialisms.' It is more global, and less fuddy-duddy, than 'Commonwealth Studies.' The term borrows, moreover, on the dazzling marketing success of the term 'post-modernism'" (1992, 93).

homi don't play that

311 But to return to Jameson's essay, what is at stake, first, in his usage of Third World theory and, second, in his comments on national allegory? I have already drawn a parallel between the use of Third World theory and what used to be called vulgar Marxism; what of this stuff on national allegory? It seems to me that Ahmad's (and, say, Suleri's) criticism of Jameson's assertion fail to read the essay in the formal way that stresses such metalinguistic themes as *register*.[7] As I argue here, the essay is the site for massive *in*security, not ease of assertion: insecurity with the U.S. hegemony, with the institutions of the academy, with the status of First World intellectuals. More specifically, Jameson introduces his theory in the most couched and "framed" manner possible: "*[L]et me now,* by way of a *sweeping* hypothesis, try to say what all third-world cultural productions *seem* to have in common and what distinguishes them radically from analogous cultural forms in the first world. All third-world texts are necessarily, *I want to argue,* allegorical, and in a very specific way: they are to be read as *what I will call national allegories*" (Jameson 1986b, 69: all but the last two words emphasized by me). The qualifications are not the mark of standard liberal self-consciousness; rather, they undermine the statements in order to open up a debate.

312 My attention to the linguistic or even typographical framing of Jameson's assertions should not be interpreted as apolitical formalism, for while it

---

7 Again, in respect to the framing that goes on in Jameson's essay, I am less interested in cataloging it—in turning the work into my own *object*—than in using the frames as the basis for an examination of some criticism of the essay.

may be a disciplinary hangover of my own work in experimental and small press poetry, the disputes over even such issues as the capitalization or hyphenation of terms like postcolonialism or postmodernism (admit it, you just ran my versions of these words against your own cerebral spell-check) show how these formal issues become the sites for larger battles. A good example of the pitfalls of typography, then, can be seen in Sara Suleri's quotation of the above passage from Jameson's essay, with the following after an ellipsis: "*The story of the private individual destiny is always an allegory of the embattled situation of the public third-world culture and society*" (Jameson 1986b, 69; qtd. Suleri 1992, 13). Evidently, some of Suleri's authority in disputing Jameson comes from the italicization of his assertion, so it seems as if Jameson is dictating what Third World intellectuals *must* produce and how these productions *must* be interpreted. Aijaz Ahmad, too, ignores some aspects of the frames in Jameson's text even while he stresses others. Most effectively, Ahmad frames his own critique in the context of the grateful or at least gracious student of Western Marxism. Indeed, his essay opens in such a tone: "In assembling the following notes on Fredric Jameson . . . I find myself in an awkward position. If I were to name the *one* literary critic/theorist writing in the USA today whose work I generally hold in the highest regard, it would surely be Jameson's" (Ahmad 1992, 95). He continues on the second page with the comment that "because I am a Marxist, I had always thought of us, Jameson and myself, as birds of the same feather, even though we never quite flocked together" (96). This might seem a little disingenuous, given the severity of the critique that follows: it resembles nothing so much as the good cop/bad cop technique of seventies television.[8] But of course we always say something is "just rhetoric" when we do not agree (as every unpopular decision at work is said to be "for political reasons").

8   When I was training to be an officer in the Canadian military in 1980–81, we were taught the same method for interviewing noncommissioned soldiers. That is, good and bad observations were to be "sandwiched" for greater effect. More recently, the "crack" Canadian Airborne Regiment, on peacekeeping duty in Somalia in early 1993, tried the same method, if more physically, against Somali "thieves" on the U.N. compound, resulting in the death of a Somali teenager and the attempted suicide of one of his Canadian "guards." I don't offer these anecdotes in any way to compare myself or Ahmad to racist soldiers, but, rather, to draw a continuum between the rhetorical or formal framing strategies to be found in various discursive practices.

313 I am not so uncomfortable with Ahmad's own framing as with what attention he does or does not pay to framing in Jameson's essay. Ahmad's first, and founding argument is that Jameson is not simply calling for curriculum reform but also formulating a cognitive aesthetics of Third World literature which depends on "a suppression of the multiplicity of significant differences among and within both the advanced capitalist countries on the one hand and the imperialized formations on the other" (Ahmad 1992, 95). In addition to criticizing Jameson's generalization, Ahmad also is critical of how this "imperialized" project is enunciated: "[It is] a much more ambitious undertaking which pervades the entire text but is explicitly announced only in the last sentence of the last footnote" (95). I have argued all along in this study that to believe a mention in the footnote is a marginal concern for Jameson: as his own work attempts to find a place for what is a matter of *taste* (enlarging the canon, mass culture, and Third World texts, and so on), so the discursive machinery of his work (which I explicate more fully in the previous chapter on *The Political Unconscious*) will typically produce such comments in footnotes, addenda, and so on. Ahmad is no more instructed to reference all of Jameson for the purposes of his critique any more than I should be told to reference more of Ahmad (or Suleri or Bhabha) for the purposes of mine, of course. Rather, I am just interested in situating a slightly variant reading of Jameson's essay.

314 The fate of the lexical framing in Jameson's essay (that is, destined to be ignored as his text is read rather literally) demonstrates or is one example of a widespread tendency in the criticism of postcolonial literature. That is, even the most sophisticated supporters of "hybridity" and anti-essentialism use the novels and texts of postcolonial authors as essentially "quotable" examples. So if Homi Bhabha is a relentless critic of the essentialist construct of nation (linking it with narrative, the *bête blanc* of pomo-poco theorizing), he will usually quote a text like Rushdie (oops, sorry, make that Rushdie's *texts*) in the following way: "Salman Rushdie's *The Satanic Verses* attempts to redefine the boundaries of the western nation, so that the 'foreignness of languages' becomes the inescapable cultural condition for the enunciation of the mother-tongue" (Bhabha 1990, 317).[9] Now, I will admit that there is

9 Bhabha offers a slightly different interpretation of this passage from *The Satanic Verses* in an interview published in *Marxism Today* (1989).

nothing like Rushdie to provide, like Joyce or Stein or Shakespeare, enough verbal flex to be quoted by anyone. He does begin *Midnight's Children* with comments about being "handcuffed to history" (1982, 9), after all, and keeps mentioning "a very Indian lust for allegory" (96) and "an Englishman's lust for an Indian allegory" (109). The eager Jamesonians among us will retreat from quotation-pillage because of the slippage of the "allegory" in those two comments, of course, or risk remaining in the magician's ghetto Saleem Sinai seems to be haunted by. Perhaps the only "lesson" of Rushdie's fate in the last six years has been not, that we "Western intellectuals" can finally see how culture *is* politicized but, rather, the meta-conclusion that "we" have to keep being taught this precisely because we have the luxury to forget it. As the Spivak/Lyotard-like character (Swatilekha) lectures in *The Satanic Verses,* "Society was orchestrated by what she called *grand narratives:* history, economics, ethics. In India, the development of a corrupt and closed state apparatus had 'excluded the masses of the people from the ethical project.' As a result, they sought ethical satisfaction in the oldest of the grand narratives, that is, religious faith" (Rushdie 1992, 537).[10] Quoting texts in support of theory might be more fruitful if the auto-parasite textuality of *The Satanic Verses*—the stuttering of S. S. Sisodia—could contaminate our usages of rue-rue Rushdie.

315 I do not mean that such framing should be another interpretive containment, and evidently Jameson's conclusions or hypothesis have been tested, and found wanting, by Ahmad and Sprinker. But the allegorical thesis is still a striking one, which does seem to describe a *tendency* or a useful way of reading a variety of texts from the Third World. In texts such as *Midnight's Children,* of course this allegory is evident and meta-fictional, down to the level of the parliament of children born when an independent India was, in 1947. So much so that Aamir Mufti argues the novel allegorizes the postcolonial position as one beyond nation, or in opposition to it (1991, 96). Or at least *Midnight's Children* and *Shame* make moves in that direction; Mufti holds that the "final difference between *SV* and the two earlier novels lies in the fact that it thematizes the hybrid identities of the post-colonial world"

10 Spivak comments on her "construction" in *The Satanic Verses* in her book *Outside in the Teaching Machine* (223), mentioning also the tendency of a critic to "quote" her character's speech as the kernel of the novel (227).

(102). Mufti speaks, then, of a pan-Islamic public sphere, traversing the globe, as evidenced in the widespread reactions to Rushdie's novel.

316 But the more recent (and aesthetically conservative) Vikram Seth novel *A Suitable Boy* (1994), pairs Lata Mehra's search (for a husband) to the first Indian General Election. Lata marries Haresh, who works for a foreign shoe manufacturer but is neither Muslim nor a poet, like two other suitors: and thus Seth posits the fate of an India attempting to maneuver between both Hindi nationalism and the legacies of British rule. That is, the suitor who wins is the democratic quasi-professional, just as Nehru returns to power with the Congress party. Haresh deals with leatherworkers and other low-caste people; so Seth holds out hope for Nehruite social-democracy. (By now a lost moment, or one only discernible in the past; this nostalgia may explain, also, the unspoken heterosexuality of the compact-allegory in *A Suitable Boy*.) But the point is less, as de Man would say, plot than character-ization, or the mutable metaphors traveling between Lata and the nation she symbolizes. If my reading is correct, and Lata is some personification of India (and, then, the other way around!), then what philosophical cheek for Seth, to flaunt the sheer immensity of the subcontinent before the English novel tradition of the heroine. The nation, however, as horizon of meaning, is inescapable.

317 The Indo-Canadian writer Rohinton Mistry's novel, *Such a Long Journey* (1993), gives us Gustad Noble, a Parsi bank clerk living in Bombay during the Indo-Pakistan war of 1971. Noble is the typical Lukácsean hero: as Parsi, he is on the edge of the historical Hindu-Muslim debates in Bombay; Mistry frequently stresses Noble's meat-eating and the custom of leaving bodies to be picked clean by carrion. Thus what Suleri calls "the post-colonial body" (1992) is in Mistry's novel foregrounded for the purpose of historical difference.[11] A key expression of that body for Noble is his mas-

---

11 And if we have learned most recently to read Naipaul's texts in terms of the post-colonial body (Suleri 1992, 149–73), surely the negative place in *An Area of Darkness* or *A Bend in the River* for India or (more fictionally, but not much) Zaire indicates the can-tankerous desire *for* placelessness (that is, the nation is allegorized precisely by its absence in Naipaul) that Naipaul mimics from Bhabha (as well as vice versa: see Bhabha 1988). Naipaul's first "India" book, *An Area of Darkness* spends a lot of time at the same lake where we start in *Midnight's Children*.

culinity, and *Such a Long Journey* can be read by comparing Noble's attempts to use his masculinity as a refuge from modernization to the Indian
government's propagandizing during the war. As both Mufti (1991) and
Ahmad (1993) have commented, neo-totalitarian Islam and Hindu nationalism acquire support precisely in their constituents' fear of a loss of identity, a
fear precisely centered on issues of gender. So the allegory derives its explanatory power from *connecting* this fear with the status of the nation; otherwise,
in the case of Mistry's novel, Gustad Noble's and other characters' misogyny—leering at a receptionist's breasts—could simply be dismissed as the
characters' (or the author's!) lack of political correctness.[12]

318 This "potted" survey is not meant to argue one way or the other, of
course, and there are many other, and better, readers of Rushdie, Seth,
Naipaul, and Mistry. Michael Sprinker, in his article (1993) on "the nation"
in Said, Ahmad, and Jameson, lays out in a fine way the precise arguments
that Ahmad makes in terms of Jameson's essay. And work on the concept of
the nation in such varying theorists as James Blaut or Partha Chatterjee, as
well as that collected in Bhabha's anthology, indicates that while "modernist" Marxist political theory may have "lost virtually all currency in the
present conjuncture within cultural studies" (Sprinker 1993, 4n3), postmodern theory, both Marxist and not, continues to circle around the nation
as signifier. James Blaut's theory in *The National Question* (1987) is based on
his own political experiences in and knowledge of the Puerto Rican independence movement. He also draws on a neo-Leninist positioning of national
struggles in relation to late capitalism. Blaut's position depends in a key way,
however, on a critique of what he terms the "metaphysical neo-Marxis[m]"
of Giovanni Arrighi and Immanuel Wallerstein, whose systemic theory of
neocolonialism, he argues "mystifies, or re-mystifies capitalism, so that it
becomes something different from and greater in scale than all the merely

---

12 But see also Michel Pharand's patient philological article on Mistry (1994). And
another observation regarding race and gender: Paul Gilroy notes that when "racial identity appears suddenly impossible to know reliably or maintain with ease, the naturalness of
gender can supply the modality in which race is lived and symbolized" (1993, 7). He is
discussing misogyny and homophobia in dancehall and rap, but the comments pertain to
Mistry's novel as well.

empirical processes taking place on the earth's surface" (43). (But see Balibar and Wallerstein 1991 for a newer formulation of Wallerstein's theories.) In effect, Blaut tries to rescue national struggles from accusations of ethnic nationalism (which he argues is "rarely the basal force" [45] of national liberation), insisting on the possibility of multinational struggles within national struggles.[13]

319　I think that part of my own feelings or thoughts on this may be determined by working in or with the legacy of a Canadian left-nationalism which, particularly in the 1960s and 1970s, was *the* hegemonic discourse for progressive intellectuals. This includes the trade unions, even today, with such figures as Shirley Carr and Bob White (former leaders of the Canadian Labour Congress)[14]; social democratic parties, including the Waffle movement (a nationalist tendency in the Ontario New Democratic Party); the media, ranging from the liberal Robert Fulford to the socialist *This Magazine* and Rick Salutin; in some ways the academy (again, see Mathews and Steele 1969); and the literati—the most well-known would be Margaret Atwood, but the working-class poet Milton Acorn was also an important figure. I suppose I mean that I see the nation still as some determinate force, a symbolic manifestation so accreted with the sweat of labor and intellect that it must be reckoned with. As a Canadian leftist I am a cultural nationalist. But this is not just frozen Canadian discourse stolen from McLuhan (he, actually, professed to be an antinationalist, and yet his communications theory, along with George Grant's, was the philosophy of the leftists, the cultural-nationalist artists, and radicals).[15] Nationalism in the Canadian

13　Blaut is also, however, wary of both assimilation and hybridization, seeing both as the two sides of the coin, or "the partial growing-together of the cultures of ghettoized communities" (1987, 167). But see also his more recent *The Colonizer's Model of the World: Geographical Diffusionism and Eurocentric History* (1993).

14　The definitive study remains Irving Abella's *Nationalism, Communism, and Canadian Labour* (1973).

15　The definitive book on these thinkers is Arthur Kroker's *Technology and the Canadian Mind* (1985). There Kroker contrasts, for instance, "Grant's reflections on technology which are particularistic and existential, following a downward spiral (the famous Haligonian 'humbug') into pure content: pure will, pure remembrance, pure duration" (58), for McLuhan, "[a]s we enter the electronic age, with its instantaneous and global

context was part of the youth generation explosion of the 1960s, which also initiated the contemporary agitation for Québecois separatism, as well as movements similar to U.S.A. phenomena.

320 If my own cultural nationalism made me more sympathetic to Jameson's thesis in that essay, what first connected, in the first text by Jameson I ever read (the postmodernism essay) must have been him mentioning the Clash and the Gang of Four. Now, we all know why a critic like Jameson would mention these two groups in particular: their lyrics and posturing are so obviously left wing. The Gang of Four took Maoism and made fun of it but at the same time criticized capitalism; the Clash named an album after the Nicaraguan Sandinistas. The bands' names, that is, stood out from the "stoic" or dialectical discourse surrounding them as examples that "spoke" to me. Fred Pfeil's various re-tellings of the story of postmodernism appear in " 'Makin' Flippy-Floppy': Postmodernism and the Baby-Boom PMC," the rather less audaciously titled "Marxism, Feminism, and Postmodern Culture" and "Postmodernism and Our Discontent," and the less hippy-than-it-sounds "From Firesign Theatre to Frank's Place: On Postmodern-ism's Career" (all Pfeil 1990, 97–148). Somewhat of a postmodernphile, the critic circles around a reading of Jameson's essay, referring to "the totalizing power of such a Lukácsian depiction [which] bid[s] to offer itself not only as final word but as full story" (97), "the pessimistic intonements of a Jameson" (135), which nonetheless "moved the term [postmodernism] out of its for-malist corral, insisting that postmodernism is not simply a name for the high art that follows in modernism's wake . . . but refers to a whole cultural condition in which the old constitutive opposition between high and mass culture has collapsed" (142). So both Bob Perelman and the Clash, in this

---

information, we are the first human beings to live completely within the *mediated* en-vironment of the technostructure" (56). Considered in Greimas's rectangle, the dystopian counter to McLuhan and Grant is H. A. Innis, famed Canadian theoretician of com-munication and political economy; Innis's work, Kroker writes, "represented an almost Weberian interpretation of the organizational strategies involved in the 'imposition' and 'cancellation' of the various communicative media" (112). But following my logic, the utopian position in this semiotic would be filled by Kroker himself, whose harnessing of Baudrillard to questions of Canadian theory serves to "contain" theory even as it "pro-duces" it via his discourse.

new postmodernism, standing out as exemplary instances, draw me into the discourse.

a sublime quilt

321 *Postmodernism, or, The Cultural Logic of Late Capitalism* and *Signatures of the Visible* are two curious, quilted books; they appear at first to be merely the joining together of various essays on film and postmodernism, a seminal essay by Jameson on each genre prefacing the respective volume, followed by a scattering of reviews, with a long essay attached to the end. The double appearance of the two books at the end of 1990 appeared superfluous, like that curious and recent mutation of the rock "double album" which is the "double release," where Guns N' Roses released simultaneously *Use Your Illusion I* and *Use Your Illusion II* (Bruce Springsteen did the same trick in 1992). Who needs to buy both? Maybe it is just a scam to get the unwary fan to shell out twice (recalling this student's chagrin when two Jameson volumes appeared from Minnesota's Theory and History of Literature series in 1988).

322 But the essays that begin the two books do not both "introduce" the respective volume's subjects. To be sure, the essay "The Cultural Logic of Late Capitalism" begins the *Postmodernism* book, the essay that first appeared, with the full title that now belongs to the book itself, in *New Left Review* in 1984 and proceeded to dominate the debate on postmodernism in Marxist theory. A vertiginous or fractalized sublime is apparent immediately, then: What is the text "Postmodernism, or, the Cultural Logic of Late Capitalism" now (let alone, how does one capitalize [on] the awkward title), or should that be *Postmodernism, or, The Cultural Logic of Late Capitalism*? Now there are two or three texts floating around with that title: the early essay,[16] the chapter in the book, the book itself. If the plethora of texts induces vertigo, resisting bibliographical and analytical categories, a fractal-

---

16 The essay in *New Left Review* in 1984 is a version of an essay that appeared in *The Anti-Aesthetic* (Foster 1983), and which was itself "originally a talk, portions of which were presented as a Whitney Museum Lecture in fall, 1982" (Jameson 1983b, 111n).

condition is also present, whereby each text, submitted to some microscope, is identical, from the text to the paragraph to the sentence and word.[17]

323 What I mean is the following. And this was an operating principle in the earlier chapters' interpretation of *Marxism and Form* and *The Political Unconscious*. A fractal is a mathematical formula that computes what was, before chaos theory, deemed to be unrepresentable: the irregularities of a cloud's edges, for instance, or a leaf. The key to a fractal illustration (as in the Mandelbrot sets) is that no matter how close you get to the "edge" (like a seashore, a leaf), the shape stays the same. So textually, any "theory" in the various "texts" called or about "postmodernism" is identical—or at least they refer to each other, and to their interpretation. Evidently, then, here I am theorizing that Jameson's writings *on* film and postmodernism are an example of his theory of the "postmodern sublime."

324 Unlike the canonical texts treated in the previous two chapters of this work, *Marxism and Form* and *The Political Unconscious*, the *Postmodernism* and *Signatures of the Visible* books are much less unified texts—which is not to say that the earlier books were "modernist," or "realist" and then "modernist." But the earlier volumes in Jameson's work were not rudely ironclad structures. What became "chapters" had first appeared as essays, and in *The Political Unconscious* Jameson notes that "a more detailed reading of the opening section of" *La Vieille Fille* is in his "first version of the present chapter" elsewhere (*PU,* 163n).[18] But *Marxism and Form* and *The Political Unconscious* are more easily *thought of* as whole *books,* a feeling I exploited in those two chapters of this work—first, by playing off against them the less canonical books on Adorno and Lewis, and second, by exploring a common formal-thematic thread (fictive and theoretical exemplification in the first book, Lacanian libidinal textuality in the second). But the repressed returns, for even as I attempt to declare *Signatures of the Visible,* one object of this chapter's gaze, to be somehow constructed in a more postmodern way, it is

17 Paul Gilroy uses this metaphor to talk about "fractal patterns of cultural and political affiliation" (1993, 139 and 144n. 22)—a reference that in the context of London also suggests Allen Fisher's stunning poem "Brixton Fractals" (1985).

18 That earlier essay is "The Ideology of Form: Partial Systems in *La Vieille Fille*" (Jameson 1976).

patently obvious that the overarching theory at work here is not unlike the great theoretical moment of film theory itself: *auteurism*.

fieldwork in mass culture

325 The center of Jameson's first book on film has to do with the retreat of the object that is constitutive both of mass culture and postmodernism. This central dictum is to be found in a footnote ("fieldwork" here refers to the role of repetition in our reception of pop songs): "My own fieldwork has thus been seriously impeded by the demise some years ago of both car radios: so much the greater is my amazement when rental cars today (which are probably not time machines) fill up with exactly the same hit songs I used to listen to in the early seventies, repeated over and over again!" (*SV,* 232n10). The serio-comic designation of listening to the radio as "fieldwork" belies the importance of this digression to the mundane and everyday. As with Sartre, driving is an important figure for Jameson, not least because of the critic's immersion in the technologized and superhighwayed North American landscape, but now a properly postmodern superhighway, one decaying as the "promise" of the futuristic fifties has given way to the degraded and cracked pavement of the Reagan-Bush eighties and nineties. For Jameson, the superhighway (in either of these manifestations) is the postmodern version of Heidegger's *feldzweg:* this " 'fieldpath' is, after all, irredeemably and irrevocably destroyed by late capital, by the green revolution, by neocolonialism and the megalopolis, which runs its superhighways over the older fields and vacant lots and turns Heidegger's 'house of being' into condominiums, if not the most miserable unheated, rat-infested tenement buildings" (*PM,* 34– 35).

326 But Bourdieu argues in *The Political Ontology of Martin Heidegger* (1991) that Heidegger's meditation on "dwelling" versus "building" represented an overcoming of the postwar German housing shortage by the essential qualities of "dwelling" (Bourdieu 1991, 127n15). As Heidegger writes, "residential buildings do indeed provide shelter . . . but—do the houses in themselves hold any guarantee that *dwelling* occurs in them?" (1975, 146). In *The Culture of Nature: North American Landscape from Disney to the Exxon Valdez,* a

recent discussion of the relationship between landscape and technology, the late Alexander Wilson argued that the modern treatment of nature essentially rationalizes the earth into commodified and discrete chunks for visual and tourist consumption. Utilizing the methodological framework of Frankfurt School critiques of late capitalism, Wilson's treatise documents the ways that scientific and popular-commercial discourses will construct "nature" and the "earth" as objects of study, interpretation, technological manipulation, and voyeuristic purchase. To give but one example, Wilson shows how the new trend in wildlife parks toward the campers' "understanding" of the environment is conflictual: "[I]nterpretive ideology has collided with the more philosophical currents of the environmental movement. Is the forest there for its own sake, or is it there to offer visitors an experience set apart from their lives in the city, or perhaps to remind them of the last example of a particular plant community in the region" (Wilson 1991, 59).[19]

327 So I stressed the "demise" of the superhighway and its futurism, as Jameson did in his footnote on his car radios. A pertinent literary formulation for this demise of a promise (and Horkheimer and Adorno have said that mass culture is characterized as a faulty promise) is a short story by William Gibson, "The Gernsback Continuum" (1986). In the story, a photographer hunts down Thirties-designed gas stations and other architectural ephemera of an "*Airstream Futuropolis: The Tomorrow that Never Was*": "[T]hey put Ming the Merciless in charge of designing California gas stations. Favoring the architecture of his native Mongo, he cruised up and down the coast erecting raygun emplacements in white stucco" (Gibson 1986, 4). That lapsed futuristic promise is now a "semiotic ghost," a character says in Gibson's story, which haunts the protagonist like the extruded superhighways today, marked by "construction" signs and flashing arrows telling us to move left or right.

328 Technology itself betrays the future, and Gibson's story is "of a promised future that would come into being only as a nightmare: . . . the streamlined cars and crystal superhighways gave the green light to postwar ecologi-

19 Wilson is particularly trenchant when it comes to the various marketing strategies of "conservation," a movement spectacular with its failures as the list of extinct species of florae and faunae grow every day and the "last remaining ones" are fetishized into T-shirts and gas station tumblers.

cal atrocities committed by General Motors under the aegis of petroleum capitalism" (Ross 1991, 101). But Gibson's critique of futurism is then betrayed, in turn, by the critic Andrew Ross, in his essay "Getting out of the Gernsback Continuum" (Ross 1991, 101–35). Ross's take on Gibson in this essay is perverted, in the Žižekian sense noted above, as he takes what this reader enjoys about Gibson—the Frederick Barthelme-like *écriture* of name-brands and international sites, the dislocated hero who is both vulnerable and techno-proficient—and says, "That's not it at all." Ross argues that the story's critique of 1930s futurism ignores the politically progressive context of the era's belief in science: "There is little to be gained, finally, from using our hindsight to excoriate the 'wrongheadedness' of 1930s progressive thinking about technology's capacity to manufacture a better social future" (Ross 1991, 134). But is this what Gibson does? The story critiques precisely where futurism has led us, and Gibson provides a genealogy of our present-day dystopia in 1930s utopias; Ross then extracts the motivational moment from the narrative and turns it into the wrongheaded project of all "[c]yberpunk literature, film, and television." What is the relationship between Ross's erudite historical survey of 1930s scientism (part of a project, *Strange Weather,* that maps out the emergence of various middlebrow "distinctions": New Age science, computer hackers, cyberpunk, futurism, and weather forecasting) and the mass culture of science fiction?

329 Jameson's anecdote about his car radios is a footnote to a deliberation on mass culture that in turn, as Michael Denning notes, was an opening move "in many recent discussions of popular culture" (Denning 1990, 4). "Reification and Utopia in Mass Culture" (*SV,* 10–34), while first published in 1979 (in the first issue of *Social Text*) was written in 1976 (*SV,* 232n8). Indeed, the essay has a 1970s flavor to it, not least when Jameson discusses "our reception of contemporary pop music of whatever type—the various kinds of rock, blues, country western, or disco" (*SV,* 20). Here Jameson stresses the importance of repetition, which, like Baudrillard's theory of simulation, "effectively volatilizes the original object . . . so that the student of mass culture has no primary object of study." With pop music, the work "by means of repetition, insensibly becomes part of the existential fabric of our own lives, so that what we listen to is ourselves, our own previous auditions." But how does pop music differ in this respect from a classical piece,

which Jameson claims is at first a "bewildering" experience? Does classical music in this sense even exist anymore? To be sure, there is a genre of music that is conversant with the Western tradition—Schnittke, Cage, Reich—but what is there in the various forms of "new" music that have been around for the last fifty years that is "bewildering"?

330 Jameson's model here is high art = difficult, low art = easy: but are not both "sides" of culture under capitalism, mass culture and high art, both easy and difficult at the same time? Hearing a pop song "the first time" is equally difficult and disturbing—in part because it is *not* a repetition, not the already heard—but in part also because without the familiar cloak of repetition, the words are not understandable, the tune is not instantly hummable, or the beat instantly danceable. And is high art always so "bewildering"? I may seem disingenuous at this point: certainly pop music exists as that which must be repeated and commodified (enacting the Freudian death drive) and hence must become banal, whereas classical music is organized around the Event, one of supreme or sublime difficulty. But surely Adorno's lesson has been that art itself is commodified by the market into "bits" of symphonic tunes (CBC-FM); and, also, a lot of pop music is difficult to listen to both cerebrally and in terms of the body (industrial-techno music, the more advanced [which is not to say politically correct, thank God] forms of rap).[20]

331 When I listen to "Protex Blue" or "White Riot" by the Clash, I can remember early or "first" times listening to the songs . . . in my bedroom as a teenager in Regina, Saskatchewan; but when I listen to Jascha Heifitz play a Beethoven concerto, that commodified record also brings back memories of listening to it in the early 1980s, when I suddenly was eager to "know" about "classical" music. This desire to know was part of my own class background and trajectory: on the one hand, I come from a lower-middle-class family— my father is an officer in the military who rose up from the ranks, my mother was a bank teller. This background was singularly lacking in cultural capi-

---

20 This has been Adorno's lesson to me, anyway. But I should add that the hyperbole encountered here and elsewhere—I originally wrote "Adorno's lesson to us all"—is only rhetorical in the sense that I (think) am aware, in my enthusiasms or dislikes, that these are contingent.

tal—Reader's Digest Condensed Books, "Hooked On Classics" albums, and paintings of fighter aircraft are still the major cultural artifacts of my father's home. As I gravitated around that dubious adolescent class-position the "bookworm," and after a short stint in the military, my trajectory was soon both artistic (I styled myself a poet from about age sixteen on) and academic, once I returned to university in my mid-twenties.

332 According to Bourdieu, this *habitus* or class background, and trajectory, can lead to one of four possible strategies: the privileging of "high art"; the turn from high art to mass culture dressed up as art; the disparagement of the avant-garde in favor of an archaic aesthetic; and/or the embrace of the university as the imaginary solution to a real contradiction. This last "real contradiction," is that while I gain a certain social prestige as an artist or academic, my class background is incommensurable with that rise; it has not prepared me for it. But the four options deserve a more complete description: the first, the turn toward high culture, is characteristic of "those who owe most of their cultural capital to the educational system, such as primary and secondary school teachers originating from the working and middle classes, [who] are particularly subject to the academic definition of legitimacy, and tend to proportion their investments very strictly to the value the educational system sets on the different areas" (Bourdieu 1984, 87). Bourdieu contrasts these adherents to the canon with another group: " '[M]iddle-ground' arts such as cinema, jazz, and, even more, strip cartoons, science fiction or detective stories are predisposed to attract the investments either of those who have entirely succeeded in converting their capital into educational capital or those who, not having acquired legitimate culture in a legitimate manner (i.e., through early familiarization), maintain an uneasy relationship with it." The third position is where Bourdieu places Heidegger: "The avant-gardism of rediscovery or restoration, notably in the case of poetry, the most academic of the arts, is perfectly suited to the first-generation academic who, being ill at ease in the intellectual world, has turned his back on all the avant-garde aesthetic movements (expressionist cinema or painting, for example) and who finds in the mode for the archaic an avant-gardist justification for his rejection of the modern" (Bourdieu 1991, 120n21). The final position is what Bourdieu calls the "oblate," after the medieval term for a lower-level priest, and designates the devoted aca-

demic, analogous to the normal technician in Kuhn's analysis: "They offer to the academic institution which they have chosen because it chose them, and vice versa, a support which, being so totally conditioned, has something total, absolute, unconditional about it" (Bourdieu 1990, 100–101; see also 49, and 291n31).

333 Michael Denning has pointed out that Bourdieu's analysis "evacuat[es] the content of cultural products and activities, by reading them as objects of consumption and markers in a symbolic class conflict" and that his "investment theory of culture mimics the capitalist culture it critiques" (Denning 1990, 16). But I would not be so hasty to dismiss either the formal elements of Bourdieu, or his use of economic figures. First, by seeing the formal *relationships* whereby mass culture is constituted over and against elite culture—class structure, an oppositional dialectics—I can rethink just why my own trajectory should have led to an overly aestheticized perspective. That position is cause in part, I think, of my affection for theory. Reflecting back onto my undergraduate career, I can see that I grabbed at theoretical terms, arguments, books, authors, and courses, precisely because class and privilege marked "traditional" English studies in a much more obvious way.[21] So I positioned myself in opposition to what I perceived to be the doughty, tried-and-true canon. The very proliferation of theory as both subdiscipline and publishing demographic has probably made it less likely an allegiance (for my reasons) for undergraduates now. The economic figures that Bourdieu uses incessantly can best be re-coded as *libidinal* investment in the sense explored in the previous chapter. Cultural investment is therefore overdetermined, and subjects do not only invest their cultural capital in a certain field, but they invest their cultural libido, or their desire to know, in the sense of Lacan and (as announced at the start of this chapter) Žižek. The

---

21 This was true even at a "provincial" university (in Victoria, British Columbia), but further problematized by the unique influx of foreign (U.S. and British) academics into Canadian universities in the 1960s and 1970s, which intellectual colonization led to a surplus of oblates devoted to a circa 1950s canon. And so when I was writing an M.A. thesis on the Canadian postmodern poets Robert Kroetsch and bpNichol, one (American-born) academic informed me that, after all, Faulkner was much more important. The canonical text on the larger debacle is *The Struggle for Canadian Universities* (Mathews and Steele 1969).

masses, as asserted earlier, are hysterical precisely because they are trapped in a desiring narrative where the object is always disappearing (repetition, simulation).

platform sneakers remix

334 As I asserted above, my notion of the hysterical, desiring masses owes something to Horkheimer and Adorno's "parable of the oarsmen." In *Dialectic of Enlightenment*, Homer's oarsmen, their ears stopped up so they cannot hear the music of the Sirens, keep rowing even though Odysseus, tied to the mast *but listening nonetheless*, begs them to untie them: "[H]is men, who do not listen, know only the song's danger but nothing of its beauty" (1972, 34). In the Frankfurt schoolmasters' remix of Homer, not only is Odysseus a figure for the twentieth-century boss, but domination implicates both the laboring masses (who, in some bizarre manner, are still thus posited as a revolutionary class) and the rulers (tied to the mast of Fortune 500). But the lexical possibilities of this section of *Dialectic of Enlightenment* notwithstanding, the discussion of Kant and Sade will more profitably aid in my discussion here of repetition and pleasure. Remarking that for Kant competition between the faculties is foreclosed, Horkheimer and Adorno note (here, I think, "Hollywood" is a metonym for the "culture industry" in general: Hansen 1993, but see also Davis 1992b, 46–54): "Intuitively, Kant foretold what Hollywood consciously put into practice: in the very process of production, images are pre-censored according to the norm of the understanding which will later govern their apprehension. *Even before its occurrence, the perception which serves to confirm the public judgement is adjusted by that judgement.* Even if the secret utopia in the concept of reason pointed, despite fortuitous distinctions between individuals, to their common interest, reason—functioning, in compliance with ends, as a mere systemic science—serves to level down that same identical interest. It allows no determination other than the classifications of the societal process to operate" (my emphasis, 84).

335 The precensorship of images and sounds endemic to the culture industry (all music is industrial music), then, supports Jameson's notion (which I nevertheless intuitively disagree with) that pop music is already a repetition,

a vertiginous repetition. "Give the people what they want" was once the slogan, it seems, but now the people must *know* what it is they want (opinion polls, *Billboard* charts, *Entertainment Tonight*). This force-feeding of knowledge is what separates our postmodern era from the dour Germans' time: since we masses desire to desire culture, various factoids are substituted for that culture, and information is substituted for knowledge.

the filmic object

336   As Raymond Bellour (1990) recently put it, film criticism has never been anything but an illusory object (19). Writing *about* film criticism can be even more of a project based on a lack, which is perhaps an unsubtle and theoretical way of rationalizing for the "turn" in this chapter away from an in-your-face treatment of Jameson's style toward what used to be called topics or themes. The three themes that haunt this chapter are mass culture, postmodernism, and film. There are various theoretical explanations for this lack in film and film criticism: historically, as Kaja Silverman has argued, critics situated film in terms of an originary lack that constituted the replacement of the referent with the celluloid image. This was then "explained" by Metz and others in psychoanalytic terms: the lack in cinema was analogous to the lack in the human subject, repeatedly castrated by the feminine, language, and so on. Bordwell has argued that the retreat of the filmic object itself is symptomatic of theory's move from the referent to the signifier to the critical apparatus. Silverman has argued that the critics' very act of focusing on a "lack" signaled an unwillingness to see the gender laws at work in cinema, as well as an overhasty and uncritical culling of psychoanalytic metaphors. For Jameson, film takes (its) place as one more cultural text in the postmodern hegemony, a totalizing world system where the divisions of mass and elite cultures exist only in the subject. Thus in his two books entirely devoted to movies, *Signatures of the Visible* and *The Geopolitical Aesthetic,* Jameson analyzes both lowbrow (*Jaws, Three Days of the Condor*) and highbrow (*Letters from Home, Days of the Eclipse*) films.[22] But here, as everywhere, the catego-

22   Another work on film in the last decade to maintain a similar *political* agenda and the same range of "quality" would be Robin Wood's *Hollywood from Vietnam to Reagan*

ries of taste are difficult simply to "browse" through, real as they are: is Brian de Palma or Hitchcock highbrow or lowbrow? Fiske (1991) has commented on the various marketing media techniques that were used to sell *The Shining* in the U.K. (125); Žižek makes the claim that in postmodernist culture, such demarcations mean little: what counts is the interpretive skill that will find in *any* text an *objet petit a* or blot. Here Fiske's concept of the "popular" is also suggestive, but if a film "fails" to be "chosen" by the "popular" bloc, is it then to be of no interest to the cultural theoretician? Or can movies only be judged or appraised as a sort of extrusion of the savage mind of the masses if they gross five million dollars in their first weekend at the box office?

337 Jameson's habit is to analyze films as the articulating reflection of a contemporary world system which derive their artistic value (or interest) from their place in a history of the form. This contemporary system is of course late capitalism, whether the system is instantiated as the crumbling national bourgeoisie as figure in *Dog Day Afternoon* or the same national bourgeoisie as Taiwanese professional (doctor) in *Terrorizer.* Jameson's history of the art form essentially boils down to the triad realism-modernism-postmodernism, a narrative that can be compressed to fit one filmmaker (as Žižek does with Hitchcock [1992a, 2–10]). This emphasis, then, suggests that politics enters the filmic-object through metanarratives of history and totality—no great surprise. But the limitations of this approach must be addressed, and I will quickly sketch them before moving on to a commentary on Jameson's readings of film.

338 The first criticism, while it now has less validity than before the publication of *The Geopolitical Aesthetic,* still must be met, and it is the observation that, as in his other cultural sets, Jameson's film canon is mostly the Eurocentric tradition of European art-cinema and Hollywood "classic realism"/auteurism. The discussion of Peruvian film in *Signatures of the Visible* and more extended treatments of individual Taiwanese and Filipino films in *The Geopolitical Aesthetic* extend Jameson's range, but as the Third (World) cinema(s) are still primarily seen as challenges *to* "white" cinema, this shift needs explaining. The most convincing argument I could make for Jame-

---

(1986), but that important volume is predominantly concerned with American film and does not pursue a *theoretical* goal.

son's approach is a global one: simply, the cultural determinant of late capitalism is itself a system centered on (North) America, Europe, and Japan, and the desire to assert some national or regional specificity (Iranian film or Canadian cinema) free from that system is to mistake voluntarism or populism for political action. Jameson puts the case elsewhere (1987c) in the following terms: "[T]he principal theoretical reply is simply that it is global capitalism which is responsible for the unification of global culture; and that this force must remain central, even if what you are concerned to study is cultural resistance and cultural innovation, since it is against this central force of unification that such resistance can alone be mentioned and cultural autonomy alone be won" (24). But the accompanying critique of difference as foundation (amid all the anti-foundationalisms) for the micropolitics of the various new social movements should neither be mistaken for a parallel dismissal of the various "new cultural objects" nor, more importantly, a dismissal of the political activities of the new social movements (feminism, gay rights, First Nations, people of color) and their international cousins, national liberation movements. Jameson's insistence, as he makes clear elsewhere (1989, 385–86) is that the new politics cannot be understood without the "vulgar" notions of class, economics, and so on (e.g., women's unpaid or underpaid labor, high unemployment for certain racial-ethnic groups), and this can surely be linked to Rorty's emphasis on cruelty.

339 But a second limitation to Jameson's work in film as framed under the rubric of mass culture has to do with his reflex of considering the filmic object as reified text. That is, his primary methodology for reading film is to interpret it as an aesthetico-political text finally "about" the vagaries of late capitalism, and to see this mostly in the intrinsic features of the film: its narrative, star system, and so on. Now, what was revolutionary in a reading of Balzac or Conrad, one might argue, is not so subversive in reading a mass cultural text, particularly if we recall Fiske's insistence on the "popular" being "made." Fiske, it is remembered, uses popular appropriations of a cultural text (jeans, Madonna, a mall) to counter the official story, the hegemonic version of the commodity purpose ("freedom" and classlessness, boy-toy, commercial center). Jameson, however, finds the oppositional reading precisely in the text as autonomous (if social) relic. For Fiske, then, the real meaning of *Jaws* lies in the appropriation of its ominous shark sound

(DUM dum, DUM dum, DUM dum) in the schoolyards of 1970s North America and not in its world-political "subtext" or political unconscious. And *The Godfather* not so much attracts an audience to its familial code of honour as finds its end in the wheezing of countless Brando imitations: "I'm gonna make you an offer you can't refuse."[23] This limitation to Jameson's take on mass culture is serious and cannot be dismissed. But the value of his work lies in precisely this lack of appropriateness. First of all, the emphasis on the object as aesthetic icon is an Adornoesque method: the introduction of the subject as aesthete is the only guarantee of objectivity (Adorno's sociology of music), where an emphasis on the empirical data of "fans" and "poaching" threatens to lapse into subjectivism (even if it does not do so in Fiske, but this is because of his feminist-Marxist metanarrative: "I write as a white male in a patriarchal culture"). Second, Jameson's method does take account of the masses precisely in terms of the compensation theory—his utopianism. That is, mass culture works by offering the view a "reward" (Fiske's "ideological free lunch") even while it adds a cheerless lesson. (To say, as Fiske does, that mass culture cannot be preachy is to miss the point: all mass culture is preachy; mass culture endlessly preaches the rewards of individualism, etc.)

miss culture

340 One of the most-cited theorists in contemporary writings on mass culture is Michel de Certeau; as is usual in the economy of citations, critics invariably appropriate a select few phrases: notably, his idea of "poaching" (de Certeau 1988, 165ff.; see Jenkins 1991 for one example). The dominant ideology of mass culture criticism is based on the romanticism of this pastoral Robin Hood figure and ends with the conclusion (or begins with it) that

---

23 Amending Fiske to the Lacanian master-code everywhere at work here, the mass cultural text can only become popular (which, after all, really means useful to the theoretician of the popular as indicating something about the masses) once it has been repeated in some form of "rewriting." The rewriting, the repetition, is analogous to the repetition of a symptom, which itself is constituted as repetition, or the obsession with an anxiety, and so on, and which, indeed, only becomes significant (decipherable) once it has been repeated.

the masses are resisting capital as they consume its products.[24] So with Fiske, this often is translated into a trope of struggle: "TV news," for example, "is the terrain over which . . . cultural struggles are waged" (1990, 185). Fiske's figure may sound like Gramsci's theory of the state as a terrain, but how does Fiske's text utilize the trope of struggle? This is part of the larger question of intellectual discourse on mass culture, and how it will (a) project manifestly romantic and/or bourgeois concepts onto the Real of the masses and their culture, and (b) more specifically, appropriate the vernacular or sociolect of the class war to valorize not so much the masses themselves but (and this is why, I think, the term now used is "popular culture") what Fiske calls the "cultural economy" (18).[25] Two processes are at work, then; one in which the subject is hypostatized into a projection of the middle-class intellectual, and the other in which the object is translated into an acceptable intellectual commodity. That is, the masses are constructed as discerning consumers (i.e., in the mode of a member of the upper class purchasing a bottle of wine or antique chair) and the cultural products, given a legitimacy by their "popularity," are reified into politico-aesthetic commodities.

341 As Susan Willis notes in her discussion of foods and drugs (1991, 133–57), "taste" does become its own law of the oral discursive field of food consumption; thus coffee is more "proper" (in a bourgeois sense) to drink for breakfast in part because of all the rituals that can be summoned up—

24 But as Jane Kuenz (1993) has recently noted, while you can claim "that poaching and other guerilla tactics intending to subvert a culture of buying only reinvent it for a new generation by confirming again the centrality of consumption, the accuracy of that conclusion is perhaps in direct proportion to its limitations" (86).

25 The economy of signifiers by which terms in various subdialects will circulate into others is not itself the problem: as I probably indicated in the early discussion of journalists' usage of "deconstruction," I do not wish to set up border patrols between linguistic states. But the circulation of signifiers is not then some utopia of "the popular" poaching on a dominant ideology. During the Persian Gulf War, for example, I was working at an office and I remember the jokes, both oral and in written communications, that would take the "mother of" phrase ("the mother of all memos," "the mother of all sales meetings"). Similarly, "Ayatollah" is now a common synonym for overbearing boss or leader; the explicit Orientalism of both examples (I do not remember jokes about "collateral damage" at that level, for example) indicates the unconscious recognition that it is all right to be irreverent (about war, suffering, and so on) if the final effect was still in line with ideology.

choosing the beans, different roasts, grinding them yourself, not to mention the entire semiotics of espresso and cappucino that recall at once both Dick Hebdige's work on Italian style in postwar Britain (1988, 77–115) *and* the foregrounding of these drinks in *My Dinner with Andre* for the express purpose of marking an Other. To digress again autobiographically, my own consumption of these forms of coffee not only marked, again, a separation from my family, but was traumatic enough to elicit Christmas gifts of pseudo-cappucino cups (inevitably with the word "espresso" or "cappucino" in flowing gold script on the outside of the cup). Coffee may once have been proper in the white-trash sense of my own class background without these rituals (a percolator and a can of Safeway's coffee in the fridge seemed to suffice for my parents), but this lower middle-class taste seemed to have been mobilized around a vulgate of health and microeconomics (caffeine is bad for children, so they cannot drink coffee; Kool-Aid is better—cheaper—than pop, and so on).

342 A brief examination of theoretico-critical reifications of the cultural products shows that, depending on the situation of the critic (a situation which, in this case, usually is a discipline), the cultural item may be seen as an intervention into the dominant ideology. This intervention is not seen as pure and politically correct, and I do not want to give the impression that it is the "objectivation" (as Bourdieu puts it) of the cultural product which I see as problematic. Instead, it is the intellectualist or theoreticist desire to find in that object a political or aesthetic agenda. "The ultimate goal" of Madonna's film *Truth or Dare*, then, "is to raise the validity of the central question of the film: Who is the public person and who is the 'real' Madonna?" (Pribram 1993, 195). Or, "*The Terminator* . . . locates the origins of future catastrophe in decisions about technology, warfare, and social behaviour that are being made today" (Penley 1989, 121–22). Or "erotic contemporary series romances which began appearing in 1981 reflect many of the ways sex roles have been redefined during this time, and the ways American women have begun to challenge the power structure of patriarchal society, both economically and sexually" (Thurston 1987, 92). Or in "*The Parallax View*, it is the disparity between the two senatorial victims of assassination that is designed to disjoin and to problematize the mystery of the private-public allegory" (*GA*, 55). Or "fantastic sit-coms [like *I Dream of Jeannie* or *The Addams Family*] presented more than just demographic changes; they provided nar-

rative situations and themes that suggested a clear departure from the conventions of the suburban family sit-coms that preceded them. These genre hybrids were parodic in nature because they retained the conventions of the previous form, but they made these conventions strange by mismatching form and content" (Spigel 1991, 216). In true Bakhtinian form, "Madonna plays with surfaces, masks, the masquerade" (Kaplan 1993, 149). Or "[David] Byrne's work involves a high degree of more or less explicit meditation on the blurring of levels, categories, signs, identities, which, as we have seen, characterise the discourse of postmodernism" (Hebdige 1988, 234). Or, in "*Duel in the Sun,* iconographical attributes of the two male (oppositional) characters, Lewt and Jesse, conform very closely to those of Ranse and Tom in *Liberty Valance*" (Mulvey 1988b, 75–76).

343 In the preceding examples, the critics attribute to mass culture either sociological interventions and enunciations (Pribram, Penley, Thurston, and Jameson) or (whether traditional or postmodern) aesthetic qualities (Kaplan, Hebdige, Mulvey) or both (Spigel). One example of how the masses are constructed as bourgeois consumers is the following: "*Star Trek,* produced in a period when 'masculine' concerns still dominated science fiction, is reconsidered in light of the newer, more feminist orientation of the genre, becoming less a program about the Enterprise's struggles against the Klingon-Romulan Alliance and more an examination of characters' efforts to come to grips with conflicting emotional needs and professional responsibilities" (Jenkins 1991, 187).

344 What must be remembered is that this knowledge-politics valorization of the object is structurally necessary: every discipline has its Law, after all, and perhaps no law is more "real" or at least demanding than the law to be epistemophilic. One of the writers in *Strangers in Paradise,* "Jane Ellen Wilson" (all names are pseudonyms), became a folklorist because of her own rural, agricultural-class origins, but had this to say: "Although I conceived of my discipline as subversive within the larger intellectual reality of our culture (as did a number of my colleagues, explicitly), on a day-to-day basis, we felt as oppressed by our own discipline as by those disciplines we had come from" (Ryan and Sackrey 1984, 213). As Bourdieu has remarked, a key to his notion of reflexive sociology (and which I would inscribe in the more general project of the dialectical and dissenting intellectual) "is that people whose profession it is to objectivize the social world prove rarely able to

objectivize themselves, and fail so often to realize that what their apparently scientific discourse talks about is not the object but their relation to the object" (Bourdieu and Wacquant 1992, 68–69).

345 Part of the difficulty encountered in nondialectical theorizing on mass culture is that the object is reified in a nonhysterical manner. That is, mass culture is hysterical not only in the sense of its femininity, its marginalization, and dominance by hegemonic elite culture in (a now unfashionable) discourse (Huyssen 1986), but also because of the following three factors: mass culture is often figured as a maw or gaping hole; it produces in the manner of the womb; it is lunatic, carnivalesque, mad, and so on. Mass culture is miss culture: it misses the point of high culture, is feminized and sterilized and marginalized, is milked for all its worth. The milk of mass culture (that glowing glass offered by Cary Grant's character to his wife in *Suspicion* is focused on by so many critics precisely because of its maternal connotations) can be immediately grasped in a few key scenes in *The Parallax View*. The hero, played by Warren Beatty, is a disreputable journalist who is "on the wagon." Tracking down a lead on a conspiracy to a small town in Washington state, he enters a bar and orders a glass of milk. Immediately a cowboy type tries to pick a fight with him, addressing the journalist as "Miss." Beatty's character does not "rise to the bait" but acknowledges that he is a girl, an acknowledgment of his femininity that will set in motion a mass cultural set piece, the barroom brawl (*GA*, 69). Indeed, throughout the film Beatty's character is punished, in the manner of the classic Hitchcock heroine, for being insufficiently socialized into the male order: he drinks milk (too childlike), but also, in two other important scenes, he is in male homoerotic idylls (Irigaray's hom[m]osexuality of power) that are brutally ruptured. First, he is pretending to fish at the bottom of a great dam, trying to ascertain how a judge was drowned, when the local sheriff throws him some lunch. Beatty's character is sincerely pleased by this, mistaking the gesture for maternal concern when in reality the sheriff is about to drown him; the dam then opens up with a roar that is more apocalyptic than maternal (Silverman 1988, 72–100). Second, the journalist is on a boat at sea, interviewing a "witness" to the original assassination; a series of well-nigh pastoral scenes ensue, with three men enjoying their day on the ocean, only to be violently ruptured by an explosion on the boat from which only Beatty's character escapes.

reification: or, the jaws of life

346 If Jameson's reification and utopia essay stands as a shrunken dwarf to his arguments on film in *Signatures of the Visible,* I would like to examine a number of slices or biopsies of the malignant mass. This figure here suggests the postmodern medicine of CAT scans and microsurgery rather than Benjamin's by now old-fashioned and mechanical notion of the filmmaker as surgeon in "The Work of Art in the Age of Mechanical Reproduction (Benjamin 1969, 233–34). First of all, I think it is important to get away from the idea that this essay is some working "between" the two extreme views, populism and elitism, the alternatives Jameson outlines quickly at the top of the article (*SV,* 9–10). The two positions are stated as binary views of mass culture at the start of the essay, but that statement can be read as a prophetic one. Two Marxist concepts—reification and commodification—act as theater ushers to the analysis of mass culture in Jameson's essay. Under capitalism, "the older traditional forms of human activity are instrumentally reorganized and 'taylorized,' analytically fragmented and reconstructed according to various rational models of efficiency" (*SV,* 10), and "by its transformation into a commodity, a thing of whatever type has been reduced to a means for its own consumption" (*SV,* 11). Art, according to the classic Frankfurt School schema, is supposed to resist reification—a new role or actant for the age-old aesthetic—because it possesses "finality without end," the Kantian sublime moment when there is no *purpose* to the activity of looking at a painting or reading a poem.

347 Jameson's mass culture essay moves from the highest reaches of Western culture—Hegel, Kant, Proust, Schoenberg—to more recent low points: Spielberg, Peter Benchley. In truth, there seems to be a desperate attempt here to be vulgar when he writes, "We suspend our real lives and our immediate practical preoccupations just as completely when we watch *The Godfather* as when we read *The Wings of the Dove* or hear a Beethoven sonata" (*SV,* 11). This—apparently—intentional vulgarism or hyperbole is like (if less snobbish than) Paul de Man's sudden lapse into television for an example of debunking and rhetoric in the seminal essay, "Semiology and Rhetoric" (de Man 1979, 3–19). Archie Bunker, in de Man's example, stands in for simplistic readers of the most sublime order: his question "What's the difference?" intends that the addressee, Edith, should know he *means,* "I

don't give a damn" (de Man 1979, 9–10). De Man sees Bunker as a figure for "[modernist] despair when confronted with a structure of linguistic meaning that he cannot control and that holds the discouraging prospect of an infinity of similar future confusions, all of them potentially catastrophic in their consequences." De Man's example demonstrates his conception of the difference between rhetoric and grammar—the incommensurability of the two modes, an incommensurability that we can either live with, like Rilke and Nietzsche, or fight futilely, like Bunker and Rousseau. Mass culture has this wonderful and heuristic side to it: the polysemous nature of its actants, the rhetorical overdrive of its registers, and its insatiable, hysteric demand to be watched without being interpreted.

348   I will take up this last condition of mass culture first, already hinted at in the discussion above of Andrew Ross. Taking for convenience's sake (and also because of its political derivations) Jameson's contention that mass culture and modernism are the two dialectical sides of the postmodern condition (and where postmodernism is, I think, slotted in as a continuing project of modernism), what are the two sides' views of interpretation? Both high culture and mass culture seem to both welcome interpretation and fear it. The hostility of many poets, painters, and musicians to criticism is well-known. And with such features of the culture industry as fan magazines or TV specials that take us "behind the scenes" of a new movie (which Paul Smith derisively refers to as the "tributary media" [1993, xvi–xvii]), mass culture would seem to welcome cheerfully the role of the critic. But high culture's hostility is only at the surface: structurally, art now (in the modern and postmodern epochs) demands to be interpreted. The novelist's use of symbols, the painter's historical references, and the pianist's use of minimal chords are just obvious examples of the shift from Kant's aesthetic to a society of criticism. And mass culture only appropriates criticism to empty it of its content: Gene Siskel and Roger Ebert or Leonard Maltin are not so much critics as phallocentric advertisements: the erect thumb speaks the truth.[26]

26 A more accurate delineation of the differences between various forms of criticism might label as "epistemophilic" the critical desire to know the object and "libidinal" the critical desire to enjoy. The first desire, then, is what is rewarded in the academy and sold in various highbrow venues; the second one is the province of the daily film critics or book

349 Baudrillard has pointed out, in various texts, the impenetrability of mass culture to the critic; graffiti, he notes, if it once was readable by and indeed intended for the "general reader," now is a cryptic sign, less signature than postmodern, neoprimitive glyph. And it is true that elite art needs to be reviewed seriously to survive, and therefore will encode its reception both within the text and without it. (Attila Richard Lukács's use of art-historical references in his skinhead paintings, an article in *The Financial Post* once commented, means that the paintings will increase in value and thus are worthy of collecting—to which it might be added that the encrypted codes also ensure showings at serious galleries like Toronto's Powerplant and appropriate critical "appreciation.") With mass culture such a desire to be interpreted is less likely (while fanzine culture attempts to transcend the division or change the reception): bucks are all that count. But the key to Baudrillard's analysis, as a glance through any of his books will signify immediately, lies in his reliance on a neoreligious vocabulary (he is the new Christ to Lyotard's new druid): mass culture, like the masses themselves, is fundamentally evil. Thus it resists the implicit morality of intellectual criticism.

350 Jameson knows that mass culture hates criticism: prepared for this eventuality by the founding masochism of Marxist theory (Lukács),[27] he responds with a text that sutures mass culture into its very fabric. Marxist criticism desires, compulsively, "to mark repeatedly the memory of a lost Cause" (Žižek 1991c, 272). Jameson then will mark, repeatedly, the trauma of the class struggle, of the failure of that class struggle, of its "impossibility"

---

reviewers. Or, as Simon Frith recently put it, "In universities . . . just as in high schools, there is still a split between what Frank Kogan describes as the discourse of the classroom (with its focus on a subject matter) and the discourse of the hallway (with its focus on one's feelings about a subject matter)" (1991, 103).

27 I should stress here that when I am using the figure of masochism for criticism at this juncture, it is in the context of the previous chapter's meditations on Lukács and *not* in the context from this chapter's opening remarks on Plato and the three types of critics. Suffice it to say that the second, Žižekian or Lacanian masochism, is founded in a repetition without closure—the Fort-da game discussed by Lacan in "The Function and Field of Speech and Language in Psychoanalysis" (1977, 30–113). Lukácsean masochism is then what Lacan calls "primordial masochism" (1977, 103).

(Žižek) or political unrepresentability, or of its necessity to somehow be *figured.* So in *Dog Day Afternoon,* the various actors are not "symbols" of classes—in the classic Lukácsean imperative—they do not "represent" the class struggle. Class struggle, or history, is in Lacan's terms the *objet a,* the little "a," which, in his example of Holbein's painting *The Ambassadors,* is exemplified by a distorted death's head in the corner of the picture (Lacan 1981, 88). Thus it is a question of a "skewed" (in Žižek's terms, "awry") unrepresentability. Lacan's formulation lays out the status of the subject (for me, the Marxist critic): "At this level, we are not even forced to take into account any subjectification of the subject. The subject is an apparatus. This apparatus is something which is lacunary, and it is in the lacuna that the subject establishes the function of a certain object, *qua* lost object. It is the status of the *objet a* in so far as it is present in the drive" (Lacan 1981, 185). The Lacan-a, the object always being lost and then found in Jameson's texts, is history, like the spool in Freud's Fort-da narrative being thrown out of the playpen of language, only to be retrieved.

search for a figure

351 This explains Jameson's extended—tortuous?—attempts to determine just how class can be figured, in "Class and Allegory in Contemporary Mass Culture: *Dog Day Afternoon* as a Political Film" (*SV,* 35–54). Here the *objet a* is class as a meaningful category for social experience, conceived of through "figurability": "[F]or genuine class consciousness to be possible, we have to begin to sense the abstract truth of class through the tangible medium of daily life in vivid and experiential ways; and to say that class structure is becoming representable means that we have now gone beyond mere abstract understanding and entered that whole area of personal fantasy, collective storytelling, narrative figurability. . . . To become figurable—that is to say, visible in the first place, accessible to our imaginations—the classes have to be able to become in some sense characters in their own right: this is the sense in which the term allegory in our title is to be taken as a working hypothesis" (*SV,* 38). This notion of the figurability of class Jameson pursues *not* through the standard post-*Cahiers du Cinema* and *Screen* tropes of spec-

tatorship and camera-fetishism (Teresa de Lauretis, Stephen Heath, and Christian Metz, for example),[28] but, as he adds in an afterword to the *Dog Day Afternoon* essay (*SV,* 54), by analyzing how characterization is created and interpreted in a filmic context that includes both late capitalism and television, that further *Aufhebung,* the degrading of an already degraded art form.

352 The first "context" for *Dog Day Afternoon,* late or multinational capitalism, is a context in the strong sense. In the post-studio era of Hollywood film, the system of multinational entertainment corporations is ontologically the origin of "blockbuster" movies like this one. And the move away from auteurism, in Jameson's reading of the film, does not mean a structuralist conclusion that history is a process without subject. Al Pacino's character Sonny, for instance, why does he rob the bank? It seems that he wants to get money for his lover to get a sex-change operation.[29] But Sonny tells the television interviewer that he has no job prospects (closed unions on the one hand, low-paying jobs like bank tellers on the other)—and even this apparent reason (which neatly demonstrates the dialectic of the revenge of content on form, in which it is not the society-of-spectacle notion of an instantaneous interview that is most relevant, but the content, Sonny's pathetic and nevertheless awe-inspiring anger) is a false lead. For the movie begins, after a sweeping and raucous series of pans around New York and Brooklyn, with the three men (Sonny, Sal, and a lad whose quick departure is foreshadowed by being the only one not "dressed for work"—not in a suit, that is); the origin of the theft of the bank, now characterizable with the benefit of Brecht's aphorism, lies in a collective revenge.

353 And so we have the crowds' sympathy for Al Pacino's character Sonny, the bank robber who signifies a sympathy born of late capitalism's "wholesale liquidation" (*SV,* 44) of older values, a liquidation that Jameson argues

28 These "semantic fields" of vision, as Bordwell puts it (1991), are displaced in Jameson's film criticism by a semantic field of transcoding (*SV,* 100) and class.

29 Like Jim's absent leap (which never takes place in the present) or Marion's (Janet Leigh's) theft of the money in *Psycho,* Sonny's apparent "reason" for robbing the bank is an absent presence in the film: it is his lover, Ernie (Chris Sarandon), who tells the police that money for an operation is the reason (or at least they infer it from his valium-induced mutterings).

we can now pin on someone responsible. Jameson bases this supposition on Stanley Aronowitz's *False Promises,* which documents the forces behind the dispersal of the white working class from city centers following World War II. But the question of somehow suturing blame onto someone responsible is once again the problem of the figurable: "[H]ow to imagine authority today," Jameson asks, "how to conceive imaginatively—that is in a non-abstract, non-conceptual form—of a principle of authority that can express the essential impersonality and post-individualistic structure of the power structure of our society while still operating among real people, in the tangible necessities of daily life and individual situations of repression?" (*SV,* 48). The movie's narrative solution to this ideological problem is the febrifuge of James Broderick's FBI agent, an actant-position that is McLuhan-cool in opposition both to the local police chief (Charles Durning) and Al Pacino: "[T]he starkly blank and emotionless, expressionless" agent thus figures a "gazing face, behind which decision making is reduced to (or developed to) pure technique" (*SV,* 49), an organization man or G-man who is beyond good and evil because he does not need those archaic emotions to drive him. The local is being blanked out, literally, by "that immense and decentralized power network" which is late capitalism, and the "very absence of [the agent's] features becomes a sign and expression of the presence/absence of corporate power in our daily lives, all-shaping and omnipotent and yet rarely accessible in figurable terms, that is to say, in the representable form of individual actors and agents" (*SV,* 50).

354 Jameson thus calls upon mass culture to provide for Marxism a figure for the manner in which class structure is changing under late capitalism. This is a three-tiered structure of proletarianized city dwellers (bank employees, the lumpen-robbers, the crowd), gormless local bourgeoisie (gutted out in the postmodernization of city and nation alike), and multinational capitalism (whose primacy, Jameson remarks, is shown in the film by "the spatial trajectory" from the bank to the pomo space of the technologized airport). A final remark on how Jameson decodes the relationship between the various actors, itself then a figure for class relations, argues that a mediation takes effect: the uneven status of Pacino, Durning, and Broderick, where the first was a Hollywood superstar, the second a "character" actor, and the third then unknown, but soon to be a television star. Thus the FBI agent's "ano-

nymity in the filmic narrative is expressed very precisely through his anonymity within the framework of the Hollywood star system. The face is
blank and unreadable precisely because the actor is himself unidentifiable"
(*SV,* 52). The second of the two contexts mentioned above, television, which
is even less amenable than film to theories of auteurism and orthodox Marxist analysis, thus is the external mediation for a late capitalism that seeks to
replace even Hollywood feature films.

355 The title of this essay, in full, is "Class and Allegory in Contemporary
Mass Culture: *Dog Day Afternoon* as a Political Film." Jameson is willfully
perverse in his attempts to find the "political" in the film not where you
would expect it, which might be, say, in the robbery as some nascent or raw
political act (which would probably be where Baudrillard, with his love of
the spontaneous and terroristic, would find it), or in the director Sidney
Lumet's liberalism, or even in the "postmodern" meta-media event of camera attention (that is more properly the focus of Heinrich Böll's novel *The
Lost Honour of Katerina Blum* and its two film versions). This Lukácsean
perversity also is apparent in the overloading of the essay with sociological
analysis and digression: the first two or three pages concentrate on how class
is obfuscated in U.S. culture, refer to Stanley Aronowitz, and then sketch out
preliminary theories of documentary and the then-nascent real-life reenact-
ments. Here Jameson is re-membering, scratching the absent member or
limb of the political in a society of the "spectacle" where, unlike the modern
period with its infamous "political unconscious" (the modern novel that
represses the representation of work, for example), culture actually brings to
the fore political issues and agendas as so much fodder for the consciousness
industry.

the heist of class

356 Jameson argues, then, that the effect of "Hollywood" (which is only a
visible arena of late capitalism), not to mention narrative resources (genres),
the star system (the *bodies* of the actors) and the filmmaker's own intents and
talents, is that class will inevitably appear as an allegory or an extended tale
of *something else.* If our contemporary world system, multinational capital-

ism, is characterized by shifting modes of production from the industrial or Fordist model to the "information age" or post-Fordist model (from Detroit and Strachan Avenue to Silicone Valley and the *maquiladoras*), then its cultural apparatchiks seem to offer narratives about the betrayal of the working class by the prime new facilitator of this shift: the Ehrenreichs's "professional-managerial class" or the new class of intellectuals-managers and their managerial revolutions.[30]

357 The heist picture, then, which has a healthy tradition in various movie cultures, has invariably concerned itself with unalienated, collective labor engaged in the Brechtian art of striking at the heart of capitalism, even if the collective usually fails (or must fail, for realism or the reality-principle to sneak in as a plot-determinant). The pleasure in watching a heist film is seeing a group of marginalized people (usually men) team their skills and talents to rip off the system. The use of technology (in particular, guns) and the role of the actors' bodies are important: the worker's body, like the criminal's body, is the final target of bourgeois economics and philosophy. Recent changes in the form of the heist picture signal the decline of even this allegory of class struggle. *Reservoir Dogs* healthily illustrates how class functions today in the late capitalist world. The film takes place in the interstices of the heist: the gang grouping together after the robbery (something you usually would see in five minutes, as Tarantino has said in an interview). This working in the margins is a filmic or cinematic analogon for the new proliferation of "gray markets" (designer label rip-offs, semi-legal computer clones) that similarly function between an outside (the black-market of crime) and the inside (the proper, official market).

358 The criminals in the film have been further reified in a particularly postmodern way: they are simulacra of the capitalist class (their uniform is a black suit, but they also modify it with cowboy boots or cuff links), and they are also nameless metonyms for our anonymous age, working with pseudonyms (Mr. Pink, Mr. White). On the one hand, the criminals relish the anonymity imposed by their boss: Mr. Pink remonstrates with Mr. White for

---

30 "Highly educated professionals spew forth from the universities in Cambridge, Boston, and Waltham. . . . The personal power seen in people of the New Class is joined to an economic fact" (Sennett and Cobb 1973, 39–40).

almost giving him his real name. On the other hand, Mr. White has told his name to Mr. Orange: "What was I supposed to do?" he asks. "I'm sorry, I can't give you that information?" The film begins with a Barry Levinson (*Diner*)-like male-bonding scene around mass culture, but one whose brutality here and throughout the film (Madonna and later black women are particularly reviled) announces the violence suffered by the working class which permeates its fantasies. Mass culture, here, is irredeemably positive: a womb or cocoon of seventies superfunk and bubble-gum pop.[31] The heist goes horribly wrong immediately, and the filmmaker's conceit that we do not "see" the robbery demonstrates the invisible nature of labor today, with offshore data processing and cottage-industry designer fashions. The film posits a schizoid betrayal of the working class: both from within, and without. The heist goes wrong because one of the "good" criminals (Mr. Blond, whose loyalty cannot be questioned) goes berserk in the jewelry store. The police show up immediately because one of the criminals (Mr. Orange) is an undercover cop.

359 The police in this film are a figure for the managerial/intellectual class, which according to the cultural logic of the film must bear political responsibility for the present-day fate of the world's proletariat.[32] Orange infiltrates the gang with two methods: First, he is helped by a snitch who we are told is true evil because he is betraying his own. Second, Orange must rehearse an anecdote to pass as a criminal: his actorly function, then (trained by the only black character in the film, who wears a Rastafarian headband, Mao cap, Che [or is it Bob Marley?] T-shirt . . . so much for the sixties!), is to "know"

31 See also *This Boy's Life* (Michael Caton-Jones, 1992), where, just after the boy has been ripped out of his almost-idyllic life with his mother (cf. Plato and Irigaray), one of a sequence of nonnarrative (i.e., in the Imaginary) shows the boy curled, fetuslike, with his radio cradled in his arms. The film also offers a textbook illustration of the *conflictual* nature of mass culture's reception, in the scene where Robert De Niro keeps turning up his Perry Como record on the hi-fi as his wife and daughter laugh over a jigsaw puzzle).

.32 This is an argument diametrically opposite to that of Pfeil in his exhaustive survey of the two PMC's (the Professional-Managerial Class and postmodern culture), " 'Makin' Flippy-Floppy' " (1990, 97–125). But then, writing in the middle of the American Reagan decade, perhaps it was necessary to state that the baby-boom PMC "is still to date most accurately characterized by its resistance to incorporation" (121).

the working (stealing) class better than they know themselves (so much for sociology). Two other points in the film support this analysis: Pink asks White if he killed cops or regular people, and when a hostage cop is being tortured by Blond and says that the criminals' "boss" doesn't think there was a setup, Blond replies that he has no boss.

360 The film also underscores the ossified morality of the working class at this late juncture. Mr. White, in particular, is a paragon, reciting U.S. Department of Labor statistics to urge Mr. Pink to tip a waitress, recommending to Mr. Orange that cutting off the finger of a store manager (!) will get you the information you want, and, in the end, when he has helped to destroy his own class solidarity protecting Orange (who he thought was not a rat—and White's moan now is the muted anguish of the proletariat, figured through Harvey Keitel's second-generation post-Method actorly style),[33] killing Orange when the latter admits he was a cop. Orange's mistake is to confuse personal ethics for class struggle.

curious georg

361 Both my present analysis of *Reservoir Dogs* and Jameson's of *Dog Day Afternoon* should point to a more general diagnosis; that is, crime drama illustrates in a total way a potentially revolutionary situation at hand. Mass culture is inevitably the masses speaking to itself: here, the cinematic collision course between the police and the criminal is telling the proletariat to destroy the new class. In *The Historical Novel* (1976), Lukács provides the following reminder on the relationship between cultural analysis and politics: "All this has very important consequences for the question which interest us here. On the one hand, we see the important connexion in life between dramatic collision and social transformation. Marx's and Engels's

---

33 Keitel's moan is not, then, an *expression* of his style (or of himself): this much, at least, is shown by comparing his performance here with that in Abel Ferrara's *Bad Lieutenant* (1992), where his various moans, "attributed" to his crack use and "disintegration," are either pathetic or, if viewed with a stern materialism, the articulation of the consumer satiated with all the object choices (gambling, drugs, women) capitalism can offer him. See the Toronto Keitel fanzine, *"You shoot me in a dream you better wake up and apologize!"*

conception of the connexions between a great dramatic period and revolution proves itself here completely; for it is clear that the social-historical concentrating of contradictions in life necessarily demands a dramatic embodiment. On the other hand, we see that the trueness-to-life of dramatic form cannot be 'localized,' as it were, in a narrow and mechanical way, round the great revolutions of human history. It is true that a real dramatic collision gathers together the human and moral features of a great social revolution, but since the portrayal aims at the human essence, the concrete conflict by no means has to reveal immediately a transformation underlying it. The latter forms the general basis of the collision, but the connexion between this basis and the concrete form of the collision can be a very complex one, with many intermediary stages" (113).[34]

362 The second comment here, Lukács's warning against a fetishistic "trueness-to-life" applies as well to two commonplaces of crime-drama analysis that must be avoided: the first, that there is a certain "mirroring" between the gang and "straight" society. While this is undoubtedly true in a sociological or historical way (and applies best to so-called "organized crime"), such an analysis forecloses any utopian view of crime. As with the vulgar psychoanalysing of youth protests (it is just Oedipal, not really important), the effect is to dismiss political interpretation and action. The hierarchy of the gang in *Reservoir Dogs* only shows the nonmonolithic nature of the working class and not that it is merely a mirror of the bourgeois order. Secondly, because of the real or biographical working-class origins of many police officers, their cultural representations are often misread as an inscription of the working class in mass culture (Aronowitz on Archie Bunker and

34 There is a passage in *The Political Unconscious* where Jameson, remarking on the importance of genre criticism to Marxism, notes that at a moment that demanded political action, Lukács "did so by sitting down at his desk and producing a piece of genre criticism" (*PU,* 105). For some reason I have been misremembering that passage as referring to *The Historical Novel,* which was written in 1937, as the Popular Front was collapsing and fascism a verifiable threat in any number of European countries. This would be nice, but it actually refers to Solzhenitsyn; nevertheless, many of Lukács's comments on the historical novel's almost Lévi-Straussian "solutions" to Balzac's or Scott's contemporary problems with imaginary, textual, deep-historical narratives, can be applied equally to his (Lukács's) own solution to the problem of aesthetics and politics in the prewar period.

De Niro makes this mistake, or perhaps the necessary first step). So, that Mr. Orange and his Black Panther-wannabe superior represent the betrayal of the working class by the professional-managerial class is indisputable. But the other major policeman in the movie is the hostage, whom Mr. Blond tortures and Michael Penn's character kills. And while Orange's betrayal of his betrayal (when he admits he is a cop) demonstrates the corruption of the new managerial class, the hostage's refusal to name the "rat," coupled with the centrality of his *body* to the film, finally show that his working class loyalty will even, and tragically, extend to the new class we (PMC's)[35] have been recruited into. The hostage cop's anger when he learns the police are waiting for the crime boss to turn up announces his self-demystification; like Bourdieu's oblate, the hostage has believed in that which did not believe in him.

triadic allegories of totality

363 It's a small world after all. Disney's inane theme song, one of many, once ripped out of the maw of the various Baudrillardean/Eco-topos of Epcot, DizWorld, DizLand (and the Mighty Ducks hockey franchise),[36] now can stand as a class anthem for postmodernism. As I noted in the preface (and return to in the conclusion) Jameson's lesson in *The Geopolitical Aesthetic* is that "totality" today is, like Foucault's famous notion of power (1980, 92–97), everywhere. "In the widespread paralysis of the collective or social imaginary, where 'nothing occurs' (Karl Kraus) when confronted with the

35 The "we" here may be problematic: self-loathing seems to be the current form of intellectual bad faith, even among the majority of intellectuals who are not tenured academics but working in the margins of the post-secondary and media institutions. But I am thinking especially of the tragic and fine ending to *Strangers in Paradise*, where the authors note that the hostility of the working class to the academy has not a little to do with their knowledge that the institution is fortified (Eugene Debs's "wall of fire" between the university and the working class is remembered) by members of their own class who have only too hurriedly made a pact with the ruling class.

36 See, for various recent discussions of Disney, "The World According to Disney" issue of *South Atlantic Quarterly* (ed. Willis, 1993).

ambitious program of fantasizing an economic system on the scale of the globe itself, the older motif of conspiracy knows a fresh lease on life, as a narrative structure capable of reuniting the minimal basic components: a potentially infinite network, along with a plausible explanation of its invisibility; or in other words: the collective and the epistemological. To put it this way is to understand how this imperfect mediatory and allegorical structure—the conspiracy, not yet even the world system itself—offers the gravest representational dilemmas, since traditional narratives have never been much good at conveying the collective" (GA, 9). So Jameson teases the allegory out of conspiracy films in the first half of his latest book (it is evident already that "the gravest representational dilemmas" in that work, stand as a shrunken dwarf and a self-referential diagnosis). A central problem in The Geopolitical Aesthetic, which Jameson acknowledges always plagues his writing on film, is that his narrator is like the specialist looking over his neighbor's shoulder in a carrel at a research library. This problematic manifests the desire to work as a literary critic—and therefore to refer to Balzac, Flaubert, Pynchon, or Gide. I would like to offer a more ambitious program for decoding the social present.

364 The past few years have witnessed a paradigm shift in how we view and use technology, a mini-revolution of sorts that figures or points to a larger shift, the postmodernization of everything (and it should be unspoken that "postmodernization" is never the same thing as "modernization" and that, most evidently, the former process will not automatically entail the "streamlining" or making new of the latter one; therefore, for example, the various vestiges of the primitive—First Nations spirituality—in the various world systems of the planet are as postmodern as the West Edmonton Mall or the latest John Woo film. The major manifestations of this shift can be seen in a few signal incidents; first, the succession of cellular phone scandals in the past year or two which had widespread publicity. In British Columbia and Québec, cell phone calls of provincial politicians were tap(p)ed by amateur (if that word any longer has any meaning) radio buffs or eavesdroppers (the shifting "guilt" or role of these key players instantiates in so-called real life the prime function Jameson sees in heroes of conspiracy films). And in Britain, both Prince Charles and Princess Di were taped as they conversed with their respective lovers. What is immediately apparent about these inci-

dents are two facts: first, that they qualify as scandals (that is, are made scandals by the mass-savage mind, or are made "popular" in Fiske's sense) because they indicate an interconnectedness of "all" communications acts today; second, that there ensued almost inevitably an immediate furor less over the actual conversations than over the issue of transcribing/translating them into some other media. In Québec, the Bourrassa conversation was banned from being published in the print/electronic media—but only in that province. So a bookstore owner took it upon himself to risk litigation by selling the transcripts at cost (a low-tech Xeroxed version: this is where the mythologies and motifs of Cold War Eastern Europe have migrated to) and by posting the conversation in his storefront window. In the U.K., too, the banal "ethics" trope, with which senior columnists like to fill space, resulted in discussions of whether the newspapers should publish the lovers' chatter (an accompanying analysis—in *The Guardian,* I think—remarked on the poverty of Charles's metaphors; again, obviously the question is really that of a dialectical translation from one medium to another).

365 The hardware half of the equation, to accompany the forgoing software concerns, then, would postulate that along with the cell phone scandals we are also witnessing a tireless (if boring) series of "technological revolutions" from microchip and microwaves in the sixties to the latest forms: interactive TV, DATs and post-CD formats, digital radio, virtual reality and the virtual office, and the forecast "explosion" of television technologies (signal compression, mini-satellite dishes, "near-video-on-demand"). These revolutions have begun the project of wiring the individual (cyberpunk, obviously) and the home, so that local forms like "home shopping" or digital radio or near-video-on-demand will attempt to de-spatialize the marketplace and replace it in the electronic environs of the home and cerebral cortex. Technological "connections" may become like genetic coding: so pervasively are we connected that it is meaningless, or at least ungraspable. Hence the turn to allegory.

366 Those two concerns, translation (and the concomitant anxieties about a pseudo-ethic of privacy, which is really a decaying individualistic paranoia about "using" any technology at all—McLuhan, Ong, Havelock, Derrida, etc.), and the contradictory indication of a growing interconnectedness of all communication acts and technology, turn out to be articulating the same

postmodern allegory of totality. That is, it suffices to offer a rough homology between the antiquarian notion of, say, exchange, communication, and sexuality. In all three domains or fields, at one time our ancestors believed that some act or one-to-one affair was taking place. Exchange was a free deal entered into between a buyer and a seller, as they exchange money for commodities or for labor. Communication, too, was theorized as some private and meaningful exchange between two intellects, with all the accompanying possibilities of understanding and intent (or their negative others). And, finally, sexuality was seen as yet another "exchange" between two adults (or whatever) taking place in some private and consensual realm. These old-fashioned views were part of and essential to the modernization of society, which defeudalized economic, linguistic, and sexual relations.

367 In the postmodern epoch, however, this has all changed. Economic transactions now take place in a throbbing network of international bank transfers, offshore data processing, and the frenetic movement of labor and capital between the North and the South, the East and the West, the First, Second, Third, and Fourth Worlds. Communication technology, and its paranoia/anxiety, through its representation as scandal is also a figure for that economic base. Forgive the vulgarism; while I still succumb here to an Althusserian nostalgia for the insistence of the economic, I also believe that the ominous structure of the simulacra will function to figure or mediate the various allegories. That is, when "the economy" is discussed in the media (as in serious scholarship, for that matter: see Thurow or Becker), such terms as command/demand economies or globalization or the "relaxation" of tariffs are themselves explicit sexualizations of the market. Once viewed dialectically, this triadic allegory is not merely a negative phenomenon. A literary bestseller a couple of years ago in the U.S.A. was Nicholson Baker's *Vox* (1992), a serious novel about phone sex. Here, the "translation" of a corrupt and symbolically marginal technology into the most venerated of media, the book, and its subsequent success, indicates the Dionysian effects of the shift.[37] But this leads to the third structure.

37 A novel about phone sex evidently anticipates the third term of my triadic allegory: sexuality and its so-called withering away in the AIDS era. But the novel also briefly documents or alludes to the economics of late capitalism when the female party says she

368 If everything stands for something else, then so too does sexuality. And now the totalization of sexuality, or AIDS, with all of its cycles of paranoia, restrictions, scientism and government, activism and puritanism, is paramount. What AIDS has demonstrated, to the good, is best illustrated in a TV advertisement (from Australia, I believe, but the trope now seems to be disseminated to various media campaigns) that begins by showing a couple in bed together and then pulls back to reveal a virtual outback of beds, a collective or dormitory or utopian space of former partners (and their former partners and so on). You are now fucking every partner your partner ever fucked.[38] Without underplaying either the rampant homophobia of AIDS-denial or the horrific effects of the disease/plague on many communities, the battle being fought on all of our behalf by AIDS activists is, in the good old Lukácsean sense, world-historical, precisely because of how it figures the importance of acknowledging the totality.[39]

allegorizing interpretation

369 In an earlier draft of this book, I described a scene from the film *Strange Brew* (Thomas and Moranis, 1983). The vagueness of that "description"

---

imagines that the packers for an erotic catalog service "are of course mostly middle-aged Laotian women" (13). These packers are on strike in the woman's fantasy, which results in the male models themselves filling orders (the semiotic become labor); but the theoretical interest in Baker's work (as in *The Mezzanine*, alluded to in an earlier chapter of this work) is not sustained by a readerly interest.

38 The spatialization of sexuality is also relevant: this is then apparent (and remembering the thesis statement of *Vox*) in the film *Bad Lieutenant* where, "all the critics agree," the best or most powerful scene is when Harvey Keitel persuades one teenaged girl to show him her ass and another to simulate fellatio while he masturbates. That is, the *separation* of the voyeur from the women is celebrated (by critics) as a new form of safe sex.

39 In this sense, Hornes's (1989, 289–97) description of Jameson's theory as prophylactic is less offensive for its misreading of Jameson's work (who cares about that?) than for its wrongheaded assumption that the various safe sex campaigns derive wholly from the top-down and not grass roots. Safe sex, beyond the metaphysics, is then a figure for a postmodern acknowledgment of the totality; new sexual practices are the road to new organic intellectuals and an activist praxis.

betrayed an unresearcherly, or nonrigorous irresponsibility. The description was from memory, from seeing the film when it came out a decade ago. I was vague because I am intrigued by Stanley Cavell's notion, in *The World Viewed* (1979), that you can talk about film as you remember it, sometimes over a span of decades. This latter possibility is interesting both for what it suggests about interpretation in general (the false specter of empirical accuracy, the use of quotation in a textual dynamic) and for mass culture. For in writing on film, the critic always has to rely on her memory: notes taken during a film are surely there to "prompt" the memory like a teleprompter or cue cards do on TV. The film is then "rescreened" in the drive-in stadium of the mind.

370   *Strange Brew*'s deconstruction of the *Screen* aesthetic is definitively populist: so what if classic Hollywood realism is fake, Bob and Doug reply, we like fakes. Mass culture is not anywhere so concerned with origins, reality, or problems of simulation as is thought by critics hung up on too much Foucault or Derrida. Donuts are the motor fuel of Bob and Doug, the donut shop the site of their offscreen adventures in the TV sketch from which the movie ensued; donuts are proudly anti-real, as exemplified by the current advertising campaign by Jos. Louis snack foods: "100% Granola-free" one bus ad claims; "No alfalfa sprouts" says another; "A good source of no soy beans" says a third. This latest product of the consciousness industry embodies the contradiction of mass culture at its center like the "crème" in a donut: populism is the ideology of intellectuals with bad faith (see Jameson's essay on *Cultural Studies* [1993b]). That is, the Jos. Louis ad campaign was created by downtown Toronto advertising "creative" and account executives, hoping to "capitalize" on what they perceive to be the masses' distrust of health food. But that distrust originates in the use by the middle classes of "health" as a token of Bourdieuesque distinction.

371   It should be clear that the use of such tokens is overdetermined and is not tied rigorously to economic status; this reaffirms both Althusserian theory and Jameson's point, in the *Dog Day Afternoon* essay, that the Marxist conception of class is relational and conflictual. So an artist having a tofu burger may not make any more money than the printer next to her on the street, who just had a Big Mac. But the ressentiment that fuels the mutual disparagement ("That's full of steroids and by-products" on one side, and "Freak food I wouldn't give a rabbit" on the other) is based on a class

struggle: *figures* that class struggle, that is. The same logic is at work in a current TV ad for a new "light" vegetable oil, where a mother, trying to cut back on cholesterol, drives her children crazy with various "health" food dishes, like a huge bean casserole. But by using the new light oil, the mother can serve up fried food ("Real food," the phallic son chirps) and keep the family ensconced in their white-trash existence.[40]

372   Film can be a privileged moment for this meditation on the (triangular?) relationship between intellectuals, mass culture, and high culture, precisely because the century of cinema has seen its "progress" from a novelty item (the nickelodeon) to, on the one hand, the trash of ironclad Hollywood genre films (including the most disreputable of genres, the sequel) and, on the other hand, the still important auteur and post-auteur notions of "world cinema" and art (i.e., "Third Cinema").[41] In this history, the work and reception of Alfred Hitchcock are exemplary; hence the importance of Hitchcock's films to various schools of contemporary criticism: auteurist (Wood or Rothman), poststructuralist (Wollen or Heath), feminist (Modleski, Mulvey), and Marxist or materialist (Jameson's essays). Typically, Jameson's essay in *Signatures of the Visible* (99–127) does not provide a new "reading" of Hitchcock; rather, he comments on how William Rothman and others have come to interpret film. The chapter, a review of Rothman's *Hitchcock— The Murderous Gaze* (1982), begins with a meditation on just what a "powerful interpretive act" can be said to be, something that can "tell us about *interpretation* as such" (*SV,* 99). The fascination with interpretation signals, I think, the retreat of the filmic object. This disappearance of film itself is the central problem of film criticism and theory today according to David Bordwell, who argues that auteur theory began (was made possible)

---

40 Lest my use of the phrase "white trash" seem unduly harsh, I should add that I take that as my own ethnic designation (especially after seeing in a British newspaper the phrase "East Anglian white trash," which is even more specific to my patrilineal heritage); Willis points out, in a chapter critical of anti-sugar moralizing: "In our society shopping in health-food stores and adopting foreign cuisines are activities that are highly defined by class and that have strong student and white middle-class associations" (1991, 135–36).

41 "Third Cinema" is a term given to revolutionary Third World cinema that rejects both the normalizing conventions of Hollywood and the personal-autobiographical rhetoric of auteur cinema. The term was coined by Argentine filmmakers/critics Fernando Solanas and Octavio Getino.

by the decline of the Hollywood studio system; the Lacanian-semiotic school that began in the late 1960s and continues as the dominant school today, was first occasioned by the decline of the European art film in general, and today is less interested in specific films than in theory itself (1991, 71–104).

373 So Jameson will ask, referring to the alternative strategies of a film theory (there is only one film theory, Bordwell argues), "[W]hat is the epistemological-cal priority of a 'semiotic' commitment to the most self-punishing frame-by-frame analysis of a given film (over and beyond the ritual of professionalism involved), as against the suggestion of Stanley Cavell (following Freud on dreams) that the filmic 'object' is whatever we *remember* the film to have been (including our mistakes, holes, substitutions), that is to say, its 'narrative' appropriated by memory and transformed into an object?" (*SV,* 100). In a sense, Jameson's essay develops into a revenge of art upon the critic, for here interpretation itself becomes a fast-receding object. Interpretation's retreat takes place in two ways: first of all, film criticism now is less interested in film itself, or in filmmakers, or even in technique, at the expense of working out a "means to elucidate issues and problems relevant to women in patriarchy," as Tania Modleski claims feminist readings of Hitchcock (including her own) attempt to do (1988, 3). So Jameson's use of Rothman is a steady and object-destroying attack on the act of interpretation—Jameson is interested in a means to elucidate issues and problems relevant to leftists in late capitalism. Second, there is the extraordinary passage in *Signatures of the Visible* which begins on page 104, with a discussion of Nabokov and Chandler and then quotes Chandler on how he tried to insert emotion into his writing for the pulps; the writing quickly moves, whole-scale and to my great surprise, into a four-page excursion or tourist-guide description of walking around in San Francisco that, like Hitchcock's films,[42] focuses on a city only to subvert its own narrative, immediately and obtrusively, with the lugubrious details of

---

42 I am thinking of, for example, the beginning of *The Birds,* where Tippi Hedren is walking across the street, and we see birds grouping (whether "we" are the 1990s viewers who already know the story, or 1963 filmgoers only prepared by the studio publicity—"*The Birds* is coming" intoned Hitchcock) so that it is not so much a "malevolence" below the surface but already apparent and used up. And when Hedren is walking along the sidewalk to the pet store, just before Hitchcock himself comes out with his dogs, a young boy whistles at the actress, which slyly refers to a television ad she was in (for a diet soft drink) when Hitchcock "discovered her."

walking around a car parked over the sidewalk (TV remote controls and garage-door openers), so that the comment that "the latter can never be *transparent*" (109) is immediately and with relief taken to refer not just to the absolute predicate but to description itself, to politics, interpretation, Jameson's text, anything we may write about it, and so on, and that the vertigo afforded by this glimpse into the rear window of theory production is less a matter of a "transcendental approach," for which Modleski reproaches Jameson (1988, 119), than a dialectics of negation that, seeing the interpreter negate the object in theory, then proceeds to negate that negation in "Allegorizing Hitchcock," where the four-page excursion, as I put it above, is almost a turn to narrative or novelistic prose.[43]

ethics and hitchcocK

374   Žižek is essentially correct in the designation of the drive to mark and to remember, to mark out on a map, a cognitive map, the route for a Marxist aesthetics of mass culture. That marking is figural, Žižek stresses: "The point is *not* to remember the past trauma as exactly as possible: such 'documentation' is a priori false, it transforms the trauma into a neutral, objective fact, whereas the essence of the trauma is precisely that it is too horrible to be remembered, to be integrated into our symbolic universe" (1991a, 272). Jameson's reading of *Dog Day Afternoon* is not, then, a lament for the failure of documentary film; the "trauma" of the disappearance of class, or, more accurately, the difficulty of articulating a class analysis, here is marked and re-membered, made possible again. But this new possibility that Jameson drives at, the sudden realization that the "superhighwayfication" of America and its concomitant effects on working-class life and radical politics derives from specific and powerful interest groups, is not, he remarks, "the result of increased information on our part . . . rather, our very possibility of rewriting

43   My use of Modleski here omits two important points: first, that she is, like Jameson, concerned with asserting the importance of interpretation; second, she is interested in "a series of readings that are *frankly* partial and 'impure' (in that they allow art and theory to intermingle freely)" (1988, 120).

history in this way is itself to be understood as the function of a fundamental change in the historical situation itself, and of the power and class relations that underlie it" (*SV,* 45). The renewed possibility of an American seeing class in everyday life is rooted in U.S. history; Canada and Britain would have very different responses and problematics, as would non-European countries. That is, the *trauma* in each case is distinct. The U.S. trauma is modernization, and it is discernible because of the decay of postmodernized society. In the United Kingdom, then, Thatcherism was probably the equivalent moment of modernization for the body politic. In Canada, the trauma is at the level of the nation as a whole: it is the trauma of a lack of trauma, the lack of a "founding revolution" or real rupture with the "mother" country; never having left the mirror stage, Canada's privileged role in postmodernity (McLuhan, Kroker, Berland) is assured because postmodernism itself is the return of the site of the mirror as "society of spectacle."

375 The case for Hitchcock was initially made in terms of *la politique de l'auteur* in general: a director working in the commercial cinema system (especially Hollywood), creating a world-vision through the use of stars and popular narratives (Jimmy Stewart, Cary Grant; Daphne du Maurier, Robert Bloch), definable technique (tracking and overhead shots, montage) and systems (color, light and dark). If I play with the orthography of his name, at least five current "Hitchcocks" can be characterized: there is HitchCOCK (feminist critiques), HITCHcock (the de Lauretis sort of deconstruction), HITCHCOCK (Wood's or Rothmanesque auteurism), hitchcock (Modleski's ambiguous use of him), Hitchcock (Jameson, the H standing as well, of course, for History), and hitchcocK (Žižek, where the last K will signal his gleeful use of Kafka and Hitchcock as neither mass culture nor high art). The first, which emphasizes Hitch's cock, is the classic (or orthodox, which is not to say either "outdated" or "naive" but "vulgar" in the antibourgeois, positive, Brechtian, *plumpes Denken* sense) feminist analysis of a Laura Mulvey: its essential (and welcome) vulgarity comes to the fore when we realize that this is probably closest to the popular present-day "forgetting" of Hitchcock. I remember when five of Hitchcock's films were rereleased in the early 1980s, I told my mother that my partner and I were seeing them at the local rep theatre (my parents have probably never gone to a "rep" house). Her response was that she remembered seeing *Vertigo* and *Rear Window* when they

first came out, but she could not understand why anyone would want to see them now; this is the essential historical truth of mass culture,[44] which refuses the nostalgia of the bourgeoisie or intellectual. So I can generalize Mulvey's analysis of *Rear Window* (Mulvey 1988a) to a masses' reading: the utopian collective subject that populates the "screen" of Jeffries' rear window, which stains Lisa as soon as she breaks the fourth wall, is figured in the movie only as a projection of Jeffries' own imprisonment. Filmically as well as semiotically (as extras as well as signs), the various cast members in their own windows are "backdrops" to the Hitchcockian plots and anguish.

376 But is Mulvey's dismissal of Hitchcock for his cock really analogous to my mother's disinterest in seeing those films again? The second spelling of his name, "HITCHcock," corresponds to the interpretations Teresa de Lauretis offers in *Alice Doesn't*. The emphasis on the "hitch" in Hitch's name signifies here a problematic of both articulation and snag. De Lauretis's interpretation in the chapter "Desire in Narrative" (1984, 103–57) is quite similar to Jameson's use of Propp and Lévi-Strauss in *The Political Unconscious;* she bases her theory of Oedipal narrative on Propp and Jurij Lotman. Especially significant is Propp's idea that "plots do not directly 'reflect' a given social order, but rather emerge out of the conflict, the contradictions, of different social orders as they succeed or replace one another; the difficult coexistence of different orders of historical reality in the long period of transition from one to the other is precisely what is manifested in the tensions of plots" (de Lauretis 1984, 113). Thus plot articulates historical change. Žižek's Kafkaesque Hitchcock is one of "blots" and "stains," or implacable presences, like the overwhelming ship at the end of the street in *Marnie* (Žižek 1992a, 119) that is "phallic" and not phallocentric because it reveals the project at work.

the existence of jameson

377 In a sense, almost everyone is a member of the masses: we all watch TV, listen to pop music, eat junk food, go to the mall, buy items made in the

44 Contrary to Tania Modleski's contention that Hitchcock ensured his popularity with "the public" by holding back the films: his popularity with critics, perhaps (Modleski

Third World. This is why Jameson can half-humorously designate driving and listening to the radio as "fieldwork": and only in feminism is the trope of autobiographical details more utilized than in cultural studies. What does it mean to be "in the masses"? First of all, this position should be viewed dialectically: while we are all in the masses today, this is objectively a characteristic of postmodern or multinational or late capitalism, and that means that our interpellation as consumers of mass culture is a serious one—hence the need to abandon high-cultural apparatuses for the interpretation of the popular. Second, the fate of a precapitalist "folk culture" is extremely uncertain: is it the darling of urban museums, an oppositional reterritorialization by diasporic ethnicities, or an atrophied, or absent, member of a commodified social Body without Organs? Third and finally, the actual possibility of being an intellectual, of there still existing an autonomous high culture, is also questionable, if not terminally ill.

378 As noted above, *Signatures of the Visible* and *Postmodernism* possess a parallel structure in that both volumes begin with a now-classic essay and end with a long "summary" of Jameson's positions on the respective topics (film and postmodernism). But while "The Existence of Italy"—the concluding chapter to *Signatures*—is often concerned with film, it also uses the field of film history and theory to reflect on aesthetics in general (and the topics of realism, modernism, and postmodernism in particular). This strategy continues a thematic concern of the book: as Jameson remarks in his essay on Rothman and Hitchcock, "I have no vested interest in this particular field, whose products I nonetheless read with a certain envy, as though it were easier to be a materialist when you had a 'really' material object to work with" (*SV,* 99). There is a certain slippage here in vocabulary: the "field" in which Jameson purports to have no vested interest is both film *and* film studies; and so the quilt-bricolage structure of "The Existence of Italy" also continues the textual field of *Signatures,* a field, then, that can finally not be located as a merely rhetorical flourish in the manner of the great Jameson sentence.

1988, 1). Another precise boundary between the masses and the intellectual: when I was writing this chapter and viewing a lot of Hitchcock I had not seen before, I mentioned to my younger brother that I was seeing *Blackmail, Murder!, The Birds, Psycho* . . . and he replied that he had seen all of them. I asked, surprised, "All of Hitchcock?" No, it turned out, all of the *Psycho* films!

379 For the sentence is an entry point into a consideration of the autonomy or semiautonomy of the modernist work of art: "[W]hen the sentence or the material signifier has won genuine autonomy over and against the semi-autonomies of the modernist work, then we are already in full postmodern-ism" (*SV,* 206). And yet this is precisely the case in books like *Signatures of the Visible* and *Postmodernism,* where such discrete units as sentence, paragraph, and chapter fling themselves against the tyranny of the book (not to mention of the author). The discourse on San Francisco in the Hitchcock chapter that I mentioned above demonstrated the autonomy present in Jameson's discourse now, an autonomy fully one of the molecular triumphing over the molar, and which is also found in the final chapter of *Signatures* with the extraordinary memory-passage initiated by a description of Chantal Aker-man's *News From Home* (*SV,* 171–73).

380 What is now apparent in the Jameson-text is the insistence on mov-ing rather more quickly with the molecular momentum into theory. Thus the discussion of Akerman's film, the occasion for a postmodern *tristesse d'Olympio* that recollects various moments of Jameson's life in New York, then rapidly shifts to a discussion of Deleuze and Guattari on the "minor" (their reading of Kafka), which turns out to be a return to the theme of restricted and elaborated codes appropriated from the linguistics of Basil Bernstein. Indeed, this linguistic turn is one of the three major thematic substrata of the chapter (the other two are, first, the linking of nostalgia films with a view of art deco as the dialectics of feudalism and capitalism, and, second, the examination of film theory auteurism). The discussion of Bern-stein begins after some false starts to the chapter:[45] a prefatory section that offers some "throwaway" observations on the relationship between realism-modernism-postmodernism and the career of capital, on the one hand, and a parallel "microchronology" (156) of film, black writing, and rock music, on the other hand; also discussed briefly is the notion that film has two histories (one silent, the other sound) and thus two microchronologies and,

---

45 The chapter is rife with phraseologies like "which will not be more than sketched here" *SV,* 205), and "cannot be dealt with further here" (157) and short-circuited refer-ences to the *Postmodernism* and Adorno books (239nn2 and 4, 243n40, 245n70, 246n71, 247n90).

in more depth, there is a reexamination of realism from a postmodern perspective. This last then leads to the proposition that realism frequently, in its project of asserting the hegemony or class-consciousness of a certain class, will say what was previously unsaid. This return of the repressed Jameson then reformulates in Bernstein's vocabulary. Restricted codes are those of a certain group and are frequently specific or only intelligible to that group, while elaborated codes will posit a certain claim to universality. Jameson sums up Bernstein's theory in his own dialectical language as follows: "[T]he restricted code corresponds to the thought patterns of pre-capitalist formations (and lower or marginal classes under capitalism), the elaborated code to the emergence of the analytic thought of the bourgeoisie; while dialectical thinking and language—or a properly dialectical code as such—projects a synthesis of both, that is to say a thinking which is more abstract and situation-specific all at once (or which, to use Marx's far more satisfactory formulation, is capable of 'rising from the abstract to the concrete')."

381 This formula—from the restricted to the elaborated—offers a promising modus operandi for rethinking the realism/modernism split, and the latter term—"the elaborated"—describes in a satisfactory manner the explosion of the sensorium we have come to expect of and associate with modernism; but, as Jameson notes, realism itself, even if it begins with a putatively "restricted" code, "the 'speech art' [or speech *act*] of a given 'restricted' social group" (*SV*, 168), may for a short period only be comprehensible to members of that group, but art involves *some* attempt to universalize that experience (and the vagaries of the term "universal," its fate to bespeak erasure of specificities of any situation so that it might appeal to the demographics of the TV movie-of-the-week, should not mean discarding the term altogether). Jameson proposes, then, that "realism is to be conceived as the moment in which a 'restricted' code manages to become elaborated or universal: something that only happens to one unique restricted code, and only for a brief historical period (the forces of the 'universal' or abstraction then dialectically undermining it and giving way to the modern)" (169). That "brief historical" realism is the realism of the middle classes, and it is not singular in the sense that realism never existed before or since (the *quijote*, twentieth-century variants), but that none achieved the *hegemony* of the nineteenth-century bourgeoisie.

382 So while the gay or post-ethnic or punk or women's films of Hanif
Kureishi or Spike Lee or Jim Jarmusch or Marguerite Duras may utilize a
realist rhetoric in the mobilization of the new social movements, such and
other "realist" projects, while undoubtedly elaborating on a restricted code,
never achieve (or even attempt to achieve) a hegemonic status. Hollywood
domination is then turned inside out: "[T]hese oppositional realisms turn
the tables on hegemonic explanation and omission, and omit the *other* explanations, which the dominant public now needs in its turn [to "explain" to
itself these queer Pakistanis or African Americans or punks or women and
their unfathomable lifestyles], and without which it feels these representations to be alien or boring, stylized or perverse, when it does not simply
classify them as 'experimental' " (*SV,* 170). It is following this excursus into
how to analyze contemporary film that the sudden consideration of Aker-
man's film, and Jameson's memories, suddenly erupts onto the page, to be
immediately followed by more theoretical connections between Bernstein
and Deleuze and Guattari. Here, then, the various apparent post-Marxisms
of the text—valorization of the new social movements, unclassifiable free
association instigated by the description of a film—are put to rest with the
use of Deleuze and Guattari's category of "the minor" to "cut across some of
our stereotypes or doxa about the political as the subversive, the critical, the
negative, by restaging an affiliated conception of art in the new forcefield of
what can be called the ideology of marginality and difference—perhaps, in
our time, the strong form of what used to be called populism and what is
probably the major ideology of the Western left today" (*SV,* 173). So minor
literatures, the cultural discourses of the diaspora and the marginalized,
appropriates hegemonic language (Creole, Yiddish, hip-hop) so that the
limits of language and representation are foregrounded and that the individual subject retreats into the collective "so that all its private utterances are at
once political."

383 This theory has a number of implications that can be explored in terms
of canonical and non-canonical literatures, film created in the First and
Second Worlds as well as in the Third World, and theories of modernism,
film, and realism. Jameson frequently refers to Raymond Chandler and
Nabokov in this book (104, 105, 211), usually in concert with Hitchcock and
around the theme of the immigrant master-artist; in both cases, then, the

writer sought to appropriate a hegemonic language, "Chandler American English" in the service of the pulps, and "Nabokov literary English" in the service of intricately plotted puzzles. To consider these authors as "minority" and "minor" writers, then, to re-place them into the context of global twentieth-century emigrations and speakers of English as a second language, would be useful as an estrangement of their (reified) style, but not, it should be warned, as a way of appropriating the politics of ethnicity and diaspora for their benefit. In the same way, to reconsider Conrad and Wyndham Lewis in the parallel context of homelessness, a project initiated in the previous chapter, only possesses value if it will subvert modernist canons and theories. Jameson's comments on Borges and his anti-canonical admiration for Robert Louis Stevenson and G. K. Chesterton accomplish similar ends. More promisingly in the field of cinema, nouvelle vague and its fetish of the handheld camera demonstrate, as Jameson remarks, an "ostentatious valorization of home movies in place of Hollywood (but also as a substitute *for* it)" (*SV*, 219) so that the "personal" films of the New Wave end up speaking with the collective voice of all of us condemned to be merely viewers of Hollywood and never its creators. When this aesthetic was appropriated by Latin American filmmakers and called "un cine imperfecto" or "third cinema," the imperfect aesthetic was then, in dialectical fashion, superseded by a desire to move away from personal stories to a cinema of the people.

the desire for nostalgia

384 There are two striking moments in Jameson's essay on Kubrick's *The Shining*. The first is when he focuses attention on what Jack Nicholson's character has actually written; then, almost immediately, Jameson inverts all of the generic codes of the movie to render it into a nostalgia film. Like the depthless characters that people the movie (the bland hotel manager, the febrile social worker, even Scatman Crothers's character), Nicholson's character's writing is both too full of content and not full enough: both " 'du texte,' as the post-structuralists put it . . . [and yet] very explicitly a text about *work*" (*SV*, 93). Remember what the character has "written": horrific repeti-

tions of "All work and no play make Jack a dull boy," page after page of various permutations and concrete poetrylike variations like a B. S. Johnson or Christine Brooke-Rose novel. Our glimpse of the pages is subjectivized or focalized through the gaze of Shelley Duvall, and here we realize most concretely the desire enunciated by Jean-Luc Godard in 1968: "When you get right down to it, the most fantastic thing you could film is people reading" (Godard 1969, 7).[46] Jameson remarks that this "work poetry" announces the impossibility of literary production, and why this is so has a lot to do with *The Shining*'s nostalgia, or, rather, with its anti-nostalgia (as is usual with these sorts of things, an anti-nostalgia film predates or anticipates the 1980s' fascination with nostalgia, be it cinematic or political). For in *The Shining* nostalgia takes the form not of some pure presence (as it does in *Body Heat* or *Ragtime*) but as a generically overdetermined series of codes: the ghostlike waiter and bartender, the "haunted" ballroom.

385 Jameson's position on nostalgia film can be also situated in terms of Žižek's distinction between *historicism* and *historicity*. In one of his readings of Benjamin, Žižek creates a Greimassian square with the antinomies historicity and repetition; the opposite of historicity is then nostalgia, and the opposite of repetition is then historicism: "The key to this enigma consists in the basic paradox of historicity as opposed to historicism: what distinguishes it is precisely the presence of an *unhistorical kernel*. That is to say, the only way to save historicity from the fall into historicism, into the notion of the linear succession of 'historical epochs,' is to conceive these epochs as a series of ultimately failed attempts to deal with the same 'unhistorical' traumatic kernel (in Marxism, of course, this kernel is the class struggle, class antagonism)—in short, to conceive the founding gesture of each new epoch as *repetition* in the precise Kierkegaardian-Benjaminian sense. The most suc-

46 In Lewis's *Tarr*, the eponymous hero similarly glances at a volume of Goethe in his German girlfriend's apartment, and the verse is described as squads of marching gothic letters. Of course, *Tarr* is not really so much a denunciation of German expressionism (which had hardly gotten off the ground in 1918 when the novel was written), although it would be interesting to see it as such in the same preemptory fashion as I describe *The Shining* here. The political unconscious of *Tarr*, however, is more likely the Soviet Union itself: the "sacrifice" hinted at in the opening of the novel then is the sacrifice of the nascent revolution.

cinct definition of historicism is therefore: historicity *minus* the unhistorical kernel of the Real—and the function of the nostalgic image is precisely to fill out the empty place of this exclusion, i.e., the blind spot of historicism" (Žižek 1992c, 81).[47] Translated into Jameson's idiolect, "historicism" is the *faux* attempt to think the historical that plagues postmodernism (and with which, perhaps, Linda Hutcheon remains satisfied in her concept of "historiographic metafiction"; see the discussion below). So the nostalgia and repetition of the postmodern epoch—perhaps its most recent example is the Clinton fixation with JFK, ranging from the 1992 campaign video at the Democratic convention, where we saw a young Clinton shake hands with JFK, to Clinton's 1994 appearance under the Brandenburg Gate in Berlin (*Ich bin ein* donut, indeed!)—are Žižek's "historicity *minus* the unhistorical kernel." That kernel is what shocks and hurts; historicism is what numbs?

386 The nostalgia here posited and deconstructed has to do, as Jameson remarks, with the 1920s, "the last moment in which a genuine American leisure class led an aggressive and ostentatious public presence, in which an American ruling class projected a class-conscious and unapologetic image of itself and enjoyed its privileges without guilt, openly and armed with its emblems of top-hat and champagne glass, on the social stage in full view of the other classes" (*SV,* 95). But the codes of genre (Jameson's essay on *The Shining* begins asking why American auteurs have turned so fruitfully to genre) demystify nostalgia as simply another lusted-for possession from the past (here the first-generation nostalgia films of the 1970s, *American Graffiti,*

---

47 Re. Žižek on Benjamin: Žižek's comments in *Enjoy Your Symptom* (1992c, 80–81) are mostly a condensed form of the more in-depth commentary in *The Sublime Object of Ideology,* where, for instance, the notion of the "unhistorical kernel" (that which in history does not change: class struggle) is first announced. Žižek analyzes the following Benjamin thesis on history (xvii): "Where thinking suddenly stops in a configuration pregnant with tensions, it gives that configuration a shock, which it crystallizes into a monad. A historical materialist approaches a historical subject only where he encounters it as a monad" (Benjamin 1969, 262–63). Žižek comments: "Here we have the first surprise: what specifies historical materialism—in contrast to the Marxist doxa according to which we must grasp events in the totality of their interconnection and in their dialectical movement—is its capacity to *arrest,* to *immobilize* historical movement and to *isolate* the detail from its historical totality" (Žižek 1989, 139).

The Way We Were, The Sting, and *The Great Gatsby,* most of them at the same time "genre" films of one type or other—teen film, romance, crime caper—are revealed to be the true object of *The Shining*'s intervention). So Jack Nicholson's character is "possessed" by "the still Veblenesque social system [of] the 1920s" (*SV,* 97), and *unlike* the nostalgia films that predecease (!) or follow *The Shining,* Kubrick's film, in Jameson's interpretation, confronts precisely that Žižekian-Benjaminian kernel: class not as sociological stratus, but rather as violent antagonism.

387 Jameson uses the generic codes of *The Shining* to reveal its political unconscious, then; it is this focus on nostalgia that provides a major thematic concern in the final essay of *Signatures of the Visible.* He begins on this theme in the fourth section of "The Existence of Italy," when he writes of Hollywood's "bourgeois cultural revolution," recalling the use of that figure in *The Political Unconscious.* There he contends that the novel plays a significant role "in what can be called a properly bourgeois cultural revolution," and "that processing operation variously called narrative mimesis or realist representation has as its historic function the systematic undermining and demystification, the secular 'decoding,' of those preexisting inherited traditional or sacred narrative paradigms which are its initial givens. . . . [The] 'objective' function of the novel is . . . producing as though for the first time that very life world, that very 'referent'—the newly quantifiable space of extension and market equivalence, the new rhythms of measurable time, the new secular and 'disenchanted' object world of the commodity system" (*PU,* 152). Only "now," in the Hollywood of the 1930s, "the social transformation of the public . . . decisively modifies the lens and begins to offer viewers glimpses of their own domestic or single-family existence" (*SV,* 174). Even as the explosion of genres in the 1930s is placed into the context of a *systemic* analysis, that system itself is replaced by "art deco," as a sort of trans-political aesthetic of the period.

388 "It is indeed no accident that a certain technology (embodied in the visible machine as it radiates speed and energy through its forms at rest) stands as the common ideological and stylistic denominator of Hollywood and Soviet socialist realism alike, when these are read together as moments of some vaster global *art deco* transition" (*SV,* 184). "Art deco," in Jameson's vocabulary—and here the impudence of a Marxist writing about hotels and

architecture is anticipated—means both WPA art (social documentary photography, murals), as well as furniture, Walt Disney, and Robert Moses (the
urban planner who destroyed working-class communities in New York with
his freeways). Jameson then sees nostalgia film and its opposite number
(punk and trash films like *Liquid Sky* or *Android*) in terms of a dialectic, whereby the historico-symbolic resonances of characters and landscapes
are developed in contradistinction to their earlier possibilities. So nostalgia
films possess that brilliant sheen characteristic of the Hollywood heyday,
with a much harder, more cynical edge, but in opposition to the sloppy
editing and imperfections of sleaze cinema. This opposition Jameson then
relates to the Third World "imperfect cinema," stressing the politics inherent
in such an allegorization of the camera. What this last phrase means is that
"form is called on to convey specific stances toward the content and as it
were to connote its essential features: thus, if technical perfection connotes
advanced capitalism—its values of profit-maximizing efficiency as much as
its technologies and the labour processes generated by such technology and
such values—the 'imperfection' can be expected, like a vow of poverty, to
connote, not merely the inert necessities of an underdevelopment that has
been imposed and 'developed' by force, but also the willingness to renounce
the surpluses of socialist development in solidarity with other Third World
countries" (*SV,* 219). So the poverty of form that characterizes "un cine
imperfecto," as well as oppositional filmmaking in the First and Second
Worlds, is not an unmediated *reflection* of either the filmmaker's politics or
her group's economics ("group" here possessing the strong, Sartrean meaning discussed above in relation to Bernstein's restricted codes); nor is it
an expression of some anti-aesthetic deemable solely on stylistic grounds.
Rather, as an allegory of formalisms, the "imperfection" is the result of a
narrative that, refused First World monies (either because of imperialistic
geography or because of the filmmaker's "independent" stance), refuses the
concomitant lust for luster.

389 Spike Lee's recent big-budget *Malcolm X* (1992) may lead some to argue
that since Lee demanded the economy of Hollywood once he had the clout,
the earlier films with their concomitant economies and styles were only
training films, or at least not so theoretically important as Jameson and I
argue. I would like to argue this point by analogy, with another artistic field

in which I have some expertise: small press literary productions. In this arena, writers self-publish or publish the works of their colleagues in small, inexpensive formats (chapbooks, broadsides, mimeo or Xerox magazines) that usually articulate some anti-aesthetic in opposition to the commodi-fied professionalism of capitalist publishing. What is significant about small press formats is that for many, if not most, of the writers involved, it does not function as a "farm team" to more respectable books: writers like Victor Coleman (Canada), Elizabeth Was (U.S.), and Tom Raworth (U.K.) con-tinue to publish small press works even as their work also appears in other formats. But it would be interesting to view the progress of such new U.S. filmmakers as Leslie Harris (*Just Another Girl on the IRT*), Nick Gomez (*Laws of Gravity*), Robert Rodriguez (*El Mariachi*) and Tarantino, as they negotiate their aesthetics with big studio film deals.

390 Jameson's final statements on nostalgia film, what he is now calling nostalgia-deco film to stress "its dependency on the earlier cultural lan-guage" (*SV,* 225) concern the relationship between film and history, or be-tween the 1920s and 1930s as a specific moment in both of those narratives. Here he recasts Lyotard's influential critique of master narratives, arguing that the ultimate metanarrative is the transition from feudalism to capital-ism, a primal scene of the political unconscious, discussed above in terms of the novel and film's respective "bourgeois cultural revolutions" of the nine-teenth and twentieth centuries. So the unwieldy dyad of the twenties and thirties and its cultural manifestations in art deco and nostalgia films "has seemed symbolically to act out that vaster historical transition between the feudal and the bourgeois period, under the guise of a twenties 'aristocratic' high life and a thirties amalgam of labour, money, and violence" (*SV,* 229).

the end of the chapter

391   There are two interpretive schemas with which to question that massive mobilization and reinterpretation of film that began in the 1950s under the rubric of the *Cahiers du Cinema* and its *politique de l'auteur:* psychoanalysis and class. In terms of a Freudian-Lacanian schema, and as discussed above in relation to Hitchcock, the filmmaker as auteur is a cinematic despot, a

father under whose authorizing signature everything in the film must be controlled—if not by the filmmaker himself, then by the willing critic. Jameson's interest in figures like Hitchcock—and his manipulation of the difference between auteurist modernism ("Hitchcock, Bergman, Fellini, Kurosawa, Renoir, Welles, Wajda, Antonioni, Satyajit Ray" [*SV,* 199]) and its Derridean supplement in the form of the French New Wave—is part of a continuing dialectic of power and creativity and their uses in capitalist society (but see Sprinker 1993, 6–7n4). That is, remembering that Jameson's various texts are as limited in their ideology as the objects of their scrutiny, they will deploy such unopposed terms as power and creativity in a manner limited by ideology, which can then be mapped out precisely by the sort of Greimassian rectangle Jameson himself uses:

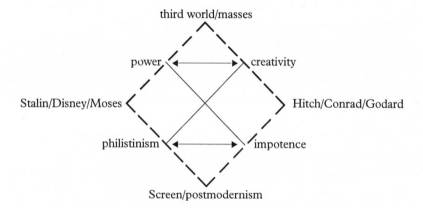

392 To think about the auteur in terms of class means entertaining Bourdieu's analyses again; in this vein, Jameson argues that the disappearance of classical Hollywood realism "constitutes a historical crisis in which the consumption of genre films becomes increasingly a matter of guilt, and in which some new legitimation must be sought for movie-going, a legitimation which will be constructed from out of the arsenal of the now traditional ways in which high modernism in the other arts dealt with analogous situations in an older cultural past" (*SV,* 182–83). Auteurism is a class alibi—"It's okay to go to a Western; it's a work of art!"—that lifts the movie out of its restricted code (generic and cheap entertainment for the masses) into an elaborated and abstracted code of Western art in general—the quest motif in the Western,

humanism in the film noir, Catholic guilt in Hitchcock. So André Bazin's determination to find a "democracy" of the filmmaker in Orson Welles's deep-focus shot (over and against the tyranny of Eisensteinian montage) is in Jameson's analysis reframed in terms of a Heideggerian ontology of the photograph: "The deconcealment of Being in the filmic image is therefore historical rather than existential" (*SV,* 193), because the film as moving image exists primarily in memory (a fact Stanley Cavell exploits to great effect, as when he remarks that contemporary actors [the early 1970s] do not seem as memorable to him as the great men of the 1930s and 1940s).

393 Our memories of film today, then, enter into a postmodern realm precisely because of how they highlight certain discontinuous or nonparallel scenes or shots (the shower scene of *Psycho,* the tennis game in *Blowup,* Grace Kelly's dresses in *Rear Window*): this is the great lesson to be learned from various subaltern or oppositional re-memberings of mass culture in general. Consider gay appropriations of film, for example: my local video store, in the Toronto gay ghetto, in addition to the standard director and genre categories, has Katherine Hepburn, Bette Davis, and Barbra Streisand sections. And two recent debates foreground the terrain at stake here: first, the question of images of drag queens in *The Crying Game* is instantly raised to a higher level of metacommentary: "I had come to think, after the debates surrounding *Basic Instinct* and *JFK,* that gay critics had transcended the positive image argument. Apparently not. We may be doomed to bicker forever about what constitutes a positive—or negative—image" (Hays 1993, 31). Another critic transcends the *mainstream* limitations of journalistic film criticism as the reviewer's own subject position is inserted ("fisted"?) into the discourse, which is a commentary on *Point of No Return:* "Granted, the film is a cheesy US remake of a much sexier French film, *La Femme Nikita,* and [Bridget] Fonda's character is designed to titillate a heterosexual male audience. Although I'm not turned on by this cock-teasing, cheesecake shit, I do appreciate a strong, nice-looking babe who knows how to use a gun" (Mills 1993, 34).[48]

---

48 Both of these critics write in Toronto's lesbian and gay biweekly *Xtra!.* The advantage to a cultural critic of working in Toronto, which possesses a rich tradition of various oppositional and 'zine "scenes" is incalculable, as the following titles attest to: *Lexicon* and

394 The present-day fetish of the discontinuous needs to be historicized and questioned. Like the contemporary disdain for "totality" or "linear history," the postmodern idea of the organic work ignores the fact that "the very language of the organic explicitly designated functional differentiation, the specialization of radically different organs within a life-totality distinct from all of them, and implying something very different from any formal homogeneity" (*SV*, 207). This statement and its accompanying discourse is focused on the notion of the chapter, suggested in some way by the punning connection between the organs just mentioned and Joyce's designation of different organs for each chapter of *Ulysses*. Thus my earlier contention of the sutured and quiltlike structure of the present volume (as well as *Postmodernism*) lies uncannily next to the statement that "Joyce's conception of the chapter as a formal unit is . . . one of the supreme philosophical achievements of the modern movement" (*SV*, 207). The unconscious self-reflexivity of the Jameson-text that I am emphasizing means that we cannot help but reflect on the status of the chapter in this book.

395 Brought to the fore in *Signatures of the Visible*, then, is the tension between such disparate textual units as the chapter, the essay, and the book. The tension is a dialectical one, which is to say that it arises out of the modes of academic production fully as much as some idealist aesthetic of textuality. The essay, then, is one of the two or three "products" that an academic humanities manager is called upon to produce (the others being "educated" students and, perhaps, some form of bureaucratic expertise). This form is

---

Quota (both lesbian-gay), *Trash Compactor* (B-movies), *Vagina Dentata* (feminist, pop culture, sex), *Drastic Solutions* (radical hardcore music), *Who Torched Rancho Diablo?* and *Mondo Hunkamooga* (litzines), *JDs* (gay skinheads), *Asian Eyes* (Asian cinema), *!*@#* (hardcore), *Vehicle* (skatepunk), etc. One of my favorite methodological choices in *Cultural Studies* (ed. Grossberg et al., 1992) was Jan Zita Grover's discussion of her grassroots use of a multitude of nonmainstream publications and discourses: changes in AIDS "keywords" are, she argues, "for the most part traceable principally at the level of everyday practices. They cannot be traced alone, as Susan Sontag obviously chose to do in her research, by clipping articles from the *New York Times*, by reading previously published studies, by consulting the etymology of 'plague' and 'epidemic.' To use only published resources . . . is to be fooled both by the centralization of the American media . . . and by the superficiality of most AIDS reporting" (Grover 1992, 230).

subject to various managerial and economic forces, notably the tyranny of the journal (and its editors and readers) and the nonexistence of a mass audience (commented on by Said [1983]). *Signatures* is divided into two parts: the second part is wholly made up of the essay "The Existence of Italy," while the various chapters in the first part, which date from 1976 to 1986, appeared in such prominent theoretical journals as *Social Text, October,* and *Critical Inquiry*.[49] These essays are not here "collected" into a book in the way that that verb could be used accurately to describe the two volumes published as *The Ideologies of Theory*. In an academic book, then, where essays metamorphose into chapters, the essays' specificities are to some extent erased, the "modes of production" concealed as the organic unity of the book is promulgated. So Andrew Ross's *No Respect* possesses a narrative thread that belies the "chapters'" initial appearances (whether at a seminar table or podium or in a journal)—and so, too, does *The Political Unconscious*. But here (and not only here and in Jameson's *Postmodernism* book) the academic "book" and the scholarly "essay" both disintegrate into the postmodern chapter. I call this postmodern because of its autonomy from the unity of the book; it is also dialectical because of its negation of the essay, which too often is fetishized à la Montaigne or Barthes as some *ne plus ultra* of intellectual discourse (even if we usually encounter the form today in one of three depressing forums: the student's essay, the academic's in some anonymous journal, or the journalist's on an op-ed page). The postmodern academic chapter is ambiguous because it depends on being in some totality (the book as physical object) while it evidently originates outside of that commodity—usually in the aforementioned and degraded realm of the "journal." Within *Signatures of the Visible*, the struggle of meanings and codes is intensified by the disparity between discrete chapters in the first part, each concerned with a film or auteur, and the much looser and more discursive second part (a structure mirrored in the *Postmodernism* book).

396 These meandering observations on the textual unit of the "modernist" chapter do have some immediate and contemporary implications, not only in how the structure of the "book" has the potential to be not merely a

49 With the singular exception of the *Dog Day Afternoon* essay, which first appeared in *College English*.

Mallarméan or Blanchotesque or Jabés-like or Derridean artifact but also the site for the return, in postmodernism itself, of memory and history, a potential that is echoed in the following closing sentences of *Signatures of the Visible* (which we now can read with a Žižekian gloss—the question of the "eclipse of historicity," that is) and that then leads, "naturally" I might say, to the beginning of a consideration of postmodernism and, of *Postmodernism, or, The Cultural Logic of Late Capitalism* (which will itself begin, of course, with "It is safest to grasp the concept of the postmodern as the attempt to think the present historically in an age that has forgotten how to think historically in the first place. In that case, it either 'expresses' some deeper irrepressible historical impulse (in however distorted a fashion) or effectively 'represses' and diverts it, depending on the side of the ambiguity you happen to favor" [*PM*, ix]): "Is this then to say that even within the extraordinary eclipse of historicity in the postmodern period some deeper memory of history still faintly stirs? Or does this persistence—nostalgia for that ultimate moment of historical time in which difference was still present—rather betoken the incompleteness of the postmodern process, the survival within it of remnants of the past, which have not yet, as in some unimaginable fully realized postmodernism, been dissolved without a trace?" (*SV*, 229).[50]

postmodernism is always in taste

397 What is surely notable about *Postmodernism, or, The Cultural Logic of Late Capitalism* is the *structure* of the book: its coffee-table booklike dimensions, first of all, then its magisterial combinations of a handful of major and influential statements on postmodernism, and, then, finally, the autotelic or destabilized status of the text itself. But since my own modus operandi thus

50 As is tediously the case throughout this book, I tend to "temporalize" chunks or segments of narratives or books according to their strict linearity within my own discourse (thus Frye may be proto-Althusserian, de Man pre-Spinozist, etc.); but here the positing of a linear or at least sequential causality *from* the close of *Signatures of the Visible* to the introduction to *Postmodernism* is chronologically (if not historically) sound given that the last section of *Signatures* is dated 1988 (*SV*, 229) and the introduction to *Postmodernism* is dated 1990 (*PM*, xxii).

far in this study has been to concentrate on that structure, with the aim of shifting attention away from the great panjandrum of "content," I would like first to take another tack in this final slice of Jameson. First, I will examine some of the key critical appraisals of the Jameson "postmodernism" essay: as I discuss below, the split in how Jameson is read on postmodernism (i.e., either for or against, whereas he has tried to position himself as neither) need not be troubling, for the readings of Jameson allow a foray into his statements on this epoch. Second, I will examine the status of "taste" in the volume. Taste can hardly be said to exist any longer, and Jameson's interrogations of various cultural forms, as well as the performative results of those interrogations, can tell us why this should be so. Third and last, I will return to the question of the rhetoric, figures, narrative, and structure of Jameson's book; topics that must crop up in the other discussions, but will be given their own full treatment.

398 Jameson's theoretical statements on postmodernism are fairly unique in that his dialectical stance results in neither a wholehearted approval of the condition nor a vociferous attack. But, in examining some of the critiques of Jameson's *New Left Review* article, surely what is most striking is how often a critic will decide that Jameson "really" is anti-postmodern—the usual term of opprobrium here will be that he is a "modernist"—or that he is too much the uncritical postmodern seducer. Those criticizing Jameson for the first fault will predictably belong to the "right wing" of deconstruction, or the theoretical camp that sees Marxism as simply another theoretico-institution of the terror: into this group, most notably, fall various contributors to Douglas Kellner's anthology *Postmodernism/Jameson/Critique:* Haynes Horne, Thomas Huhn, for instance. Other critics who share the technique but not the theoretical bent would be Charles Bernstein and Linda Hutcheon. Attacks on Jameson for his addiction to the postmodern image come from various traditional and post-traditional sectors of the Left, and include Terry Eagleton, Mike Davis, and Russell Jacoby. A dialectical account of this range of critiques, then, should not be satisfied with "answering" the criticisms, but instead should examine the contradictions in the various positions taken relative to Jameson's work on postmodernism.

399 Engaging with a text or theory via its critics, be they the severest, the merely incompetent, or the most friendly, may seem unsatisfactory; issues

are filtered through another layer of discourse, there is no "getting at the original," and vital points may be lost. But part of the lesson of postmodernism as Jameson presents is a certain unrepresentability of its own artifacts, which then will embody that unrepresentability thematically and formally. Duane Hanson's figures, which cause us to suffer a momentary delusion about the real people in a museum, are such an artifact, and only because they are metonyms or synecdoche for a larger cultural process. In this way, then, the exact opposite of my attack on Horne, below, holds for the Jamesonian concept of the postmodern sublime: Jameson's work must of necessity fall into the postmodern culture he describes, if only because his texts are about the problem of description.

vertiginous slime

400 At one time, it seems, it was possible or even necessary to sweat—dirt existed then, too, and not merely as post-Beuys lumps of simulated graves, but as something that got under your fingernails (whereas now, indisputably, dirt is a code, "Workplace Hazardous Materials Information System" or WHMIS)—now, we only sweat via the Daniel Bell information-age medium of electronic exercise, where our bodies are displayed as watts or calories burned off on a rowing machine, where sweat is a sign of self-referential exertion ("burn, baby, burn" refers both to L.A. and to that nagging roll of flesh around your bellybutton).[51] Sweat exists in two states (like all the great, transforming materials): the slime of activity, the crust of rest.

401 In this context or epoch, Sartrean slime (and the concomitant problems of its misogyny and anti-lesbianism) has been replaced by postmodern slime, a commodity designed less to épater le bourgeoisie than to gross out your parents. Vertiginous slime is variously easy or difficult to pull off of sur

---

51 The Canadian feminist writer Patricia Seaman confronts precisely this problematic—postmodern exercise as emergent or perhaps even hegemonic praxis even while patriarchal scopophilia remains "residual"—in her short story "Facts about Shriners": "At the gym I can only bench press 22.5 kg. when I tried to press 30 kg. I needed one of the guys to coach me. So, I asked one of them and he said, Sure honey, it's the only time I get to see you lying down" (1991, 83–84).

faces (depending on the accompanying postmodernity: presumably hair that is "natural"—relatively untreated—will stick more than hair suitably coated or surfaced with half a can of spray or mousse), rather like that great invention Silly Putty (glazier's slime meets Baudrillardean process: Silly Putty's real function, it will be remembered, was less to be formed into some object than to roll over the color comics, thence to "transfer" them onto one's arm. And these temporary tattoos, like self-mutilation via adolescent girls' ear-piercings, set the stage for the present-day vogue for body-piercing). This revelation of toy theory makes explicable what was previously a mystery, that is, the apparent shift in rebels' energy from shocking or disturbing "society" (be it *Gemeinschaft* or *Gesellschaft*, late capitalism or state capitalism, social democracy [as Simon Frith notes, punk rock, it should be remembered, did not start during Thatcher, but during the mid- or late-seventies Labour government; punk rock anticipated Thatcher, perhaps, fully as much as the CCCS] or actually existing socialism [which no longer exists, of course]) to grossing out one's parents, which latter dialectic, then, finds its expression in theory in the Bloomian cycles of theory's great Oedipal conflicts—Derrida versus Sartre or Foucault, Eagleton versus Williams, Aijaz versus Jameson, Sedgwick versus Bloom, Glucksmann versus Althusser.

402 Postmodern slime does not stick, however: criticism or theory as vertiginous slime sticks to oneself (I'm rubber, you're glue, etc.) to be then peeled off, or sticks momentarily to an image (à la Silly Putty) and less temporarily transfers that text to one's own body: "A dialectics no longer 'glued' to identity will provoke either the charge that it is bottomless—one that ye shall know by its fascist fruits—or the objection that it is dizzying. In great modern poetry, vertigo has been a central feeling since Baudelaire; the anachronistic suggestion often made to philosophy is that it must have no part in any such thing. Philosophy is cautioned to speak to the point; Karl Kraus had to learn that no matter how precisely each line of his expressed his meaning, a materialized consciousness would lament this very precision was making its head swim. . . . But a cognition that is to bear fruit will throw itself to the objects *au fond perdu*. The vertigo which this causes is an *index veri;* the shock of inconclusiveness, the negative as which it cannot help appearing in the frame-covered, never-changing realm, is true for untruth only" (Adorno 1987, 31–33).

flannelized jameson

403 As I mentioned in the first chapter, I neither welcome nor disparage the current inflation of signification in the mass media, under which ostensibly "theoretical" words like "deconstruction" or "postmodernism" will acquire a variety of meanings. If, therefore, a newspaper editorial will speak of the "deconstruction of Yugoslavia" (or of Canada during the Meech Lake/Charlottetown Accord debates), and meaning something like a breakup, the dialectical response, it seems to me, is not then to praise journalism and the slippery signifier; nor is it sternly to rebuke the editorialist for branch-Derridean behaviour. The dialectical response is to track the vagaries of a word's career, or the positions and uses to which a word will be put, and to ponder on the desire of a journalist to reach for what still has some sorry luster, this word, to dignify a text that will, in twenty-four hours, be lying in a recycling box.

404 The past couple of years has also seen an inflation of the word "flannel" to become a stock-in-trade of mass culture, the constellation, as it were, around or of "grunge," an early-nineties version of punk and hardcore. Referring at first to plaid or flannel lumberjack's shirts worn by youth tied around the waist and featured in Nirvana and Pearl Jam videos and the movie *Singles*, the word (as verb) now also connotes the "engrungefication" of music, a process that, predictably, elicits both negative and positive responses.[52] On the one hand, various older fans or critics (like myself) will

---

52 Susan Willis, in "Hardcore: Subculture American Style" (1993), discusses what is locally (in North Carolina) termed "hardcore," or the contemporary metal-punk-grunge-alternative music and style scene (North Carolina is one of the post-Seattle, decentered, centers of grunge—bands like Superchunk—just as Halifax, Canada, is now producing bands like jale, Hardship Post, and Sloan). Willis's perception that her daughter Cassie's (her primary informant) "style choice is partially motivated by the desire to differentiate herself from her younger and therefore loathesome siblings . . . [but] has much more to do with the way she positions herself with respect to consumer society" (368) would seem to contradict my from-anti-society-to-anti-family thesis above. However, as Willis makes clear, her own position *in the family* would serve to occlude her own theorizing; Cassie's quoted remark "Mom, you know I don't want to be taken for a redneck" (367) articulates Cassie's hysterical desire that the academic parent *not* know (i.e., in direct opposition to the statement's "content"). But Willis's article is also useful for its comments on Hebdige and on the U.S. appropriation of de Certeau.

bemoan the loss of memory entailed in grunge: kids were wearing the clothes and playing the music in the early eighties in Victoria, B.C., the argument will go; or, in a new version of the hipper-than-thou argument parodied by the seventies' Tubes song "I Was a Punk Before You Were a Punk," Lou Koller (of the heavy metal group Sick of It All) remarks, "I find it funny that just because bands like Pearl Jam and other groups have stage diving in their videos a lot of clubs now allow stage diving that wouldn't let us at previous shows. That's ridiculous, but it's funny, because all these so-called grunge kids and even hip hop kids dress like hardcore and metal kids dressed three or four years ago" (Lynne and Ruiz 1993, 39). A positive response is to salute the recent border-blur between genres (which is of course only a symptom of the worldwide, late capitalist, structural dissolution of borders, from "infotainment" and MacJournalism to theory-fiction and free trade); whereas during my formative years one marked one's place in the musical spectrum by *not* listening to disco or heavy metal (*only* Elvis Costello and the Ramones), the confluence of various "-metals," "-cores," and "-hip-hop" (speed, death, grind, hard, heavy, homo) bespeaks a certain solidarity of the "heavier" forms of rock (but see also "speedballads" and "cuddlecore").

405 This analysis and response, which is a second-rate version of Jameson's more magisterial attitudes toward both structuralism and postmodernism, is also my reaction when I come across precisely this sort of wild lexigraphy in theoretical contexts. In his essay "Jameson's Strategies of Containment" (1989), Haynes Horne glosses Jameson's comment (*PM*, 7) on the inertness of reproduced works of art—Van Gogh's *A Pair of Boots*—with the following comment: "[I]t would appear that even works of high modernism face the fate of having their expression deconstructed, not just by the critical climate of the age, but merely by the passage of time itself" (Horne 1989, 287). Now, *if* Van Gogh can be seen as an avatar of high modernism—and it is interesting that Horne accepts this contentious placement by Jameson—how is that what Jameson calls "a reified end product" (*PM*, 7)? How is it, that is, that the passage of time and reification can be called *deconstruction?* If deconstruction is merely (or ominously) a process of reification, a process whereby we become so used to an artistic image that it is as commonplace as a calendar picture or place mat, then there was no need for Derrida to conduct his interventions into the philosophical traditions—Plato, Rous-

seau, Husserl. Surely, the hallowed and ossified place those philosophers had in well-thumbed paperbacks meant they were already "deconstructed"? I am not arguing against a multiplicity of meanings for the word "deconstruction," any more than Jameson would bemoan the fact that Van Gogh's image is available in books and on posters instead of just at the Baltimore Museum of Art. But within the context of a theoretical argument or critique, like Horne's or mine, it is important to choose one's vocabulary carefully, especially when *tone* is at such a highly sardonic register—evinced by the succession of qualifiers in the sentence: "*So* it *would appear* that *even* works of high modernism" (Horne 1989, 287).

406 It may be argued that Horne means, in his condensed way, that the process Jameson is out to subvert by restoring the situation of the artwork is the Benjaminian de(con)struction of aura. That is, the sublime multiplicity of Van Gogh's image deconstructs the originary fetish of the painting's thingness, its oily texture or ideology of oil, and makes the image available to the masses. But even if this is Horne's point, what does it have to do with Jameson's agenda in the postmodernism essay? Jameson's essay begins with the question of whether we are now in a new epoch or period or stage of world history; does the list of newer cultural styles "imply any more fundamental change or break than the periodic style and fashion changes determined by an older high-modernist imperative of stylistic innovation? . . . Consider, for example, the powerful . . . position that postmodernism is itself little more than one more stage of modernism proper (if not, indeed, of the even older romanticism)" (*PM*, 2–4). Jameson asks this question because he sees cultural production today as ensconced in commodity production: this insight, revolutionary or not, should remind us that at least since the Industrial Revolution the main role of art has been to construct some sort of avant-garde with the end of working outside of capitalism: from the *Lyrical Ballads'* appropriation of the language of the marginalized to the Cubists' restructuring of our visual perceptions. And it is also important to remember that this structural position had little to do with the "politics" of the producer— Pound no less than Dos Passos was disgusted with capitalism.

407 Jameson's list of cultural artifacts that immediately prefaces the quotation, then, is not so grand a document: it is not, that is, some demonstration of the author's notorious aesthetic breadth. For, *if we take Jameson at his*

word, and even if we do not reach for the predictable Bourdieu analysis or diagnoses, the ability to discuss the following is no more astonishing than a salesman knowing his product: "Andy Warhol and pop art, but also photo-realism, and beyond it, the 'new expressionism': the moment, in music, of John Cage, but also the synthesis of classical and 'popular' styles found in composers like Phil Glass and Terry Riley, and also punk and new wave rock (the Beatles and the Stones now standing as the high-modernism moment of that more recent and rapidly evolving tradition): in film, Godard, post-Godard, and experimental cinema and video, but also a whole new type of commercial film (about which more below); Burroughs, Pynchon, or Ishmael Reed, on the one hand, and the French *nouveau roman* and its succession, on the other, along with alarming new kinds of literary criticism based on some new aesthetic of textuality or *écriture*" (*PM,* 1–2). Jameson is not Dwight Macdonald and *New Left Review* is not the *Partisan Review:* there is little stature to be gained by being aware or by postulating that the Clash is to the Stones as Godard is to Hitchcock. A mistake many make and will continue to make in reading Jameson on postmodernism, in reading any critic on postmodernism for that matter, or even in writing about postmodernism, if need be, is that to be a critic today has little or nothing to do with criticism in the past. There is no need for some guardian of the language to go to battle to protect and explicate the novels of Burroughs or E. L. Doctorow in the way hordes of criticasters did fifty years ago for *Ulysses.* There will be no Armory Show in the 1990s, no Ballet Russe, no censorship battles. Or, rather, when battles do take place, as in the p.c. debates or the *Piss Christ* kerfuffle, the players tend to be engaged in postures instead of outrage: "[T]oday, NEA controversies notwithstanding, we would hesitate to call the aesthetic political, not because the categories have become genuinely distinct, but, on the contrary, because we can no longer tell the difference" (Rolleston 1991, 88). Now the humanists (William Bennett, Robert Hughes, Alan Bloom, E. D. Hirsch) take the position of the censor, and the barbarians or philistines (flag-burners, gay/black/leftist artists) take the position of rebels: from identity to practice. The shift is a Gramscian one from a battle of terrain to a battle of positions. The politics of an artist or a writer, if at one time they existed (only to have little effect on one's art), remained his or her private hobby (and therefore didn't really exist), are now more like occupation codes—the feminist performance artist Annie Sprinkle, the Trotskyist flag-burner, the body-piercing Ron Athey.

408 But the question of whether or not postmodernism is a definitively new period in history, *that* question, is important for Jameson because, as tied as the culture is to a new stage in capitalism—late or multinational capitalism— what is then evident is that "this whole global, yet American, postmodern culture is the internal and superstructural expression of a whole new wave of American military and economic domination throughout the world: in this sense, as throughout class history, the underside of culture is blood, torture, death, and terror" (*PM*, 5). The Benjaminian statement, then, should dispel fears that attention paid to Warhol or Jonathan Demme or Paul de Man are somehow frivolous for a proper Marxist; its very specificity, Jameson's grounding, as it were, in the economic analysis of Mandel, also abrogates any illusion that postmodern culture is not really that much different than modernism and, further, we therefore can maintain the modernist distinctions between the elite and the popular and turn onto that proper object of study, culture, our scholarly spectacles—in the celebrated A. M. Klein poem, "Portrait of the Poet as Landscape," they are "the mirroring lenses forgotten on a brow / that shine with the guilt of their unnoticed world." Those modernist glasses have been replaced, in the figure of cyberpunk, by "mirrorshades"; as Bruce Sterling puts it in a quintessentially Deleuzed moment of schizoid theory, "Mirrorshades have been a Movement [meaning, cyberpunk] totem since the early days of '82. The reasons for this are not hard to grasp. By hiding the eyes, mirrorshades prevent the forces of normalcy from realizing that one is crazed and possibly dangerous. They are the symbol of the sun-staring visionary, the biker, the rocker, the policeman, and similar outlaws" (Sterling 1988, xi).[53] Sterling's intimations of paranoia

53 In *Femmes Fatales: Feminism, Film Theory, Psychoanalysis* (1991), Mary Ann Doane notes how *women* wearing glasses, in classic Hollywood cinema, was an image that was "a heavily marked condensation of motifs concerned with repressed sexuality, knowledge, visibility, and vision, intellectuality, and desire. The woman with glasses signifies simultaneously intellectuality and undesirability; but the moment she removes her glasses (a moment which, it seems, must always be *shown* and which is itself linked with a certain sensual quality), she is transformed into a spectacle, the very picture of desire . . . the cliché has a binding power so strong that it indicates a precise moment of ideological danger or

as well as the stereotypical self-designation of marginality are a clear thesis-statement of an objective truth in Jameson's analysis. If the figure of glasses or spectacles has now shifted from an inquiring male scholar to a furtive biker or outlaw, then the globe-trotting cyberpunk ethos is evidently a so-matic manifestation of the pervasive and not-so-hidden hand of capital and the market, a hand clothed now for Daniel Bell and Bruce Sterling in the fine weave of postindustrial informationism, and for less fortunate persons in Chiapas or Pakistan in a slightly different fabric.

the revenge of the content

409   This narrative, then, has been the context in which Jameson begins, as an object-lesson, his discussion of Van Gogh and Warhol; and it is telling that he starts this discussion with the admission that Van Gogh's painting is "an example which, as you can imagine, has not been innocently or ran-domly chosen" (*PM*, 6). In part, the fact that Heidegger also wrote on the painting in his essay "The Origin of the Work of Art," guided Jameson in his choice. Like Jameson, Heidegger was concerned with the status of art in a world of commodities and capital: "If we consider the works in their un-touched actuality and do not deceive ourselves, the result is that the works are as naturally present as are things. The picture hangs on the wall like a rifle or a hat. A painting, e.g. the one by Van Gogh that represents a pair of peasant shoes, travels from one exhibition to another. Works of art are shipped like coal from the Ruhr and logs from the Black Forest. During the First World War Hölderlin's hymns were packed in the soldier's knapsack together with cleaning gear. Beethoven's quartets lie in the storerooms of the publishing house like potatoes in a cellar" (Heidegger 1975, 19). As is usual with titles, Heidegger's essay has little to do with his: his *Ursprung* is neither a Nietzschean spring nor a Foucauldean genealogy, and it certainly is not a source of the artwork in any normative sense. But his stultifying list aims to

---

threat—in this case, the woman's appropriation of the gaze. Glasses worn by a woman in the cinema do not generally signify a deficiency in seeing [as they would in the "feminiz-ing" of men, for instance] but an active looking" (27).

re-place the work of art in a world oscillating between the banality of the potatoes, knapsacks, and coal, and the sublime of the hymn, forest, and river. Or, rather, in Jameson's terms, "these henceforth illustrious [!] peasant shoes slowly re-create about themselves the whole missing object world which was once their lived context" (*PM*, 8). And Heidegger's list is no more aleatory than Jameson's choice of Van Gogh: surely the Black Forest, the coal, the potatoes, and the soldier are all places or environs for the boots and their cousins.

410 Heidegger's analysis accomplishes much the same as Jameson's re-creation: but it is Jameson's desire to restore some of the mystery of the painting and its origins that is so troubling to Horne. He argues that "Jameson seeks to restore 'the whole object world of agricultural misery,' thus creating without acknowledging it, a text of the painting which is extended to the sociohistorical. Thus it regains its 'expression,' which is one of 'backbreaking peasant toil, a world reduced to its most brutal and menaced, primitive and marginalized state,' *a world Jameson fails to recognize as based largely in the text created by his own semantic enrichment*" (Horne 1989, 287; my emphasis). Even before descending to the quagmire of textualism, consider the logic of Jameson's apparently "creating without acknowledging . . . a text of the painting." What, precisely, is this "text of the painting" that Jameson does not know he is creating . . . keeping in mind his statement that he wants "to propose two ways of *reading* this painting" (*PM*, 6; italics mine); and in addition, just how does Horne *know* that Jameson does not know? Finally, what exactly is the meaning of the statement where Horne alleges that the peasant world where life is reduced to bare essentials is based on Jameson's text? This seems to be the sort of apolitical deconstruction, William James meets Derrida where "it's text all the way down" in Christopher Norris's recent phrase (1992). But my quarrel is not with this matter of interpretation; Horne implies that his textualist view is not a matter of interpretation at all: Jameson, Horne writes, "fails to recognize" it, a phrase that suggests little willingness to engage in debate.

411 This examination of Horne's rhetoric lays out the general methodology of his article, in which he outlines the various "strategies of containment" whereby Jameson seeks to control postmodernism, or theory, or poststructuralism. Horne's article, indeed, is called "Jameson's Strategies of Contain-

ment," which raises an interesting dilemma for Horne (which he fails to recognize, as it were)—a dilemma that relates to an important technique of deconstruction. The motivation behind titling a paper as Horne does is to demonstrate how a writer or theoretician's figures can be turned against her or him.[54] But, using Jameson's notion of "strategies of containment" against his own text is as epistemologically problematic as positing that Marx or Marxism is ideological. To demonstrate by analogy: if I use the Marxist idea of ideology—baldly put, false consciousness—to critique or "deconstruct" a text by Marx or "Marxism itself," then my point of critique (ideology) loses its heuristic value. *If Marxism is ideological, then ideology as a Marxist concept has no meaning.*[55] In a similar fashion, taking a figure from Jameson's own theory to argue the following becomes epistemologically fallacious: "Health officials seek to contain the spread of the AIDS virus in a way similar to that in which Jameson's strategy of periodizing seeks to contain the dissemination of poststructuralist theory, which in its solvent form endangers the project of reviving the revolutionary subject" (Horne 1989, 289).

4l2 From a certain poststructuralist or deconstructive viewpoint, there is nothing troubling with Horne's methodology; the Derridean technique, after all, is simply a matter of pushing a philosopher's thought up to and beyond its self-imposed limits. If Jameson posits strategies of containment, then they ought to apply equally to his own texts. This is true to an extent, except that Jameson's theories, as I have examined them throughout this work, are not simply textual machinations. Like cognitive mapping, another key Jameson figure, the strategies are in some ways simply an updated version of false consciousness. The strategies of containment Jameson outlines

54   For some reason, Jameson's "strategies of containment," a notion he presents in *The Political Unconscious,* is also used as a critique by Dowling (55) and Bennington (as discussed in the second chapter).

55   Of course, there are a few non-Marxist meanings of the term "ideology," both those that predate Marx's use (Antoine de Stutt de Tracey, for instance) and those that have acquired legitimacy in the thought of non-Marxist thinkers like Paul Ricoeur (see Eagleton 1991). And I would also agree with Jameson's contention that varieties of Marxism—his, Eagleton's, Perry Anderson's (*LM,* 6)—are ideological in the weak sense, meaning that they are "working theories." But in the strong or global or totalizing sense, and logically, my argument above still stands, I believe.

in bourgeois ideology are present because of the limits of bourgeois thought itself as it attempts to legitimize the heroic mission of capital. But Horne's comparison of poststructuralism to AIDS misinterprets the role of the state in AIDS-prevention—a role it enters into only with great pressure from grass-roots activist groups. This is all in the context of Horne's contention that Jameson is a dyed-in-the-wool modernist and thus is motivated by "an unmistakably modernist design . . . the attempt to legitimate, in the face of the epistemological break defining postmodernism, political involvement in mass movements" (Horne 1989, 270). What kind of "modernist design" is this—T. S. Eliot as union organizer?

413 Horne believes that it is "clearly trying to [Jameson] to discuss Warhol's painting 'Diamond Dust Shoes' in the same section as Van Gogh's 'Peasant Shoes.' Jameson is able to do this, but not without a few nasty remarks about soup cans and tinsel" (286). I cannot find any remarks, nasty or otherwise, about tinsel (and a soup can is mentioned as part of Warhol's silk-screen images), but a reading of how Jameson turns from his and Heidegger's remarks on Van Gogh toward a consideration of Warhol may be less "clearly trying": "At any rate, both readings may be described as *hermeneutical,* in the sense in which the work in its inert, objectal form is taken as a clue or a symptom for some vaster reality which replaces it as its ultimate truth. Now we need to look at some shoes of a different kind, and it is pleasant to be able to draw for such an image on the recent work of the central figure in contemporary visual art. Andy Warhol's *Diamond Dust Shoes* evidently no longer speaks to us with any of the immediacy of Van Gogh's footgear: indeed, I am tempted to say that it does not really speak to us at all. Nothing in this painting organizes even a minimal place for the viewer, who confronts it at the turning of a museum corridor or gallery with all the contingency of some inexplicable natural object. On the level of content, we have to do with what are now far more clearly fetishes, in both the Freudian and the Marxian senses (Derrida remarks, somewhere,[56] about the Heideggerian *Paar Bauernschuhe,* that the Van Gogh footgear are a heterosexual pair, which

---

56 "Restitutions," in *The Truth in Painting* (Derrida 1987, 286–87). Derrida says that a boot opened up in the manner of the one on the right in Van Gogh's painting is vaginal, while one more footlike would be phallic.

allows neither for perversion nor for fetishization)" (*PM*, 8). At this point, a clarification of Horne's use of the "deconstruction of expression" is in order. The phrase was originally a section title in the *New Left Review* essay, and while section titles did not survive in the *Postmodernism* book's version of the essay, Jameson does still use the phrase, as in the *NLR* version, but not in Horne's meaning. Here, then, Edward Munch's painting *The Scream* is "read as an embodiment not merely of the expression of [anxiety] but, even more, as a virtual deconstruction of the very aesthetic of expression itself, which seems to have dominated much of what we call high modernism but to have vanished away—for both practical and theoretical reasons—in the world of the postmodern" (*PM*, 11). This is very different from Horne's reification-as-deconstruction. But what is finally most important about Horne's series of takes on Jameson is the desire to see Jameson as an anti-postmodernist, a pathological sanitation inspector trapped in humanistic categories. If Munch's painting finds its greatest postmodern embodiment in the child-actor's scream in *Home Alone,* Horne's self-designated role as point man for postmodernism is probably adequate.

postmodernism as liberalism

414 One of the most influential apologists for postmodernism is probably Linda Hutcheon. In *A Poetics of Postmodernism* (1988), Hutcheon's strategies are several: to provide a working definition for postmodern fiction based on architecture (basically, "historiographic metafiction"); to argue that the "paradoxical, contradictory" nature of the postmodern means that it is implicated in and critical of the dominant culture; and, finally, to defend postmodernism against its critics, who come primarily, although not exclusively, from the Left. Thus, to elaborate on this last proposition, Hutcheon devotes some time to discussing Habermas, Eagleton, and Jameson. Habermas is read, as he usually is in the poststructuralist orthodoxy, as some avatar of old-fashioned Enlightenment values. The following passage, in which Hutcheon offers a commentary on some words used by Habermas, is not untypical of her methodology: " '*Common sense,' be it Leavisite or Habermasian* [linking Habermas with Leavis is a cunning, or, in Hutcheon's code,

"sly," strategy, for nothing is closer to out-and-out antiquity for today's theorist than FRL], *has been revealed as anything but 'common'* [presumably "common" is meant in a Hutcheonesque, and not Gramscian sense] *and shared:* [an adjective which is meaningless in this context] *it is the ideology* [it is difficult to understand how, if Hutcheon nowhere has any real use for Marxist critiques, she can still use this term and idea] *of the dominant group* [since thinkers of such various theoretical tendencies stripes as Gramsci, Althusser, and Barthes would all say that there is no "dominant ideology" or group, why is Hutcheon clinging to such an apparently pre-postmodern notion?]. *'Historical consciousness' cannot be an unproblematic issue* [who has said that historical consciousness is unproblematical?: surely Lukács's entire project was to determine the problems in that concept; here is a key Hutcheon tactic: to take what is actually a real point of contention for the Left and turn it into a monolithic and heretofore unexamined proposition—it should be noted that Hutcheon will make all of the proper noises about *not* taking the Left for a monolith (215), but this appears to be a superficial comment and not a wide-ranging commitment; again, the study apparently is as complicit and critical as she claims postmodernism to be] *after historio-graphic metafiction's questioning"* (Hutcheon 1988, 209).

415 Hutcheon's take on Eagleton's postmodernism essay works in a similar fashion and thus contends that he discusses only theory and not "postmodern practice" in a "strategy . . . clever and certainly convenient" (18) that is no more than "absolutist binary thinking." Ignoring the real problem of using such *moral* and political terms like "absolutist," how is Eagleton's separation of postmodernism from modernism *more* binary than Hutcheon's claim on postmodernism or, for that matter, her fetish of theory and practice? But her discussion of Jameson's postmodernism article demonstrates in a thorough manner the essential liberalism of Hutcheon's take on postmodernism. The two first characteristics of Hutcheon's book, I noted above, were that she sees a prime example of postmodernism in historiographic metafiction and that the entire set of cultural practices is somehow and simultaneously complicit and critical of the dominant culture. So, in discussing E. L. Doctorow's novel *Ragtime* (1976), which Hutcheon sees as intrinsically historiographic and metafictional (she discusses or cites it eighteen times in her study), she argues that "there can be no single, essen-

tialized, transcendent concept of 'genuine historicity' (as Fredric Jameson desires), no matter what the nostalgia (Marxist or traditional) for such an entity. . . . Jameson has asserted that Doctorow's *Ragtime* is 'the must peculiar and stunning monument to the aesthetic situation engendered by the disappearance of the historical referent' [*PM*, 25]. But it is just as easy to argue that, in that very novel, the historical referent is very present—and in spades. Not only is there an accurate evocation of a particular period . . . but historical personages also appear within the fiction" (Hutcheon 1988, 89). Besides Hutcheon's apparent slip into a sort of pre-structuralist faith in the referent and accuracy, her reading of Jameson on *Ragtime* as a lament (Hutcheon, 212) or negative critique (Hutcheon, 89) is not surprising, although I would not call her interpretation of Jameson's work a misreading, except in the late-seventies sense that every reading is a misreading. Rather, what Hutcheon does is to lay over Jameson's text a linguistic grid, which has everything to do with register or tone. That is, Hutcheon does not get Jameson factually wrong when she understands him to be saying that Doctorow's novel is not dealing with a genuine historicity. What happens, however, is that Jameson's response becomes an *objection*. Hutcheon writes the following confident statement: "Of course, it is this mixing of the historical and the fictive and their tampering with the 'facts' of received history that Jameson objects to" (Hutcheon 1988, 89). But Jameson argues that *Ragtime* is both thematically *and* formally about "the disappearance of the historical referent" in that it tells the story of the shift from a representable and real urban squalor to the more ambiguous economy of the image (the character Tateh's trajectory from Jewish resident of the Lower East Side to pioneer of cinema) but *not* in an ambiguously realistic style: "[F]or one thing, the objects of representation, ostensibly narrative characters, are incommensurable and, as it were, of incomparable substances, like oil and water—Houdini being a *historical* figure, Tateh a *fictional* one, and Coalhouse an *intertextual* one" (*PM*, 22). Paradoxically, Hutcheon sees postmodernism primarily as a cultural or aesthetic phenomenon confined to high culture, and therefore maintains the traditional position of the critic "explaining" it even while she pretends not to be. On the other hand, Jameson's more totalizing viewpoint, which sees postmodern cultural artifacts as part of a global economic-political-cultural epoch, would then be more capable of locating the place of the postmodern "theorist."

prolegomena to any fugue of the postmodern

416 Ethics might seem to be a singularly unpromising venue for an inquiry into *Postmodernism:* a dilatory glance through chapter headings and the index leads to the pages 289–90, hardly a good start, and there only the Chomskyan remark that U.S. inventions of villains in the 1970s and 1980s ("mostly Arabs or Iranians for some reason"), which may be explained by American guilt over its middle-class comforts, also "depend for their effects on the revitalization of *ethics* as a set of mental categories." But here two unequal developments do lead in promising directions. The first is the explosion in the past fifteen years or so of what we can now call "postmodernist ethics": Irigaray, MacIntyre, Rorty, Levinas, for example. The second is the continuing binarization of world politics into the "West" and whatever is not the West. The East refers variously and depending on the demands of the day to Communism, Islam, Communist China, capitalist Japan, the Middle East, and eventually, whatever is not the West will include such internal threats as p.c.-ism, Native Americans, Rigoberta Menchú (see Beverly 1993, 12–22), or whoever else such avatars of the intellect as Alan Bloom or William Bennett determine. At various levels, then, the dirty world of politics and the clean world of ethical philosophy have mobilized popular and elite opinion in the class wars and imperialist gestures of late capitalism. In the case of defending the West in its various guises, surely nothing is easier to decode than the overdetermined semiotics of dirtiness: from Yasser Arafat's bristle (which is echoed and postmodernized in Don Johnson's chin on *Miami Vice*) and the squalor, achieved through a full-dress assault on the sixties, that is now attached to "activism," so that any modern-day activist almost inevitably is thought to inhabit a fetid commune with half-naked savages—all of these examples and more, then, mean that both the class and sexual connotations of dirtiness are harnessed to the project of setting up discrete epistemological *maquiladoras* of imperialism.

417 Ethics gets scanty mention in *Postmodernism* when compared with the earlier essay on MacIntyre (*IT,* 1:181–88), the contention in *The Political Unconscious* that ethical criticism has been a dominant form of bourgeois theory, and the attention paid in that book to questions of the ethical in Conrad. And what is also briefly glossed over is the question of taste. But two textual conditions of Jameson's postmodernism book must be noted, two

modi operandi that differentiate it from a certain film book examined earlier in this chapter, even if the overall structure of both books are parallel.
That is, first of all, there is in *Postmodernism* a curious redoubling of chap-
ter/essay title and sur-title or subtitle: in the table of contents, each chapter is
given a double-barreled appellation—"Ideology: Theories of the Postmodern," or "Theory: Immanence and Nominalism in Postmodern Theoretical
Discourse."[57] Each chapter will then feature as its head-title, what was the
so-called subtitle in the table of contents: chapter 9, for instance, is headed
"Nostalgia for the Present." And then, at the top of each recto page, the
putative title of the chapter reappears, like a tardy translation supplied to
monolingual operagoers courtesy of the technology of Sur-Titles. This
focus on the textual machinations of Jameson's book may be justified on at
least three counts. First, in his essay on Negt and Kluge in *October* (1988b),
Jameson comments upon the still-radical importance of typographical sub-
versions. Second, the Ong-McLuhan tradition of questioning the rational
hegemony of the printed page, which I would argue to be a Canadian tradition, holds that the appearance of the text on the page is as arbitrary and as
constructed as such objects of the deconstructive impulse as "voice" or
"presence." Third, that selfsame deconstructive impulse, not least in the
work of Derrida himself, has continually stressed the relevance of marginalia
itself, both literal and metaphorical.

418 The second obstacle to be noted or overcome before moving to questions of taste is the place of the discussion of taste in Jameson's book; it
comes at the start of the final chapter, the paradoxical "Conclusion: Secondary Elaborations," the first section of which is "Prolegomena to Future Con-
frontations Between the Modern and the Postmodern." Complications continue with the first two allegories offered in the chapter: one, the comparison
of Marxism and hotels; the other, the autobiographical positioning of the
writing subject. That "Marxism" and "postmodernism" seems to be incom-
patible terms for many people, Jameson remarks, means that, on the one
hand, he must have lapsed from the Catholicism of the former in order to

---

57 Here already a certain vertigo creeps into my text, for the chapter titles are "really"
typeset on two lines, with no "colon" separating them, and I merely have followed the
tradition for citing books' titles: placing a colon between what seems to be a title and its
subtitle.

embrace the catholic taste of the latter; while, on the other hand, the semiotic connotations of the two terms suggests a mnemonic assemblage whereby a Leninist and faded restaurant, "decorated with old photographs, with Soviet waiters sluggishly serving bad Russian food" (*PM*, 297) is tucked away in a properly shiny and pomo hotel extravaganza. This brief paragraph might serve as one more of those many self-reflexive or self-referential moments in Jameson's writings: here, the proper referent is the surprising luxuriousness of Jameson's postmodernism book itself, encountered in a bookstore first in hardcover with a glossy Andy Warhol cover.

419 The second allegory that opens the final chapter to Jameson's postmodernism book is a brief narrative of his own vicissitudes as both critic of postmodernism and of structuralism. Here a certain coyness enters the text: "[A] book I published years ago on structuralism [meaning, of course, *The Prison-House of Language*] elicited letters, some of which addressed me as a 'foremost' spokesperson for structuralism, while the others appealed to me as an 'eminent' critic and opponent of the movement" (*PM*, 297). In both cases, he suggests, some unnamed people will simultaneously mistake Jameson for both critic and proponent of structuralism or postmodernism, and this interesting error is caused, finally, because of his Marxist stance. That is, the historical and dialectical opportunities that are seldom found other than in Marxism—the insistence on grounding theory in practice, the necessity for a historical situating—mean that a mindless dualism of either being "for" or "against" such movements is irrelevant.

taste and liberalism

420 As Peter Nicholls has noted (1991), the wide range of cultural artifacts that Jameson analyzes in *Postmodernism* allows him "to stage a fuller characterization of some of the dominant modes of postmodernism" and "gives the whole account of postmodernism a stronger developmental thrust than it had before" (1). So what is notable about this latest book is the typical Jameson breadth: what was a range of Continental Marxist traditions in *Marxism and Form* or a competence across a range of literary criticisms in *The Political Unconscious* here is an unabashed *aesthetic* competence.

421 If we are now ready for the glimpse of Jameson's putatively "private"

taste, the catalog of it then is designed to disappoint, even as the notion of an autobiographical moment in a Jameson text, for all of its alluring novelty, gives way to bittersweet regret. For the discussion of his own taste is anti-climactic: "[C]ulturally I write as a relatively enthusiastic consumer of post-modernism, at least of some parts of it" (298). This is really all we need to know, since the "opinions" of various art forms—the novel, photography, music—can be easily turned upside down or dismissed with the reader's own catalog, as Christopher Norris has shown in *Uncritical Theory* (1992). So taste is now *only* some dreaded Bourdieu class marker.

422   I would argue that Jameson's position here bespeaks a radical plurality of taste that cannot be lightly dismissed or glossed over, as we search for either the correct Marxist message of his tome (the modus operandi both of his would-be "simple-hearted comrades" and of those who come not to praise Jameson, but to bury him) or its mindless hedonism (a Marxist writing about hotels and pop art?). That is, the remark "As far as taste is con-cerned," or, the apparent casual tone of the line, indicates not its unim-portance but its primacy. Textually, the casual tone is necessary so that Jameson's taste (architecture, music, film) cannot be allowed to be granted an overwhelming importance. The theme is the following: economic free-dom is inseparable from aesthetic bliss. This is not Lyotard's message, which is that the economic can no longer be said to exist. Jameson's statement is an invitation for every reader to situate her own taste: to investigate its etiology and its implications. The question of taste usually leads to the Kantian tradition of aesthetic inquiry: how am I reflected in my "knowledge" of what is beautiful, and so on. But, as Jameson argues both here and in his book on Adorno, such old-fashioned philosophy has been outdated by the consolida-tion of late capitalism in its present form. It was still possible for Adorno to stimulate the last twinges of activity in that aesthetic dead horse. Now, how-ever, the routinization of the subject under bureaucratic capitalism, to better extract value, and the concomitant dismantling of the aesthetic "project" in favour of such unintended methodologies as surrealism or abstract painting, necessitate new theories of the relationship between subjectivity and taste. My point is not some full-scale poststructuralist ejection of the subject; there are still sufficient *radical* reasons for maintaining notions of an autonomous subject, and the frigid dismissal of all subjectivities as so much socially constructed signs can sometimes lead to quiescence of the worst sort.

423 Another way of coming at this problem in Jameson is to be found in the notion of the collective subject, which would seem to be a Marxist way of incorporating poststructuralist attacks on the bourgeois subject, since, as Jameson remarks, it often seems "that, for poststructuralism, all enemies are on the left" (*PM*, 217). In a discussion of Walter Benn Michaels's book on Frank Norris, *The Gold Standard,* Jameson comments on the dialectic of person and corporation. In typical bourgeois fashion, we can now think of a corporation as a "person" and bemoan the transgression of the human ineffable. What if it is the other way around, and individualism itself is a sort of corporation, and what if that corporation is not a capitalist or modern invention but one stretching back through the Middle Ages? Jameson quotes Michaels: "Hence the corporation comes to seem the embodiment of figurality that makes personhood possible, rather than appearing as a figurative extension of personhood" (Michaels 1987, 205; qtd. *PU,* 216).

424 Jameson's text is valuable precisely because here is a Marxist critic presenting himself as a "consumer," but in ways that circumvent notions of professionalism or discipline (the comment in *Signatures of the Visible* regarding English professors watching film critics with envy is pertinent). *Postmodernism,* like the essay from which the book takes its lengthy title, is a hodgepodge of opinion, taste, ideas received and fixed, theories, and asides. Norris, however, interprets Jameson's aesthetic breadth rather differently. He begins with the passage from *Postmodernism* cited above (Jameson's taste marginalized into a question of "consumership"), and remarks, "I happen to differ rather sharply with Jameson's stated preferences here, finding the music (or most of it) unlistenably vapid and trivial, the poetry (Ashbery excepted) pretty undistinguished, the architecture far more interesting in the idea than the execution, and the fiction—at any rate in writers like Calvino, Pynchon, Barth and Bartheleme—by far the most accomplished and distinctive body of work. But of course this is precisely Jameson's point: that in matters of 'taste' there is always room for differences of view. . . . And at this point issues of 'taste' become largely irrelevant, since we are obliged to confront postmodernism as something indisputably *there,* an aspect (so to speak) of the way we live now, and not as a 'position'" (Norris 1992, 159–60).

425 Taste today, as either a class or Kantian moment (in Bourdieu's view, both are the same thing) no longer exists. Jameson's Hegelian postmodern-

ism-as-spirit position, Norris argues, then is almost like, on the one hand, Bell, Fukuyama, and the other end of the ideology apparatchiks and, on the other hand, Rorty and Fish of the pragmatist school (Norris 1992, 162). The great philosophical "tic" of the dialectician is to see connections everywhere; this is not quite the same as seeing conspiracies; the latter come about, like religion, when political impulses toward the collective cannot reach their fruition through an authentic means. But this desire to totalize, a necessity, goes a long way toward accounting for the wide range of reference one will always find in Jameson's work, and most recently in the aesthetic forms dealt with in the postmodernism book.

the rhetoric of taste

426 Throughout Jameson's secondary elaborations, the taste of the collective subjectivity makes its mark. That is, before the attempts to devise a theory of modernism, Jameson's remarks on music do, as he says they ought to, "lead us into something more interesting and complicated than mere opinion" (*PM*, 299), and this is the *effect* of the statement that music "remains a fundamental class marker, the index of what Pierre Bourdieu calls social 'distinction.'" What, precisely, does this mean—or, what is it about music that it is so much that "fundamental class marker" unlike, say, painting or poetry or film? For Jameson, as I argued briefly in the previous chapter, music's ability to "mediate our historical past along with our private or existential one" (299) suits the art form admirably to the dialectics of mem-ory and history. We remember every time we have heard a piece of music and thus feel either disenfranchised (the oarsmen's stopped-up ears) or exalted (the bourgeois at a concert or listening to a CD player). But surely other art forms will pose as complicated a problem for a Marxist aesthetic. Poetry, for example, seems to possess none of the economic prestige that accrues to either music or the visual arts in their high forms. The odd Ted Hughes or Joseph Brodsky will become poet laureate, but these awards are almost embarrassing for the holders, who themselves tend to be outmoded avatars of premodernist verse. Whereas a rigorous avant-gardism in paint-ing is no obstacle to wealth, the equivalent poets either live on the pleasure of the academy or in impoverished notoriety.

427 For poetry, then, the modern slide toward difficulty has in postmodern-ism meant either a quasi-return to populism (the poetries of the various constituencies: feminists, workers, blacks, gays and lesbians) or a continua-tion of obscurities. The debates over Language poetry in the U.S., for in-stance, tend to be between very similar modernist positions, so that Barrett Watten's "constructivism"—influenced by Stein and the Russian Formal-ists—is not that different from Tom Clark's Williamesque populism. "Po-etry" is then an elite art form with almost no popular equivalent—given that rap or folk are properly musical forms—and any interest in poetry imme-diately marks the aesthete off from the masses.

428 Perhaps this is too harsh. The appropriateness of Jameson's insights into music can be judged for how they apply to poetry, and thus the re-mark that music today is increasingly spatialized is also pertinent to poetry. For what will link many disparate "trends" or "styles" of poetry (here Jame-son's invective against mere opinion returns) is the attention in the past thirty years to "modes of production." The appearance of Allen Ginsberg's *Howl* in the City Lights Pocket Poets format signaled to the popular con-sciousness the reality that poetry was no longer a casebound fetish for aes-thetes.[58] The explosion of mimeo magazines from the 1950s on meant that such various avant-garde traditions as U.S. Black Mountain writing, the L=A=N=G=U=A=G=E poets, the British new wave, Brazilian concrete poets, and the Canadian small presses all ensued, if in very different aes-thetic directions, out of a common literary format. The move away from the left margin, the use of the "book" as a unit of measure, various visual tech-niques and formalisms, a dialectic of clean and dirty (concrete) poetics: these and more signaled the arrival of space as a formal element of poetry, and perhaps as *the* formal element.

429 Thinking these thoughts, I find Jameson's casual mention of Bob Perel-man—"surely only a very old-fashioned critic or cultural journalist [Hilton Kramer?!] would be interested in proving the obvious, that Yeats is greater

58 Jerome McGann's recent work on Pound (1989, 96–128), and on the importance of seeing Pound's work in the original format, bears witness to a happy influence of contemporary poetry upon bibliography and theory, and the other way around (McGann has been a strong supporter of L=A=N=G=U=A=G=E poetry for some years). In regard to Ginsberg, see Michael Davidson's genealogical *The San Francisco Renaissance: Poetics and Community at Mid-Century* (1991).

than Paul Muldoon, or Auden than Bob Perelman" (*PM*, 300)—is essentially correct in its main point, even if critics of my generation would not hold such a nostalgic place in their hearts for Yeats or Auden. But the recognition that it is not a matter of taste in reading postmodern poetry does not or should not lead to the essentially liberal position that taste is, after all, a private affair, owing allegiance to no higher authority, or that tastes are "incommensurable" to each other and cannot be judged by a higher power. For if a Marxist literary theory is to have any interpretive value, it must posit some objective reasons for why Perelman is so different from Auden.

430 Jameson's celebrated raising of a poem by Perelman to international notoriety—his analysis of the poem "China" in the original postmodernism article in the *New Left Review*—is well-known for three salient points: his labeling of the L=A=N=G=U=A=G=E aesthetic as fundamentally "schizophrenic fragmentation" (*PM*, 28); his laying over the poem a thematic grid of the emergence of Red China; and Jameson's admission that Perelman had written the poem based on a book of photographs he found in Chinatown in San Francisco (and whose Chinese captions he could not read). The first point is the object of George Hartley's critique in his study *Textual Politics and the Language Poets* (1989). In the chapter "Jameson's Perelman," Hartley argues that Jameson's "importation of Lacan's discussion of schizophrenia leads him to the traditional Marxist denunciation of modernist (and now postmodernist) fragmentation, rather than to an appreciation of Perelman's particular use of the material signifier as a political critique" (45). But Jameson's use of the Lacanian analysis argues that Lacan's view of schizophrenia diagnoses that condition as paradigmatic of how communication works in general. That is, "personal identity is itself the effect of a certain temporal unification of past and future with one's present; and, second, that such active temporal unification is itself a function of language, or better still of the sentence, as it moves along its hermeneutic circle in time" (*PM*, 26–27). So the breakdown in the signifying chain characterized by schizophrenia is analogous to the structuralist notion that language is not a matter of a signifier referring to a referent, but to another signifier. And therefore postmodern poetry of Perelman's type is notable for how it foregrounds this breakdown, displays the rhetorical effects at work in our notion of personality, and so on. At this point it is evident that Jameson is not really the latter-

day Lukács that Hartley accuses him of being (or at least not for Hartley's reasons), for what Jameson finds in Perelman's poem, in postmodern culture in general, is that when "schizophrenic disjunction or *écriture* . . . becomes generalized as a cultural style, [it] ceases to entertain a necessary relationship to the morbid content we associate with terms like schizophrenia and becomes available for more joyous intensities, for precisely that euphoria which we saw displacing the older effects of anxiety and alienation" (*PM*, 29). For the joy in Perelman's poem "China" is not a prim and modernist irony, whether in its hegemonic manifestations in Eliot, Woolf, or Joyce, or in its more subversive places like Lewis, H. D., or Stein. Perelman's line "A sister who points to the sky at least once a decade is a good sister" plays both with the economy of the sentence (like elsewhere in the poem, there is little sense of meaning-climax to the phrase) and with a minimalist humor. This "euphoria . . . high . . . intoxicatory or hallucinogenic intensity" (*PM*, 28) is precisely why Jameson turns our attention to culture.

431 For Jameson's next point is that in spite of the attenuated style of Perelman's poem, a global thematic can be detected. Now, an important aspect of postmodern cultural artifacts, Jameson argues, is their "derealization" of the Real, which leads to the notion of the postmodern sublime. Duane Hanson's polyester figures, Jameson notes, will for a short period cause us to think that the other museum-goers around us are also statues; most of us have probably had the experience of wondering if the air-humidity monitor in a museum is some "conceptual" work, or of coming up to a label or brass plaque and attempting to read it "ironically." Such a museum experience only foregrounds the contemporary vertigo of cityscapes; wearing a Walkman, who has not wondered if the noise she was now hearing was the street (truck, conversation, music from a storefront) or the headphones? This is also the supreme fictional effect of much contemporary poetry, whether it is the collage-effect of concrete poems that make store signs (with all of their wonderful illiterate spellings and phonetic grammar) suddenly works of art, or a poem like Charles Bernstein's "Contradiction turns to rivalry" (1983, 25–28), which is a list of what seem to be *TV Guide* plot summaries of movies and TV shows: "A grim smuggling operation and a dead hippie lead to intrigue in Malta" (26), or "It's the dog pound for Roger when Jeannie turns him into a poodle" (27). So now TV listings can be L=A=N=G=U=A=G=E poems. But Bern-

stein's poem or text makes the same argument that Jameson does: many of the plot synopses show how popular culture will feed on the social movements of the 1960s (hippies, feminism, student movements) or turn various tragedies into fodder for a comedic mill (*SV,* 38–39).

sublime hysteria

432 Jameson's intervention into the various contemporary discussions of the sublime characteristically raises the debate to a higher level, for his conclusion is that the postmodern version of the sublime, in its very fetishization of the failure of representation, itself indicates some important truth about our culture and society today. Comparing postmodernism with the abandon of futurism and Marinetti, he writes, "[T]he technology of our own moment no longer possesses this same capacity for representation: not the turbine . . . not the baroque elaboration of pipes and conveyor belts, nor even the streamlined profile of the railroad train . . . but rather the computer, whose outer shell has no emblematic or visual power" (*PM,* 36–37). But this is not to say that the proper response is the feeble variants of thematized media-society one sees in popular culture, or that technology is now the Mc-Luhanesque or Baudrillardean engine of society. Evidently, if the second were true, then the very plethora of the first in mass culture would indicate that representation is doing very well today (the valorization of metafiction is a similar wrongheaded proposition). Instead, "our faulty representations of some immense communicational and computer network are themselves but a distorted figuration of a present-day multinational capitalism" (37), and the fetish of technology appeals precisely because it *is* a fetish in all of the Pascalian-Marxian senses: it inverts the process and makes us think it is technologies of reproduction that drive the world economy and not the other way around.

CONCLUSION:

THE SYNOPTIC JAMESON

It has always seemed to me that what is most interesting and, finally, relevant about Jameson's work has been its effect of an allegory-vertigo; indeed, this postmodern vertigo makes itself known in a memory-effect so that, in my own little career through learning theory in the past ten years, I cannot remember *not* having read Jameson. But it is the allegory in the allegory-vertigo that interests me here; that is, the way in which, after reading a certain amount of Jameson, not only does everything suddenly start seeming like an allegory for something else (if I might paraphrase from *The Geopolitical Aesthetic*, if everything means something else, then so too does Jameson), but any given text of Jameson's starts being able to stand in for any and all of Jameson's writings. So there is no "recent" Jameson, just as there is no "legacy" of Jameson but in the most superficial sense, or the more obsolete meaning of the word, a delegate as opposed to a bequest. That Jameson's work "delegates" responsibility even as it is a delegate to a higher authority— that it allegorizes even as it argues that the old-fashioned narratives of totality, the economic, and revolution still hold sway—seems to me to be a more satisfactory way of putting it.

This is to say the following: I'd rather get a "synoptic" Jameson than a "recent" Jameson; even if, as most theory junkies, I buy or check out the "new" Jameson, I will be disappointed if this text does not, in some ways, disappoint, if it does not repeat Jameson himself, if it cannot be lined up in a synoptic edition like the Gospels or Chandlers and compared, passage for passage, phrase for phrase, with "earlier" or "classic" Jameson. This, then, is the first sense in which I'd like to consider "space" in regard to Jameson: the space of his books, which are in some ways palimpsests and in other ways hypertexts, some kind of bedeviled layering where, like superhighways or information superhighways in America over Heideggerian forest paths, the nonsynchronous is suddenly immediate and simultaneous.

So too, then, I would argue that many intellectuals of my generation read the work of Jameson, and theory in general (Jameson means something else) as mass culture; by my generation I suppose I mean those born in the late-fifties or in the sixties, Generation X as my fellow Canadian put it. I don't know if this generation is more specific ethnically or sexually or nationally (I refuse to explain obscure Canadian references in Canada, but being a Canadian, I probably won't make any) than I'm letting on here. But my point is that in this milieu, Jameson and Butler and Spivak and Barthes are on the same plane as Shabba Ranks and PJ Harvey and *Deep Space Nine* and John Woo: cultural signifiers of which one is as much a "fan" as a "critic," driven as much by the need to own or see or read the "latest" (or the "classic" or the "original") as by the need to debate it on Internet and in the seminar room. You think *Rid of Me* is good? Check out *4-Track Demos*. *True Romance* is more of a John Woo film than *Hard Target*. If you like *Gender Trouble,* check out *Bodies that Matter*. Jameson's piece of Chandler in *Shades of Noir* is a remix of his older essay and samples some of the comments on modernism at the end of *Signatures of the Visible*.

I'd like to include here a brief comment on totality that Jameson makes in *Late Marxism:* "The summary deictic indication in passing of late capitalism, system, exchange, totality, is not a reference to other sets of thoughts or concepts . . . which can be criticized in their own terms for their coherence and validity and their ideological quotient. It rather gestures toward an outside of thinking—whether system itself in the form of rationalization, or totality as a socioeconomic mechanism of domination and exploitation—which escapes representation by the individual thinker or the individual thought. The function of the impure, extrinsic reference is less to interpret, then, than to rebuke interpretation as such and to include within the thought the reminder that it is itself inevitably the result of a system that escapes it and which it perpetuates: even there where it seeks radically to grasp and confront the element in which it bathes and which infiltrates and determines its subjective processes fully as much as the objects for which it seeks to account" (30–31).

Jameson's comments introduce the tack I would like to take on what I see as a shift in his recent writings on mass culture: a thematic-theoretical figuration of totality and space that confronts more fully and radically the unrepresentability of those systems even as it pushes the mass cultural objects—primarily film, but also cyberpunk and Raymond Chandler—in the direction of meta-interpretive allegories.

What I am most interested in is Jameson's recent book on film, *The Geopolitical Aesthetic*, which in the first half looks at conspiracy as an allegory for totality in North American films of the past two decades. Jameson argues that Alan J. Pakula's films like *The Parallax View* and *All the President's Men* (his latest movie is *The Pelican Brief*) and Cronenberg's *Videodrome* represent or re-figure a way of conceptualizing the totalizing effects of late capitalism. And this has not a little to do with their status as mass cultural texts. This is made clear in his discussion of Cronenberg: "Here a Western, commercial version of the Third-World political aesthetic of Cuban 'imperfect cinema' is deployed, and not only in the function of B-film generic signals (the shoestring horror film, and so on). In another place, I argued something pre-eminently relevant here, namely, that the ideologeme of elegance and glossiness, expensive form, in postmodernism, was also dialectically at one with its opposite number in sleaze, punk, trash, and garbage art of all kinds. . . . [T]his production also re-enacts those more humble predecessors, which are, in *Videodrome*, pornography as such. . . . Here too, then, authenticity in the grain and in the camera work means a gradual approximation to the palpable grubbiness of the archetypal model, not excluding a wonderfully garish and cheap color. . . . Finally, the positioning of this film and its production in the world system is no mere external accident either. . . . [E]ven in terms of a signal system, the Canadian provenance of *Videodrome* (and of Cronenberg himself) marginalizes the work internally and assigns it a semi-peripheral resonance, particularly since it is not designed to exemplify some national . . . cultural production, even though its deeper ideological values (a horror of US pornography, for example) are very Canadian, or at least Torontonian, indeed" (23–24).

This passage argues that it is precisely Cronenberg's carnifying cinema's situating on the margins of even B-grade movies which allegorizes both his own filmic aesthetic (horror and porn: Marilyn Chambers was in Cronenberg's *Rabid*) and Canada's position as colony of the U.S. (In Canadian video stores, Canadian films are still frequently shelved in the "foreign cinema" section.) In fact, like three earlier Cronenberg films (*Fast Company, The Brood, Scanners*) *Videodrome* was financed under a Canadian tax-shelter experiment of the late 1970s and early 1980s (Cronenberg's were among the few from that system to make money and be artistically worthwhile). The film's cheap look, determined by the economics of making movies in a country where 97 percent of the screens are dominated by American films, is then called into service by Jameson's allegorizing, so that mass cultural aesthetics articulate the space of the contemporary world system.

With more rarefied senses of space, Jameson extends the totality notion literally to its own edge. In his essay "Spatial Systems in *North by Northwest*" (1992), he analyzes the film's movement across the United States, remarking that "this sequence of spaces generates a sense of completeness (or a 'totality-effect') which can scarcely be explained by content alone. Comparable formal problems (and 'solutions') can be found in Raymond Chandler's equally episodic (and spatial) detective stories, where the successful mapping of the Los Angeles region—in other words, our sense that, in spite of necessary selectivity, 'totalization' has been achieved, is structurally dependent on the inclusion of some ultimate boundary or verge of Being itself. . . . In the Hitchcock film, the stereotypical or imaginary frame is clearly some phantasmic United States, about which one might argue that the open-field sequence sets the Midwest in place, while the mountainous landscape of North Dakota does double duty for the Rockies. . . . Yet here too, as in Chandler, the completeness of the enumerated elements (of such a map-phantasm) is not enough: we must also come to the ultimate edge of all this, in order for it to recohere retroactively as a satisfyingly exhaustive itinerary" (56). With Chandler, that reterritorialization is carried out by its Adornoesque outside, a garage as a "place at the very edge of Being" in *The Big Sleep* or the sea in *Farewell My Lovely*. As Jameson writes in "The Synoptic Chandler" (1993a), "[T]he liquid element does not exist here within the narrative world, is not a part of its semiotic system, but rather lies beyond it and cancels it as such. . . . In other words, death itself is in Chandler some-thing like a spatial concept" (52–53).

These two themes, then, space and mass culture, are brought together by Jameson at the conclusion of his analysis of *Videodrome:* "[T]he conspiracy plot of *Videodrome* can now be seen as something like a formal pretext to touch all the bases in the urban landscape itself. . . . This spatial closure is formally necessary precisely because the narrative itself cannot know any closure or completion of this kind. [Jameson makes a lot of how in these films the protagonists seem to flip from hero to villain to pursued; the arbitrary nature of conspiracy or thriller plots, then, is a formal analogon to the over-determination of subjectivity and agency by the structure of totality.] Only in the cheapest generic Science Fiction does the revolution triumph, sweeping the conspiratorial present away. . . . But *Videodrome* is a kind of realism: it . . . seeks urgently to convince us that on some level, in the superstate, the conspiracies are real and already with us" (*GA*, 32–33).

I'd like to finish here, finally, with two examples of these expressions in mass culture. The first is Richard Benjamin's film *Made in America* (1993). I liked how the movie presents as everyday certain aspects of African Ameri-can culture. I didn't like how it allegorized race relations into, on the one hand, sexual congress and, on the other hand, running a car dealership to fight off imports. The allegory of the failure of the black family in the U.S. as source for everything from the L.A. rebellion to Anita Hill is addressed, or further displaced, perhaps, in *Made in America* via the trope of technology. Here Jameson's remark that "if everything stands for something else, so too does technology" is pertinent; or, to put this in the form of a question, why was the Goldberg character *artificially* inseminated? Why, indeed, if not to, on the one hand, avoid the question of miscegenation and then, on the other hand, with the "coming together" of the characters, to argue that there has been progress in the fated twenty or so years (almost a Watts-to-L.A.-rebellion lifespan?) since the fatal injection was made. This interracial ro-mance, real as it is (was) in what we call "real life," is designed to accomplish the financial rearming of America; this is first signaled in the title credits, where "Made in America" announces its double meaning (conceived and also manufactured), and then changes from red-white-and-blue colors to Afrocentric yellow and green.

But I'd like to examine the film through another prism: offshore labor markets. In the movie, Whoopi's daughter Zora finds out (in quotation marks) her sperm bank father is Ted Danson, a car dealer, and not a black guy. So much for the crisis of the missing African American patriarch, or so it seems. Whoopi and Ted start out hating each other, then fall in love, and together they can save America from import cars. Turns out, though, it's a mistake—the postmodern sublime—Zora had located Ted by going through the computers at the sperm bank, but the data had been sent offshore to be computerized, and mistakes were made. Late capitalism rears its ugly head; the errors are blamed on poor Third World labor. That is, this addresses two key features of multinational capital, which are, first, the international division of labor, where the manufacturing process is divided into different regions or countries, and thus information will be processed wherever keystrokes are cheapest and, second, information itself is now a commodity. It functions as plot determinant and is also that edge or outside that Jameson identifies.

A final example I'd like to offer of current articulations of Jameson's praxis is the recent novel *Snow Crash* (Stephenson 1993). Here what is exemplary is not the by-now classical notion of cyberspace per se, but rather the way in which cognition (which is to say ideology) is materially rendered in a textual sense. I mean this last phrase literally: the U.S.A. of the novel is a conglomeration of franchises, in which even the nation-state or government has been replaced by Mr. Lee's Hong Kong, for instance. Space thus is thoroughly commodified, normalized, and reified. And to run the franchise-spaces, the operators rely on binders, which trope is, ironically, the least fantastic device of the novel. Such binders or manuals are now the norm for corporate and franchised and bureaucratic capitalism, as writing them is the likely job for many of the students we teach. I have some experience with writing manuals for the provincial government, and the dirty secret of the business is that often they are not really used. But their function in the novel is to materially offer a textual site for ideology in action, as practice. Thus when a stove overheats, the franchise operator of the pizza place (or whatever) is seen hurriedly riffling through his binder (which is undoubtedly not kept up to date). Binders are also the Third World's entry point to a simulacra of America in *Snow Crash*. It is no accident that many of the franchise operators are Armenian (a geography that in the political Symbolic is both Soviet and Third World: rather like Florida, say, or our own Labrador). Like the old-fashioned Pledge of Allegiance, the binder offers a performative and ideological misrecognition for sutured identification with the nation/empire.

To conclude: as I remarked earlier in this book, the key moment in *Signatures of the Visible* for me was the footnote where Jameson remarks that his field research into mass culture has been hindered by the fact that his car radio has not worked for years. (Perhaps he should have bought a Volvo.) Similarly, my favorite moments in *The Geopolitical Aesthetic* are the still photographs from *The Parallax View*. A parallel series of photographs are in the liner notes for a recent CD from Chicago punk-rock group Urge Overkill. The synoptic Chandler or Jameson is that outside; and my own position as fan and critic is itself an attempt to rebuke interpretation even while I perpetuate it.

WORKS

CITED

WORKS BY JAMESON

Books

Fables of Aggression. Berkeley: U of California P, 1981.

The Geopolitical Aesthetic: Cinema and Space in the World System. Bloomington: Indiana UP, 1992.

The Ideologies of Theory. 2 vols. Theory and History of Literature, nos. 48 and 49. Minneapolis: U of Minnesota P, 1988.

Late Marxism: Adorno, or, the Persistence of the Dialectic. London: Verso, 1990.

Marxism and Form: Twentieth-Century Dialectical Theories of Literature. Princeton: Princeton UP, 1974.

The Prison-House of Language: A Critical Account of Structuralism and Russian Formalism. Princeton: Princeton UP, 1974.

Postmodernism, or, The Cultural Logic of Late Capitalism. Durham: Duke UP, 1991.

The Political Unconscious: Narrative as a Socially Symbolic Act. Ithaca: Cornell UP, 1981.

Sartre: The Origins of a Style. 2d ed. New York: Columbia UP, 1984.

Signatures of the Visible. New York: Routledge, 1990.

Other Works

1972a. "Three Methods in Sartre's Literary Criticism." In John K. Simon, ed., *Modern French Criticism: From Proust and Valéry to Structuralism*. Chicago: U of Chicago P.

1972b. "The Great American Hunter, or, Ideological Content in the Novel." *College English* 34.2: 180–97.

1976. "The Ideology of Form: Partial Systems in *La Vieille Fille*." *Sub-Stance* 15: 29–49.

1979a. "Reification and Utopia in Mass Culture." *Social Text* 1: 130–48.

1979b. "Towards a Libidinal Economy of Three Modern Painters." *Social Text* 1: 189–99.

1982a. "Interview." *Diacritics* 12.3: 72–91.

1982b. "Progress Versus Utopia, or Can We Imagine the Future?" *Science Fiction Studies* 27: 147–58.

1982c. "*Ulysses* in History." In W. J. MacCormack and Alistair Stead, eds., *James Joyce and Modern Literature*. London: Routledge. 126–41.

1983a. "On Raymond Chandler." In Glenn W. Most and William W. Stowe, eds., *The Poetics of Murder: Detective Fiction and Literary Theory*. New York: Harcourt. 122–47.

1983b. "Postmodernism and Consumer Society." In Hal Foster, ed., *The Anti-Aesthetic: Essays on Postmodern Culture*. Port Townsend: Bay. 111–25.

1984a. "Flaubert's Libidinal Historicism: *Trois Contes*." In Naomi Schor and Henry F. Majewski, eds., *Flaubert and Postmodernism*. Lincoln: U of Nebraska P. 76–83.

1984b. "Rimbaud and the Spatial Text." In Tak-wai Wong and M. A. Abbas, eds., *Rewriting Literary History*. Hong Kong: Hong Kong UP. 66–93.

Ed. 1985a. *Sartre after Sartre*. Yale French Studies 68. New Haven: Yale UP.

1985b. Introduction. In Jameson 1985a, iii–xi.

1985c. "Baudelaire as Modernist and Postmodernist: The Dissolution of the Referent and the Artificial 'Sublime'." In Chaviva Hosek and Patricia Parker, eds., *Lyric Poetry: Beyond New Criticism*. Ithaca: Cornell UP. 247–63.

1986a. "The Realist Floor-Plan." In Marshall Blonsky, ed., *On Signs*. Baltimore: Johns Hopkins UP. 373–83.

1986b. "Third-World Literature in the Era of Multinational Capital." *Social Text* 15: 65–88.

1987a. "A Brief Response." *Social Text* 17: 26–27.

1987b. Foreword. In Algirdas Julien Greimas, *On Meaning: Selected Writings in Semiotic Theory*. Minneapolis: U of Minnesota P. vi–xxii.

1987c. "The State of the Subject (III)." *Critical Quarterly* 29.4: 16–25.

1988. "On Negt and Kluge." *October* 46: 151–77.

1989. "Afterword—Marxism and Postmodernism." In Douglas Kellner, ed., *Postmodernism/Jameson/Critique*. Washington, D.C.: Maissoneuve. 369–87.

1990a. "Modernism and Imperialism." In Terry Eagleton, Fredric Jameson, and Edward Said. *Nationalism, Colonialism, and Literature*. Minneapolis: U of Minnesota P. 43–66.

1990b. "Clinging to the Wreckage." Interview with Stuart Hall. *Marxism Today* (September): 28–31.

1991. "Thoughts on the Late War." *Social Text* 28: 142–46.

1992. "Spatial Systems in *North by Northwest*." In Žižek, Slavoj, ed., *Everything You Always Wanted to Know about Lacan (But Were Afraid to Ask Hitchcock)*. London: Verso. 47–72.

1993a. "The Synoptic Chandler." In Joan Copjec, ed., *Shades of Noir*. London: Verso, 33–56.

1993b. "On 'Cultural Studies.'" *Social Text* 34: 17–52.

1993c. Address to the Marxist Literary Group session ("The Jameson Legacy") of the Modern Languages Association. 27–30 December, Toronto.

WORKS BY OTHER AUTHORS

Abella, Irving. 1973. *Nationalism, Communism, and Canadian Labour: The CIO, the Communist Party, and the Canadian Congress of Labour, 1935–1956*. Toronto: U of Toronto P.

Adorno, Theodor. 1967. "Sociology and Psychology." *New Left Review* 46:

———. 1973. *Philosophy of Modern Music*. Trans. Anne G. Mitchell and Wesley V. Blomster. New York: Continuum.

———. 1987. *Negative Dialectics*. Trans. E. B. Ashton. New York: Continuum.

———. 1989. *Minima Moralia: Reflections from Damaged Life*. Trans. E. F. N. Jephcott. London: Verso.

Ahmad, Aijaz. 1992. *In Theory: Classes, Nations, Literatures*. London: Verso.

———. 1993. "Culture, Community, Nation: On the Ruins of Ayodhya." Unpublished MS.

Althusser, Louis. 1965. "Théorie, Pratique Théorique, et Formation Théorique. Idéologie et Lutte Idéologique." Unpublished MS.

———. 1971. *Lenin and Philosophy*. Trans. Ben Brewster. New York: Monthly Review.

———. 1986. *For Marx*. Trans. Ben Brewster. London: Verso.

———. 1990. *Philosophy and the Spontaneous Philosophy of the Scientists and Other Essays*. Trans. Ben Brewster et al. London: Verso.

———. 1993. *The Future Lasts Forever: A Memoir*. Trans. Richard Veasey. New York: New P.

Althusser, Louis, and Étienne Balibar. 1979. *Reading Capital*. Trans. Ben Brewster. London: Verso.

Anderson, Jason. 1994. "Long Live the Revolution: Killdozer's War on Wimp Rock and Wal-Mart." *eye* (30 June): 30.

Anderson, Perry. 1988. *In the Tracks of Historical Materialism*. London: Verso.

———. 1992. *English Questions*. London: Verso.

Andrews, Bruce, and Charles Bernstein. 1984. *The L=A=N=G=U=A=G=E Book*. Carbondale: Southern Illinois UP.

Arac, Jonathan. 1987. *Critical Genealogies: Historical Situations for Postmodern Literary Studies*. The Social Foundations of Aesthetic Forms. New York: Columbia UP.

Aronson, Ronald. 1985. "Sartre and the Dialectic: the Purposes of Critique, II." In Fredric Jameson, ed., *Sartre after Sartre*. New Haven: Yale UP. 85–107.

Ashcroft, Bill, et al., eds. 1989. *The Empire Writes Back: Theory and Practice in Post-Colonial Literatures*. New York: Routledge.

Austin, J. L. 1975. *How to Do Things with Words*. Ed. J. O. Urmson and Marina Sbisà. Cambridge: Harvard UP.

Baker, Nicholson. 1987. *The Mezzanine*. New York: Vintage.

———. 1992. *Vox*. New York: Vintage.

Bakhtin, M. M. 1985. *The Dialogic Imagination: Four Essays*. Trans. Michael Holquist. Austin: U of Texas P.

Balibar, Étienne. 1994. *Masses, Classes, Ideas: Studies on Politics and Philosophy Before and After Marx*. Trans. James Swenson. New York: Routledge.

Balibar, Étienne, and Immanuel Wallerstein. 1991. *Race, Nation, Class: Ambiguous Identities*. London: Verso.

Balzac, Honoré de. 1968. *Oeuvres Complétes*. Vol. 6. Paris: Club de L'Honnête Homme.

———. 1970. *The Black Sheep*. Trans. Donald Adamson. Harmondsworth: Penguin.

Barrett, Michéle. 1991. *The Politics of Truth From Marx to Foucault*. Stanford: Stanford UP.

Barthes, Roland. 1984. *Mythologies*. Trans. Annette Lavers. London: Paladin.

———. 1985. *S/Z: An Essay*. Trans. Richard Miller. New York: Hill and Wang.

———. 1986. "The Reality Effect." In *The Rustle of Language*. Trans. Richard Howard. New York: Hill and Wang. 149–54.

Baudrillard, Jean. 1988a. *The Ecstasy of Communication*. Trans. Bernard and Caroline Schutze. Foreign Agents. New York: Semiotext(e).

———. 1989b. *Selected Writings*. Ed. Mark Poster. Stanford: Stanford UP.

Bazin, André. 1974. *What Is Cinema?* 2 vols. Trans. Hugh Gray. Berkeley: U of California P.

Bell, Daniel. 1976. *The Coming of Post-Industrial Society: A Venture in Social Forecasting*. New York: Basic.

Bellour, Raymond. 1990. *L'Entre-Images: Photo, Cinéma, Vidéo*. Paris: La Différence.

Benjamin, Walter. 1969. *Illuminations: Essays and Reflections*. Ed. Hannah Arendt. Trans. Harry Zohn. New York: Schocken.

———. 1985. *The Origin of German Tragic Drama*. Trans. John Osborne. London: Verso.

———. 1986. *Reflections: Essays, Aphorisms, Autobiographical Writings*. Trans. Edmund Jephcott. New York: Schocken.

Bennett, Tony. 1990. *Outside Literature*. New York: Routledge.

Bennington, Geoff. 1982. "Not Yet." *Diacritics* 12.3: 23–32.

Bennis, Phyllis, and Michel Moushabeck, eds. 1993. *Altered States: A Reader in the New World Order*. New York: Olive Branch P.

Berger, John. 1980. "Why Look at Animals?" In *About Looking*. New York: Pantheon. 1–26.

Berland, Jody. 1992. "Angels Dancing: Cultural Technologies and the Production of Space." In Grossberg et al., 38–55.

———. 1993. "On the Politics of Representing (Canadian) Culture." *Alphabet City* 3: 58–63.

Bernstein, Charles. 1983. *Islets/Irritations*. New York: Jordan Davies.

———. 1986. *Content's Dream: Essays 1975–1984*. Los Angeles: Sun and Moon.

———. 1992. *A Poetics*. Cambridge: Harvard UP.

Berthoud, J. A. 1985. "Narrative and Ideology: A Critique of Fredric Jameson's *The Political Unconscious*." In Hawthorn, 101–16.

Beverley, John. 1993. *Against Literature*. Minneapolis: U of Minnesota P.

Bey, Hakim. 1991. *T. A. Z.: The Temporary Autonomous Zone, Ontological Anarchy, Poetical Terrorism*. New York: Autonomedia.

Beynon, Huw, ed. 1985. *Digging Deeper: Issues in the Miners' Strike*. London: Verso.

Bhabha, Homi K. 1988. "Of Mimicry and Man: The Ambivalence of Colonial Discourse." In Annette Michelson, Rosalind Krauss, Douglas Crimp, and Joan Copjec, eds., *October: The First Decade*. Cambridge: MIT P. 317–25.

———. 1989. "Identities on Parade." Interview with Bhikhu Parekh. *Marxism Today* (June): 24–29.

———. ed. 1990. *Nation and Narration*. New York: Routledge.

———. 1992. "The World and the Home." *Social Text* 31/32: 141–53.

Blackburn, Robin, ed. 1991. *After the Fall: The Failure of Communism and the Future of Socialism*. London: Verso.

Blaut, James. 1987. *The National Question: Decolonising the Theory of Nationalism*. London: Zed Books.

———. 1993. *The Colonizer's Model of the World: Geographical Diffusionism and Eurocentric History*. New York: Guildford.

Bloch, Ernst. 1989. *The Utopian Function of Art and Literature*. Trans. Jack Zipes and Frank Meclenburg. Studies in Contemporary German Thought. Cambridge: MIT.

Bloomfield, Terry. 1991. "It's Sooner Than You Think, or Where Are We in the History of Rock Music?" *New Left Review* 190: 59–81.

Bonitzer, Pascal. 1992. "Hitchcockian Suspense." In Žižek 1992a, 15–30.

Bordwell, David. 1991. *Making Meaning: Inference and Rhetoric in the Interpretation of Cinema*. Cambridge: Harvard UP.

Borge, Tomás. 1984. *Carlos, the Dawn is No Longer Beyond Our Reach: The Prison Journals of Tomás Borge Remembering Carlos Fonfeca, Founder of the FSLN*. Trans. Margaret Randall. Vancouver: New Star.

Boschetti, Anna. 1988. *The Intellectual Enterprise: Sartre and Les Temps Modernes*. Trans. Richard C. McCleary. Evanston: Northwestern UP.

Bottomore, Tom, ed. 1983. *A Dictionary of Marxist Thought.* Cambridge: Harvard UP.

Bourdieu, Pierre. 1984. *Distinction: A Social Critique of the Judgement of Taste.* Trans. Richard Nice. Cambridge: Harvard UP.

———. 1990. *Homo Academicus.* Trans. Peter Collier. Stanford: Stanford UP.

———. 1991. *The Political Ontology of Martin Heidegger.* Trans. Peter Collier. Stanford: Stanford UP.

———. 1992. *The Logic of Practice.* Trans. Richard Nice. Stanford: Stanford UP.

Bourdieu, Pierre, and Loïc J. D. Wacquant. 1992. *An Invitation to Reflexive Sociology.* Chicago: U of Chicago P.

Brennan, Tim. 1992. "Rushdie, Islam, and Postcolonial Criticism." *Social Text* 31/32: 271–76.

Breton, André. 1972. *Manifestoes of Surrealism.* Trans. Richard Seaver and Helen R. Lane. Ann Arbor: U of Michigan P.

Callinicos, Alex. 1985. *Marxism and Philosophy.* Oxford: Oxford UP.

Castoriadis, Cornelius. 1984. *Crossroads in the Labyrinth.* Trans. Kate Soper and Martin H. Ryle. Cambridge: MIT.

Cavell, Stanley. 1979. *The World Viewed: Reflections on the Ontology of Film.* Rev. ed. Cambridge: Harvard.

Chatterjee, Partha. 1986. *Nationalist Thought and the Colonial World: A Derivative Discourse?* London: Zed Books.

———. 1993. *The Nation and Its Fragments: Colonial and Postcolonial Histories.* Princeton: Princeton UP.

Chicago, Judy. 1980. *Embroidering Our Heritage: The Dinner Party Needlework.* New York: Anchor.

Cockburn, Alexander. 1990. "The Blindness of Intellectuals." *Z Magazine,* April, 65–66.

Cohen, G. A. 1994. "Amartya Sen's Unequal World." *New Left Review* 203: 117–29.

Colás, Santiago. 1992. "The Third World in Jameson's *Postmodernism, or, the Cultural Logic of Late Capitalism.*" *Social Text* 31/32: 258–70.

Collits, Terry. 1989. "Imperialism, Marxism, Conrad: A Political Reading of *Victory.*" *Textual Practice* 3: 303–22.

Conrad, Joseph. 1985. *Nostromo: A Tale of the Seaboard.* Harmondsworth: Penguin.

———. 1989. *Lord Jim.* Harmondsworth: Penguin.

———. 1990. *The Secret Agent.* Harmondsworth: Penguin.

Coste, Dider. 1989. *Narrative as Communication.* Theory and History of Literature 64. Minneapolis: U of Minnesota P.

Crichton, Michael. 1991. *Jurassic Park.* New York: Ballantine.

Culler, Jonathan. 1984. *On Deconstruction: Theory and Criticism after Structuralism.* Ithaca: Cornell UP.

Davidson, Michael. 1991. *The San Francisco Renaissance: Poetics and Community at Mid-Century.* New York: Cambridge UP.

Davies, Alan. 1991. "Peer Pleasure." Unpublished MS.

Davis, Mike. 1992a. "L.A. Inferno." *Socialist Review* 22.1: 57–80.

——. 1992b. *City of Quartz: Excavating the Future in Los Angeles.* New York: Vintage.

——. 1992c. *L.A. Was Just the Beginning: Urban Revolt in the United States: A Thousand Points of Light.* Open Magazine Pamphlet 20. Westfield: Open Media.

——. 1992d. *Beyond Blade Runner: Urban Control, the Ecology of Fear.* Open Magazine Pamphlet 23. Westfield: Open Media.

Dawson, Ross. 1992. "British Cultural Studies and its American Journey." *Mediations* 17.1: 102–6.

De Certeau, Michel. 1988. *The Practice of Everyday Life.* Trans. Stephen Randall. Berkeley: U of California P.

Decker, Jeffrey Louis. 1993. "The State of Rap: Time and Place in Hip Hop Nationalism." *Social Text* 34: 53–84.

de Lauretis, Teresa. 1984. *Alice Doesn't: Feminism, Semiotics, Cinema.* Bloomington: Indiana UP.

——. 1987. *Technologies of Gender: Essays on Theory, Film, and Fiction.* Bloomington: Indiana UP.

Deleuze, Gilles. 1989. *Cinema 2: The Time-Image.* Trans. Hugh Tomlinson and Robert Galeta. Minneapolis: U of Minnesota P.

——. 1990. *Expressionism in Philosophy: Spinoza.* Trans. Martin Joughin. New York: Zone.

Deleuze, Gilles, and Félix Guattari. 1987. *A Thousand Plateaus: Capitalism and Schizophrenia.* Trans. Brian Massumi. Minneapolis: U of Minnesota P.

de Man, Paul. 1979. *Allegories of Reading: Figural Language in Rousseau, Nietzsche, Rilke, and Proust.* New Haven: Yale UP.

——. 1988. *Blindness and Insight.* 2d Ed. Theory and History of Literature 7. Minneapolis: U of Minnesota P.

DeMott, Benjamin. 1990. *The Imperial Middle: Why Americans Can't Think Straight About Class.* New Haven: Yale UP.

Dempsey, Anna. 1991. Review of *The Sublime Object of Ideology,* by Slavoj Žižek. *Sociological Review* 39.1: 172–74.

Denning, Michael. 1990. "The End of Mass Culture." *International Labor and Working-Class History* (spring): 4–18.

Derksen, Jeff. 1993. *Selfish.* Vancouver: pomflit.

Derrida, Jacques. 1982. *Margins of Philosophy.* Trans. Alan Bass. Chicago: U of Chicago P.

——. 1987. *The Truth in Painting.* Trans. Geoff Bennington and Ian MacLeod. Chicago: U of Chicago P.

——. 1993a. "Interview." In Kaplan and Sprinker, 183–231.

——. 1993b. *Spectres de Marx.* Paris: Galilée.

De Souza, Edward. 1992. *Girls Lean Back Everywhere: The Law of Obscenity and the Assault on Genius*. New York: Random.

Diggins, John Patrick. 1992. "Power, Freedom, and the Failure of Theory." *Harper's*, January, 15–19.

Doane, Mary Ann. 1991. *Femmes Fatales: Feminism, Film Theory, Psychoanalysis*. New York: Routledge.

Doctorow. E. L. 1976. *Ragtime*. New York: Bantam.

Dowling, William C. 1984. *Jameson, Althusser, Marx: An Introduction to "The Political Unconscious."* Ithaca: Cornell UP.

Eagleton, Terry. 1986. *Against the Grain: Essays 1975–1986*. London: Verso.

———. 1987. *The Function of Criticism: From "The Spectator" to Post-Structuralism*. London: Verso.

———. 1990a. *The Ideology of the Aesthetic*. Oxford: Basil Blackwell.

———. 1990b. *Criticism and Ideology: A Study in Marxist Literary Theory*. London: Verso.

———. 1990c. "Defending the Free World." In Ralph Miliband et al., eds., *Socialist Register 1990*. London: Merlin. 85–94.

———. 1991. *Ideology: An Introduction*. London: Verso.

———. 1992. "The Crisis of Contemporary Culture." *New Left Review* 96: 29–43.

Eagleton, Terry, and Derek Jarman. 1993. *Wittgenstein: The Terry Eagleton Script/The Derek Jarman Film*. London: bfi.

Eagleton, Terry, et al. 1990. *Nationalism, Colonialism, and Literature*. A Field Day Company Book. Minneapolis: U of Minnesota P.

Eastwood, Clint. 1993. "Interview." *Psychology Today* 26.1: 38–41, 75–78.

Ehrenreich, Barbara, and John Ehrenreich. 1979. "The Professional-Managerial Class." In Pat Walker, ed., *Between Labour and Capital*. Boston: South End, 5–45.

Elliott, Gregory. 1987. *Althusser: The Detour of Theory*. London: Verso.

———, ed. 1994a. *Althusser: A Critical Reader*. Oxford: Blackwell.

———. 1994b. Preface. In Elliott 1994a, vii–xv.

———. 1994c. "Analysis Terminated, Analysis Interminable: The Case of Louis Althusser." In Elliott 1994a, 177–202.

Ellis, John. 1982. *Visible Fictions: Cinema, Television, Video*. London: Routledge.

Farred, Grant. 1994. "'Victorian with the Rebel Seed': C. L. R. James, Postcolonial Intellectual." *Social Text* 38: 21–38.

Fields, Belden. 1985. "French Maoism." In Sohnya Sayres et al., eds., *The 60s Without Apology*. Minneapolis: U of Minnesota P. 148–77.

Fisher, Allen. 1985. *Brixton Fractals*. London: Aloes.

Fiske, John. 1990. *Reading the Popular*. Boston: Unwin.

———. 1991. *Understanding Popular Culture*. New York: Routledge.

Flieger, Jerry Aline. 1982. "The Prison-House of Ideology: The Critic as Inmate." *Diacritics* 12: 47–56.

Foster, Hal, ed. 1983. *The Anti-Aesthetic: Essays on Postmodern Culture*. Port Townsend: Bay.

Foucault, Michel. 1979. *Discipline and Punish: The Birth of the Prison*. Trans. Alan Sheridan. New York: Vintage.

———. 1980. *The History of Sexuality*. Vol. 1: *An Introduction*. Trans. Robert Hurley. New York: Vintage.

———. 1984. "What Is an Author?" Trans. Josué V. Harari. In Paul Rabinow, ed., *The Foucault Reader*. New York: Pantheon. 101–20.

———. 1991. *Remarks on Marx*. Trans. R. James Goldstein and James Cascaito. New York: Semiotext(e).

Frank, Tom. 1993. "Rock n Roll is the Health of the State." *The Baffler* 5: 5–14, 119–28.

Freud, Sigmund. 1988. "Creative Writers and Day-Dreaming." In *Art and Literature*, ed. Albert Dickson, trans. Angela Richards. The Pelican Freud Library, 14. Harmondsworth: Penguin. 131–41.

Frith, Simon. 1983. *Sound Effects: Youth, Leisure, and the Politics of Rock 'n' Roll*. Rev. ed. of *The Sociology of Rock* (1978). London: Constable.

———. 1988. "Art Ideology and Pop Practice." In Nelson and Grossberg, 461–76.

———. 1991. "The Good, the Bad, and the Indifferent: Defending Popular Culture from the Populists." *Diacritics* 21.4: 102–15.

———. 1992. "The Cultural Study of Popular Music." In Grossberg et al., 174–86.

Frow, John. 1986. *Marxism and Literary History*. Cambridge: Harvard UP.

Frye, Northrop. 1973. *Anatomy of Criticism: Four Essays*. Princeton: Princeton UP.

Gibson, William. 1984. *Neuromancer*. New York: Ace.

———. 1988. "The Gernsback Continuum." In Bruce Sterling, ed., *Mirrorshades: The Cyberpunk Anthology*. New York: Ace. 1–11.

———. 1991. "Academy Leader." In Michael Benedikt, ed., *Cyberspace: First Steps*. Cambridge: MIT. 27–30.

Gilroy, Paul. 1993. *Small Acts: Thoughts on the Politics of Black Cultures*. London: Serpent's Tail.

Gleick, James. 1987. *Chaos: Making a New Science*. New York: Penguin.

Godard, Jean-Luc. 1969. *Masculine Feminine*. New York: Grove.

Gramsci, Antonio. 1975. *Selections from the Prison Notebooks*. Ed. and trans. Quentin Hoare and Geoffrey Nowell Smith. New York: International.

Greimas, Algirdas Julien. 1987. *On Meaning: Selected Writings in Semiotic Theory*. Trans. Paul J. Perron and Frank H. Collins. Theory and History of Literature 38. Minneapolis: U of Minnesota P.

Grossberg, Lawrence, Cary Nelson, and Paula Treichler, eds. 1992. *Cultural Studies*. New York: Routledge.

Grover, Jan Zita. 1992. "AIDS, Keywords, and Cultural Work." In Grossberg et al., 227–34.

Guha, Ranajit. 1988. "The Prose of Counter-Insurgency." In Guha and Spivak, 45–86.

Guha, Ranajit, and Gayatri Chakravorty Spivak, eds. 1988. *Selected Subaltern Studies*. New York: Oxford UP.

Hansen, Miriam. 1993. "Of Mice and Ducks: Benjamin and Adorno on Disney." In Willis, 27–61.

Hartley, George. 1989. *Textual Politics and the Language Poets*. Bloomington: Indiana UP.

Harvey, David. 1990. *The Condition of Postmodernity*. Oxford: Blackwell.

Havelock, Eric A. 1963. *Preface to Plato*. Cambridge: Belknap.

Hawthorn, Jeremy. 1985. *Narrative: From Malory to Motion Pictures*. London: Edward Arnold.

Hays, Matthew. 1993. "Whatever Turns You On: *The Crying Game* Deserves a Second Glance." *Xtra!* (16 April): 31.

Hebdige, Dick. 1988. *Hiding in the Light*. A Comedia Book. London: Routledge.

Heidegger, Martin. 1975. *Poetry, Language, Thought*. Trans. Albert Hofstadter. New York: Harper.

Henderson, Greig. 1991. "Eagleton on Ideology: Six Types of Ambiguity." *University of Toronto Quarterly* 61.2: 280–88.

Hindess, Barry, and Paul Hirst. 1975. *Pre-Capitalist Modes of Production*. London: Routledge.

Hobsbawm, E. J. 1994. "The Structure of *Capital*." In Elliott 1994a, 1–9.

Hollier, Denis. 1986. *The Politics of Prose: Essay on Sartre*. Trans. Jeffrey Mehlman. Theory and History of Literature 35. Minneapolis: U of Minnesota P.

Horkheimer, Max, and Theodor Adorno. 1972. *Dialectic of Enlightenment*. Trans. John Cumming. New York: Continuum.

Horne, Haynes. 1989. "Jameson's Strategies of Containment." In Kellner 1989b, 268–300.

Hutcheon, Linda. 1988. *A Poetics of Postmodernism: History, Theory, Fiction*. New York: Routledge.

Huyssen, Andreas. 1986. *After the Great Divide: Modernism, Mass Culture, Postmodernism*. Bloomington: Indiana UP.

Irigaray, Luce. 1987. *Speculum of the Other Woman*. Trans. Gillian C. Gill. Ithaca: Cornell UP.

Jenkins III, Henry. 1991. "*Star Trek* Rerun, Reread, Rewritten: Fan Writing as Textual Poaching." In Penley 1991, *Close Encounters*, 171–205.

Johnson, Barbara. 1985. *The Critical Difference: Essays in the Contemporary Rhetoric of Reading*. Baltimore: Johns Hopkins UP.

Kaplan, E. Ann. 1993. "Madonna Politics: Perversion, Repression, or Subversion? Or Masks and/as Master-y." In Schwichtenberg, 149–65.

Kaplan, E. Ann, and Michael Sprinker, eds. 1993. *The Althusserian Legacy*. London: Verso.

Kellner, Douglas. 1989a. *Critical Theory, Marxism and Modernity*. Baltimore: Johns Hopkins UP.

——, ed. 1989b. *Postmodernism/Jameson/Critique*. PostModernPositions 4. Washington, D.C. Maisonneuve.

Kiernan, Victor. 1983. "History." In McLellan, 57–102.

Kroker, Arthur. 1985. *Technology and the Canadian Mind: Innis/McLuhan/Grant*. Montréal: New World Perspectives.

Kuenz, Jane. 1993. "It's a Small World After All: Disney and the Pleasures of Identification." In Willis, 63–88.

Kuhn, Thomas S. 1968. *The Structure of Scientific Revolutions*. Chicago: U of Chicago P.

Kurzweil, Edith. 1992. Review of *Looking Awry: An Introduction to Jacques Lacan through Popular Culture*, by Slavoj Žižek. *American Journal of Sociology* 97.6: 1786–88.

Lacan, Jacques. 1977. *Écrits: A Selection*. Trans. Alan Sheridan. New York: Norton.

——. 1981. *The Four Fundamental Concepts of Psycho-Analysis*. Trans. Alan Sheridan. New York: Norton.

LaCapra, Dominick. 1983. *Rethinking Intellectual History: Texts, Contexts, Language*. Ithaca: Cornell UP.

Laclau, Ernesto, and Chantal Mouffe. 1987. *Hegemony and Socialist Strategy: Towards a Radical Democratic Politics*. London: Verso.

Laplanche, J., and J. B. Pontalis. 1973. *The Language of Psychoanalysis*. Trans. Donald Nicholson-Smith. New York: Norton.

Larrain, Jorge. 1983. "Base and Superstructure." In Bottomore, 42–45.

Larsen, Neil. 1990. *Modernism and Hegemony: A Materialist Critique of Aesthetic Agencies*. Theory and History of Literature 71. Minneapolis: U of Minnesota P.

Lefort, Claude. 1988. *Democracy and Political Theory*. Trans. David Macey. Minneapolis: U of Minnesota P.

Lenin, V. I. 1985. *The State and Revolution: The Marxist Theory of the State and the Tasks of the Proletariat in the Revolution*. Moscow: Progress.

Lentricchia, Frank. 1980. *After the New Critics*. Chicago: U of Chicago P.

——. 1985. *Criticism and Social Change*. Chicago: U of Chicago P.

Leupin, Alexandre. 1985. "A New Sartre." In Fredric Jameson, ed., *Sartre after Sartre*. New Haven: Yale UP. 226–38.

Lévi-Strauss, Claude. 1966. *The Savage Mind*. Chicago: U of Chicago P.

——. 1967. "The Structural Study of Myth." In *Structural Anthropology*, trans. Claire Jacobsen and Brooke Grundfest Schoepf. Garden City: Anchor, 202–28.

——. 1971. *Tristes Tropiques: An Anthropological Study of Primitive Societies in Brazil*. Trans. John Russell. New York: Atheneum.

Lewis, Wyndham. 1968. *Tarr*. London: Calder and Boyars.

——. 1983. *The Revenge for Love*. Harmondsworth. Penguin.

Li, Victor. 1991. "Naming the System: Fredric Jameson's 'Postmodernism.'" *Ariel* 22.4: 131–41.

Lothe, Jakob. 1985. "Repetition and Narrative Method: Hardy, Conrad, Faulkner." In Hawthorn, 117–32.

Lubiano, Wahneema. 1992. "Black Ladies, Welfare Queens, and State Minstrels: Ideological War by Narrative Means." In Toni Morrison, ed., *Race-ing Justice, En-Gendering Power: Essays on Anita Hill, Clarence Thomas, and the Construction of Social Reality*. New York: Pantheon. 323–63.

——. 1993. "Standing in the State: Black Nationalism and 'Writing' the Black Subject." *Alphabet City* 3: 20–23.

Lukács, Georg. 1976. *The Historical Novel*. Trans. Hannah and Stanley Mitchell. Harmondsworth: Penguin.

——. 1978a. *Studies in European Realism*. Trans. Edith Bone. London: Merlin.

——. 1978b. *The Theory of the Novel*. Trans. Anna Bostock. London: Merlin.

——. 1983. *History and Class Consciousness: Studies in Marxist Dialectics*. Trans. Rodney Livingstone. London: Merlin.

Lynne, Heidi, and Ivette Ruiz. 1993. "Violence and Heavy Metal Music: A Combustible Combination?" *Screamer* 6.3: 36–43.

Lyotard, Jean-François. 1974. *Economie Libidinale*. Paris: Minuit.

——. 1984. *The Postmodern Condition: A Report on Knowledge*. Trans. Geoff Bennington and Brian Massumi. Theory and History of Literature 10. Minneapolis: U of Minnesota P.

——. 1988. *The Differend: Phrases in Dispute*. Trans. Georges Ven Den Abbeele. Theory and History of Literature 46. Minneapolis: U of Minnesota P.

McCaffery, Steve. 1986. *North of Intention: Critical Writings 1973–1986*. Toronto: Nightwood.

——. 1992. "Interview." *Paragraph* 14.2: 14–18.

McCaffery, Steve, and bpNichol. 1992. *Rational Geomancy: The Kids of the Book-Machine: The Collected Research of the Toronto Research Group 1973–1982*. Vancouver: Talonbooks.

McClintock, Anne. 1992. "The Angel of Progress: Pitfalls of the Term 'Post-Colonialism.'" *Social Text* 31/32: 84–98.

McGann, Jerome. 1983. *The Romantic Ideology: A Critical Investigation*. Chicago: U of Chicago P.

——. 1989. *Towards a Literature of Knowledge*. Chicago: U of Chicago P.

McGowan, John. 1991. *Postmodernism and Its Critics*. Ithaca: Cornell UP.

Macherey, Pierre. 1979. *Hegel ou Spinoza*. Paris: Maspero.

——. 1989. *A Theory of Literary Production*. Trans. Geoffrey Wall. London: Routledge.

——. 1990. *A quoi pense la littérature?*. Paris: PUF.

McLellan, David, ed. 1983. *Marx: The First Hundred Years*. London: Fontana.

McLuhan, Marshall. 1968. *The Gutenberg Galaxy: The Making of Typographic Man*. Toronto: U of Toronto P.

McRobbie, Angela. 1991. "The Revenge of the 60s." *Marxism Today* (December): 24–27.

Mamet, David. 1992. *Homicide*. New York: Grove.

Mao Ze-dong. 1970. *Mao Tse-Tung on Revolution and War*. Ed. M. Rejai. New York: Anchor.

Mathews, Robin, and James Steele, eds. 1969. *The Struggle for Canadian Universities*. Toronto: New P.

Marcuse, Herbert. 1974. *Eros and Civilization: A Philosophical Inquiry into Freud*. Boston: Beacon.

Marx, Karl. 1973. *Grundrisse*. Trans. Martin Nicolaus. New York: Vintage.

———. 1977. *Selected Writings*. Ed. David McLellan. Oxford: Oxford UP.

Metz, Christian. 1982. *The Imaginary Signifier*. Trans. Celia Britton, Annwyl Williams, Ben Brewster, and Alfred Guzzeti. Bloomington: Indiana UP.

Michaels, Walter Benn. 1987. *The Gold Standard and the Logic of Naturalism*. Berkeley: U of California P.

Middleton, Peter. 1990. "Language Poetry and Linguistic Activism." *Social Text* 25/26: 242–53.

Miller, J. Hillis. 1982. *Fiction and Repetition: Seven English Novels*. Cambridge: Harvard UP.

———. 1987. *The Ethics of Reading: Kant, de Man, Eliot, Trollope, James, and Benjamin*. The Wellek Library Lectures. New York: Columbia UP.

Miller, James R. 1989. *Skyscrapers Hide the Heavens: A History of Indian-White Relations in Canada*. Toronto: U of Toronto P.

Mills, Sonja. 1993. "Guns and Groin Appeal: Lesbians Lust after Hollywood Heroines." *Xtra!* (16 April): 34.

Mistry, Rohinton. 1993. *Such a Long Journey*. Toronto: McClelland and Stewart.

Mittenzwei, Werner. 1973. "The Brecht-Lukács Debate." In Gaylord C. LeRoy and Ursula Beitz, eds., *Preserve and Create: Essays in Marxist Literary Criticism*. New York: Humanities. 199–230.

Modleski, Tania. 1988. *The Women Who Knew Too Much: Hitchcock and Feminist Theory*. New York: Methuen.

Moylan, Tom. 1986. *Demand the Impossible: Science Fiction and the Utopian Imagination*. London: Methuen.

Mufti, Aamir. 1991. "Reading the Rushdie Affair: An Essay on Islam and Politics." *Social Text* 29: 95–116.

———. 1992. "The Satanic Verses and the Cultural Politics of 'Islam': A Response to Brennan." *Social Text* 31/32: 277–82.

Mulvey, Laura. 1988a. "Visual Pleasure and Narrative Cinema." In Penley 1988, 57–68.

——. 1988b. "Afterthoughts on 'Visual Pleasure and Narrative Cinema' Inspired by *Duel in the Sun*." In Penley 1988, 69–79.

Naipaul, V. S. 1986. *A Bend in the River*. Harmondsworth: Penguin.

Negri, Antonio. 1991a. *Marx Beyond Marx: Lessons on the Grundrisse*. Trans. Harry Cleaver, Michael Ryan, and Maurizio Viano. New York: Autonomedia.

——. 1991b. *The Savage Anomaly: The Power of Spinoza's Metaphysics and Politics*. Trans. Michael Hardt. Minneapolis: U of Minnesota P.

Nelson, Cary, and Lawrence Grossberg, eds. 1988. *Marxism and the Interpretation of Culture*. Urbana: U of Illinois P.

Nicholls, Peter. 1991. "Divergences: Modernism, Postmodernism, Jameson and Lyotard." *Critical Quarterly* 33.3: 1–18.

Norris, Christopher. 1987. *Derrida*. Fontana Modern Masters. London: Fontana.

——. 1991. *Spinoza and the Origins of Modern Critical Theory*. Oxford: Blackwell.

——. 1992. *Uncritical Theory: Postmodernism, Intellectuals, and the Gulf War*. Amherst: U of Massachusetts P.

Norton, Bruce. 1994. "Late Capitalism and Postmodernism: Jameson/Mandel." In Antonio Callari, Stephen Cullenberg, and Carole Biewener, eds., *Marxism in the Postmodern Age*. New York: Guildford P: 59–70.

O'Connor, Chris. 1994. "New Kids on the Glock: Gunning Down the Humorless with YAP." *eye* (7 April): 26.

Palmer, Michael, ed. 1984. *Codes of Signals: Recent Writings in Poetics*. San Francisco: North Atlantic Books.

Parenti, Michael. 1986. *Inventing Reality: The Politics of the Mass Media*. New York: St. Martins.

Parker, Andrew. 1994. "Teaching Foucault." Talk delivered at the Institute for Culture and Society, Hartford, 21 June 1994.

Parks, Brian. "Bay Watch: *The Real World 3*." *Village Voice* (12 July): 39.

Parry, Benita. 1992. "Overlapping Territories and Intertwined Histories: Edward Said's Postcolonial Cosmopolitanism." In Sprinker 1992, 19–47.

——. 1993. "A Critique Mishandled." *Social Text* 35: 121–33.

Penley, Constance, ed. 1988. *Feminism and Film Theory*. New York: Routledge.

——. 1989. *The Future of an Illusion: Film, Feminism, and Psychoanalysis*. Media and Society. Minneapolis: U of Minnesota P.

Penley, Constance, and Andrew Ross, eds. 1991. *Technoculture*. Cultural Politics 3. Minneapolis: U of Minnesota P, 135–62.

Penley, Constance, Elisabeth Lyon, Lynn Seigel, and Janet Bergstrom, eds. 1991. *Close Encounters: Film, Feminism, and Science Fiction*. Minneapolis: U of Minnesota P.

Perelman, Bob. 1981. *Primer*. Berkeley: This.

Pfeil, Fred. 1990. *Another Tale to Tell: Politics and Narrative in Postmodern Culture.* London: Verso.

Pharand, Michel. 1994. "The Road to Salvation: Mythological and Theological Intertextuality in Rohinton Mistry's *Such a Long Journey.*" *Open Letter* 8.8: 107–16.

Plato. 1968. *The Republic.* Trans. Allan Bloom. New York: Basic.

Prasad, Madhava. 1992. "On the Question of a Theory of (Third World) Literature." *Social Text* 31/32: 57–83.

Preminger, Alex, et al., eds. 1986. *The Princeton Handbook of Poetic Terms.* Princeton: Princeton UP.

Pribram, E. Deidre. 1993. "Seduction, Control, and the Search for Authenticity: Madonna's *Truth or Dare.*" In Schwichtenberg, 189–212.

Readings, Bill. 1989. "The Deconstruction of Politics." In Lindsay Waters and Wlad Godzich, eds., *Reading de Man Reading.* Theory and History of Literature 59. Minneapolis: U of Minnesota P, 223–43.

Rée, Jonathan. 1985. "Marxist Modes." In Roy Edgley and Richard Osborne, eds., *The Radical Philosophy Reader.* London: Verso, 337–60.

Resnick, Stephen, and Richard Wolff. 1991. "Althusser's Contribution." *Rethinking Marxism* 4.1: 13–16.

Robbins, Derek. 1991. *The Work of Pierre Bourdieu: Recognizing Society.* Boulder: Westview.

Rolleston, James. 1991. "The Uses of the Frankfurt School: New Stories on the Left." *Diacritics* 21.4: 87–100.

Rorty, Richard. 1980. *Philosophy and the Mirror of Nature.* Princeton: Princeton UP.

———. 1990. *Contingency, Irony, Solidarity.* Cambridge: Cambridge UP.

———. 1992. "The Intellectuals at the End of Socialism." *Yale Review* 80.1 and 2: 1–16.

Ross, Andrew. 1991. *Strange Weather: Culture, Science and Technology in the Age of Limits.* New York: Verso.

Rothberg, Michael. 1992. "Marxism after Post-Marxism." *Socialist Review* 22.1: 113–20.

Rothman, William. 1982. *Hitchcock: The Murderous Gaze.* Cambridge: Harvard.

Rowbotham, Sheila. 1990. "Clinging to the Dream." *Z Magazine,* June, 25–30.

Rubin, Joan Shelley. 1992. *The Making of Middlebrow Culture.* Chapel Hill: U of North Carolina P.

Rushdie, Salman. 1982. *Midnight's Children.* London: Picador.

———. 1992. *The Satanic Verses.* Dover: Consortium.

Ryan, Jake, and Charles Sackrey. 1984. *Strangers in Paradise: Academics From the Working Class.* Boston: South End.

Said, Edward. 1979. *Orientalism.* New York: Vintage.

———. 1983. "Opponents, Audiences, Constituencies and Community." In Foster, 135–59.

——. 1990. "Figures, Configurations, Transfigurations." *Polygraph* 4: 9–34.

——. 1993. *Culture and Imperialism.* New York: Knopf.

Sartre, Jean-Paul. 1963. *Saint Genet: Actor and Martyr.* Trans. Bernard Frechtman. New York: Mentor.

——. 1965. *What Is Literature?* Trans. Bernard Frechtman. New York: Harper.

——. 1966. "Interview." *Revue d'esthétique* 19: 3–4.

——. 1968. *Search for a Method.* Trans. Hazel Barnes. New York: Vintage.

——. 1969. *The Words.* Trans. Bernard Frechtman. New York: Fawcett.

——. 1977. *Life/Situations: Essays Written and Spoken.* Trans. Paul Auster and Lydia Davis. New York: Pantheon.

——. 1991. *Critique of Dialectical Reason.* 2 Vols. Trans. Alan Sheridan-Smith and Quentin Hoare. London: Verso.

Schiller, Friedrich von. 1966. *Naïve and Sentimental Poetry and On the Sublime.* Trans. Julias A. Elias. New York: Ungar.

Schwichtenberg, Cathy, ed. 1993. *The Madonna Connection: Representational Politics, Subcultural Identities, and Cultural Theory.* Boulder: Westview.

Seaman, Patricia. 1991. "Facts about Shriners." In Douglas Glover and Maggie Helwig, eds., *Coming Attractions 91.* Ottawa: Oberon P. 82–88.

Searle, John. 1977. "Reiterating the Differences: A Reply to Derrida." *Glyph* 1: 198–208.

Segal, Lynne. 1991. "Whose Left? Socialism, Feminism, and the Future." In Blackburn, 274–86.

Sennett, Richard, and Jonathan Cobb. 1973. *The Hidden Injuries of Class.* New York: Vintage.

Seth, Vikram. 1994. *A Suitable Boy.* New York: Little, Brown.

Shields, Rob. 1991. *Places on the Margin: Alternative Geographies of Modernity.* New York: Routledge.

Shohat, Ella. 1992. "Notes on the 'Post-Colonial.'" *Social Text* 31/32: 99–113.

Showalter, Elaine. 1985. "Toward a Feminist Poetics." In Elaine Showalter, ed., *The New Feminist Criticism.* New York: Pantheon, 125–43.

——. 1987. "Critical Cross-Dressing: Male Feminists and the Woman of the Year." In Alice Jardine and Paul Smith, eds., *Men in Feminism.* New York: Methuen. 116–32.

Silliman, Ron. 1984. "IF BY 'WRITING' WE MEAN LITERATURE. if by 'literature' we mean poetry. if . . ." In Andrews and Bernstein, 167–68.

——. 1987. *The New Sentence.* New York: Roof.

Silverman, Kaja. 1988. *The Acoustic Mirror: The Female Voice in Psychoanalysis and Cinema.* Bloomington: Indiana UP.

Simont, Juliette. 1985. "The Critique of Dialectical Reason: From Need to Need, Circularly." In Jameson 1985a, 108–26.

Smith, Paul. 1993. *Clint Eastwood: A Cultural Production.* Minneapolis: U of Minnesota P.

Soper, Kate. 1992. Rev. of *The Ideology of the Aesthetic* and *Ideology: An Introduction*, both by Terry Eagleton. *New Left Review* 192: 120–32.

Soja, Edward W. 1990. *Postmodern Geographies: The Reassertion of Space in Critical Social Theory.* London: Verso.

Spigel, Lynn. 1991. "From Domestic Space to Outer Space: The 1960s Fantastic Family Sit-Com." In Penley 1991, *Close Encounters*, 205–35.

Spinoza, Benedict de. 1951. *A Theologico-Political Treatise.* Trans. R. H. M. Elwes. New York: Dover.

Spivak, Gayatri Chakravorty. 1987. *In Other Worlds: Essays in Cultural Politics.* New York: Routledge.

——. 1988. "Subaltern Studies: Deconstructing Historiography." In Guha and Spivak, 3–32.

——. 1990. *The Post-Colonial Critic: Interviews, Strategies, Dialogues.* Ed. Sarah Harasym. New York: Routledge.

——. 1993. *Outside in the Teaching Machine.* New York: Routledge.

Sprinker, Michael. 1982. "The Part and the Whole." *Diacritics* 12: 57–71.

——, ed. 1992. *Edward Said: A Critical Reader.* Oxford: Blackwell.

Sprinker, Michael. 1993. "The National Question: Said, Ahmad, Jameson." *Public Culture* 6: 3–29.

Stephenson, Neal. 1993. *Snow Crash.* New York: Bantam.

Sterling, Bruce, ed. 1988. Preface. *Mirrorshades: The Cyberpunk Anthology.* New York: Ace.

Storr, Robert. 1994. "An Interview with Mike Kelley." *Art in America* 82.6: 90–93.

Suleri, Sara. 1989. *Meatless Days.* Chicago: U of Chicago P.

——. 1992. *The Rhetoric of English India.* Chicago: U of Chicago P.

——. 1994. "Woman Skin Deep: Feminism and the Postcolonial Condition." In Williams and Chrisman, 244–56.

Szélenyi, Iván. 1991. "The Intellectuals in Power?" In Blackburn, 269–73.

Thurston, Carol. 1987. *The Romance Revolution: Erotic Novels for Women and the Quest for a New Sexual Identity.* Urbana: U of Illinois P.

Turner, Bryan S. 1983. "Asiatic Society." In Bottomore, 32–36.

Verdery, Katherine. 1994. "Beyond the Nation in Eastern Europe." *Social Text* 38: 1–19.

Waters, Christopher. 1994. Rev. of *Crooklyn* (soundtrack). *!*@#* (July): 30.

Watkins, Evan. 1978. *The Critical Act: Criticism and Community.* New Haven: Yale UP.

Watt, Ian. 1981. *Conrad in the Nineteenth Century.* Berkeley: U of California P.

Weber, Samuel. 1987. *Institution and Interpretation.* Theory and History of Literature 31. Minneapolis: U of Minnesota P.

Wells, Susan. 1985. *The Dialectics of Representation.* Baltimore: Johns Hopkins UP.

West, Cornel. 1986. "Ethic and Action in Fredric Jameson's Marxist Hermeneutics." In

Jonathan Arac, ed., *Postmodernism and Politics*. Theory and History of Literature 28. Minneapolis: U of Minnesota P. 123–44.

——. 1988. "Interview." In Andrew Ross, ed., *Universal Abandon? The Politics of Postmodernism*. Minneapolis: U of Minnesota P. 269–86.

White, Keith. 1993. "Burn Down the House of Commons in Your Brand New Shoes." *The Baffler*: 7–12.

Wicke, Jennifer, and Michael Sprinker. "Interview with Edward Said." In Sprinker 1992, 221–64.

Williams, Patrick, and Laura Chrisman, eds. 1994. *Colonial Discourse and Post-Colonial Theory*. New York: Columbia UP.

Williams, Raymond. 1988. *Marxism and Literature*. Oxford: Oxford UP.

——. 1990. *Culture and Society: Coleridge to Orwell*. London: Hogarth.

Willis, Susan. 1991. *A Primer for Daily Life*. New York: Routledge.

——. 1993. "Hardcore: Subculture American Style." *Critical Inquiry* 19.2: 365–83.

——, ed. 1993. *The World According to Disney*. South Atlantic Quarterly 92.1.

Wilson, Alexander. 1991. *The Culture of Nature: North American Landscape from Disney to the Exxon Valdez*. Toronto: Between the Lines.

Wodsku, Chris. 1994. "Indie Pop." Paper delivered at Socialist Scholars Association, Calgary, June.

Wood, Robin. 1986. *Hollywood from Vietnam to Reagan*. New York: Columbia UP.

——. 1989. *Hitchcock's Films Revisited*. New York: Columbia UP.

Woolen, Peter. 1982. *Readings and Writings: Semiotic Counter-Strategies*. London: Verso.

Worpole, Ken. 1983. *Dockers and Detectives: Popular Reading: Popular Writing*. London: Verso.

Yeghiayan, Eddie. 1991. *A Fredric Jameson Bibliography*. Irvine: Critical Theory Institute.

Žižek, Slavoj. 1989. *The Sublime Object of Ideology*. London: Verso.

——. 1991a. *For They Know Not What They Do: Enjoyment as a Political Factor*. London: Verso.

——. 1991b. *Looking Awry: An Introduction to Jacques Lacan through Popular Culture*. Cambridge: MIT.

Žižek, Slavoj, ed. 1992a. *Everything You Always Wanted to Know about Lacan (But Were Afraid to Ask Hitchcock)*. London: Verso.

——. 1992b. "Alfred Hitchcock, or, The Form and Its Historical Mediation." In Žižek, ed., 1–12.

——. 1992c. *Enjoy Your Symptom: Jacques Lacan in Hollywood and Out*. New York: Routledge.

——. 1993a. "From Courtly Love to *The Crying Game*." *New Left Review* 202: 95–110.

——. 1993b. *Tarrying with the Negative: Kant, Hegel, and the Critique of Ideology*. Durham: Duke UP.

INDEX

BIOGRAPHICAL NOTE

Clint Burnham was born in Comox, British Columbia.
He has edited literary magazines and published chapbooks
in the Toronto small press community. Burnham's
monograph on Canadian writer Steve McCaffery
will be published in 1995.

Library of Congress Cataloging-in-Publication Data
Burnham, Clint.
The Jamesonian unconscious: the aesthetics of
Marxist theory/Clint Burnham.
p. cm.—(Post-contemporary interventions)
Includes index.
ISBN 0-8223-1585-8 (hard). — ISBN 0-8223-1613-7 (pbk.)
1. Marxist criticism.   2. Jameson, Fredric.   I. Title.
II. Series.
PN98.C6B87 1995
801'. 95—dc20   94-41965   CIP